COLLABORATIVE THERAPY
WITH MULTI-STRESSED FAMILIES

THE GUILFORD FAMILY THERAPY SERIES
Michael P. Nichols, Series Editor

Collaborative Therapy
with Multi-Stressed Families

From Old Problems
to New Futures

WILLIAM C. MADSEN

THE GUILFORD PRESS
New York   London

© 1999 The Guilford Press
A Division of Guilford Publications, Inc.
72 Spring Street, New York, NY 10012
http://www.guilford.com

Printed in the United States of America

This book is printed on acid-free paper.

Last digit is print number: 9 8 7 6 5 4 3 2 1

Library of Congress Cataloging-in-Publication Data

Madsen, William C., 1954–
    Collaborative therapy with multi-stressed families: from old
problems to new futures / William C. Madsen.
      p. cm. — (The Guilford family therapy series)
    Includes bibliographical references and index.
    ISBN 1-57230-490-1 (hardcover : alk. paper)
    1. Family psychotherapy. 2. Family counseling. 3. Problem
families. I. Title. II. Series.
RC488.5.M332 1999
616.89′156—dc21
                                   99-39708
                                     CIP

About the Author

William C. Madsen, PhD, is Training Coordinator at the Family Institute of Cambridge. He has spent most of the last 20 years working in public sector mental health with "high-risk," multi-stressed families. Currently a provider of training and consultation to agencies and organizations, Dr. Madsen has developed and administered innovative programs that combine outpatient and home-based services. He has written and presented extensively about the development of strengths-based, collaborative partnerships between families and helpers.

Acknowledgments

There are many people whose work has profoundly influenced me over the years both directly, through conversations and workshops, and indirectly, through books, articles, and videotapes. Rather than acknowledge them all, I would like to focus on a few whose ideas have especially influenced the development of this book. Michael White's and David Epston's conceptual ideas and presence with clients have radically transformed my work and provided me with a way of thinking and practicing that allows me to bring the best elements of myself into my work. The clarity and continual evolution of Karl Tomm's ideas inspire me. Evan Imber-Black's commitment to public sector families and efforts to expand our conceptual analysis to include the larger helping systems have long influenced my work. And the elegantly simple shift in this book from working on problems to envisioning and building new futures has its foundation in the work of Insoo Kim Berg, Michael Durrant, Wynx Lawrence, and David Waters.

The expression of ideas in this book has been immeasurably enriched by colleagues, students, and representatives of consumer self-help groups, who read and commented on portions of the book in various stages. However, the efforts of four people—Meg Bond, Bill Lax, Sallyann Roth, and Kathy Weingarten—stand out in particular and deserve my recognition and great appreciation. I gratefully acknowledge the incredible detail, precision, and thoughtfulness of Kathy's comments, Sallyann's pivotal notations, Bill's consistent conceptual and emotional support offered with a loving sense of humor, and Meg's ever present availability to play with ideas and ways of expressing them.

The book that now exists is worlds apart from the one I originally submitted. The editorial comments of Kitty Moore, my editor at The Guilford Press, and Mike Nichols, editor of The Guilford Family Therapy Series, have tightened the conceptual framework of this book and made the expression of ideas significantly more accessible. I am grateful for their efforts in helping me clarify my writing.

Over the time that I have worked on this book, I have been extremely fortunate to develop a narrative community that has thoroughly enlivened my work and life. I want to express my appreciation to Janet Adams-Westcott, Gene Combs, Vicki Dickerson, Jill Freedman, Bill Lax, Stephen Madigan, and Jeff Zimmerman for their love, support, and both actual and virtual presence in the all too strange world of mental health. Their conceptual rigor, political commitment, and ironic sensibility permeate this book.

Throughout this book, I have attempted to translate somewhat esoteric concepts into readily accessible language. While the success of that endeavor remains to be seen, the process grew out of my work as a supervisor, administrator, and consultant in a variety of community agencies. I would like to acknowledge and thank the staff and management of FCP, Inc.; Baystate Community Services; the Metrowest Inter-Agency Council; Wayside Youth and Family Services; The Home for Little Wanderers; and the Beal Street Program of South Shore Educational Collaborative for their provision of opportunities to develop and "field test" the ideas and practices discussed throughout this book.

This book is dedicated to those individuals and families who have shared aspects of their lives with me and allowed the inclusion of their stories. Many of them have not fared well within the servile systems designed to "help" them, and their willingness to share their experiences represents a level of grace and generosity that I find inspiring. I hope that we can honor that gift by building a professional culture anchored in connection, respect, curiosity, and hope.

I also want to acknowledge my own family: my spouse, Meg Bond, and our children, Arlyn Madsen-Bond and Erik Madsen-Bond, who have both tolerated my obsession with this book and simultaneously refused to let it pull me away from them. They have kept me anchored in the "real world" and helped me appreciate its wonder. Meg has been a constant source of support, encouragement, and thoughtful criticism. Her presence permeates this book, and she has been a partner in this process in every sense of the word. Arlyn and Erik have been two of my best mentors about the spirit behind this work and teach me daily about curiosity and hope.

Finally, to family, friends, colleagues, mentors, and clients, I offer my deepest appreciation and thanks.

Contents

Introduction

This book describes a way of working with families in difficult clinical situations. It examines contexts in which overextended workers in under-resourced organizations with continually shifting mandates attempt to help families beset by overwhelming problems and crises. It critically examines many of the assumptions that traditionally organize our work with "difficult" families; highlights the importance of the stance, attitude, or emotional posture we take in relation to families; and outlines conceptual models and clinical practices that support the development of respectful, constructive, and effective relationships with families. The title *Collaborative Therapy with Multi-Stressed Families: From Old Problems to New Futures* reflects three shifts that anchor this book. This "Introduction" briefly introduces those three shifts and presents an overview of the book.

FROM TECHNIQUE TO ATTITUDE

The phrase "collaborative therapy" reflects a focus on the attitude or stance we take in relation to clients. That stance is the foundation for all subsequent clinical work. This book will examine what I have come to call a relational stance of an appreciative ally. The phrase "relational stance" refers to the way in which we approach clients. We can choose how we position ourselves in relation to others. We can position ourselves in ways that strengthen respect, curiosity, and connection in the therapeutic relationship. We can also position ourselves in ways that inadvertently pull us toward judgment, disconnection, and disapproval. The stance we

1

take in relation to clients has profound effects on the relationship and is shaped by the values and conceptual assumptions with which we enter.

The phrase "appreciative ally" refers to an approach in which clients experience us as "on their side." This approach necessitates a continual search for elements of competence, connection, vision, and hope in our work with families. Those elements help us to better anchor ourselves in this type of relationship. Such an approach has both pragmatic and aesthetic benefits. The work with families is more efficient and effective when anchored in this relational stance and it better reflects how many of us generally prefer to be with people in the world. Chapter 1 "Working with Multi-Stressed Families: From Technique to Attitude," explores the importance of how we position ourselves in relation to families.

FROM MULTI-PROBLEM FAMILIES TO MULTI-STRESSED FAMILIES

The phrase "multi-stressed families" reflects a shift from identifying families with the problems they face (as characterized by the common phrase "multi-problem families") to viewing family members as more than the problems in their lives. Most of the clients in this book have been described in multiple ways by professionals. Some of the adjectives typically attached to them include highly resistant, noncompliant, dysfunctional, high risk, chaotic, disorganized, and multi-problem. At times, families behave in ways that make these kinds of labels extremely compelling. At the same time, these labels organize how we view families and what we attend to in our interactions with them. As a result, these labels have a tendency to become self-fulfilling prophecies. When we view families only through such pejorative labels, we strip away the richness and complexity of their lives and demean the integrity of our work.

This book proposes an alternative to the traditional description of multi-problem families. If we are going to refer to families in difficult situations with some kind of label, a more appropriate one might be "multi-stressed families." This phrase better captures the stresses and pressures that operate on these families. "Multi-stressed" recognizes the difficult realities of their lives yet also orients us to the strengths, resources, and knowledge that families possess in addressing those stresses.[1]

Although the word "multi-problem" has a tendency to objectify families and promote a certain distance between "us" and "them," the word "multi-stressed" holds the potential to help us transcend this unfortunate division in order to better appreciate their humanity and strengthen our mutual connection. As an example, several years ago I taught a graduate family therapy course titled "Working with Multi-Stressed Families." As I dealt with the registrar's office in setting up the course and as I talked to students coming into the course, each person with whom I had contact was intrigued by the title and wanted to hear more about the content of the course. Many commented that they probably came from a multi-stressed family and talked with ease about the multiple pressures facing families today. It's doubtful a course titled "Working with Highly Dysfunctional, Multi-Problem Families" would have generated the same response. Although the shift from multi-problem to multi-stressed may seem to be simple semantics, it has profound implications, which are further examined in Chapter 2, "What We See Is What We Get: Reexamining Our Assessment Process."

FROM OLD PROBLEMS TO NEW FUTURES

The third shift is captured in the phrase "from old problems to new futures" and reflects a movement away from trying to correct problems in families' lives to building on life outside those problems as a foundation for moving forward. Often therapy is framed in terms of problems that need to be addressed. There is an understandable focus on what needs to be changed. However, this orientation may have the inadvertent effect of contributing to a continued focus on the problem. Such a focus may not help a client or family develop a sense that things could be different. As David Waters and Edith Lawrence (1993) put it: "One of the great deficits of most therapy is the lack of a proactive vision of what people need to move towards instead of a sense of what they need to move away from" (p. 9). Michael Durrant (1993) suggests that we shift from focusing on what needs to change to focusing on what that changed state will look like; in other words, focusing on the *nonproblematic future*. When we begin with a focus on the futures that clients would prefer to move toward, we establish a positive momentum that builds connection and minimizes "resistance." Chapter 4, "Envisioning New Futures: Developing Collaborative Therapy Contracts with Families," explores this shift in more detail.

OVERVIEW OF THE BOOK

This book begins by examining some of the options available to us in how we position ourselves with families. Arguing that we have choices over how we position ourselves with families and consequently need to attend to the effects of those choices, Chapter 1 outlines a series of four conceptual assumptions that help anchor us in a relational stance of an appreciative ally and examines the ways in which these assumptions reflect a shift from more traditional thinking about families and the process of therapy. Our conceptual models (how we think about families) and our clinical practices (how we act with families) invite the enactment of particular relational stances. We can think and act in ways that support how we would like to be with clients, or we can draw on ways of thinking and acting that can organize us into less constructive relational stances. Chapters 2 through 4 outline conceptual models that are useful in thinking about families, problems, and therapy. Chapter 2 presents a conceptual framework for understanding problems in people's lives. It focuses on a resource approach to family assessment, examining the degree to which our assessments have the potential to become self-fulfilling prophecies and highlighting ways to understand family difficulties in nonblaming and nonshaming ways. Chapter 3 outlines a conceptual framework for understanding what has traditionally been called resistance and offers ideas about how to successfully engage reluctant families. It views therapy as a cross-cultural negotiation between a particular therapeutic microculture and a particular family microculture and specifically addresses the vexing question of how to engage families that either minimize difficulties or stubbornly insist that the problem lies with one particular family member who they would like "fixed." Chapter 4 builds on the previous two chapters to offer an organizational framework for therapy with particular focus on the process of goal setting. It examines the ways in which therapy is affected by how treatment goals are framed and highlights ways to collaboratively develop treatment contracts that are consistent with the relational stance outlined here.

The subsequent five chapters examine clinical practices that build on these conceptual frameworks and support the core values and basic assumptions outlined in Chapter 1. Chapter 5 continues a cross-cultural metaphor to examine therapy as an anthropological expedition in which the therapist's task is not to "fix" dysfunction but to help families bring forth untapped strengths. Drawing on narrative ideas, it outlines a questioning process to help people experience themselves as separate from the problems in their lives in order to help them develop and enact new life stories. Chapter 6 continues this discussion with a focus on taking apart the old stories that have organized family lives and putting together new alternative ones that open more possibilities for them. Chapter 7 examines ways to elaborate and solidify new life stories. Chapter 8 highlights innovative ways to constructively draw on clients' natural communities to support them in building preferred lives. And Chapter 9 examines our work with other helpers, with a focus on developing an appreciative professional audience for the enactment of new stories.

The book concludes by bringing these assumptions, conceptual models, and clinical practices back home to our own agencies. Chapter 10 raises questions about how we can begin to develop institutional structures and organizational climates that fully support the implementation of the ideas throughout this book.

EVOLUTION OF THIS BOOK: BOUNDARY SPANNING IN CONFLICTING WORLDS

This book both grows out of and reflects my own professional history over the last 20 years of working with multi-stressed families. It represents an attempt to bring together ideas and experiences from multiple sources. For much of my professional career, I have stood with a foot in the quasi-academic world of the family therapy community and a foot in the "trenches" of community agencies. In the former, I have found fascinating ideas and stimulating interchanges; in the latter, I have found a community of relentless commitment, gut-based intuition, and crisis-driven adrenaline rushes. All too often the two worlds replicate the class polarization within our society at large. The esoteric conferences at high-priced hotels are inaccessible to the worker with 12 years of inner-city home-based experience, and the crisis team going out to see a family at 2:00 A.M. is convinced that the conference presenter with a degree and numerous publications is too removed from the "real world" to offer something useful to its members. This division is unfortunate because each of these worlds has its own contributions as well as blind spots. The two worlds can enrich each other and there exists the possibility for a mutually enhancing dialogue between them. This book attempts to blend esoteric philosophical ideas with "whatever works" practicalities. Moreover, it attempts to present this blend in readily accessible language with concrete applications.

Over the years, I have developed a strong interest in expanding professional knowledge by bringing in clients' experiences and expertise. A number of years ago, I helped to organize a conference titled "Beyond Us and Them: Building True and Effective Partnerships with Families." As family members and helpers came together to puzzle out how services could become more helpful to *all* families, an interesting synergy occurred. The emerging wisdom transcended ideas brought in by helpers or parents alone. In the space between us, new ideas, realizations, and opportunities emerged. I was profoundly moved by the collective wisdom that develops when different bodies of knowledge are honored. My greatest teachers (aside from perhaps my children) about the important elements of doing this work have been clients. Clients have much to teach professionals about how to be more effective in our roles as helpers. Increasingly within the fields of child welfare, mental health, and health care, professionals are finding ways to better include client voices in clinical discussions, professional education, and program design (due in no small part to client demands to be included more). This development holds the prospect of another mutually enhancing dialogue in the bridging of these worlds. This book has made a concerted effort to bring clients' voices into the text and is enriched by their contributions.

Much of my work with families has been in community agencies that have specialized in working with marginalized and severely pathologized families. Many of these families have not been well served by our "helping" systems, and at times I have referred to them as Adult Survivors of Pathologizing Ideas. This book offers a strong critique of predominant ideas and practices within the fields of mental health, social services, and health care. The force of that critique is fueled by a passionate outrage about the inadvertent negative effects that many of our taken-for-granted ideas and practices have had on clients. I hope that the concerns raised will be considered thoughtfully, and I also hope that they will be seen as examinations of ideas and practices rather than critiques of individuals. In many ways, we are all to varying degrees Adult Survivors of Pathologizing Ideas (clients and helpers alike). This book examines a number of common assumptions about professional identity that have taken a significant toll on helpers as well as families and offers ideas to rehumanize therapeutic relationships.

The ideas in this book are anchored in my daily experience of initially working, then supervising and administering, and now consulting in community agencies typified by huge workloads, woefully inadequate resources, and maddening bureaucratic requirements. The ideas in this book have been profoundly influenced by my exposure to and involvement in home-based family therapy and the family-centered services movement. Conceptually, this book is anchored in a theoretical approach to therapy that I am describing as "collaborative therapy" (a rubric referring to narrative, solution-focused, and collaborative language systems therapies). This is where I currently locate my thinking, but I have also been profoundly influenced by structural, strategic, and Milan systemic therapies over my career. My current philosophical predilection sits on the shoulders of these earlier ideas (just as my subsequent thinking on down the line will undoubtedly be informed by collaborative therapies). It is important to acknowledge and honor my own professional lineage as well as that of much of the family therapy field. Another mutually enhancing dialogue would be one across ideological lines within the various professions.

This book is anchored in my experiences from numerous different worlds. The difficulty of straddling those worlds lies in the periodic uncertainty about where I belong. The joy lies in the expanded opportunities for connection.

NOTES

1. We could conceivably use the phrase "multi-problem families" to refer to families encountering multiple problems in their lives and still think of the families as distinct from and more than those problems. However, the phrase as traditionally used has such a strong connotation of locating problems within families and collapsing families' identities into their problems that I prefer the phrase "multi-stressed families." This phrase tends to orient us to the external stresses impinging upon families and better supports a separation between people and the problems in their lives.

1

❧

Working with
Multi-Stressed Families

From Technique to Attitude

Most people who have worked in clinical agencies are probably familiar with situations such as the following three true stories.[1]

> Linda is notorious among the staff of a local mental health clinic. Mere mention of her name elicits a collective groan. She is a single parent of three children from different fathers, none of whom know their father. Linda came from an abusive, alcoholic family and grew up in multiple foster homes. She has an extensive drug history, widely fluctuating mood swings, and a vicious temper. She is often explosive and verbally wields her tongue like a sharp knife. She has more helpers than one can keep track of and routinely calls them in crisis with demands for immediate responses. Members of the crisis team refer to her as a "frequent flyer" and administrative staff developed a luncheon support group to deal with her irate phone calls. At the same time, Linda doesn't follow through with appointments that are set up for her and numerous clinic staff are alarmed about her parenting. They see her as a "help-rejecting, hostile borderline who is in denial about her substance abuse." The clinic director has placed numerous calls to protective services, but has been unable to get them to remove her children. Her oldest son's therapist views her as intrusive and is frustrated by her refusal to respond to the limits he sets around the confidentiality of her son's treatment. Linda keeps demanding to know what they are talking about and on several

occasions has ended up screaming obscenities at the therapist in the waiting room. At this point, the clinical staff is debating whether to demand an apology for her behavior or ban her from the clinic.

Bryan is a 16-year-old biracial boy who no one can figure out. He's had multiple hospitalizations for suicidal ideation, out-of-control behavioral difficulties, and bizarre sexually provocative behavior (he often wears dresses, high heels, and multicolored nail polish). He has been variously diagnosed as gender identity disorder, attention-deficit disorder, oppositional defiant disorder, bipolar disorder with psychotic features, schizoaffective disorder, and schizotypal personality disorder. He is isolated and preoccupied and describes hearing voices. He's considered sexually deviant with possible homicidal tendencies. His local school is unwilling to admit him and his mother, a quiet passive woman, is paralyzed with fear. She continually looks to helpers for advice but has difficulty following through on any of their suggestions. Phone calls between Bryan's mother and various workers are punctuated with a litany of ever-changing concerns and crises. Out of desperation, Bryan and his mother have been referred to a short-term intensive family stabilization program for help. When asked what she hopes will come out of the referral, his case manager replies, "I have no idea. I really try to avoid thinking about this case."

Crystal is a woman who never seems to catch a break. She has two sons and an estranged daughter. She lost a fourth child to heart disease at an early age. In fact, the whole family is in poor health. They are all obese, and diabetes and high blood pressure run through the family. Crystal's life has been an endless series of trauma and tragedies. She grew up in an alcoholic household and was sexually abused by her father and four older brothers. Two of her brothers died in accidents as teens. Six months ago, her live-in boyfriend shot himself. Since then her sons' behavior has steadily deteriorated. Crystal lost her job because of the time she has spent dealing with her sons. She is impoverished and socially isolated. When referred for family therapy, Crystal accepts the referral with the same fatalistic resignation that has permeated her life. The therapist assigned to the family returns after the first meeting to present the case to her team. As she goes through the family history, a pervasive gloom settles in the room and she notices team members one by one beginning to space out. That night, she tries talk to her husband about the difficulty of listening to so many painful stories in her work. He responds by shaking his head and saying, "God bless you honey. I don't know how you do it." Strangely, she doesn't feel comforted and wonders whether her parents were right that she should have gone into banking.

RELATIONAL DIFFICULTIES IN THERAPY

These stories highlight some of the relational difficulties that can develop between clients and helpers and the effects that these difficulties can have on our work with multi-stressed families. Let's examine these difficulties.

Loss of Connection

Clinical situations such as the stories just described can be emotional roller coasters. Our reactions to them can run the gamut from critical judgment to fear to despair to resignation. The ways in which we make sense of and handle these reactions shape how we interact with clients and influence our developing relationship. Our reactions to situations such as these may threaten our connection with clients. Therapists don't go into this work to be sworn at by clients like Linda, just as Linda didn't go to a mental health clinic to end up being humiliated. The frustration that emerges when conflicts arise can fracture relationships and lead to adversarial interactions that polarize parties, resulting in escalating anger and blame. Difficult clinical situations can also provoke the fear evidenced in people's reactions to Bryan's appearance and potentially alarming symptoms. These reactions often encourage helpers to keep their distance, making it difficult to develop open, appreciative relationships. Finally, the relentless trauma and sorrow in lives such as Crystal's can become too painful to bear. As we seek to protect ourselves from overwhelming despair, avoidance becomes an appealing coping strategy. Each of these situations presents a danger of losing our connection with clients and finding ourselves in a position of attempting to manage them or going through the motions of helping them or simply avoiding them.

Loss of Competence

The overwhelming nature of the problems confronting multi-stressed families and the woefully inadequate patchwork of services now available to them can also pull us into feelings of incompetence. In hearing stories such as Crystal's, we can become captured by tragedy and victimization and lose sight of client resourcefulness. (How is it that Crystal still continues to function in her life?) As we work hard to help families make changes in their lives, we can reflect on the apparent lack of progress and begin to question our own competence. Improvements seem so minimal, especially when compared to the videotapes of magical interventions by the "masters" of family therapy. We can blame ourselves, clients, or the system, but we become profoundly attuned to what is not working. In addition, we're constantly subjected to pressures to do more with less resources. Managed care wants a 30% increase in functioning in 40% less time, agency mandates shift without notice, and paperwork swallows up more and more hours. Amidst all this, we can end up wondering why we ever got into the field in the first place. We lose sight of our own abilities and then have difficulty seeing competence in clients.

Loss of Vision

Folk singer Steve Goodman's song, "The I Don't Know Where I'm Going But I'm Going Nowhere in a Hurry Blues," captures another feeling that can often accompany work with multi-stressed families. This feeling is also summed up in the resigned statement, "I have no idea," by Bryan's mental health worker quoted earlier. Often we don't even know where to start. We feel overwhelmed by the multitude of problems. Every time we think we have a direction, a new crisis hits and we end up feeling like we're starting from scratch. In response, we can become frustrated with clients and blame them for the crises, referring to them with such phrases as "crisis prone." Or we can drift into resignation, going through the motions of talking with clients and wondering when our session is going to end. In either case, any thought of actual change becomes a distant possibility.

Loss of Hope

The magnitude of problems confronting families can at times become overwhelming. As we listen to Crystal's endless series of traumas and tragedies, it is easy to become caught up in despair and resignation. Reflection on the system's apparent inability to adequately respond to clients only exacerbates these feelings. We can feel dismayed by the task of trying to help people in situations such as these and wonder about our own audacity in taking on this work. We can lose hope that things could be different and begin to search for ways to protect ourselves from both the wrenching pain in clients' lives and our own sense of impotence. The loss of hope makes it extremely difficult to continue doing this work.

Loss of Balance

In an attempt to deal with these dangers of losing connection, competence, vision, and hope and to provide better services to families, numerous calls for strengths-based, collaborative treatment approaches have arisen. Although this book reflects such a shift, a danger of a loss of balance in these efforts can arise. We can enter into families' lives romanticizing the strengths we credit them with and ignoring or minimizing the limitations, difficulties, and pain that also exist in their lives. In the process, we may avoid difficult but important conversations with families. This lack of balance may leave the family feeling we don't understand the severity of the difficulties in their lives, or it may direct us away from taking real risk factors into account. If we only focus on family strengths, we risk missing situations in which children are being abused, women are being battered, or individuals are doing substantial harm to themselves.

Isn't this a cheerful beginning? Aren't you glad you picked up this book? I wanted to start here to acknowledge that this work has many potential dangers. It is hard work and ripe for cynicism, despair, and resignation. Yet, working with families such as these can also be curiously challenging, highly stimulating, and richly rewarding. This book describes a way of thinking about and working with families that have not been well served by mental health, social service, and medical systems. It attempts to do so in a way that acknowledges the difficulties that can accompany this work and yet emphasizes the potential reward and personal gain for therapists working with them. Having considered some potential dangers of working with multi-stressed families, let's begin to examine a way of approaching clients that will help us avoid these dangers and stay anchored in our hopes and values. The following story provides a context for the foundation of this approach.

A LESSON IN HUBRIS

A number of years ago, I took a job in a large agency to help staff providing home-based therapy develop their family therapy skills. I was greeted enthusiastically by workers who welcomed my expertise in family therapy, and I entered with a certain amount of hubris. I had a lot of family therapy experience and believed the staff would benefit greatly from it. Although many of the front-line staff were experienced in home-based therapy, they were not "technically proficient" therapists. They had neither an articulated conceptual framework nor a set of techniques from which to draw. And yet, they were doing remarkable work with families. They were going into difficult situations and helping families make significant changes in their lives. This was puzzling. It challenged much of what I had learned as a family therapist. These folks knew very little about family therapy and yet were doing great work with families. How was I to make sense of this?

As I talked to both staff members and families, I was struck by consistent themes. The staff, by and large, didn't see the families with which they worked as "resistant" or "pathological." Rather than view families as some strange or dysfunctional "other," they described them as "regular folks." Some might describe these staff members as inexperienced or naïve, but they preferred to think of themselves as "experienced optimists." The families, in describing their experience of receiving services, repeatedly said such things as, "The workers were so respectful. I know we gave them a hard time, but they just kept coming back." "They were the first professionals who really listened to me." "They treated my kid like a normal kid, not a mental case." and "I liked talking to them because no matter how hopeless I felt, they always believed I could do better."

ATTITUDE AS THE FOUNDATION
OF CLINICAL WORK

As I pondered the apparent paradox of staff without formal training doing effective work with families once considered unreachable, I became convinced that the foundation of clinical effectiveness lies in the basic stance we hold in regard to clients and the way we position ourselves in relation to them. I think this is particularly true with families we designate "difficult." Our most important clinical quality is the attitude, stance, or emotional posture we take in relation to clients. That stance is the foundation for all subsequent clinical work. Although this assertion is a simple and perhaps commonsensical one, I believe it has profound implications and represents a significant change from how most of the mental health system currently operates.

Over the years, numerous authors have highlighted the importance of the therapeutic relationship (e.g., Aponte, 1992; Duncan, Hubble, & Miller, 1997; Rogers, 1957, 1961; Sullivan, 1953). Empirical studies on therapy outcome have consistently revealed the overwhelming importance of relationship factors such as therapist empathy, respect, warmth, and genuineness in therapy (Bordin, 1979; Dore & Alexander, 1996; Duncan, Solovey, & Rusk, 1992; Lambert, 1992; Lambert, Shapiro, & Bergin, 1986; Patterson, 1984; Truax & Carkhuff, 1964). Families are more likely to put a therapist's suggestions into practice when family members perceive their therapist as understanding them and caring about them (Kuehl, Newfield, & Joanning, 1990). In fact, clients' perceptions of therapists' attitudes better predict successful therapy outcome than do therapists' perceptions (Bachelor, 1991; Free, Green, Grace, Chernus, & Whitman, 1985). The hope that therapists bring to therapeutic interactions also contributes to change. Successful therapists hold greater hope for clients (Frank, 1982), and efforts to heighten client hope may be as genuinely therapeutic as specific techniques (Connor-Greene, 1993; Lambert, 1992).

Although many have recognized the importance of the stance or attitude with which we approach families, less attention has been paid to the implications of this realization. For example, despite years of research showing that relationship factors play a powerful role in therapy outcome, the development of therapist attitudes has, by and large, received little attention in professional education and training. In an era of cost containment and the search for more effective techniques, we may be losing sight of the simple fact that *respect is cost-effective*. Unfortunately, the fundamental importance of how we approach clients gets easily lost when dealing with clients such as Linda, Bryan, and Crystal. We may begin with a commitment to curiosity, openness, and respect, but the frustration engendered by these types of situations often pull us away from being the clinicians we would prefer to be. This book describes ways to keep us rooted in an approach to clients that reflects our best selves.

Throughout this book, the phrase "relational stance" is used to refer to the ways in which we approach clients. This phrase has also been described as a philosophical stance (Anderson, 1997), an emotional posture (Griffith & Griffith, 1992, 1994), a conceptual posture (Tomm, 1995), and a position (Elliot, 1998; Winslade, Crocket, & Monk, 1997). Each of these descriptions emphasizes a "way of being in relationship with our fellow human beings, including how we think about, talk with, act with, and respond to them" (Anderson, 1997, p. 94). Whereas this way of being has been in the background of collaborative approaches to therapy (an umbrella term referring to narrative, solution-focused, and collaborative language systems therapies), I want to move it to the foreground in order to evaluate our ways of *thinking* and *acting* in terms of their potential to support this way of being.

The stance we take in relation to others reflects a choice. We can choose how we position ourselves in relation to others. We can position ourselves in ways that invite respect, curiosity, and connection. We can also position ourselves in ways that invite judgment, disconnection, and disapproval. The stance we take has profound effects on the relationship and is shaped by our values and conceptual assumptions.

ON BEING AN APPRECIATIVE ALLY

It is important and useful to position ourselves as an appreciative ally with clients. This description refers to a stance in which we position ourselves in alliance with clients and in which clients experience us as "on their side." Drawing on more politicized language, this stance could be described as *standing in solidarity with clients* as they resist the influence of the problems in their lives. Appreciation is an integral part of this stance. We can begin with a focus on what is working in clients' lives and seek to support and elaborate on that. We can continually search for elements of *competence, connection, vision,* and *hope* in our work with families. Those elements help us to better anchor ourselves in this type of relationship. This stance has both pragmatic and aesthetic benefits. The work with families is more efficient and effective when anchored in this relational stance, and it better reflects how many of us generally prefer to be with people in the world.

It is important to note that the emphasis on this stance is not an injunction that we have to like our clients or that we have to unconditionally accept how they are in their lives. The demand that we have to like our clients can be quite oppressive. In my own work, there have been clients whom I have found initially quite distasteful, and there are actions (e.g., violence and abuse) I find unacceptable. The demand that we like people whose actions we cannot tolerate can be experienced as invalidating and shaming of our reactions as helpers. However, in working with clients who shock, offend, infuriate, or sadden me, I have repeatedly found that significant work only begins after I have been able to find something (however small) that I can appreciate and respect about them. That kernel of appreciation and respect is the foundation for an alliance and subsequent work. Valuing a stance of an appreciative ally does also not restrict us to only this stance. There are times when I will confront clients about the effects of their actions on others and times when I will decide to act in ways that I realize will be experienced by clients as "not being on their side" (e.g., hospitalizing someone who is considering suicide). However, in these situations I aspire to position myself as an appreciative ally to the extent that I act out of caring and respect for them as full human beings. I hope that my confrontations of clients and my attempts to restrict their choices reflect a process that is as appreciative and supportive as possible. This is not just the right thing to do; it is also an effective thing to do. As Alan Jenkins (1996), who works primarily with abusive men, has put it:

> I remain convinced that I cannot assist a man to give up patterns of abusive behavior by abusing him in return. I cannot assist a person to respect other's personal boundaries by violating his own. Respectful therapy involves a process of knocking on doors and waiting to be invited in, rather than breaking them down, barging in, and then expecting to be welcomed with open arms. (p. 122)

I want to acknowledge that positioning ourselves as an appreciative ally with clients is often easier said than done. The clinical situations described in this book are complex and difficult ones. The stresses the families face are overwhelming and their behavior can be outrageous. In addition, the ways in which we are encouraged by many of our traditional models to make sense of and respond to problematic client behavior often exacerbate the problem.

An Appreciative Ally Stance in Action

To concretize the relational stance of an appreciative ally consider the following discussion with two staff members of a home-based program in the Midwest that worked with Bryan (who was discussed earlier) and his family. I had worked with these two women some years back and went back to talk with them about their work. Louise begins the discussion.

> "When this young man was referred to us, the intake information looked pretty alarming. He was described as a bizarre and dangerous cross-dresser. Both his family and providers were very frightened of him. None of the schools wanted him and people were reacting like crazy to this kid. So we went out, met the family, and saw a very different picture. We saw this cute, curly-haired waif with purple nail polish. You know, he was a little provocative in his dress, but we just continued along and as a result, four months later with substantial work with both the family and the other providers, he now seems to be doing a lot better. His family is less scared of him, though he still makes them nervous. His outbursts have settled and providers have a whole different attitude toward him. He's now interviewing for a day school and being seriously considered which is a gigantic thing because nobody would touch this kid with his so-called provocative sexual stuff. So, he still has a long way to go, but he's doing a lot better now than you would have predicted from looking at his intake sheet."

I thought that was a pretty remarkable shift from the intake sheet to the outcome described 4 months later and asked how they thought it had been accomplished. Heidi chimed in.

> "Well, this was a case in which attitudes played a huge part. We work as a team and the team's way of looking at this family was very different from what had happened with other providers in the past. From the beginning, we made up our minds that we were going to

look differently at this kid because it was just too hopeless to look at it any other way. So we began by taking the time to get to know the family as best we could and we just looked for ways to connect with them. You know, these kids develop reputations that are larger than life. And we went out looking for the kid rather than looking for the reputation. I think if you look for the reputation you'll find it, but that's nothing new. Our job is to find something new, something that's going to be more useful than just the same old story."

As I listened to this story, I was reminded of their remarkable ability to connect with clients. It seemed just like them to describe a "bizarre, dangerous cross-dresser" as a "curly-haired waif with purple nail polish." But I wondered, have they minimized his difficulties? How is it they're the only ones who view him this way? Are they really "experienced optimists" as they claim or simply misguided Pollyannas who won't face real difficulties. I posed the question to them, "But what about this kid's problems? He had some pretty concerning symptoms. How did you make sense of those and how did you handle them?" Heidi responded:

"Well, there were three things that we were concerned about, the reports of voices, the reports of the sexually provocative behavior, and the reported homicidal ideation. You know everyone saw him as a monster, as a very scary kid and as a perpetrator, but nobody had ever really talked to him. There was no evidence that he was a perpetrator, it was just assumptions that everyone held because he acted bizarre. A lot of the providers looked at his hearing voices as a problem. We looked at the family as not having a family language. For instance, Bryan would come into the house with a dress and high heels on and mother had never said to him, 'Why are you wearing high heels?' We'd assume that it would be a normal reaction for a mother to ask 'Why are you dressed like that?' but she never said it. So we thought there's fairly obvious stuff here that doesn't get stated in the family and this kid doesn't have a language and maybe he's looking for a voice and maybe the voices that he hears are helping him to come up with language to sort out this stuff. And so the work then became to examine his voices and see where they could be useful for the family. Our goal was to basically open up everybody's voices."

I looked over at Louise who was smiling at this and she chimed in: "But if it comes down to voices, he was hearing our voice as a noncritical voice." Heidi continued:

"You know, there was other stuff going on that the team actually paid more attention to. There was some racial stuff that was happening.

He's half black and half white. He looks white. His sister looks black. There's a father who's black, a mother who's white. And he would paint his face half black and half white, and wear black nail polish, so we thought well the most obvious thing to begin to take a look at here was whether he was trying to find some expression for his racial identity as part of his adolescent identity piece. We saw beyond the sexually provocative stuff which allowed us to not be afraid of him I think."

Curious about this, I asked them, "So, how did you talk with him about that?" Louise simply replied, "We just addressed it head on. We took the time to talk to him about it, like it was okay to talk about. You know, I said to him one day, I'm confused. What's the story with you dressing like that?"

Heidi laughed and added:

"You see everyone was afraid of him and no one would talk to him. Nobody would come in and talk to him. Early on, we saw his provocative behavior as setting out to solicit a reaction and it made sense not to react to that. But sometimes, to get people to not react to a boy in a dress with purple nail polish and high heels is not an easy thing to do."

We all laughed and then I asked, "It sounds like a lot of the ways in which providers made sense of this kid distanced them from him. How did you move beyond that and stay connected to him?" Heidi again replied:

"Well, all of these assumptions were pathologizing and not helpful and if we bought them we wouldn't have a job. We wouldn't have anything to do in the family that would be useful. And, I just think it's what we do. I mean we were able to take it all and put it into a category and say okay, so he behaves in a very provocative way and we didn't overreact to the sexual stuff, maybe it's just a liberal stance I don't know. Maybe because we've always worked with scary people or people who present scary, and we don't get usually scared by that. To me it's just kind of a description of how we work."

By now they were on a roll. Louise chimed in:

"I think one of the things is that all of the providers were so focused on this kid's 'pathology.' To me pathology is an attacking position. I think to pathologize is to attack. And I think to go in and state what's real is the beginning of the work. We don't pathologize, but we don't ignore problems either. I don't know. I think we state what's real in a non-attacking way so that families have some room and energy left to quit defending themselves and start addressing their difficulties. I don't know. I think there's no other way to explain why they connect so quickly to us."

Heidi added:

"Louise, I think the other thing that's real critical is that when we think about people, we think about what it is really like for them in their lives. You know, like what's it like for Bryan to be shunned at school? And, how is it for his mother to be so frightened that she won't even ask her son why he's wearing a dress, but she'll consult with a thousand people around him? Our assumption is there's an enormous amount of pain here and we want to go in and as much as we can alleviate some of it or at least have a healthy respect for it without creating more pain. You know, I think sometimes therapists can go out and create a lot more pain than they find. You know it's like the 'first do no harm kind of thing' that you always talk about. We have a healthy respect for what people are feeling at any given time. By the time they come to us, there are lots of open wounds and it just doesn't make sense for us to ignore that or to rub salt in them."

Louise came back with "We also take the time to sit with people and really connect with them as human beings," which prompted the following response from Heidi: "And I think too, the ability to see beyond behavior. We try to not get stuck with overanalyzing behavior and symptoms. We look beyond their problems and they become more than their problems. They become people we get real interested in. It helps us to get to the heart of things."

Let's look at some of the qualities in the relational stance taken by Heidi and Louise with Bryan and his family. First and foremost is an *emphasis on connection*. As Heidi put it, "We began by taking the time to get to know the family as best we could and we actively looked for ways to connect with them." In this attempt to connect, there's a deliberate decision to emphasize our similarities with clients. Clients are not seen as diagnostic categories or as some dysfunctional other. They are seen as regular human beings struggling with problems in the same way that we all do. In this view, Bryan shifts from a "bizarre, dangerous cross-dresser" to a "cute, curly-haired waif with purple nail polish," a description that better facilitates a connection. They actively look beyond his reputation. They go out "looking for the kid rather than looking for the reputation."

This emphasis on connection is supported by *respectful curiosity*. Again, in Heidi's words "When we think about people, we think about what it's really like for them in their lives. You know like what's it like for Bryan to be shunned at school? And, how is it for his mother to be so frightened that she won't even ask her son why he's wearing a dress, but she'll consult with a thousand people around him? . . . We have a healthy respect for what people are feeling at any given time." There is a strong attempt to enter into clients' experience, to "sit in their shoes," and to experience their pain and joy in the world with an emphasis on validating and honoring that experience. What comes through in this interview is an honoring of the privilege of being invited into and having an opportunity to share in these clients' lives. Their appreciation of clients is coupled with an active curiosity to develop an understanding of client experience. These workers thrive on the opportunity to get to know people and learn about their lives. Again, "we look beyond their problems and they become more than their problems. They become people we get real interested in. It helps us get to the heart of things."

There is also a quality of *openness* in this description of their work, openness both in the sense of sincerely being open to another's experience and in the sense of candid honesty. These individuals aren't afraid of "difficult" clients. They're willing to take on the hard conversations and initiate them in a way that allows them to take place successfully. As Louise puts it, "We don't pathologize, but we don't ignore problems either. I think we state what's real in a nonattacking way so that families have some room and energy left to quit defending themselves and start addressing their difficulties." These helpers draw on their faith in client resourcefulness to assume that difficult conversations can take place and then set about initiating them with a directness and sensitivity that provides a safe "holding environment" in which the conversation does take place.

Finally, Heidi and Louise exude a continual sense of *hopefulness*. Despite Bryan's alarming symptoms, they have an unshakable faith that he can do more in his life. They focus on what could be rather than on what isn't. Hopefulness opens new possibilities.

These qualities of connection, respectful curiosity, openness, and hopefulness comprise elements of a stance of an appreciative ally. Whereas these qualities could be seen as inherent personality characteristics of these two women, it is more useful to view them as ways of being in the world that are actively formed by how Heidi and Louise position themselves as they interact with clients. This second conceptualization draws from social constructionist approaches to psychology that view the "self" not as an inherent essence but as something we construct in social interaction with others. This shifts the focus from "who" we are with clients to "how" we are with clients. I prefer this focus because it opens more possibilities for us in how we position ourselves with clients. If the qualities of this relational stance are personal characteristics, we may be in a position of either having them or not (e.g., she "is" empathic, he "is" judgmental) and then we're stuck with that situation. If we consider our relational stance a way that we choose to position ourselves with clients, it opens up space for us to create very different relationships with clients. Heidi's description of their thinking as they first met Bryan reflects a deliberate choice: "From the beginning, we made up our minds that we were going to look differently at this kid because it was just too hopeless to look at it any other way. . . . Our job is to find something new, something that's going to be more useful than just the same old story." That choice positions them in a certain relationship with clients and supports the emergence of qualities such as connection, respectful curiosity, openness, and hopefulness.

The stance we take in relation to clients is the foundation for our work with them. Our conceptual models and clinical practices shape that stance. The ways in which we think about clients and families (our conceptual models) and the ways in which we act with them (our clinical practices) invite the enactment of particular relational stances. We can think and act in ways that support how we would like to be with clients or we can draw on ways of thinking and acting that can organize us into less constructive relational stances. In this sense, we are responsible for the relational stance we construct with families. In an attempt to provide some direction for the development of an allied stance, this chapter examines four conceptual assumptions that anchor it. These assumptions include a Belief in Resourcefulness; a Commitment to Empowering Processes; a Preference for Partnership; and a Striving for Cultural Curiosity. These assumptions require a shift from traditional thinking. The conceptual shifts could be described as a shift from emphasizing problems to emphasizing competence, a shift from the role of an expert to the role of an accountable ally, a shift from working on professional turf to working on family turf, and a shift from teaching to clients to learning with them.

BELIEVING IN RESOURCEFULNESS: SHIFTING OUR FOCUS FROM PATHOLOGY TO COMPETENCE

In their work with families, therapists are faced with a fundamental choice that guides all subsequent action. This choice involves whether to operate from a deficit model or a resource model of family functioning. A deficit model assumes certain knowable norms for family organization and interaction. Whatever deviates from these norms is assumed to be defective. Therapy then focuses on fixing that which is in need of repair, inadvertently reinforcing a focus on dysfunction. The therapist is then in a position of identifying what is missing or broken in families and attempting to address that. In contrast, a resource model of family functioning assumes the following:

> A family is continually generating its own norms in an interacting context of history, culture, ethnicity, social class, politics, interpersonal relationships and individual quirks. The therapist searches for strengths, and attempts to remain respectfully curious and open to difference. Diversity is welcomed. Therapy is seen as that which facilitates the family's creative capacity to solve problems, to effect healing, to generate development and to gain new knowledge, first with the therapist and then without the therapist. (Imber-Black, 1986, p. 149)

This choice of emphasizing resources or deficits is a foundation for the rest of our work with families. Subsequent work is both informed by and reinforces this choice.

Increasingly, the field of family therapy has embraced a commitment to the belief that all families are resourceful and have the capacity to grow, learn, and change. The core of this belief holds that the families with which we work often have more competence than we realize and often have significant untapped abilities, resources, and knowledge that, if acknowledged and drawn upon, can be useful in their lives. A resource model does not ignore pathology and dysfunction but emphasizes strengths. From this perspective, services begin with a focus of building on competence rather than correcting deficits.

A deficit model and a resource model can be thought of as stories or narratives held by therapists that organize what is seen. Our stories about families shape our view of them and promote selective attention to particular factors and selective inattention to others. Linda, described earlier, exemplifies the effects of how we view clients. The clinic staff viewed Linda as a "help-rejecting, hostile borderline who was in denial." This story promoted attention to Linda's "borderline" nature, her interpersonal difficulties, and her incompetence as a parent. This story became a self-fulfilling prophecy and organized the staff's interactions with her. Linda was expected to be out of control and yet was also asked to publicly apologize to staff for her behavior. Her interactions with staff in turn confirmed their story about her. Clearly, this situation was extremely frustrating for everyone involved.

Linda was later referred to another clinic for family therapy. Her experience at this clinic was quite different. Two therapists were assigned to her family. One worked with Linda, a second with the children, and the two therapists met conjointly with the whole family. Knowing Linda's experience with the first clinic, these therapists decided to approach her quite differently. They viewed Linda as a trauma survivor whose whole childhood had been a fight to stay alive. They saw her as driven by shame and humiliation and viewed her substance abuse as a way to soothe her shame. They were impressed with her ability to quit drugs cold turkey and risk confronting the shame of having lost her children. They saw her movement to sobriety as testimony to her commitment to her children. Although they were concerned about her attempts at recovery on her own, they respected her approach as long as it seemed to work for her. They knew that Linda had a long history of bad experiences with mental health helpers and saw her as fiercely protective of her children. The first meeting with her was held with the protective worker who Linda saw as a supportive ally because "she listens and doesn't judge me." The meeting became an extensive interview of the therapists by Linda to see if she felt comfortable entrusting her "intimate life" in their care. Rather than see her questions about her children's therapy as intrusive, the therapists drew on her as a consultant for the ongoing therapy. Linda's relationship with these therapists had its ups and downs. She was volatile and often challenged them. The therapists appreciated Linda's strong feelings and saw her as someone who gave them lots of practices sitting with intense affect. However, Linda's trust grew slowly but surely. As she came to believe that the therapists' faith in her was real, she began showing more and more competence. Shortly before one Easter, she showed up at the second clinic and gave chocolate Easter bunnies to every member on the team that supported the therapists working with her.[2] The story about Linda developed by these therapists was quite different from that of the first set of therapists and the resulting interactions between her and the team reflected that difference.

It is important in contrasting a narrative of pathology and a narrative of resourcefulness to avoid a polarization in which clients are seen as simply dysfunctional or simply resourceful. Linda had significant problems that had entered her life. These problems had wreaked havoc on the life of her family. A deficit model often situates client lives in a story of tragedy. There is a focus on what is missing and what has been lost. A tragic story can hold significant appeal. There is a certain drama that accompanies it. However, it can also invite pity or protectiveness on the therapist's part and close down rather than open up possibilities for clients. A resource model often situates client lives in a heroic story that acknowledges the tragedies in their lives but also emphasizes their courage in confronting multiple stresses. A heroic story pulls for a different kind of connection with clients.

A deficit model is a strong organizing assumption in our field and is supported by a number of factors. One of the most pressing is the immediate context of our work. Mark Karpel (1986) points out that clients typically go to therapists because they (or someone) feel something is wrong. They arrive unhappy in some way and the purpose of therapy can easily be seen as trying to understand what is "wrong" and do something about it. Because we are being asked on a daily basis to "fix" something that is "wrong," it makes sense that we have developed a language for this endeavor. By the time clients get to therapy, the problems that bring them have often become entrenched and occupy significant space in their lives. In the words of Michael White and David Epston (1990), clients' lives have become "problem-saturated." Michael Durrant (1993) suggests that therapists' views of clients are derived from inadequate or skewed data. We see people when things are not going well, and such a skewed sample easily leads us to see the world in terms of dysfunction, pathology, and deficit. As a couple I saw put it, "You know, you really see us at our worst." We could view this statement as a minimization of their situation or as a sobering comment on the limited views we get of people in a clinical setting. Our immediate work context often promotes selective attention to problems and inattention to strengths and resources.

Our work is embedded in professional assumptions that strongly support our adherence to a deficit model. The field of mental health has a long tradition of attempting to identify, categorize and describe pathology. When conducting professional workshops, I often ask how many participants have taken a course in psychopathology. Virtually everyone raises his or her hand. Then I ask how many have taken a course in individual or family resourcefulness. Silence. We seem to know a lot more about what is wrong with people than what is right with them.

Much of our adherence to a deficit model can be traced to the evolution of a medical model as a metaphor for understanding problems in living. The medical model, which was developed to address physical maladies, describes symptoms, groups them into syndromes, and seeks to understand their etiology in order to develop cures. It has proved useful in the treatment of acute and infectious diseases. For example, from 1900 to 1980, the development of antibiotics and improved immunological measures brought most infectious diseases under control (Burish & Bradley, 1983). However, this stunning success in addressing acute physical maladies has not translated well into addressing chronic physical illnesses (which have replaced infectious disease as the most prevalent form of sickness in the United States) and is even less applicable as a metaphor for problems in daily living. The application of a medical model to social functioning has encouraged us to view human life through a lens of disease with a strong focus on the individual and presumed pathology. In the process, the broader context of social interaction and meaning is obscured. The family as a social context is essentially ignored except as the locus and source of trauma (which positions therapists and families in an adversarial relationship). In addition, the influence of broader social, economic, and cultural factors disappears almost entirely. As a result, what began as a major triumph in one arena (infectious and acute physical illnesses) has become quite limiting in the field of mental health.

Much of family therapy has also replicated this search for pathology. Attempts to view individual clients within a family context have often shifted from labeling the patient as the problem to labeling the family as the problem. Earlier family systems thinking could be characterized as "let's work with the family because they are the problem" rather than "let's work with the family because they are the most powerful solution." Family therapy began from research on the etiology of schizophrenia, and the thrust of most early family formulations was to better understand and spell out the roots and persistence of pathology. Increasingly, there has been a gradual shift from identifying pathology to eliciting family resourcefulness; however, we have a historical trail littered with such fault-finding concepts as schizophrenogenic mothers, enmeshment, and function of the symptom. The legacy of those concepts continues to affect our thinking.

Finally, as a participant in a workshop I once led, put it: "Competence is quiet, it is difficult to hear." I like that quote. I have two children. When they are getting along well and playing together, it's easy for me to not notice (despite my best intentions to pay attention to those times and remark on them). However, when they are fighting, it's impossible to not notice. Is that true in your life? In your own clinical supervision, do you talk more about the aspects of your work that are going well or the problems you encounter? If you drive to work, are you more likely to notice when traffic flows smoothly or creeps at a snail's pace? Are you more likely to write a letter to your congressional representative when he or she does something you like or when he or she does something you dislike? Again, competence is quiet. The trick is to listen very carefully for it.

Advantages of a Belief in Resourcefulness

Conducting therapy with a belief in people's resourcefulness offers a number of advantages. When we begin with a focus on strengths and resources, we are less likely to provoke resistance. I assume for most of us that it is easier to introduce ourselves to strangers by talking about what we do well than by leading with our deepest, most shameful secrets. Building therapy on a foundation of competence provides a reminder when exploring problems that families have strengths as well as difficulties. Recognizing these strengths sets a stage of competence and pride which is a much stronger foundation from which to derive future solutions to the problems in their lives. Focusing only on problems leads to demoralization. Recognizing strengths and resources invites hope and opens possibilities.

A belief in resourcefulness also provides direction to our work. Waters and Lawrence (1993) point out that many models of diagnosis and treatment offer elaborate schemas for investigating what's wrong with a person but virtually none for what's functional or effective. We are likely to study people's difficulties ad absurdum but altogether ignore their assets. A focus on deficits and dysfunction doesn't provide us with a map for moving toward new behaviors. When we begin therapy with a strong awareness of family strengths and resources, we are better positioned to help them draw on those resources to confront the problems in their lives.

In addition, a focus on client resourcefulness adds to the accumulated wisdom brought to clinical situations. Clifford Geertz (1973) draws a distinction between expert and local knowledge. Expert knowledge includes those bodies of professional knowledge that have been written, published, and given credence in our society. Local knowledge is that wisdom that grows out of people's daily lives and experiences. A focus on resourcefulness encourages us to elicit clients' local knowledge. In the example with Linda described earlier, the second team's consultations with her about their work with her son resulted in a number of creative ideas that they would never have developed on their own. In addition, as clients and professionals share knowledge, new ideas are generated. This newly emerging wisdom does not preexist in either clients or helpers but grows synergistically out of the interaction between them. As the second therapy team and Linda discussed her family's situation, together they generated new ideas for helping her son that far exceeded the usefulness of any prior attempts by either party.

Finally, a belief in resourcefulness has the potential to enrich our clinical work. If you think back to the two Lindas described previously, would you rather work with the help-rejecting, hostile borderline or the trauma survivor who is intensely committed to her children and desperately searching for a helper she can trust? When we focus on client resources, clients become more intriguing as human beings. They become easier to respect and appreciate. We begin to realize that we may also learn something from them. It offers the potential for this work to be something that is quite remarkable.

I am not romanticizing clients' lives here. Let me reiterate that a belief in resourcefulness need not minimize the difficulties that exist in people's lives. It is important to avoid a dichotomous way of thinking in which clients are seen as either dysfunctional or resourceful. We need to acknowledge both family strengths and the difficulties they confront. The important conceptual shift lies in beginning with a strong appreciation of family competence as a foundation for helping them address the problems that enter their lives.

ENGAGING IN EMPOWERING PROCESSES: SHIFTING OUR ROLE FROM EXPERT TO ACCOUNTABLE ALLY

When we begin with a belief in resourcefulness, our work can be seen as eliciting and elaborating clients' knowledge and abilities in order to support them in building the lives they would prefer. This section focuses on empowering and disempowering processes, highlighting some of the ways in which our actions may inadvertently undermine clients and examining how we can shift our role with clients to make our work more accountable to them.

The phrase "empowering processes" is used to refer to ways of thinking and acting that acknowledge, support, and amplify people's participation and influence in developing the lives they prefer. Disempowering processes refers to ways of thinking and acting that may disqualify, constrain, or supplant people's participation and influence in their lives. The focus on empowering processes rather than empowerment is deliberate. Although empowerment is often used to refer to a state of being produced by empowering which directs our attention to what is happening for clients (e.g., she is empowered, he is not), a focus on empowering processes tends to orient us to what we are doing and the effects of our actions on clients. This latter focus is more useful to help organize the relational stance we take with clients. It orients us to the process of our interactions with clients and the consequences of those interactions.

As we interact with clients, our actions have certain effects on them. These effects may be empowering or inadvertently disempowering. For example, consider the different consequences for a mother's sense of competence with her son when a male therapist sets limits on her son's rowdy behavior in a family therapy session versus when he helps *her* to set limits. In addition, the way in which he chooses to attempt to help her may have differential effects. The therapist may draw upon her past successes with her son and the wisdom she holds about him to help her develop more effective ways of dealing with him or he may offer her suggestions from a parenting training manual that, while effective, disqualify her knowledge and violate her preferred ways of being with her son. His actions can *support* her or inadvertently *supplant* her.

It is useful to draw a distinction between the *intent* behind our actions and the *effects* of those actions. Helpers generally attempt to act in empowering ways, but our actions may have inadvertent disempowering effects on clients. For example, in meeting to discuss a boy's return to his old school, a therapist begins a description of her work with the family by glancing at the mother and then saying to the team, "I began working with this case when the Department filed a C & P and the son was placed in an ASU to assess suicidality and impulse control." He continues while everyone except the mother nods knowingly. What impact do you think that experience might have on this mother? How might it be for her to be referred to as "this case" followed by a string of unintelligible acronyms? If you were in her shoes, how would you feel about being in a room and hearing your life described in unfamiliar words to a group of strangers, believing that you were the only one who didn't understand what anyone was saying? The mother who related this incident to me described her reaction, "I thought we were coming to the meeting to all talk about my son's future and when the therapist started, I realized that it didn't matter if I was in the room or not. They were just going to talk to each other and I sat there trying to figure out how I could gracefully get out of the meeting." No one in the meeting intended to negatively affect this mother. The way in which they were talking is a fairly common practice in "case discussions." However, that manner of talking had a devastating impact on her participation and sense of influence in both the meeting and her life at that moment.

Here's another example. I used to provide family therapy supervision using a one-way mirror. Often students would ask what families thought about that setup, and I gave them the party line (at the time) that families didn't mind the mirror and that although they might be a little uncomfortable at the beginning, they would quickly forget about it. I felt assured that because families had signed a consent form and had been introduced to the team members behind the mirror, they were not troubled by it. Then I began asking families about their experiences with one-way mirrors and discovered that many of the concerns raised by students which I had so casually dismissed were in fact shared by many families. A number of families described feeling paranoid that an unseen and unknown group of "professionals" was sitting behind the mirror judging them. My intent in using a one-way mirror was never to promote paranoia or critical judgment, but unfortunately our actions had that effect in some situations. Learning about the discrepancy between my intent and the effects was sobering. The best judge of the effects of our actions are those on the receiving end of them. It is important not to lose sight of the good intentions behind our actions, but it is also important to be accountable for the effects of our actions despite our intentions.

Our actions with clients are organized by the ways in which we think about our role. Our conceptualization of our role with clients can also have empowering or disempowering effects on them. Therapy can be seen as a process in which therapists act upon clients to change them or to repair damage, or it can be seen as a process in which we work with clients to assist them in making changes in their lives (Durrant, 1993). The former view emphasizes professional knowledge (what we know about human development, pathology, family functioning, etc.). From this, we are positioned in front of clients, leading them or *working on* them based on our knowledge. The latter view appreciates our professional knowledge, clients' local knowledge, and the knowledge that jointly develops between therapists and clients. We are positioned beside clients, supporting them and *working with* them based on shared knowledge. The latter position fits with an allied stance. A working-on model of therapeutic process fits with a deficit model of client functioning in which clients are viewed as damaged or disturbed and requiring our intervention. That view invites a role in which we as the experts operate upon clients to fix or cure something. One unfortunate effect of such attempts is that we may lose sight of client resourcefulness and inadvertently supplant their knowledge and functioning in our attempts to help them.

This inadvertent supplanting of clients is encouraged on many fronts. In our professions, we are taught specialized expert knowledge about individual and family development, functioning, and pathology. This training has the potential to invite us into an authoritarian stance in which we know and clients would be best served by submitting to that knowledge. This stance is supported culturally by professional titles ("the Doctor will see you now") and by the semimystical aura of therapy (I once told a neighbor that I was a therapist and he replied, "Oh, so that means when I say 'Good Morning,' you'll know what I *really* mean."). In the process, our professional knowledges are elevated and clients' local knowledges are obscured.

Our inadvertent supplanting of client functioning may also be encouraged by our good intentions and the organizational pressures we face. Many of us come to mental health and social services out of a strong desire to help others. As we stand a little bit outside clients' lives and view their pain and distress, it may appear to us that there are some obvious solutions that would alleviate their distress. There is a strong pull to fix things. The "fix-it" mentality also receives significant support from the current push for empirically validated treatment approaches and the search for replicable procedures for specific conditions that will save time and money. It is also important not to lose sight of the pressures that clinicians in community agencies are under to produce and document quantifiable changes in client functioning in a shorter and shorter amount of time. As public-sector therapy (and increasingly private practice) takes on an assembly-line ethos, we are encouraged into an instrumental orientation that focuses on product.

However, despite our helpful intentions and the pressures we face, the fact remains that we are ill positioned to make decisions for others' lives. This realization is helpful both politically and pragmatically. A value for client self-determination is a crucial element of a commitment to empowering processes. Clients know more about their lives and are in a better place to decide on their life directions. At the same time, our attempts to get clients to do things that reflect our preferences for them often result in frustrating interactions that we can come to see as dysfunctional resistance. An orientation to competence supports our commitment to empowering processes. Our faith in client resourcefulness eases our anxiety in difficult situations and supports a *working-with* rather than a *working-on* approach to clients. For example, when we believe a father has some threads of competence as a parent, we are less likely to take over for him as he tries to work with his children than when we only see his parenting difficulties.

Our conceptualization of our role also influences how we think about and draw on clients' broader communities. All too often, we are aware of the professional resources available to clients but ignore the power of their natural networks. We make a point of coordinating our work with other helpers but neglect to find out about the self-help group that a mother attends, the church with which a grandmother is intimately involved, or the neighbors who look after the children every afternoon while the mother and grandmother are away. We are only a temporary presence in people's lives; resources such as self-help groups, community institutions, and support networks are embedded in the fabric of their lives. One concept that can help us remember our place in clients' lives is a distinction between *primary* relationships (consisting of an individual's relationships with family and household members, kin, friends, neighbors, associates and acquaintances, and community members) and *secondary* relationships (consisting of relationships with representatives of social institutions which includes mental health, social service, and health care workers) (Kliman & Trimble, 1983). It is important that we remain secondary and do not inadvertently undermine clients' primary relationships. Within a commitment to empowering processes, our job is to *support*, not *supplant*, the knowledge and functioning of clients and their existing communities.

Although we are often encouraged into a role of *working on* families, we have choices about how we position ourselves. We can instead relate to clients as allies who actively support them in building the lives they prefer. Some useful guidelines for this endeavor can be framed as a series of questions to examine the effects of our actions on clients:

- How do I think this client or family is experiencing our interaction right now?
- What is their experience of themselves in that interaction?
- Is our interaction acknowledging, supporting, and amplifying their knowledge?
- Is our interaction acknowledging, supporting, and amplifying their participation and influence in their life?

One way to help us answer these questions is to put ourselves in clients' shoes and imagine how we might react. How would you want to be regarded and treated by someone who was helping you with a difficult time? How might clients' reactions and preferences be similar or different from yours? If you reflect on your own experiences at work, how is it different talking to a supervisor who tells you what you should do with a family than one who first solicits your ideas? How is it different when supervision proceeds at your pace and follows your agenda? The way we would prefer to be treated in supervision may also hold true for clients' preferences regarding how we treat them in therapy. At the same time, although it is useful to try to step into clients' experience, it is important not to assume that our guesses actually reflect their experience. We need to continually ask ourselves how clients' reactions and preferences might be similar to or different from ours.

The questions listed provide a way for us to continually reflect on the effects of our actions on clients. They are rooted in an assumption that the best judges of the effects of our actions are the people most affected by them, that is, those human beings who come to be called clients. We can minimize inadvertent disempowering processes by actively inviting feedback from them about their experience of our actions and evaluating our work in terms of the degree to which they are experienced by clients as empowering, respectful, connecting, and hopeful. One way to do this is to make our work more accountable to clients.

Accountability structures are an attempt to amplify the voices of those who have less power in interactions and to ensure that those with more power have opportunities to receive feedback about inadvertent negative effects of their actions along with a consequent responsibility to acknowledge and deal with those effects (Hall, 1996; Tamasese & Waldegrave, 1993; Tamasese, Waldegrave, Tuhaka, & Campbell, 1998). Often, accountability is seen as a unidirectional flow in which those in hierarchically subordinate positions are accountable to those in positions of more power or responsibility (e.g., workers are accountable to supervisors). However, accountability in this context refers to partnership accountability in which parties are mutually accountable to each other with a particular emphasis on amplifying voices less likely to be heard.

We can make our work accountable to clients by routinely inviting their feedback on the effects of our actions in ways that convey an agreement to act in accordance with the information we receive. One way to do this is to include clients in clinical discussions in ways that client feedback about the process is taken seriously and acted upon. When clients are unable to attend such meetings, we can include "client voices" in clinical discussions through having someone listen to the discussion as the client being presented and then be interviewed about their experience of the discussion (Anderson, 1997; Madsen, 1996). Additional ways to make our work accountable to clients are discussed throughout this book. These efforts provide ways to give us feedback about the effects of our thinking and acting on clients and offer opportunities to organize our work in ways that are experienced by clients as connecting, empowering and hopeful. In the process, we move from experts to accountable allies.

We can also make our work more accountable to the clients we serve by "situating" our questions, thoughts, and suggestions. Situating refers to the practice of clearly identifying the experiences, ideas, and intentions that guide our work. David Epston introduced the term "transparency" to refer to this process of sharing our organizing thoughts and assumptions with clients (White, 1993). We can situate our work throughout the course of therapy ("Would you be interested in what's organizing this question?" or, "I'm thinking about pursuing this line of questioning, how would that work for you?"). We can also check in with clients at the end of sessions to get their feedback on what they've found more and less useful about the meeting and offer them opportunities to better understand (if they desire) the rationale behind particular questions or comments (Madigan, 1993; Nylund & Thomas, 1997). I've often thought of this process as conducting therapy with subtitles that show our thinking.

Accountability structures, the process of situating our ideas, and therapist transparency are all ways to demystify our thinking and anchor it in a specific context rather than contribute to the belief that it arises out of some distant "truths" that are inaccessible to clients. These practices contribute to a context in which clients are better able to decide for themselves how they might want to respond to our effort. They give us feedback on the effects of our actions on clients and offer opportunities to organize our work in ways that may be experienced by clients as more empowering.

WORKING IN PARTNERSHIP:
SHIFTING OUR WORK
FROM PROFESSIONAL TURF
TO FAMILY TURF

If we have a commitment to empowering processes, the relationships we develop with clients are of crucial importance. Therapy proceeds much better when based on a collaborative partnership in which the nature of the relationship is jointly defined rather than unilaterally determined. Research studies have found the degree of client collaboration to be the best predictor of successful treatment outcome (e.g., Hartley, 1985; Stiles, Shapiro, & Elliot, 1986). If collaborative therapy relationships are jointly defined, cooperation becomes a two-way street and clients are not the only ones who can be "noncompliant." Clinicians, with our culturally conferred status, are typically in a position to determine the prevailing definition of therapeutic relationships, but it behooves us to attend to the way in which clients define these relationships. Linda's experience with the first clinic is a good example. Typically, clinicians are the ones who present workshops at professional conferences. However, if Linda was presenting a workshop at a client-organized conference on "New Strategies in Managing Noncompliant Therapists," what do you think she might say? How would she describe the therapist who sought to manage her "intrusiveness" in her son's individual therapy? Would she define the relationship as collaborative?

This is not to suggest that clinicians should simply conform to client dictates any more than clients should simply conform to therapist dictates. Partnership is an interactional process. However, because we as therapists hold a leadership position in the relationship, a collaborative partnership begins with us finding ways to cooperate with clients rather than simply expecting them to cooperate with us. For example, the therapists on the second therapy team who worked with Linda were willing to spend a portion of the first session being interviewed by her in order to address the concerns she raised. Their willingness to take her concerns into account contributed to the development of a collaborative partnership and enhanced her subsequent cooperation with some of their requests.

Collaboration begins with honoring the expertise of all involved parties. Clients are the best experts on their experience. When that expertise is acknowledged, they are more able to recognize and experience their knowledge and abilities. Therapists have expertise in creating contexts that help clients to envision preferred futures and draw on their resourcefulness to address the problems that stand between them and those futures. Michael

White (1995) refers to clients as the *senior partner* in therapeutic relationships as a reminder that we are in *their* lives and that they are the best judges of the direction for their lives. In my own work, I find that I can be more helpful to families when I stay anchored in my area of expertise (supporting them in their life journey). I often become less useful when I stray into their area of expertise (determining the direction of that journey).

A collaborative partnership is enhanced when we come across as regular human beings rather than distant professionals with clients. In daily practice, this connection is supported by talking in a conversational ways rather than conducting interviews, checking our use of jargon, and attempting to match clients' language. The process of connection is facilitated by emphasizing our similarities with clients while acknowledging and becoming curious about our differences. For example, refer back to Heidi's and Louise's attempts to view Bryan as a 16-year-old boy rather than a "bizarre, dangerous cross-dresser," while also raising questions about his cross-dressing in a curious, straightforward manner.

Finally, the connection we make with clients is influenced by our assumptions about our place in their lives. In community agencies, clients are often referred by third parties and assigned to therapists with very little choice in the process. We can fall into assuming that because we have been given their name and have read their intake sheet we have a right to enter their lives and ask personal questions. We need to be careful about such assumptions. A conceptual device that can help us stay anchored in collaborative partnership is to refer to clients in our heads as "the people we work for," and to see our presence in their lives as a privilege that needs to be earned.

In collaborative relationships, there are attempts to acknowledge and minimize the power differential between clients and therapists. Therapists, even though we may not experience it at times, are in a privileged position in our relationship with clients. Therapy occurs typically in our space, at a time we largely set, and in a structure we largely determine. We diagnose clients and keep the official record of our work together in our charts. We are the ones who are paid for being in the relationship (albeit at times, not much). Clients are culturally defined as being in need of help, are in a position of being expected to disclose potentially embarrassing aspects of their life (even though they may choose not to), and are more likely to feel vulnerable in the interaction. As we will see shortly, attempts to flatten the hierarchy in the relationship and make our actions in the relationship more accountable to clients have beneficial effects. At the same time, it is important to acknowledge that given the structural power differential in therapy, it is impossible to have a totally egalitarian relationship. It would be a mystification to pretend the relationship could be an equal one, and it runs the risk of obscuring the responsibilities that accompany our privileged position.

One conceptual shift that can help us develop more collaborative partnerships is a shift from working on *professional turf* to working on *family turf*. This can be viewed both literally and metaphorically. The development of home-based therapy serves as an example of this shift. Home-based therapy has emerged as an effective alternative for clients who have not been well served by the traditional mental health system. This approach to service delivery has been variously referred to as home-based therapy, family preservation, family-based services, and family-centered services. Family-centered programs typically include short-term intensive services that are delivered primarily in clients' homes, a focus on the whole family as the client, 24-hour availability so that services are delivered according to the family's schedule rather than the provider's schedule, a strong focus on integrating concrete services as well as traditionally defined "clinical" services in an attempt to respond to a broad range of family needs rather than narrowly defining their needs in ways dictated by the professionals, and the active involvement of families in their own treatment (Berg, 1994a; Berry, 1992; Hartman, 1992; Kaplan & Girard, 1994; Kinney, Haapala, & Booth, 1991; Sandau-Beckler, Salcido, & Ronneau, 1993).

Home-based services have come to be known as family-centered services because they are based on an attempt to fit services to families rather than families to services. The phrase "family-centered services" represents a shift from working on professional turf to working on family turf. The provision of therapy in clients' homes has resulted in a radical reorientation of services. Many home-based workers have been profoundly affected by the context of working in clients' homes rather than professional offices and have come to view both their work and their relationships with clients in quite different ways. There is something profoundly different about doing therapy in their home (family turf) than in our offices (professional turf).

The *context* of home-based work structures the therapeutic relationship in a distinct way. For example, think about how it is different when it is the therapist who shows up out of breath late for an appointment after hitting bad traffic, and it is the family who is wondering what the "real" meaning of the lateness might be. The power hierarchy is significantly flattened in home-based therapy. While an office-based therapist might announce to the family that he or she is going behind the mirror to consult with the team, a home-based therapist is much more likely to encounter family "team members" (such as the chatty next-door neighbor or the teenager's boisterous friends) who drop by unannounced and join the session or bring it to a close.

The context of home-based therapy also makes it difficult to hold a disengaged expert stance. For example, consider the effect of any of the following situations on the therapeutic relationship:

> At the end of a session, you have to ask the family if you can use their bathroom, which unfortunately doesn't have a door.
>
> Immediately after a difficult session, you return to ask the family's assistance in jumping your car battery because you inadvertently left your lights on.
>
> Finally, a family suggests that their 13-year-old boy walk you to the subway stop because they don't think you'd be safe walking there by yourself.

The context of home-based therapy exposes our own vulnerabilities and offers opportunities to come across as a regular human being. For many home-based therapists, collaboration is a daily practice rather than an abstract clinical idea. Conversations in home-based work occur over coffee around a kitchen table, or perhaps in a living room surrounded by family photos. We are a guest rather than an expert and need to conduct ourselves differently.

Finally, in home-based therapy, the therapist is much closer to the family's lived experience. For example, a therapist is told, "You might not want to sit by that window. A bullet came through there last week." The family goes on to describe how the police have been inadvertently busting into the wrong apartments recently as part of a crackdown on drugs in the projects and one of the family members jokingly says, "If they kick in our door tonight, do you think they'll believe you're our therapist?" As the therapist has difficulty holding his train of thought while staring at the door, he suddenly feels in his gut what the family experiences on a daily basis. He begins to wonder what they draw on to cope with their living situation. In this way, the context of home-based work offers helpers an intuitive grasp of client experience that is less accessible in other contexts and supports the development of our appreciation for clients' knowledges and expertise. This immersion in family experience is a significant aspect of the power of home based treatment. In my experience with family-centered services, families often express the sentiment, "You folks were the first helpers who really understood us."

These contextual elements that flatten hierarchies, humanize our interactions with clients, and invite us more directly into an appreciation of family experience all contribute to a collaborative partnership. A preference for partnership is reflected in attempts to work on family turf by making ourselves relevant to families and fitting services to them. This can be reflected in the design of all services ranging from user-friendly waiting rooms and intake procedures to family involvement in clinical discussions to being accountable to clients for how meetings are conducted. (Ideas for developing institutional structures that support collaborative partnership are discussed at the end of this book.)

Advantages of Collaborative Partnership

The advantages of partnership for clients can best be described by clients. The following exchange comes from an interview I did with two women from Parents Anonymous (a national self-help parent group) about their experiences receiving mental health services. In this section, they talk about the importance of partnership between helpers and parents.

KAREN: I think what you're talking about is what I call breaking down the barriers and equalizing the relationship between professionals and parents. When you're sitting in a therapist's office and the therapist is sitting across from you in his or her professional attire and you're the person with the problems and you're feeling very ashamed about yourself in the first place, there's a definite hierarchy. It feels like this person sitting across from me has his or her life all together and I'm a mess, even though rationally we know that's not true. But, that's what it feels like, and to have somebody be able to meet you on an equal footing and connect as a human being, well it just changes everything.

BILL: How does that change things? If helpers connect with you as human beings rather than as the expert, how does that change things?

KAREN: I think it decreases the feelings of shame and helplessness. To me, it gets rid of the feeling of I'll never be able to live up to where this person is or I'll never be able to get it as together because no matter what I do, I'm always going to be one step below.

NAOMI: I think what happens in that situation for me when professionals are more human is I'm more prone to being honest and to really be who I am. A lot of times, I carry around this image of myself. You know, how I'm supposed to behave, and what a good parent is, and I'm always doing, doing, doing. And the bottom line is I'm always feeling less than, like I'm not up to par. My image of professionals is that they're smart, they're put together, they're just all that I would like to be and when I see that they're human and have their own struggles, I learn from that. I learn that I'm OK. I learn that we're all in this together. Nobody is perfect and so I'm more honest.

KAREN: I think there's a huge difference in focusing on what a person needs help with in a way that makes them feel less than because they have problems and in a way that makes them feel human because they have strengths and weaknesses, which we all do.

Clearly, conducting therapy on family turf, humanizing the relationship, and acting in partnership have powerful effects for these women. This way of working also holds potential risks and powerful opportunities for therapists. There is a certain amount of vulnerability when we step out from behind our professional roles. We run the risk of not knowing ahead of time how to respond to clients, of feeling on the spot, and of having to acknowledge our own uncertainties. We also run the risk of more deeply connecting to clients' painful experiences as well as to our own feelings that get triggered in the process. These risk are also opportunities. The development of collaborative partnership holds the potential to become a transformative process for us as well as for clients. We have opportunities to make powerful connections, to be profoundly moved, and to learn important lessons about ourselves, others, and life.

STRIVING FOR CULTURAL CURIOSITY: SHIFTING OUR DIRECTION FROM TEACHING TO LEARNING

A number of years ago, when I was training family practice and pediatric residents in a large public hospital, I heard a story of a woman who came to the hospital to have a baby. The delivery went without complications until the physician who delivered the baby congratulated the mother exclaiming, "You have a beautiful baby boy. In fact, he is one of the most beautiful babies I've ever seen." Rather than joining the physician in his appreciation of her son, the mother became apprehensive and retorted, "No, it's an ugly baby." The physician was perplexed and sought to reassure the mother that her new son was perfectly healthy, quite normal, and very beautiful. However, the more he attempted to reassure her, the more upset she grew. She became agitated and began crying, "Get out of here. Leave me alone. He is an ugly baby; ugly, ugly baby." The physician wondered about the mother's emotional state. He thought she might have an "attachment problem" and became concerned for the baby's well-being. He decided to separate them in order to give the mother time to calm down. However, the attempted separation backfired and resulted in the mother desperately clinging to the baby and trying to hide him under the bed sheets. At this point, the physician retreated to consider his options. He thought the woman might be psychotic and potentially abusive. He considered a referral to the hospital's social work department in anticipa-

tion of postpartum depression. He considered contacting protective services. He was quite puzzled and very alarmed.

This is a perplexing situation until one puts it into a particular context. The woman was a Southeast Asian woman who believed in the existence of "evil winds" that can steal away the souls of beautiful babies.
Within this prevailing cultural belief, it is important to camouflage the
beauty of your baby. From this perspective, the mother's actions become
protective and caring, while the physician's proclamations of the baby's
beauty become neglectful and potentially abusive. This story highlights an
unfortunate cultural mismatch.

A cross-cultural metaphor can be useful when applied to the therapeutic process. We can view both families and helpers as distinct cultures
with particular beliefs and preferred styles of interacting, embedded in a
wide range of taken-for-granted assumptions. Therapy can be seen as a
cross-cultural negotiation in which the two cultures interact in a mutually
influencing relationship (Harkaway & Madsen, 1989; Madsen, 1992). In
this interaction, the beliefs and interactions of a client or family may be
more understandable through their perspective than through ours. In the
previous example, the mother's emotional outburst makes sense in her
cultural context. She is not a "crazy" mother but a concerned and protective mother who is pursuing her only option in the face of the physician's
wanton disregard for her baby's welfare. Similarly, the physician's actions
make more sense within his cultural context than within the mother's. In
this situation, the difficulties that developed did not stem from a "crazy"
mother or a "malevolent" physician but grew out of a cross-cultural
exchange that went awry.

Although a cross-cultural metaphor has been most commonly
applied at a macrolevel to refer to broader ethnic or sociological differences, it is also useful with any family we encounter. To encourage our
consideration of each family as a distinct culture, we can refer to individual clients or families as "microcultures." This usage is an attempt to promote awareness of and respect for their distinctiveness and avoid confu-
sion with the larger sense in which culture is used. In thinking about
particular families as a microculture, it is important to enter into their life
with an attitude of curiosity, seeking to learn about them while developing a keen sensitivity to the influence of broader macrocultures.

The concept of microcultures can be particularly applicable with
families who seem most like us. Because they seem like us, we can fall
into the mistake of thinking we know who they are, that we (metaphorically) speak the same language, and that their taken-for-granted assumptions are the same as ours. It is important to remind ourselves that we
don't know them and that we need to figure how the world looks from
their perspective. Viewing each family as a foreign microculture encour-

ages an attitude of cultural curiosity in which we actively try to elicit that family's particular meaning rather than assume we already know it or that it is the same as ours.

To fully understand the complexity of each family, it is useful to approach them as a unique culture and to learn as much as possible about that culture. Much of this learning can be accomplished by asking the family to teach us about them. It can be useful to think about entering each family as an *anthropologist* looking to discover their meaning rather than as a *missionary* looking to assign our meaning. Such an endeavor can be supported by entering with a stance of "not knowing" (Anderson & Goolishian, 1992). I have come to refer to this as an attitude of cultural curiosity. Just as anthropologists (or more accurately ethnographers) immerse themselves in a foreign culture in order to learn about it, therapy from an anthropological stance can begin with immersing ourselves in a family's phenomenological reality in order to fully understand their experience. Within family therapy, a cultural metaphor has been proposed as an alternative to the prevailing systems metaphor with the idea that families may be more usefully viewed as cultures than systems (Pare, 1995, 1996).

Clifford Geertz (1973), a prominent cultural anthropologist, differentiates between thin and thick description in considering an anthropologist's task. Thin description refers to those portrayals of other cultures that are arrived at through categories derived by the anthropologist (e.g., the physician viewing the Southeast Asian mother's response to his declaration of her baby's beauty as evidence of a "dysfunction"). Thick description is arrived at through interpretations that are anchored in the other culture's own categories of understanding (e.g., searching for the cultural belief within which the mother's actions make sense). Clinically, thin descriptions attempt to fit clients to professional categories, whereas thick descriptions attempt to understand people within their own experience. Geertz is critical of thin description. He regards any descriptions of an action that "attempt to cast what it says in terms other than its own is regarded as a travesty—as the anthropologist's severest term of moral abuse, ethnocentric" (Geertz, 1973, p. 24).

Ethnocentrism is the emotional attitude that one's culture is superior to all others. At times, we in the therapeutic community can fall into "therapeucentrism," referring to the tendency to privilege our categories of understanding clients' lives above all others. We can mistake our categories for objective facts rather than interpretive frameworks that have been developed to support our work. We can lose sight of the existence of multiple perspectives and become oblivious to clients' perspectives, either assuming they are the same as ours or simply placing more stock in our values and beliefs. Therapeucentrism inadvertently suppresses the reality of different perspectives. In the process, valuable information is lost and we risk cross-cultural negotiations that are experienced by others as dishonoring.

An example of therapeucentrism is reflected in Linda's previously discussed experience with two different mental health clinics. Linda had many questions about what was happening in her son's individual therapy. His first therapist viewed her demands to be more involved in that therapy as evidence of an enmeshed mother with poor boundaries. He responded by working harder to keep her out of the therapy to protect the confidentiality of that relationship. If we focus on the question, "In what context does this action make sense?" we realize that Linda had a long history of physical and sexual abuse in various foster homes as well as emotional abuse from previous helpers. Within that context, her demand to know what a stranger whom she doesn't trust is doing all alone with her son in a locked room makes perfect sense. Her fury and verbal assaults on the therapist when he tells her he can't tell her what is going on and implies that she should not be asking that question takes on a whole different light in this context.

When we enter into clients lives attempting to get them to conform to our rules rather than attempting to learn more about their microculture, we risk descending upon families in much the same way as colonists descend upon a new land (Amundson, Stewart, & Valentine, 1993). Families may respond to this experience of being colonized by acquiescing (e.g., Linda could simply comply with the therapist's demand that she not question his rules, which might feel to her like yet another experience of abuse at the hands of an authority figure) or rebelling (e.g., Linda could refuse to comply with a rule of confidentiality that she fears puts her son at risk). Viewing Linda's actions within the context of her experiences, values, and beliefs supports us in developing a more compassionate view of her actions and helps us to interact with her in more constructive ways.

This example highlights the importance of an anthropological approach, but it is often difficult to stay anchored in cultural curiosity when we observe events that challenge our own values and beliefs. The following questions may provide some help in this process:

- In what context might this behavior make sense?
- What might be the positive intent behind the behavior I find frustrating?
- How can I come to respect and appreciate that positive intent even if I don't condone the behavior?
- What do I not know about this family that would change my opinion of them?
- What could I learn from this family?

If we begin with an assumption that clients are experts on their own experience, our job shifts from putting information *into* them to bringing forth their expertise and jointly developing new ideas *with* them. This shift in the flow of information invites a parallel shift in roles. We, as therapists, move from being teachers to being learners. Instead of us having privileged expert knowledge that we impart to clients, we become curious questioners eliciting clients' experience and expertise. In this process, we shift from "teaching to" clients to "learning with" them. As we invite clients to teach us about their competence, connection, vision, and hope, they begin to experience themselves in new and important ways. The art and skill of this process lies in how we organize our questions to elicit information. In the process, new experiences of self emerge for clients and new knowledge is co-constructed between clients and therapists. Chapters 5 and 6 examine a questioning process to accomplish this end.

SUMMARY

This chapter has highlighted the importance of the relational stance we adopt with clients. That stance is the foundation for our clinical work. A stance of an appreciative ally is grounded in the active development of qualities such as connection, respectful curiosity, openness, and hope. Four conceptual assumptions that support the development of an allied stance include a Belief in Resourcefulness, a Commitment to Empowering Processes, a Preference for Partnership, and a Striving for Cultural Curiosity. These four assumptions help us to maintain this type of relational stance. These assumptions are supported through a series of conceptual shifts: from emphasizing problems to emphasizing competence, from the role of an expert to the role of an accountable ally, from working on professional turf to working on family turf, and from teaching to clients to learning with them.

Our relational stance begins with "how we are" with clients. It underlies and informs our conceptual models or "how we think" about clients, as well as our clinical practices or "what we do" with clients. Graphically, it could be illustrated in the following way:

Clinical Practices
"How We Act"
Conceptual Models
"How We Think"
Relational Stance
"How We Are"

The remainder of this book explores ways of thinking about and working with multi-stressed families that help position therapists as appreciative allies.[3] The next chapter presents a conceptual framework for understanding problems in people's lives. It focuses on a resource approach to family assessment, examining the degree to which our assessments have the potential to become self-fulfilling prophecies and highlighting ways to understand family difficulties in nonblaming and nonshaming ways.

NOTES

1. All the clients discussed in this book have had their names and identifying details about their lives changed in order to protect their confidentiality.

2. One way to make sense of this present would be to see it as evidence of "splitting," which confirms Linda's "borderline" nature. If we assume this description of her is a story we tell to organize our understanding of Linda rather than an objective fact about her, we can raise questions about the implications for the therapeutic relationship of viewing Linda as engaging in an act of gratitude or an act of pathology. Each description organizes a different response to Linda and gives rise to a different interaction with her.

3. I do not in any way want to imply that the conceptual models and clinical practices described in this book are the only ones that invite the enactment of the relational stance I'm proposing. They are simply ones I have found particularly useful.

2

※◆※

What We See Is What We Get

Reexamining Our Assessment Process

In most agencies the need for assessments is a taken-for-granted fact of life. Many programs separate out a distinct assessment phase of treatment. However, the process of conducting an assessment is also a profound intervention. Consider Jeffrey, a 14-year-old boy who has been hospitalized 12 times in the last 3 years. At his most recent psychiatric admission, an intake worker is collecting his previous hospitalization history. As the worker methodically obtains the details of precipitant, treatment course, and discharge plan for each hospitalization, he notices Jeffrey's presence in the room increasingly shrinking. The intake worker is only collecting information, not "intervening," and yet is it any wonder that by the time Jeffrey describes his 11th unsuccessful hospitalization, his sense of self has shrunk to microscopic level? The questions we ask in an assessment not only collect information but also generate experience. The process of answering those questions shape clients' experience of self and powerfully affect how subsequent work unfolds. This chapter critically examines the effects of our conceptual formulations on clients and the process of therapy. It offers a conceptual map for thinking about family difficulties in nonblaming, nonshaming ways and outlines a collaborative assessment process that promotes particular attention to family knowledge, abilities, and resourcefulness.

EXAMINING THE EFFECTS
OF OUR ASSUMPTIONS

In the first chapter, Linda encountered two different mental health teams. The first team viewed Linda as a help-rejecting borderline with inappropriate boundaries, whereas the second team saw her as a survivor of serious abuse who was desperate for help but very suspicious due to a long history of previous negative experiences with helpers. As we reflect on Linda's interactions with the two different teams, several important points emerge. Different observers "see" different things in a situation. Perception is not a passive process of observation but an active drawing of distinctions (Tomm, 1992). The distinctions we draw as therapists are profoundly organized by our conceptual models, our own history, the institutional contexts in which we work, and broader cultural assumptions that shape our interpretation of the world. The different views of Linda and the problems in her life were shaped by the context of the respective teams' interactions with Linda and the clinical orientations within which those interactions were interpreted. The first team operated within a medically oriented outpatient clinic in which Linda felt very uncomfortable. Their work was organized by an assumption that treatment must begin with a thorough diagnostic assessment. This assumption encouraged a particular set of questions and organized a particular relational stance with Linda. The second team saw Linda in her own home, and while they valued the importance of clearly understanding situations, they organized their work around an assumption that therapy must begin with a compassionate connection. That different priority positioned them in a different relational stance with Linda. In turn, Linda interacted quite differently on her own turf than on professional turf and the different organizing assumptions encouraged the respective clinicians to draw quite different conclusions about those interactions.

Our distinctions promote selective attention to particular events and inattention to others. Those distinctions organize our experience of what we are observing. The respective stories about Linda influenced the various responses to her. The first team anticipated her outbursts and described themselves as stiffening up in anticipation of Linda's "inappropriateness." The second team, whose perspective emphasized her resilience and commitment to her children, had a different reaction to Linda. They admired her persistence in continuing to seek out help and wanted to help her have a different experience in their interactions with her.

Our formulations about clients position us in particular relationships with them. Our reactions to them are often communicated in subtle ways and, in turn, invite client reactions that develop into repetitive interactions. For example, Linda thought the first clinical team was uneasy around her, perceived them as critical of her, and viewed them as "uptight and judgmental." She responded with suspiciousness and defensiveness, and an interaction developed that was characterized by mutual mistrust, blaming, and antagonism. As the interaction became more polarized, each party became more entrenched in their negative view of the other. In contrast, Linda felt understood and validated by the second team and responded with "more appropriate" behavior with them. Although she had a fiery temper and reacted strongly to perceived slights, she also recovered quicker and the interactions between the second team and Linda were largely characterized by mutual appreciation. Their respective views of each other led to a more constructive interaction. Our formulations have strong effects on our views of clients, on clients' views of us, and on our developing relationships.[1]

If we accept this premise, it makes sense that we need to be conscious about how we choose to view clients, understand problems, and organize our work. The questions we ask and the ways in which we organize the information we receive have a profound effect on our subsequent work. At the same time, it is important to not simply view this process in a strictly linear fashion. Clients' actions organize helpers' views of them. Helpers' views of clients organize what they attend to while relating to clients. There is a recursive interaction between the two. Because we have a degree of control over our attention, we can decide to attend to things that will be most constructive and therapeutic. Our conceptual frameworks can highlight the similarities between clients and us and humanize our relationship with them or they can highlight our dissimilarities, objectify clients, and invite us to treat them as "other." These interactions have the potential to invite the enactment of particular life stories for clients. If we use pathologizing categories to understand families, we run the risk of bringing forth pathology. Conversely, if we use categories that highlight clients' resourcefulness, we increase the chance of bringing forth competence. In short, what we see shapes what we get and where we stand shapes what we see.

EXAMINING THE CONTEXT
OF OUR ASSUMPTIONS

Our views of clients are embedded in and profoundly shaped by taken-for-granted professional and cultural assumptions about clients, problems, and the process of therapy. For example, treatment traditionally proceeds through a process of conducting an assessment, developing a treatment plan, and implementing a set of interventions organized by that treatment plan. This process is anchored in a number of assumptions. It begins with an assumption that a client's condition can be "objectively" studied and identified in order to treat it. This assumption itself is embedded within a broader assumption that "reality" is knowable and its elements can be accurately and reliably discovered and described, and that the observer who is describing it stands outside the observed system. These assumptions are anchored in a set of beliefs about reality that reflect a modernist world view. Kathy Weingarten (1998) has concisely summarized the implications of a modernist approach for family therapy: "Within family therapy, a modernist approach entails the observation of persons in order to compare their thoughts, feelings, and behaviors against preexisting, normative criteria. The modernist therapist then uses explanations, advice, or planned interventions as a means to bring persons' responses in line with these criteria" (pp. 3–4).

This process of entering into a family system, observing how it functions, comparing that to our theories of "appropriate" behavior, and then developing a series of interventions to tinker with the system so that it functions more "appropriately" puts us in a particular relational stance with families. It positions us as an outsider acting on the system. This stance may provoke a response from families that don't particularly appreciate the experience of being acted upon. We may interpret their response through our perspective as "resistance" or "noncompliance," leading us to either pathologize or try to counter that response. (Chapter 3 examines this process in more depth.)

As described in the previous chapter, it is helpful for both pragmatic and aesthetic reasons to position ourselves as insiders *working with* families rather than outsiders *acting on* them. In my own efforts to develop conceptual models and clinical practices that fit with a relational stance of an appreciative ally, I have been drawn to narrative, social constructionist, and postmodernist ideas. These ideas can be both frustratingly abstruse and wonderfully liberating. They offer a way of thinking about clients and interacting with clients that allow us to bring more of ourselves into our work and position ourselves in ways that clients seem to find very helpful. Much of the material in this book is profoundly influenced by narrative, social constructionist, and postmodernist ideas. At the same time, I also describe ideas that reflect my original grounding in modernist approaches to family therapy. In attempting to draw from both world views, I am not striving for conceptual purity but rather utility. Even though my work is largely anchored in a postmodern world view, I want to acknowledge and honor both my own history and much of the field's history.

I am not going to describe postmodernist, social constructionist, or narrative world views in great depth in this book.[2] Instead, I will try to avoid offputting jargon and yet bring to life the rich possibilities of these ideas through concrete applications. Social constructionist inquiry focuses on the processes by which people come to describe, explain, and account for the world and their position in it (Gergen, 1985). Social constructionist ideas are embedded in a postmodern world view in which there are no essential truths and in which the therapist is no longer the expert who knows how families should solve their problems. Rather than developing a series of interventions designed to bring clients in line with normative standards, the therapist is, in the words of Kathy Weingarten (1998), a "fellow traveler," listening carefully and participating in conversations that generate many possible ways forward. Anchored in a lateral relationship in which our thinking is made visible to clients, there is an attempt to honor clients' abilities to develop solutions and move forward in their lives and to draw on their immediate experience as the criterion against which we measure our efforts rather than normative models. This world view fits well with a relational stance of an appreciative ally.

A social constructionist conception of the self can be helpful in thinking about the effects of our conceptual frameworks on clients. Many individual psychology models assume that what we call the "self" consists of innate personality characteristics that represent the true essence of the person (e.g., Linda is a "borderline"). These models often take an ahistorical, acontextual approach that isolates individuals from their social context. Social constructionist approaches view the "self" as constructed in social interaction (e.g., Linda would become a very different women in different cultures and different historical periods). Our ways of understanding ourselves and our relationship to the world develop in the course of our interactions in the world and are profoundly shaped by those interactions. We are continually creating our identities *in the moment* as we interact with others. This perspective shifts the focus from "who we are" (as a preexisting quality) to "how we are" (our ways of being that are continually being reinvented). However, the person we are becoming is profoundly shaped by and inseparable from our social context.

We grow up in a world of conversations, some involving us, some simply about us. These external conversations become internalized and begin to comprise the stories we tell about ourselves (Tomm, 1992). For example, Linda has heard all her life that she was "a good for nothing, out-of-control bitch who was going nowhere in her life." She heard it from her family, from various boyfriends, and from a culture in which outspoken, assertive women often come to be labeled strident or a "bitch." Over time, those conversations become internalized and operate as a framework for making sense of her life. The conversations that helpers have with and about clients contribute to the construction of their identities and experiences of self. The Linda who interacted with the second team was a different woman from the Linda who interacted with the first team. In the course of her interactions in each context, Linda and the two teams shaped her respective identities. This process occurs in and is profoundly influenced by the broader sociocultural context of those interactions. This assumption that the self is constructed in social interaction rather than preexisting can be perplexing and challenging. The claims of social constructionism violate fundamental cultural assumptions. However, they provide a useful guideline for approaching clients. If we assume that our conversations about and with clients have important effects on how they become in their lives, it behooves us to think carefully about how we organize both our internal conversations about clients and the external dialogues we have with them.

Our conceptual models organize our internal conversations about clients. We can think about these conversations as the stories we develop about clients in the course of interacting with them. The stories that we carry with us organize what we see and shape how we react in our interactions with clients. It is inevitable that we develop such stories in our interactions with clients and it is inevitable that those stories have a profound effect on us, on clients, and on our relationship. Given this, we can attempt to develop conceptual models (or professional stories about clients, problems, and therapy) that will have the most useful effects. From a social constructionist perspective, our hypotheses or formulations can be seen as stories we are creating in the course of our interactions with families to organize our work. Within this perspective, it is particularly important to think about the effects of the formulations we are developing. The following questions provide criteria for evaluating the effects of our formulations:

- What are the effects of our formulations on our view of clients?
- What are the effects of our formulations on clients' views of themselves?
- What are the effects of our formulations on our relationships with clients?
- Do our formulations invite connection, respectful curiosity, openness, and hope?
- Do our formulations encourage the enactment of our preferred relational stance with clients?

In an attempt to be sensitive to the effects of our formulations on the relationship we develop with clients, this chapter highlights ways of understanding problems that are nonblaming and nonshaming and that pay particular attention to family wisdom and competence. The concept of constraints provides one foundation for a new way of conceptualizing families and problems.

FROM DISCOVERING CAUSES TO IDENTIFYING CONSTRAINTS

Many of our attempts to understand situations involve a search for causality (e.g., Why did X happen?). Another way of attempting to understand a situation draws on the concept of constraints (e.g., What prevented something other than X from happening?). When applied to problems in life, the concept of constraints shifts the organizing question, from *What caused the problem?* to *What constrains an individual or family from living differently?* We can identify constraints at a number of levels, including a biological level, an individual level, a family level (which includes family of origin), a social network level (which includes helpers as well as neighbors, friends, and relevant others), and a sociocultural level (the taken-for-granted cultural assumptions that organize our sense of self and the world around us). At each level, we can examine those factors that constrain people from addressing a problem differently. The following example highlights constraints across multiple levels.

Constraints Across Levels

Charlie is a hyperactive 7-year-old boy in foster care who was removed from his home 3 years ago for neglect. Both biological parents currently have no contact with him. For the past year, he has lived with his second foster mother and father, Maria and Joey, a childless couple who hope to adopt him. He has been referred for therapy by Maria for help with his attentional and behavioral difficulties. When he is alone with his foster parents, he does fine. However, at school and when they visit Maria's large family, Charlie becomes scared and out of control and ends up fighting with other children. His foster parents, who normally are nurturing, firm, and consistent, become tentative with him, alternately pleading and threatening. Charlie recently disclosed being sexually abused by an older sibling in his previous foster home which held a total of eight natural and foster children. His disclosure has prompted a crisis for Maria who was willing to take in any child except one who was sexually abused and who now feels trapped by discovering Charlie was abused after growing so attached to him. She fears that the abuse has scarred Charlie for life and yet is in great conflict with the school who she sees as scapegoating him after they were told by his protective worker, Pam, that he had been sexually abused. Maria feels little support from Pam whose office is a great distance away and feels very alone in now dealing with Charlie's disclosure.

If we pose the question of what constrains Charlie from better managing his behavior, we can identify constraints at a number of levels. Charlie does fine in a small, structured setting. However, in larger chaotic situations, he loses his focus and becomes fearful and easily distracted, and his behavior becomes unmanageable. At a biological level, attentional difficulties may constrain him from more effectively organizing the myriad stimuli impinging upon him. Perhaps, Ritalin or another medicine would help bolster his ability to manage chaos.

At an individual level, Charlie states that "he can't trust adults." This belief, anchored in his traumatic experiences of being neglected by his biological parents and abused in his first foster home, constrains his ability to turn to Maria and Joey for support when he feels overwhelmed. The lack of support and resulting sense of isolation leaves him even more vulnerable to the disorganizing effects of chaos at school and when he visits Maria's large family. In this way, the effects of trauma may further constrain his ability to manage his behavior in less structured settings.

At a family level, we can identify a number of interactional constraints that hinder Joey and Maria's effort to help Charlie better manage his behavior. When Charlie begins acting out, Joey watches while Maria pleads with him. As Joey gets frustrated with the ineffectiveness of Maria's pleading, he begins to threaten Charlie that they will go home if he doesn't straighten out. Maria, anxious to avoid a scene, responds with further pleading, which invites further threats from Joey. This interaction undercuts each parent's efforts and constrains their ability to more effectively parent together. Their parenting is further hampered by Maria's family's dismay at Charlie's behavior. As Maria's mother becomes more judgmental, the foster parents become more tentative, which invites increased judgment. The cumulative effect of these patterns constrains Joey and Maria from effectively supporting Charlie in managing his behavior.

At a social network level, there is a constraining interaction between the protective services worker, Pam, and Maria in which Maria feels lied to and not supported by Pam around Charlie's abuse disclosure, who in turn sees Maria as exaggerating Charlie's difficulties. The more Pam minimizes Maria's concerns, the more Maria maximizes her frustrations; the more Maria expresses her frustrations, the more Pam views Maria as a "problem" and dismisses her concerns, and on and on.

Finally, at a sociopolitical level, we can identify a number of ways in which gendered beliefs support particular family interactions and constrain alternate possibilities. Maria's pleading and Joey's threatening are embedded in their respective ideas about being a woman and a man and cultural ideas about men's and women's roles and power in relationships. Consider Joey's statement, "I hate it when Charlie doesn't listen to his mother. I can't just sit by and let him do that to her." When asked about that statement, he replies, "What kind of man would I be if I just sat back and let her take that." This response is strongly influenced by broader cultural ideas about how men, women and children "should" be and act. Examples of such ideas include "men should be in charge," "men should protect and rescue their women," and "children should be seen and not heard." These ideas can be seen as cultural specifications that encourage particular ways of being and discourage others. Often they are unspoken but extremely powerful. They specify normative roles for men and women and construct anyone who lives outside those specifications as abnormal (Freedman & Combs, 1996b). In that sense, they constrain alternative possibilities.

Another example of the constraining influence of taken-for-granted cultural assumptions is the way in which Maria experiences significantly more judgment than Joey from her family. She says, "Joey doesn't notice, but when Charlie starts acting out, I can feel their eyes on me. It's not enough I couldn't have my own kids, now I can't even manage this one." This statement is embedded in strong premises that evaluate Maria's adequacy as a woman in terms of her ability to conceive children and manage them. These premises in turn, are embedded in cultural ideas about Maria's role as a woman and mother. For both Joey and Maria, these broader cultural ideas both shape and constrain their options.

Discourse as a Way to Understand Cultural Influences

Numerous authors have suggested the usefulness of "discourse" as a way to examine the influence of our broader culture on individuals and families. Rachel Hare-Mustin (1994, p. 19) defines discourse as a "system of statements, practices, and institutional structures that share common values." In this definition, discourse includes our taken-for-granted cultural assumptions (e.g., in Joey's and Maria's situation, the cultural "truths" that "men should protect their women" and "a mother is responsible for her child's actions"), our unexamined daily habits (e.g., Joey steps in to discipline Charlie when he talks back to Maria and Maria apologizes to her mother when Charlie misbehaves), and the economic, political, and cultural institutions within which these assumptions and actions exist. These are all intertwined and we both participate in and are the recipients of them. Taken-for-granted cultural assumptions about men's and women's roles shape how Joey and Maria interact when Charlie misbehaves. In turn, their interactions around his misbehavior maintain those prevailing gender assumptions.

Discourses can be seen as "presumed truths" that are part of the fabric of everyday life and become almost invisible. They are difficult to question, shape our identity, and influence attitudes and behaviors. In our lives, we are subjected to multiple and often conflicting discourses. However, over time, certain discourses become dominant and take up more space in our culture. Discourses are often prescriptive and include cultural specifications about how people should be and against which people compare themselves. They both reflect the prevailing social and political structures and tend to support them. Michel Foucault, a French social philosopher, examined the way in which cultural discourse is internalized by individuals. He suggests that people monitor and conduct themselves according to their interpretation of cultural norms (Foucault, 1980). Through this process, discourse shapes our sense of who we are and who we "should" be. When cultural discourses become a framework for making sense of our lives, those experiences that do not fit become invisible. This process has marginalizing effects on some individuals and families. Their own knowledge is obscured and their life is interpreted through the lens of dominant discourses. In this way discourse contributes to the construction of identity and constrains alternate possibilities.

The Constraint, Not the Person, Is the Problem

The family just described highlights interlocking constraints at multiple levels. Anchored in a theory of constraints, therapy can become a collaborative effort in which the therapist works with the family to help them identify and address the constraints in their lives. In Charlie's family, constraints included Charlie's possible attentional difficulties at a biological level ("hyperness" as they called it), Charlie's mistrust and suspiciousness at an individual level, a threatening/pleading interaction between Joey and Maria at a family level, a minimize/maximize interaction between Maria and the protective worker at a social network level, and the influence of gender discourses at a sociocultural level. We can think about each of these constraints as a distinct entity separate from the people involved rather than viewing the constraint as part of the person or family. This conceptualization opens space to examine the relationship between the family and the particular constraint. At times it is helpful to personify problematic constraints. For example, we could think about hyperness (or mistrust or suspicion) as an entity that has come into Charlie's life and now wreaks havoc. We can then think about Charlie as being in a relationship with hyperness (which wreaks havoc in his life) rather than being hyper or having an attention deficit disorder. The process of talking with clients in this way is referred to as "externalizing conversations." This profound shift in thinking about problems was originally developed by Michael White and David Epston (1990) and has been subsequently elaborated by many others within the narrative therapy community. Externalizing conversations consist of questions that move from the internalizing language of clients (e.g., I'm depressed and bring this misery on myself) to externalizing questions (e.g., What does depression get you to do that you might otherwise not prefer?). Externalizing is not simply a therapy technique but a way of organizing our clinical thinking. It offers a way to separate (in our own minds) persons from the problems in their lives. From this perspective, *the person is not the problem, the problem is the problem.* This conceptualization organizes our thinking differently. The goal is to separate people from problems in order to challenge ways of thinking that are blaming and unhelpful and to open ways for people to experience their association with a problem as a relationship with the possibility of developing a different, preferred relationship with that problem.

We can also externalize constraining interactions and beliefs. For example, the threatening/pleading interaction between Joey and Maria can be thought of as a pernicious pattern that gets hold of them and significantly interferes with their joint parenting. Likewise, the prevailing cultural belief that "men should protect their women" and a "mother is responsible for her child's actions" can be seen as separate from Joey and Maria and taking a significant toll on their sense of self. This way of thinking is radically different from our traditional internalizing assumptions (he *is* schizophrenic or he *has* schizophrenia) that locate problems in individuals and is often difficult to incorporate. However, this way of thinking can be extremely useful. It offers a way to disentangle blame and responsibility (which are so tightly intertwined in our culture). If we think about problems, interactions, and beliefs as separate entities that take a toll on clients, we can avoid blaming clients for the difficulties in their lives. This approach positions us in a different relationship with clients. At the same time, thinking about clients as being in a relationship with problems allows us to examine both the problem's influence on them (which avoids blame) and their influence on, resistance to, or coping with the problem (which promotes responsibility from a supportive rather than demanding position). The use of externalizing conversations to simultaneously avoid blame and invite responsibility is explored in depth in Chapter 5.

The shift to a conceptual model based on constraints in which individuals are seen as distinct from those constraints has a number of advantages. By shifting from causes to constraints, we orient ourselves to context as well as internal qualities and thus expand our unit of analysis. By seeing people as distinct from and more than the constraints in their lives, we open space to connect with them as human beings and appreciate their resourcefulness in addressing constraints. Finally, this focus can unite therapists and family members as they struggle together against constraints rather than against each other. This focus invites a stance of solidarity in which our task with clients becomes identifying constraints and then standing with them to support and assist them in challenging those constraints.

This section has focused on constraints across multiple levels. We can also think of constraints as existing in realms of action (interactional patterns) and meaning (beliefs and life stories). To pursue this distinction in more depth, let's now examine ways to better understand constraints in realms of action and meaning.

CONSTRAINTS IN A REALM OF ACTION

People's actions are often embedded in interactional patterns that constrain alternate possibilities. One of family therapy's great contributions to the field of mental health has been the shift from focusing on individuals to focusing on interactions. However, we can take that shift even further and begin to view the people caught in such patterns as distinct from those patterns. One organizing schema that is particularly useful for distinguishing and externalizing interactional patterns was developed by Karl Tomm (1991). Rather than diagnosing individuals, Tomm sought to diagnose what he refers to as pathologizing interactional patterns (PIPs). This section draws heavily on his organizational system.

Over time, the ways in which people interact repeat with some regularity and develop into a pattern. Patterns of interaction have a major influence on individual experience and mental health. Some patterns can help us feel competent and connected to others. For example, every time Jane brings home a test with a B, her father compliments her on her effort and she responds by asking for help with the questions she got wrong. His compliments make it easier for her to ask for help, and her requests for help make it easier for him to compliment her. In the interaction, both feel competent and connected. Other patterns can help us feel incompetent and disconnected from others. For example, every time John brings home an A-, his father chastises him for not getting an A. John responds by declaring that school doesn't mean anything anyway, which confirms for the father that he's not working hard enough. The father's criticism invites the son's defensiveness, and the son's defensiveness invites further criticism. The outcome of the sequence leaves both John and his father feeling incompetent in their respective roles as student and father, and disconnected from each other. The effects of patterns depend on the nature of the actions and the meanings attributed to them. In the second example, the effects of the interaction on John would depend on how his father criticized him and what meaning the boy made of his father's criticism (e.g., the effects of his father's criticism would be quite different if John saw it as confirmation that he just wasn't good enough than if he simply saw his father as an old perfectionist who can't help himself).

Interactional patterns can be seen as a series of mutual invitations in which the actions of one person invite a particular response from the other and the response in turn invite a counter response. In the previous example, the father's criticism invites the defensiveness on John's part. John's defensiveness ("School doesn't mean anything anyway.") in turn invites further criticism from the father ("See, you're not taking your studies seriously."), and on and on. Over time, these patterns can take on a life of their own and induct participants into them. John and his father each "know" the other's response before they even hear it. As the pattern becomes stronger, it develops into a major organizing component of their relationship and has significant influence over their experience of each other and their relationship. The pattern could be diagrammed as follows:

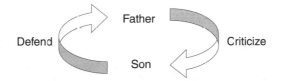

In examining this interaction, it is important to acknowledge that the participants do not have equal opportunities to contribute to the interaction. Although both the father and son contribute to this interaction, their participation and influence in the interaction is not equal. Fathers (as a cultural group) have more power and influence than sons (as a cultural group). Preexisting power differences bias participation and need to be taken into account. As a result, these diagrams are organized with the father placed vertically above the son to remind us of the broader cultural power relations.

The Pattern, Not the Person, Is the Problem

Focusing on the pattern rather than simply the people involved represents a fundamental shift in perspective. In this shift, we are moving from diagnosing and labeling people to diagnosing and labeling patterns. As we separate the pattern from the family members caught up in it, we can focus on the pattern rather than the person as the problem. From this perspective, the family is not doing the pattern; rather, the pattern is doing them. The pattern can be seen as separate from the persons captured by it and having strong effects on them. At the same time, the people caught by the pattern are not passive victims of the pattern. While the pattern may pull them into it, they have opportunities to resist that pull and often have numerous experiences with each other outside of the pattern. Our work can focus on eliciting and elaborating those experiences outside the pattern as a foundation for resisting the pull of the pattern.

Some Examples of Constraining Patterns

Karl Tomm (1991) and his colleagues have distinguished over 200 specific PIPS that generate or support common problems. Similar patterns have also been described elsewhere (e.g., Cade & O'Hanlon, 1993; Madsen, 1992; Watzlawick, Bavelas, & Jackson, 1967; Watzlawick, Weakland, & Fisch, 1974; Zimmerman & Dickerson, 1993). The following are examples of interactional patterns that often constrain effective management of problems faced by multi-stressed families. I will briefly describe several patterns to highlight the shift from locating problems in individuals to locating problems in patterns and then address the usefulness of this schema for addressing patterns.

Overresponsible/Underresponsible

Jim is a stubborn, independent old guy who smokes like a chimney and insists that his chronic lung disease is not a problem. A retired assembly-line worker, he describes himself as a "hardworking guy who just ran out of gas and retired." Given his family history of early deaths, he sees himself as "more or less living on borrowed time" and accepts his situation fatalistically. He doesn't let things bother him and his attitude toward life is visible in the wry smile that accompanies his persistent refrain, "The rain's gonna fall, nothing to do about it." His wife Chris, also a smoker, is very worried about his medical condition. She left her family-of-origin role as a caretaker to become an emergency medical technician and is proud of the fact that "no one has ever died on her watch." After Jim's forced retirement due to health issues, she took on his medical condition as a project, minimizing her own health concerns. However, the harder she tries to get him to stop smoking, the more he smokes, and the more he smokes, the harder she tries to get him to stop. We could make sense of this situation in a number of ways. Jim could be seen as "in denial" about his medical condition or Chris could be seen as "codependent," using her husband's health crisis to conveniently avoid her own issues. We could also focus on the interactional pattern between them that constrains effective management of his medical condition. Jim's underresponsibility for managing his medical condition invites Chris' overresponsibility. As she puts it, "I have to nag him about smoking because he won't take it seriously." Chris' overresponsibility for the management of his medical condition invites Jim's underresponsibility. In Jim's words, "She worries enough for both of us. Why should I add to that?" Paradoxically, the interactional pattern rigidifies Jim's stance that his smoking is not a problem and constrains his management of his medical condition.

Minimize / Maximize

Mary is a 43-year-old teacher who suffers from progressive kidney disease and deteriorating eyesight due to unmanaged diabetes. She hides her medical problems from her Christian Scientist parents who she thinks view illness as a weakness of character. She lives with her husband, Bruce (45), and their three children. There have been numerous crises in the family over the years, and Mary, in her role as family manager, has had little time to focus on her own medical condition. When she does, she alternates between obsessively worrying about her declining health and berating herself for being out of control. Bruce's concerns about her medical condition are eclipsed only by his fears about her pessimistic attitude, which lead him to continually encourage her to be more optimistic. When Bruce, distraught about her pessimism, tells her she's got to be more positive, Mary responds, "What's there to be positive about? The only thing that's positive is that I'm gonna get sicker, I'm gonna need a kidney transplant, and I may die." Bruce, as a Pop Warner football coach, tries to tell her that with that attitude, she'll never win the game and she responds with, "Oh you want optimism, how about this. The good news is when I lose my kidneys, I'll have already lost my eyesight, so I won't have to watch the gruesome scene." This, of course, confirms Bruce's belief that she needs an attitude transplant. Bruce's attempts to help her are experienced by Mary as minimizing her concerns (e.g., "it's not that big a deal, just get a better attitude"), which invites her to respond by maximizing her concerns ("you don't realize how bad it is, let me explain it to you"), which invites more minimizing ("now honey, get a grip, you'll never win the game with a losing attitude"). As the sequence unfolds, both Mary and Bruce feel increasingly misunderstood and compelled to state their case more strongly. In the process Mary is continually emphasizing how little control she has over her medical condition. In this way, the pattern rigidifies her stance that her medical condition is beyond her control and constrains effective management of it. When describing sequences such as this, it's common to describe the reaction to the "identified patient" first in an attempt to move from focusing on the individual to focusing on the interaction. This is not meant to imply the pattern starts with minimizing. Such a pattern could also be described as maximize/minimize.

Pursue/Withdraw

Susan and Richard are an upper-middle-class white couple who both work and share parenting responsibilities for their two children. Each morning at breakfast, Richard reads the newspaper, while Susan tries to talk to him about their plans for the day while also getting the kids ready for school. At night, when work is over and the kids are asleep, Susan wants to talk about their respective days, while Richard wants some down time after a stressful day at work and would rather watch his favorite sports team on TV. Periodically, Susan complains, "We never talk anymore." Richard feels backed into a corner and doesn't know how to respond. He retreats into his newspaper or sports, and Susan, feeling increasingly alone in the relationship, tries various ways to connect with him. The more she pursues him, the more he withdraws and the more he withdraws, the more she pursues. The pattern organizes the responses of each and their actions intensify the pattern. While focusing on the pattern allows us to shift away from locating the problem in individuals, it is also important to take the broader cultural context of the pattern into account and acknowledge the ways in which gender roles and expectations con- tributes to the construction of this pattern.

Demand Disclosure/Secrecy and Withholding

Denise is an African American 12-year-old, brought to therapy by Yolanda, her single-parent, working-poor mother, after Denise was arrested for shoplifting. Yolanda is irate about her daughter's arrest and the fact that Denise keeps lying to her. Yolanda worries about the preva- lence of gang activity and drugs in their inner-city neighborhood and keeps a tight rein on her daughter. Denise is furious that her mother doesn't trust her more and periodically sneaks out at night to "get some space." She's spending more and more time locked in the bathroom, the only private room in their apartment; and Yolanda is very worried about what she's doing in there. However, the more Yolanda demands answers, the more Denise clams up and tells her mother to get out of her face. Denise's secrecy drives Yolanda crazy and sends her into a flurry of accu- sations and interrogation. Yolanda's interrogations reciprocally enrage

Denise who experiences them as statements of mistrust and responds by refusing to answer them. The shift to a focus on the pattern rather than the individuals holds the potential to depersonalize and deescalate their interactions.

Correction and Control/Protest and Rebellion

Bart Jr. is a 12-year-old working-class white boy who has been brought to therapy by his single-parent father who is fed up with his son's absolute refusal to respond to limits. Bart Sr. describes himself as "growing up in a rough neighborhood, falling in with the wrong crowd, and doing time in prison as a young man before seeing the light and turning his life around." He has vowed that his son will not repeat his same mistakes and keeps his son on a strict regimen of chores and studying in an attempt to keep him away from bad influences. However, the more chores assigned to Bart Jr., the more he refuses to do them and the more he refuses to do the chores, the longer the list of demands on him grows. Another less extreme version of this pattern is reflected in a conversation between my preteen daughter and I that has become a running joke between us. The conversation goes, "Arlyn, you need to clean your room." "Dad, if you got off my back, I'd clean it." "Arlyn, if you'd clean it, I wouldn't be on your back," and on and on.

Addressing Interactional Patterns

This shift from assessing people to assessing patterns holds significant advantages. It allows clinicians to make sense of families in ways that objectify patterns rather than individuals. It positions clinicians in a different relationship with families, inviting more compassion and empathy, and minimizing judgment and blame. It helps families to resist self-stigmatization and to join together against the pattern rather than against each other. It also creates space for them to distance themselves from the pattern and develop a new relationship to it. Finally, a focus on patterns implies directions for intervention. For example, in the overly harsh/overly soft sequence, we could, from a structural family therapy perspective, set up an enactment in which the therapist invites either party to shift his or her response as the pattern is played out in the session. The therapist could ally with the mother and unbalance the couple in an attempt to shift the pattern. From a strategic family therapy perspective, a therapist could prescribe and exaggerate the pattern in an attempt to disrupt it. From a solution-focused perspective, the therapist could inquire about exceptions in which the couple's stances are less polarized or when their responses support each other. And, from a narrative perspective, one could externalize the pattern; examine the effects of the pattern on the husband, wife, and their relationship; examine the ways in which cultural discourses coach the father and mother into those patterns; and support them in their development of preferred patterns which would contribute to a restorying of their relationship in a preferred direction. The particular approach chosen will depend on the therapist's theoretical orientation, but this categorization schema has heuristic value across orientations. It provides a concise model for assessing patterns that reinforce particular ways of interacting and constrain alternatives. Once these patterns have been clearly described, strategies for addressing them follow fairly easily.

In each of these situations, the pattern could have been described in a number of ways. There is significant overlap between these patterns. It's important to note that these patterns do not represent real, objective facts but, rather, distinctions drawn by the therapist. In this sense, this taxonomy of pathologizing interpersonal patterns is no more real than the traditional *Diagnostic and Statistical Manual of Mental Disorders* (DSM) used to diagnose individuals. Any assessment or formulation consists of distinctions drawn by the worker. The important question becomes how useful are they and what are the consequences of using them? For example, what are the effects of thinking about a family this way? How does it help us to understand them and guide us in our work with them? What view of them does it give us? What is the impact of that view on our relationship with them? Does this formulation invite respect, connection, and curiosity or does it invite disrespect, distance, and judgment. A number of patterns are highlighted here to help orient the reader toward possible patterns; however, in distinguishing these patterns it is important to construct them with families, drawing on their language. Otherwise we run the risk of debating among ourselves which is the real pattern and then imposing that description on the family.

CONSTRAINTS IN A REALM OF MEANING

We can also distinguish constraints in a realm of meaning. The beliefs we hold constrain us from alternative possibilities. Potentially constraining client beliefs that are worthy of consideration include beliefs about the problem, beliefs about treatment (or what should be done about the problem), and beliefs about roles (or who should do what about the problem) (Harkaway & Madsen, 1989; Madsen, 1992). Within these three broad areas, we can identify a number of important questions. Relevant beliefs about the problem include the following:

- Is this a problem? For whom? In what way?
- How did this come to be a problem?
- Does the client have any control over the problem?
- Are there any special meanings associated with the problem?

These questions are sequential because the answers to each question profoundly affect the framing of subsequent questions. For example, if the "problem" is not defined as a problem, then the question of client influence over the problem is irrelevant.

Is this a problem, for whom and in what way? If a client does not view what appears to us to be a problem, it makes sense that they may not be invested in addressing that problem. Jim, the smoker with chronic lung disease did not view *his* smoking as a problem. He did, however, see smoking as a problem for his wife (because she was "still young and healthy"). Jim would be willing to stop so that his wife would get off his back and address her own smoking. Knowing this belief allows us to shift our efforts and engage Jim around quitting to help his wife's health (which generates more interest for him) than to improve his own health.

A second question is, How did this come to be a problem? The way in which family members view the evolution of a problem profoundly shapes their attempts to manage the problem and their expectations of treatment outcomes. For example, Thomas misbehaves. His mother views his restlessness and behavioral difficulties as signs of an undiagnosed attention-deficit disorder and seeks medication for him. The psychiatrist they go to see is ambivalent about prescribing medication in this instance but goes along with the mother's request. Later he learns that the mother never filled the prescription. Initially, annoyed with her noncompliance, he decides to investigate the situation further. He calls their home and when the father answers, finds out that the father, who is adamantly opposed to medication, threw out the prescription when the mother brought it home. The father views Thomas as a spoiled brat and contends that Thomas just needs some limits set on him. The parents' differing views of the etiology of Thomas's behavioral difficulties lead them to different preferred treatment protocols (medication for a biological problem vs. consequences for a behavioral problem). Paradoxically, the way in which they manage their different opinions constrains their attempts to parent together. The psychiatrist schedules an appointment with the parents and, taking some time to enter into their respective views of the evolution of this problem, develops a better appreciation for their respective beliefs. From within their logic, he emphasizes the importance of a containing environment to help manage a potential biological problem and the way in which medication may help Thomas better respond to limits.

The parents develop a mutually acceptable plan for dealing with their
son.

A third question is, Does the client have any control over the problem? Donna was a single-parent mother of four strapping adolescents
who drank heavily and terrorized the neighborhood. Donna grew up in
an alcoholic household and was repeatedly abused by her father until she
left home, marrying a man who later came to periodically rape and batter
her when he was drunk. When he abandoned the family, she was left to
raise four large adolescent boys who scared both her and the neighborhood. Attempts to get her to set limits on the boys and hold them
accountable for their actions devolved into a minimize/maximize
sequence in which the therapist's plans for consequences were repeatedly
met with a litany of the boys' infractions. When the therapist addressed
Donna's belief that she had no control over her boys and shifted to the
effects of her multigenerational story of victimization on her parenting,
Donna began to identify times when she didn't feel completely victimized
by her sons' actions and used that as a foundation to begin to demand
that they at least treat her with respect in her house. That demand represented an important first step in their development of accountability.

A fourth question is, Are there any special meanings associated with
the problem? Often problems carry with them issues of family membership and loyalty, for example, "All the boys in the family have done time
in juvenile hall," or "He's just like Uncle Joe." The following situation
highlights another example of special meanings of problems. Mark was
having difficulty finishing high school when his father's sudden death
threw the entire family into a panic. Mark became very depressed and
was hospitalized. At the hospital, he complained of vague hypnagogic
hallucinations as he was falling asleep where he would have visions of his
father, which terrified him.[3] He was prescribed an antipsychotic medicine
which he refused to take. His family's support of this stance precipitated
significant conflict between the family and the hospital staff. However,
this decision became understandable in the context of a long family history of having conversations with dead relatives and seeking their advice.
The boy needed his father's advice about surviving his death and graduating high school and feared that the medication would take his father
away yet again. Within this context, Mark's resistance to medication
becomes more understandable. When a consultation interview elicited the
special meaning associated with Mark's "visions," the psychiatrist was
able to discuss with Mark and his family ways in which medication might
be able to take the edge off his conversations with his father without
eliminating the possibility of such conversations and the family's resistance to medication eased.

We can also frame questions about beliefs about treatment. The first question is, Is treatment effective?, or Can something be done about this problem? I used to consult to a large public hospital and met with Samuel, a 70-year-old African American man with chronic hypertension. Partway through a consultation, he turned to the resident working with him and said, "You know son, I've been coming here for 30 years, and each year I get one of you young fellows telling me to take these pills and stop eating salt. Salt ain't got nothing to do with my tension and these pills ain't nothing but sugar. I'm old, but I ain't a dead horse, so when you gonna stop beating your head against me?" When the resident heard this, he realized the futility of prescribing a treatment that only he believed useful. He began to inquire about Samuel's belief that hypertension medication was not useful and learned that he only took it when he got heartburn. The physician continued to ask Samuel what he thought should be done about hypertension and learned a wealth of interesting folklore and alternative treatments. Out of a discussion about their respective beliefs, a joint mutual respect and trust emerged that allowed Samuel to give the medication a chance, even though he was skeptical. Repeated experiences of treatment failures may contribute to a belief that treatment isn't effective. Understanding such a belief makes a client's unwillingness to pursue a particular course of action understandable and may suggest different ways of framing suggestions.

A second question is, What is the most appropriate treatment?, or What would be the best thing to do about this problem? Clients' explanations of the problem and their views about its etiology profoundly affect their ideas about how the problem should be addressed. As we saw in the example of the mother and father who disagreed over the cause of their son's misbehavior, different family members may hold divergent beliefs about what should be done about a problem. Conflicts over the "appropriate" treatment may constrain effectiveness and polarize the participants, inadvertently rigidifying each person's position. Understanding clients' beliefs about treatment allows us to work within clients' logic, which is often more effective.

Finally, we can identify beliefs about roles or who should do what to address the problem. We can identify beliefs about who in the family should do what. In the family discussed previously, the parents not only disagreed about what the treatment should be (medication or limit setting), but also roles. The father thought the mother should provide more discipline, the mother thought the father should get more involved with his son and fill the prescription. It is also useful to explore family beliefs about the role of the family and the role of the professional. Some families may think it is more appropriate to handle a situation themselves than ask a professional who is an "outsider and doesn't know our child the way we do." It is important that we not move in too quickly in our attempts to be helpful. We are better positioned when we first obtain an invitation to help before proceeding. However, the process of getting such an invitation is not a time-consuming, passive process. We need to actively work to get invited in to help. Chapter 3 on engaging reluctant families outlines concrete, active steps to accomplish this task. At the other extreme of beliefs about roles, some families may feel profoundly disempowered and believe they should place their child's care in the hands of an expert who will take charge. The mother with four strapping adolescents continually looked for a therapist who would successfully tell her boys to stop being rowdy. At the same time, she didn't trust that any-one could really help and found herself continually second-guessing every helper involved with her family. In the context of her history, that combi-nation of personal disempowerment and protectiveness for her boys becomes very understandable.

In medicine, it is considered unethical to prescribe a medication without knowing some basic biological facts and what other medications a patient is taking. It is important to have a full understanding of the receiving context into which a medication is introduced as well as be aware of it's potential interaction with other medications. Likewise, in psychosocial interventions, it is important to fully understand the receiv-ing context and potential interaction effects between therapist interven-tions and client meaning systems. Assessing client beliefs about problems, treatment and roles helps us to do this.

Meaning and Clients' Life Stories

As we focus on constraints in the realm of meaning, we can also examine the constraining effects of personal narratives or life stories. A narrative approach begins with a belief that people are interpretive beings continu-ally trying to make sense of their experiences in life. Human beings orga-nize their experiences in the form of stories (Bruner, 1990). Life stories provide frameworks for ordering and interpreting our experiences in the world. At any point, there are multiple stories available to us and no sin-gle story can adequately capture the broad range of our experience. As a result, there are always experiences that fall outside any one story. How-ever, over time particular narratives are drawn on as an organizing frame-work and become the dominant story. These dominant stories are double-edged swords. They make our world coherent and understandable and yet, in the words of White and Epston (1990), "prune, from experience, those events that do not fit with the dominant evolving stories that we and others have about us" (p. 11). Narratives organize our field of expe-rience, promoting selective attention to particular events and experiences and selective inattention to other events and experiences. In this way,

much of our lived experience goes unstoried, is obscured, and phenomenologically does not exist. Particular narratives can become problematic
when they constrain us from noticing or attending to experiences that
might otherwise be quite useful to us.

We can refer back to Charlie, Maria, and Joey for an example of this
process. Maria described growing up as the "lost child who could never
quite measure up" in her family. Her two older brothers were encouraged
to make something of their lives in the United States by their Italian
immigrant father. Her older sister was considered eccentric and Maria
took care of her two younger sisters who were considered quite gifted.
Maria grew up in a traditionally gendered household. Her father worked
hard and was seldom home. Her mother worked at home as a housewife
and devoted herself to the children. Maria developed a strong internalized
voice that "a mother's life is her children." This voice received significant
support from her family of origin, her ethnic culture, and dominant cultural ideas about the role of women in families. Maria was the first to
marry and her parents eagerly awaited grandchildren. When she found
out she was unable to bear children after years of unsuccessful attempts,
shame kept her from telling her mother for 2 years. When she finally told
her mother, the mother wept uncontrollably for 3 days. Maria blamed
herself for this effect on her mother, which only enhanced her shame and
strengthened her story of "not measuring up."

Charlie entered Maria and Joey's life as an explosion of joy. However, that joy was shattered when he disclosed sexual abuse in a previous
foster home. Once again, Maria felt lost, unable to measure up, shamed,
and isolated. As Charlie began "not measuring up" at school and in
Maria's family of origin, she feared he was scarred for life. This story of
not measuring up and being a victim to lifelong scarring resonated for her
and led to incredible despair for Maria in thinking about both Charlie's
plight and her own.

This story of "I'm alone and I can't measure up" organized Maria's
experience of herself and of Charlie. It led to great distance from her husband who worried that she was slipping away from him. Maria's understanding of her life was filtered through this story. Those events that fit
were reinforced. She was acutely aware of her family's response to Charlie's misbehavior. She was furious with Pam (the protective worker) for
her lack of availability to Charlie and the family, and she was in a pitched
battle with the school over their scapegoating of Charlie. However, the
events that fell outside the story of "I'm alone and can't measure up"
were rendered almost invisible. Maria was a wonderfully competent parent to Charlie. She was adept at sensing his needs and had a deep connection to him. Her home was the first place he felt secure enough to disclose
the abuse. She had two friends who marveled at how she parented Char-

lie (a fact she minimized until the two friends were brought into sessions). And yet, within her life story, there was no way to make sense of these experiences.

Much of our work with families can focus on helping them to challenge the constraining effects of dominant life stories by inviting them to attend to events that fall outside those stories as a foundation for constructing new stories within which to interpret their lives. For example, as the therapist elicited Maria's experiences of competent parenting and her thoughts about those instances, Maria began to organize her perception of herself and her life in a radically different fashion. As her two friends were asked to comment on those instances of competence, the emerging threads of a new story could be woven together in a tighter, more complex pattern. A colleague of mine once described that process as "shining a light on instances of competence and asking clients what they notice." Concrete clinical practices to invite this process are further examined in the latter half of this book.

Returning to the constraining effects of dominant life stories, the phenomenological disappearance of instances of competence from Maria's life raises a question of how the story of "I'm alone and can't measure up" developed and how other events in Maria's life were "pruned from experience." To address this question, we need to return to an examination of the internalization of cultural discourses and consider the ways in which broader cultural narratives constrain the development of an alternative story that might bring Maria's connection and competence to the fore.

The Sociocultural Context of Life Stories

The stories that shape our lives are not simply our own. In many ways, they are received from and embedded in family and cultural stories that organize our sense of self and our relation to the world. Stephen Madigan (1997) quotes feminist author Jill Johnson (1973) who claims "identity is what you can say you are, according to what they say you can be" (p. 18). The "they" in this case, refers not to particular individuals but to cultural assumptions and practices passed on through those around us. As described earlier, cultural discourses are internalized by individuals. Weingarten (1998) describes internalized discourse as "the kinds of self-statements that can be produced by incorporating dominant cultural messages" (p. 9). These self-statements are comparative and evaluative, filled with shoulds and oughts. We all live with internalized discourses and they usually leave us believing that we, just like Maria, have not measured up to them.

Maria's story that she couldn't measure up or look to others for assistance is shaped by cultural shoulds and oughts for women in our culture. Her sense of being defective because of her inability to bear children and then her anticipated adoption of a "broken" child is embedded in a cultural story that often equates womanhood with motherhood and a family-of-origin story that a "mother's life is her children." Women are encouraged in our culture to take care of others and regard their own needs as secondary (Bepko & Krestan, 1990). Within that cultural idea about how women should be, bothering her husband or her friends with her troubles was an unthinkable option for Maria. She couldn't impose on others and yet was furious at feeling so alone and unsupported. She had no way of making sense of that fury and it confirmed for her that she didn't measure up as a good wife or mother.

Throughout the stories we hold about ourselves, we find repeated examples of the influence of our broader culture. Gender, race, class, and culture permeate our everyday life. Problematic interactional patterns and belief as well as constraining life stories are embedded in cultural specifications or ideas about who we should be that are taken for granted and go unexamined. These cultural specifications often support problems in people's lives.

In this way, we can see these cultural shoulds and oughts as separate from the people affected by them and again locate the problem in discourse rather than in individuals. Putting constraints in a broader cultural context has a number of effects. It alleviates blame and shame, it counters isolation (e.g., We are not the only ones struggling with this; maybe it's not simply about our inadequacies), it allows the emergence of personal agency to resist constraints, and it counters the invisibility of cultural specifications by naming them. Placing constraints in a cultural context also enriches our understanding of the fabric of clients' lives. Such an endeavor allows us to develop stronger conceptual understandings of clients and families and to intervene more effectively on their behalf. A broader understanding of clients' context also helps us to connect to them in more humane ways.

RECURSIVENESS OF ACTION AND MEANING

This discussion of constraints has separated out realms of action and meaning. However, they are actually complexly interwoven. The way in which we make sense of the world profoundly influences how we interact in it, and our interactions, in turn, either support or challenge our beliefs. We enact or play out the stories we hold about our lives. In the process, we invite others to participate in the performance of our life stories. Their participation shapes those life stories. The ways in which others respond may either confirm or challenge our life stories. However, at the same time, others' actions are interpreted within the predominant story. As a result, actions that fall outside that narrative may not be noticed.

As helpers, we are often invited to participate in the enactment of existing family narratives, and the way in which we respond to that invitation can have a profound effect. In fact, we are often simultaneously invited into several possible family narratives, and we can respond by noting the range of possible narratives into which we have been invited and selecting which ones we will respond to and in what ways. Our interactions with clients can inadvertently invite the enactment of pathologizing and constraining life stories. Our interactions with clients can also invite the enactment of healing and empowering life stories. Those interactions are shaped by the way in which we enter them and reflects a choice on our part. However, our interactions with clients are influenced by our conceptual models and, in many contexts, channeled through the assessment process.

EXAMINING OUR ASSESSMENTS

As highlighted previously, the need for writing assessments in most agencies is a taken-for-granted fact of life. As we have seen, assessments are also interventions. As such, it is important to examine the effects of both the content and process of our assessments. The most frequent misuse of assessments is when they become a laundry list of all the things that are wrong with clients. Ironically, the field of mental health has been much better at emphasizing illness than health. We have many more tools for discovering how things went wrong with clients than for identifying steps to help them do better in their lives. If assessments are to be an effective guideline for therapy, we need to understand problems in ways that are nonblaming and nonshaming, and we need to promote particular attention to the strengths and resources possessed by families. If we think about problems as ruts in clients' lives, a strengths-based focus helps us not to become further mired in the rut. Promoting particular attention to family competencies and knowledges helps us to identify the quickest way out of the rut. This section examines the effects of the content of our assessments and leads into an assessment outline that attempts to address some of the concerns raised. That outline follows with a discussion of the process of conducting assessments and a proposed framework that positions us as collaborators with families who together assess the problems in their lives rather than experts who assess families.

Traditionally, our assessments are organized in a close approximation of the following sequence: Problem and Precipitant, History, Current Functioning, Medical Condition, Risk Factors, Mental Status, Formulation, and Diagnosis. We begin with the problem and its precipitants. We then go back to examine the history that led up to this problem. After examining current functioning and relevant medical information, we assess risk factors and mental status. Finally, we develop a formulation which leads to and justifies a particular diagnosis. Although this approach has a long history, I have a number of concerns about it. Briefly, the initial focus on the problem, precipitant, and history entrenches us in a problem focus. It promotes selective attention to pathology and dysfunction and selective inattention to health and competence. It organizes us around a search for causality and locates problems primarily in individuals. This framework organizes us to think in ways that run counter to the conceptual models proposed here. Developing formulations that justify a diagnosis runs the risk of simplifying and trivializing clients' lives. Michael White (1997), expanding on the work of cultural anthropologist Clifford Geertz (1973), has drawn a distinction between thin conclusions and thick descriptions. Thin conclusions refer to the quick formulations we reach about clients that encapsulate their lives within our frameworks. Describing Linda as a "help-rejecting borderline" obscures the richness of her life. Likewise, simply describing her as "wonderfully resourceful" is also a thin conclusion. Thick descriptions refer to the richly developed descriptions of people's lives that incorporate many aspects of their lived experience and are anchored within their own meaning systems. We are pushed toward thin conclusions by many forces. Some examples include the obligation to diagnose, the pressure to do more with less resources, the demand to manage costs and increase productivity, and the requirement to demonstrate empirically valid, measurable outcomes.[4] However, assessments can also be a vehicle for thick description. We can use them to develop richer understandings of clients' lives. One way to use assessments toward this end is to develop formats that invite rich description rather than thin conclusions.

The traditional assessment outline is anchored in the medical model. Its continued use is encouraged by licensing and reimbursement regulations that mandate the inclusion of particular sections. The forms we use organize our thinking. To complete the forms, we need to ask particular questions. If we accept the assumption that the questions we ask generate experience as well as yield information, then assessment questions shape our experience of clients, clients' experience of self and us, and structure our relationship in particular ways. The forms we use shape our interactions with clients in ways that contribute to their experience of self. This is not to say we are bound like automatons to forms and that the forms determine our interactions with clients. The forms we use invite us into particular interactions with clients and we can accept or decline those invitations. For a fine example of engaging in a postmodern practice within a traditional modernist context, I recommend Glen Simblett's

(1997) chapter on "Narrative Approaches to Psychiatry." However, if we want our forms to support our work rather than simply meet bureaucratic requirements in documenting it, we can consciously develop forms that invite the ways of thinking about and interacting with clients that represent our preferred models and practices. The following assessment outline organizes our understanding of families in ways that support the ideas in this book. It is offered not as *the* way to conduct assessments but as one example of various alternatives we could derive.

An Assessment Outline

The following assessment outline grew out of an endeavor to rewrite forms for a community agency that was integrating home-based and clinic-based therapy. Previously, the agency had one set of forms for the home-based family therapy teams and a second set of forms for the clinic staff based on a medical model and driven by licensing and reimbursement regulations. This outline has been subsequently adapted by a variety of agencies. The suggested assessment outline is a modification of forms developed to conform to licensing regulations and yet encourage the enactment of conceptual ideas presented here. The outline is a generic form that can be used with some modification for children, adolescents, and adults and in both individual and family therapy, and it has been adapted by a variety of agencies. The distinction between individual and family therapy is an unfortunate one. It pushes us to define therapy in terms of who is in the room. If we consider family therapy as a way of thinking about our work rather than a modality of therapy, the distinction between individual therapy and family therapy begins to dissolve. In many ways, "family therapy" is an unfortunate term that runs the risk of arbitrarily limiting the relevant system of conceptualization to simply the family. It is important that we broaden our thinking beyond families to social networks and that we include the sociocultural context of people's lives in our thinking as well. The following outline has been profoundly influenced by the work of Alexander Blount (1987, 1991) and builds on an assessment form he developed. The outline of the form is followed by brief explanations of each section.

One Assessment Format

Identifying Information
• Demographic information

Description of the Family
• Brief description of members of family network that brings them to life (attach genogram or eco-map)

- Living environment and recent changes in household composition
- Family hopes and preferred futures

Presenting Concerns
- Presenting concerns in the words of the referral source
- Client/family response to referral
- Client/family definition of their concerns (in rank order)
- Client/family vision of life when concerns are no longer a problem

Context of Presenting Concerns
- Situations in which problem(s) is most/least likely to occur
- Ways in which client and others are affected by problem(s)
- Client/family beliefs about the problem(s)
- Interactions around the problem(s)
- Cultural supports for the problem(s)

Family's Experience with Helpers
- Client's/family's current involvement with helpers
- Client's/family's past experience with helpers
- Impact of past experience on view of helpers

Relevant History
- Multigenerational history related to important theme regarding presenting concern, constraining interactions, beliefs and life stories, and experience with helpers

Medical Information and Risk Factors
- Status of physical health
- Suicide–Violence–Sexual Abuse–Neglect–Substance Misuse

Mental Status

Protective Factors
- Personal, familial and community characteristics, skills and knowledges that protect from risk and promote resilience
- Improvements noticed since first contact

Diagnosis

Formulation
- Include information that addresses biological, individual, family and sociocultural factors

Identifying Information

This section contains the relevant demographic information typically used. In discussing demographic information, it is particularly important to locate a family in terms of race, class, culture, and sexual orientation. We often launch into a description of families in which these elements only become important if individuals represent a nondominant group (e.g., we'll note when a family is African American but not white, or when a family member is gay but not straight). The assumption that families are white and straight unless otherwise specified contributes to the marginalization of nondominant groups. In addition, culture and class are factors that profoundly affect families' experience, and it is important to contextualize families within these factors.

Description of the Family

This section begins with a brief description of the important persons in a client's life in ways that bring them to life and attempt to portray their humanity. We can move away from sterile descriptions, such as "the identified patient is a 15-year-old girl who presents with oppo-sitional defiant disorder," to richer descriptions that capture their pas-sions, hobbies, idiosyncrasies, and quirks (e.g., Lira is a 15-year-old white, working-class girl with flaming red hair, multiple piercings, caus-tic humor, and a flamboyant disdain for authority figures). By including the important persons in a client's life, this section attempts to move beyond predetermining our unit of conceptualization as simply the fam-ily. "Family therapy" is perhaps an unfortunate term that risks arbi-trarily limiting the relevant unit of conceptualization. This outline draws on the concept of the "problem-determined system," which sug-gests that the relevant unit of conceptualization includes whomever is involved with or talking about the problem (Anderson, Goolishian, & Winderman, 1986). The inclusion of significant others outside the household pushes us to think beyond the family. Who else might be involved in this client's life? What neighbors or relevant members of the family's network would be important to include in our thinking? Who are we not including that we should? The description of the living envi-ronment (their home and neighborhood) helps us get the flavor of the family's life space. Do they live in a cramped apartment in public hous-ing with leaky windows in the winter? Are they renting the upstairs apartment in a two-family home with the landlords living downstairs with a newborn who cries continually? Do they own their own home? Is the home filled with photographs and children's artwork or is it a finely decorated space with white carpets and fine antiques populated by a couple with a new young child? Recent changes in the household composition is included to highlight any notable transitions in the fam-ily life and in their social environment. Finally, family hopes and pre-ferred future help us to get to know the family outside the concerns that bring them to therapy and help us identify some goals that we can begin moving toward. (The usefulness of this future orientation is fur-ther examined in Chapter 4.)

Presenting Concern

This section begins with a description of the presenting concerns in the words of the referral source or whoever initiates contact. Beginning in this way highlights that someone is describing the problem in a particular way. It sets the stage to examine how concerns are defined and reminds us that the description we've received of the problem is an opinion rather than an objective declaration. Describing the family's response to the referral helps us to avoid beginning to work on a problem that is not defined as such by the family (see Chapter 3) and leads naturally into the family's definition of their concerns (which may be to get the referral source "off their backs"). This sequence aids in developing an agreed-upon focus with the family that will serve as the basis for a therapy contract (explored more in Chapter 4). The presenting concern is the hanger that holds the rest of the assessment. The more clearly the problem can be concretely described, the easier it will be to write the rest of the assessment. Finally, including a description of how life will look different when these concerns are no longer a problem shifts us from a problem focus to a future focus.

Context of Presenting Concerns

This section includes the situations in which the most pressing problem(s) is more or less likely to occur (e.g., Freddie's tantrums are more likely to happen when his father is on the road and his mother is home alone and exhausted and least likely to happen when both parents have more energy and are more available to him). This section gives us information about the interactional context of the problem and opens space for eliciting and building on exceptions. The examination of ways in which the client and others are affected by the problem begins a process of labeling the problem as the problem rather than the person as the problem. It allows us to examine the effects of the problem on individuals and relationships (e.g., the tantrums scare Freddie who fears losing control, distance his father who becomes angry and spends more time at work, pull his mother into hopelessness, and lead to fights between the parents about how to manage Freddie). Client/family explanations of the problem elicits family beliefs about the problem and how they shape the family's experience and handling of the problem (e.g., Freddie has no idea where the tantrums come from, his mother believes he's cursed, and his father thinks Freddie's mother is just spoiling him). Describing such beliefs highlights constraints in a realm of meaning. Examining interactions around the problem elicits constraints in a realm of action (e.g., When Freddie's mother expresses her belief that he is cursed, his father tells her to stop acting so stupid and says he just needs a good "whupping." The mother defends Freddie and they escalate into an overly harsh/overly protective pattern.). The questions about cultural support for the problem encourage us to take a broad conceptualization and include constraints at a sociocultural level (e.g., the father's culturally embedded belief that he should be able to just tell his son to knock it off and get more respect from his son and wife because he's working hard to build a life for them).

Family's Experience with Helpers

This is one of the most useful sections for clinicians. It seeks a description of clients' current involvement with helpers along with their previous positive and negative experiences with helpers. It is important to include the impact of these past experiences on the family's current view of helpers. For example, we might learn about a family's previous experience with a helper in which they felt interrogated and judged that has led them to believe that you can't trust helpers but have to go through the motions of talking to them. Alternatively, we might learn that a family had a previous helper who was nice and listened attentively but never offered the suggestions they desperately sought and have concluded that therapy is supportive but basically a waste of time. This section is helpful because it gives us a coming attraction of difficulties we may fall into with a family. In this way, we can benefit from the efforts of previous helpers and enter the relationship differently, if necessary. In this process, it's important to draw a distinction in our own heads between the "facts" of a situation and a family's experience of it. Acknowledging a family's negative experience of a particular situation does not mean agreeing that another helper is "bad." It simply means accepting the validity of their experience. For families that have had multiple negative experiences with helpers, the process of asking about their previous experiences may help to define this current relationship as different. The simple fact of asking often opens the possibility of developing a different relationship with them.

Relevant History

After getting this initial information, we can move into relevant history. Traditionally, historical information has followed presenting problem and preceded current functioning and social information. I find it more useful to have a history follow the presenting concern, its context, and the family's experience with helpers. In this way, the history becomes theme driven rather than an outpouring of every piece of data available about this family. This sequencing helps us to focus our work and avoid overly long assessments. We can focus our history taking on the elaboration of relevant themes related to the presenting concern, constraining interactions, beliefs and life stories, and the family's experience with helpers.

Medical Information and Risk Factors

"Medical Information" includes information about family members' health and its relationship to the presenting concerns. "Risk Factors" include issues such as suicide, violence (by others or toward others), sexual abuse, physical abuse, neglect and substance misuse. In our attempts to emphasize family resourcefulness, it is important that we not lose sight of risky situations and insure that risk factors are being adequately addressed.

Mental Status

"Mental Status" is traditionally included in individually focused assessments and is typically required by licensing regulations. Blount (1987) has reframed mental status as the ways in which the problem(s) impairs the day-to-day functioning of those people affected by it and suggests expanding a consideration from just the identified client to all affected members. This can include the usual categories such as appearance and behavior, general orientation, thought content and organization, attention, concentration, memory, intellectual functioning, mood and affect, and judgment and insight.

Protective Factors

"Protective Factors" include the personal, familial, and community characteristics and skills that promote resilience and protect clients from risk (Walsh, 1996, 1998). Whereas risk factors provoke our anxiety and alert us to how worried we should be about clients, protective factors have the potential to contain our worry by identifying the resources clients have available to them to manage the risks and highlight what we can build on to further strengthen their coping. This section also includes other family strengths, resources, and knowledge as well as improvements noticed since our initial contact that can serve as a foundation for continued progress.

Diagnosis

Most assessment forms in public agencies require a diagnosis from the fourth edition of the *Diagnostic and Statistical Manual of Mental Disorders* (DSM-IV; American Psychiatric Association, 1994). DSM-IV is the major classification system of "mental disorders" used in North America. The question of how to incorporate DSM-IV diagnoses in family assessments is a thorny one. Many family therapists find DSM-IV to be of limited use in understanding families or planning family treatment. Family systems theory and DSM-IV are based on different epistemological paradigms, and Denton (1989, 1990) has raised a number of ethical questions around using DSM-IV in family therapy. Numerous authors have also raised serious questions about the negative effects of the use of DSM-IV labels (e.g., Gergen, 1990; Tomm, 1990). A thorough consideration of these concerns is beyond the scope of this section, but I will briefly review some of them. (For an incisive critique of DSM-IV, I'd refer interested readers to Tomm, 1990.) DSM-IV locates problems within individuals and obscures the influence of social context. It promotes selective attention to deficits and selective inattention to client competence and knowledge. The labeling process is often stigmatizing and pathologizing. It creates a relationship that can be objectifying and dehumanizing of clients who are subjected to professional classification. Personally, I have not found it useful in the determination of a specific treatment plan. It tends to support thin conclusions rather than thick descriptions. And, most important, it invites us into relationships with clients that may not support the development of a relational stance that we would prefer. Based on concerns such as these, a number of clinicians have refused to use DSM-IV diagnoses. I think this is a courageous stand and one that I support. At the same time, in many settings, the use of DSM-IV diagnoses is an implicit condition of employment. For many clinicians, the decision to not use diagnoses is not a viable option. If we are using it, it is important to see it as one of a number of possible stories about a client and to be clear about why and in what manner we are using it. Blount (1991), in his development of a systemic mental health center, has recommended the inclusion of the following category after a diagnosis: "Ways in which the experience of the person(s) diagnosed is different from the standard description of that diagnosis." I think this is an interesting addition to a diagnosis and would encourage others to utilize it. It helps to remind us that people are more than the diagnoses we assign them and pushes us to move from thin conclusion to thick description.

Formulation

The formulations we develop about a family can be thought of as a story we have created to organize our thinking about that family in our efforts to be helpful to them. Our formulation is not "objective truth" but one of a number of possible stories. Our formulations have the potential to become self-fulfilling prophecies. Once again, what we see is what we get.

Given this, it is important to consider the consequences of the formulations we develop. One useful way to organize formulations is to attempt to address three questions:

- Where would the client/family like to be at the end of therapy?
- What constraints impede them getting there?
- What strengths, resources and knowledges might they draw on or construct to address those constraints?

In addressing these questions, it is important to include information that addresses multiple levels, including biological, individual, family, social network, and sociocultural factors. Chapter 4 examines these three questions in more detail.

EXAMINING THE PROCESS OF ASSESSMENTS

This assessment format may encourage the development of different descriptions of clients and families, but the process through which we obtain the information is critically important. The assessment process places therapists and clients in a particular power relationship in which client experience often is organized into professional categories. This process runs the risk of obscuring and marginalizing client expertise and knowledge and can have inadvertent disempowering effects on clients. In this relationship, professionals are in a position to "know" and clients in a position to receive that knowledge. (Often when clients don't "appropriately" receive that knowledge, they are labeled "resistant.") Although there is a distinct power difference between therapists and clients in therapy that cannot be erased, there are many ways in which we can make therapeutic interactions more egalitarian in order to honor and celebrate client wisdom and to avoid inadvertently disempowering clients. It is important to consider the effects of assessment processes on clients and to be aware of their implications. There are several inherent risks in a process whereby one party assesses another. One is that clients, as the object of assessment, will feel objectified and disempowered. A second is that the process encourages a distancing in the relationship between the assessor and the assessed.

One way to address these concerns might be to decide not to conduct assessments, declaring that they are an oppressive exercise of professional privilege. However, that is a difficult option for most therapists in community agencies and the public sector. Most clinics and community agencies are bound by licensing and funding regulations that require particular types of information in forms. Deciding not to participate in the generation of those forms presupposes a certain privilege that many clinicians who have decided to work with families typically served by such agencies do not have. Those clinicians are bound to comply with paperwork requirements as a condition of employment. In addition, assessments can help us to organize our thinking and ensure that we have a full understanding of clients' lives. An important question becomes how can we use traditional forms to organize our thinking about clients and our interactions with clients in ways that we find ethically and politically palatable and that promote partnership and accountability?

Shifting Our Role in the Assessment Process

One way to use forms to reorganize our thinking as well as our interactions with clients is to shift from a role in which therapists as professional experts assess families to a role in which therapists and families together draw on their mutual expertise to collaboratively assess the problems that have come into their lives. In this process, the concerns raised here about the assessment process can be used to mutual advantage. As therapists and clients jointly become the assessors of problems, they increase the possibility that problems will become objectified and disempowered. A joint assessment of problems that are seen as separate from families may also encourage a distancing in the relationship between families (the assessors) and problems (the assessed).

The next section contains a series of questions that can be asked of families to engage them in this type of assessment process. The particular questions outlined here represent questions therapists might hold in their heads and clearly need to be adapted to the language of any particular client or family. As therapists engage in this type of a questioning process with families, it is important to keep in mind that as descriptions of clients' lives, these assessments are really their property. They are written documents of clients' life experiences. Therapists may want or need to keep a copy for agency records, but the original (even if the "original" needs to be a photocopy to maintain compliance with licensing regulations) should remain with clients.

Questions to Assess Problems
Rather Than Families

Description of the Family
- Who are the important persons in your life? (You/your refers to the plural you.)
- What are you like outside the influence of the problem that brings you to therapy?

- As I get to know you, what do you think I will particularly appreciate about you?
- Where would you like your lives to be headed?

Presenting Concerns
- What is the referral source's biggest concern?
- What is your reaction to that?
- What are your concerns? (in rank order)
- How will your life look different when these concerns are no longer problems?

Context of Presenting Concerns
- In what situations is the problem most/least likely to occur?
- What is the effect of the problem on you and your relationships?
- How does this problem interfere with your preferred life?
- How do you explain the problem?
- How have you attempted to cope with the problem?
- What broader cultural support does the problem receive?

Family's Experience with Helpers
- What helpers are currently involved with you?
- What has been your past experience with helpers (good and bad)?
- What impact does that have on your view of helpers?
- What are the implications of this for our work together?

Relevant History
- What is the history of the relationship between the problem and you?
- When has the problem been stronger/weaker in the history of that relationship?
- When have you been stronger/weaker throughout the history of that relationship?
- What has supported the problem's influence on you? (family-of-origin level, family–helper level, broader cultural level)
- What has supported your influence on the problem? (family-of-origin level, family–helper level, broader cultural level)

Medical Information and Risk Factors
- What effects has the problem had on your physical health? Has it exacerbated existing medical concerns for you or others?
- What, if any, interactions has the problem had with suicidal ideation, violence, substance misuse, sexual abuse or neglect in your lives?

Formulation
- What future would you like to have?
- What constraints stand in the way of you getting to that future?
- What strengths, resources and knowledge do you have to deal with those constraints?

When I have used this framework, I have often begun with a contextualizing introduction that goes something like this:

> "As you probably know, one of the things I'm required to do is write up an assessment of your situation. I have often found that this process can be very helpful to me in organizing my work with families. However, because this assessment is a story about your lives, I would like to propose that we do it together. What I would like to do is ask you a series of questions to get some information and write down much of what you say so I can make this assessment as close to your words as possible. After we are done here, I will write it up and we can go over it and see what you think. We can see what fits for you, what doesn't and what you think we should add. How does that sound to you?"

I often give families an outline of the categories and offer some explanation for their inclusion. In my experience, clients have found this a valuable and empowering experience. The framework begins with a focus on getting to know families outside the problems in their lives and views those problems as separate from families. As a result, clients who may be initially quite suspicious about the process become engaged. If, in the course of a discussion of the draft assessment, differences of opinion emerge, these can be discussed and brought into the final assessment. In this way, the assessment becomes an acknowledgment of multiple perspectives rather than an imposition of a homogeneous single perspective.

This process takes more time but leads to the creation of assessments that organize and support our work. In this way, paperwork becomes intimately connected to the process of therapy rather than something that is done the night before a paperwork audit.

The framework laid out here does not include information on mental status or diagnosis. If, as described in the first assessment framework, we think about mental status as including some of the effects of the problem(s) on individuals, that section can be captured in the context of the presenting concern. I do not find diagnosis useful, and in fact, I find it potentially quite harmful for families for the reasons laid out earlier. My preference would be to not include mental status or diagnosis as separate sections in an assessment that I would write with families. However, if we are required to include them as separate sections, I would recommend a frank discussion with families about that requirement and our thoughts about how to handle it.

As a collaborative process, paperwork can channel our work with clients and help to keep us anchored in the relational stance we would prefer. This process can also lead to interesting though potentially difficult discussions between clients and therapists that make visible the power dynamics in the relationship in ways that may become uncomfortable. However, these issues are in the room and are an important part of multi-stressed families' experience with the helping network. Raising them to an explicit level can be a productive experience for everyone involved.

SUMMARY

This chapter emphasized how our conceptual models shape our views of clients and our resulting interactions with them. A social constructionist approach highlights the ways in which the assessment process *constructs* rather than *discovers* realities. If we accept that assumption, we have a particular responsibility for developing conceptual models that promote nonshaming and nonblaming ways of understanding problems and focus particular attention on family strengths, resources, and wisdom. Drawing on the concept of constraints, we examined constraints at a level of action (problematic interactional patterns) and meaning (constraining beliefs and personal, family, and cultural narratives). That examination provided a foundation for an assessment framework that attempts to objectify and disempower problems rather than families.

Throughout this process, it is important to keep in mind that the attitude with which we conduct assessments is a powerful intervention (Madsen, 1998). It is important that we conduct assessments in a friendly, positive atmosphere, that we use normal everyday language, that we maintain a positive and hopeful view of clients and families, that we acknowledge their expertise on their lives, and that we attempt to put ourselves in their shoes and conduct ourselves in ways that we would want others to treat us. Finally, it is important to keep in mind the honor and privilege of being allowed to enter people's lives. It is useful to receive the information shared with us as a gift and to keep in mind that we need to "earn the right" to conduct an assessment. We are not just due this information because of the role we are in. It's helpful to pose to ourselves the question, How would a complete stranger need to act with us for us to share our life story with him or her? The next chapter examines ways to engage clients who may be understandably reluctant to begin that process.

NOTES

1. This comparison of Linda's different reactions to these two teams should not be taken as a description of a "good" team and a "bad" team. It is an attempt to highlight that our conceptual frameworks have effects on clients (and thera-

pists as well), that these effects may be positive and/or negative. It behooves us to acknowledge and address those effects. This section is not a comment on individuals but, rather, on prevailing conceptual frameworks and the taken-for-granted cultural assumptions that inform them. This distinction should become more evident as the book unfolds.

2. For readers interested in one accessible discussion of social constructionism, see *An Introduction to Social Constructionism* (Burr, 1995).

3. Hypnagogic hallucinations can occur in that nebulous area between wakefulness and sleep and are normal phenomena.

4. The end point of many traditional assessments is a DSM diagnosis, which is represented on Axis I or II in a numerical fashion (e.g., 313.81 for oppositional defiant disorder or 301.83 for borderline personality disorder). This encapsulation of an individual's life and experience into a five-digit number may be the ultimate thin conclusion.

3

⟐⟐⟐

Collaboration
Is a Two-Way Street

Engaging Reluctant Families

In working with multi-stressed families, we often encounter situations in which families minimize problems or insist that the problem lies with only one particular family member. In both situations, such families may be reluctant to actively engage in family therapy. We also encounter families who seem grateful for our suggestions but somehow never follow through on any of them. Attempts to engage reluctant families are informed by our beliefs about "resistance."[1] This chapter examines various conceptualizations of resistance and their effects, proposes a model for collaborative relationships, and explores ways to develop collaborative relationships with reluctant families. As a starting point, consider the following clinical situation.

Carolyn is a 35-year-old mother who looks beaten down by life. She's on medication for depression and anxiety and has difficulty venturing out of her house. She grew up in a working-class family of heavy drinkers and went on welfare when her husband abandoned the family. She lives in a subsidized apartment with her four children (ages 13, 11, 8, and 2) and her brother Frank who is on disability for a back injury. Frank drinks heavily and has physically beaten Carolyn in the past. The family has a long history of involvement with protective services because of neglect concerns. Maura is a hyperactive 11-year-old with a genital abscess that hasn't healed over a long period. Carolyn emphatically declares that Maura got the wound when she fell on her bed frame, but various helpers are concerned about possible sexual abuse by Frank. Despite the presence of home health aides to help monitor her progress, Maura's wound has not healed and medical personnel are concerned about infection. The home health aides complain that the house is filthy and dangerous. The kitchen is infested with cockroaches and the bathtub is black with grime.

Medical personnel are frustrated in their attempts to teach Maura daily hygiene skills and furious with Carolyn for her lack of support for their efforts. They complain that she refuses to carry out their instructions to keep Maura off her bicycle to avoid reopening the wound. Maura's physician at a prestigious hospital an hour away has given Carolyn several stern lectures on the need to better care for her children's health and has strongly recommended that Frank leave the house. The physician orders a psychiatric hospitalization to get a better assessment of Maura. Carolyn, concerned about losing her children to protective services, reluctantly agrees but then refuses to cooperate with the discharge plan of outpatient family therapy. The physician is concerned about Carolyn's apparent unwillingness to help her daughter and demands that Carolyn bring Maura to the hospital twice a week in order to better monitor her progress. For her part, Carolyn is furious and disgusted with the medical personnel. She feels demeaned by the way she is treated and makes a point of rubbing dirt on her hands in the parking lot just before she takes Maura into appointments just to annoy them. The physician seeks a consultation to help the family see the need for outpatient treatment.

We could make sense of Carolyn's reluctance to engage in therapy in a number of ways. We could focus on Carolyn, seeing her as "in denial" about her daughter's condition and "resistant" to services. We could focus on the medical personnel, saying that in their alarm over the lack of healing and possible sexual abuse issues, they began intrusively imposing their ideas. We could focus on the interaction between Carolyn and medical providers in which their intrusiveness invites her resistance and her continued resistance invites escalating intrusiveness. Finally, we could focus on the professional and cultural assumptions that specify roles and organize the relationship between the physician and the family. In this context we might examine the effects of the medical model, according to which helpers diagnose problems and prescribe treatment and patients follow the prescribed treatment. Seeing that definition of the relationship as a cultural construction, we might examine the effects of that definition on Carolyn's interactions with helpers and on the consequences for Carolyn of challenging that particular construction. Each of these different ways of viewing this situation affects how subsequent interactions will unfold and has distinct consequences for how we understand and evaluate both helpers and families. The next section delineates various ways in which resistance has been viewed in family therapy and examines the effects of these conceptualizations on Carolyn and her family.

WHAT DO WE DO ABOUT "RESISTANCE"?

Within family therapy, there are a variety of available formulations of resistance. These formulations can be seen as metaphors that organize our thinking about resistance. The way in which we understand resistance organizes how we respond to it, influences how clients respond to our responses, and shapes the resulting therapeutic relationship. While our understanding of resistance may be a metaphor to guide our thinking, the metaphors we choose have *real* effects on us, our clients, and our relationship. These effects may be positive or negative. Our understanding of resistance may invite connection, appreciation, and respect or evaluation, judgment, and criticism. This section explores some of the metaphors of handling resistance in family therapy and examines some of their possible effects. Although some of these metaphors may initially appear to be objective truths, it can be helpful to consider them as one of a number of possible guiding formulations.

We Can Try to Interpret Resistance

Sigmund Freud developed the concept of resistance. He found that individuals who approached him for help were at times hesitant to reveal their thoughts and feelings to him, not accepting of his interpretations, and reluctant to explore their relationship to him. Freud believed that, despite their desire for help, patients unconsciously employed a host of defensive maneuvers to avoid becoming aware of unresolved intrapsychic conflicts or unacceptable thoughts and impulses (Freud, 1949). The concept of resistance became a cornerstone of psychoanalytic thought. Resistance was seen as residing in the patient's unconscious and being expressed in the treatment relationship through transference. A major focus of treatment became the analysis of resistance as it manifested itself in the treatment relationship. The analyst, through interpretation would attempt to "make the patient *aware* that he (sic) had the resistance, *why* he had the resistance, and why he had it in that form" (Fenichel, 1954, p. 201). Offering interpretations (generated by the analyst based on psychoanalytic theory) to help patients work through resistance and gain insight into underlying conflicts, thoughts, and impulses organized the therapeutic endeavor.

Within this conceptualization, Carolyn's resistance to therapy might be seen as a defensive avoidance of the anxiety provoked by having to face her daughter's possible sexual abuse by Frank as well as her own trauma history. Although this is a reasonable hypothesis, it is important to not mistake our hypotheses for reality. Assessing Maura's safety in this situation is extremely important, but it is also important that we don't enter with an assumption of "guilty, until proven innocent." Maura's physician saw Carolyn as a fragile, anxiety-ridden woman with primitive defenses. She adamantly believed Carolyn needed to kick Frank out of the house but lacked the emotional resources to do so. We could draw an important distinction here between what Carolyn *needs* to do and what the professionals *would like* her to do. We don't know whether Maura is at risk. We don't know whether Frank is currently abusive to Carolyn. We don't know what positive effects Frank's presence has on the family. Possible distinctions between what we as helpers think families need to do and what families really need to do have the potential to get lost when the therapeutic relationship is structured in a way in which the professional "knows" and has the role of interpreting that knowledge to clients.

In this situation, the physician pushed Carolyn to do what the physician assumed was the right thing and then considered it resistance when Carolyn didn't comply. Two thorny issues emerge here. First, a series of ethical questions arise. Is the physician in a position to know what the right thing to do is? Does the physician know Carolyn's ideas about the right thing? Does the physician know why Carolyn might disagree with her ideas? Without a fuller appreciation of Carolyn's experience of the situation, snap judgments about who Carolyn is and what she should do in her life are potentially arrogant and intrusive. Second, methodological issues arise. If we were to assume that kicking Frank out of the house were the best thing to do (a questionable assumption without further information), simply attempting to get Carolyn to do that without understanding her thoughts about the matter and appreciating what might constrain her from that action is likely to be a fruitless and frustrating endeavor. We can run into serious problems when we as therapists come to believe that we know what is best for clients.

A danger in this metaphor of interpreting resistance is the way in which it highlights professionals' ideas and obscures clients' ideas. When therapists are the ones who define the meaning of resistance and then help clients to come to that realization, they run the risk of coming to know more and more about their categories of understanding the world and less and less about clients' categories. This emphasis on professional definitions has the potential to obscure and invalidate client experience and mystify power differences in the therapeutic relationship. Clients' protests against perceived abuses of those power differences may then be dismissed as pathological resistance.

For example, in various educational settings, I have periodically interviewed members of a client self-help group about their positive and negative experiences with helpers. The purpose of these interviews was to help students (and me) learn about positive and inadvertently negative effects of our practices from clients who had not been served well by the mental health system. Routinely, these interviews have been profoundly moving for students, group members, and me. In one setting in which I proposed such an interview, there was concern that the proposal would make students too self-conscious about their work. One faculty member, who is a very gentle, respectful individual, declared that doing such an interview ran the risk of inviting the women being interviewed to "act out the transference." When asked about that statement, he expressed a concern that questions about their experience with helpers might provoke comments that reflected projections from their experience with other authority figures that would interfere with helping them to accept and work through those other issues. The group's reaction (including mine) was to nod sagely and move on. As I later reflected on the comment, I realized the way in which that formulation transformed legitimate grievances of clients who had been mistreated by the mental health system into dysfunctional projections of their unresolved psychopathology. The important point of this story is not to focus on the faculty member but on the formulation that organized his thinking. In this sense, the formulation, not the person, is the problem. Although none of the women were directly affected by the comments in that meeting, their lives have been profoundly affected by similar comments in various case conferences and team meetings in which their resistance to treatment was discussed by similar groups of professionals. Their experience of abusive aspects of the mental health system is invalidated by such a formulation. The structural power difference that puts professionals in a position of defining the legitimacy of client experience is mystified by such a formulation. The profoundly disempowering effects of that way of thinking are obscured by such a formulation. And, finally, defining legitimate grievances as pathological projections has the potential to become a self-fulfilling prophecy and to exacerbate resistance.

We Can Try to Challenge Resistance

The concept of resistance is often seen as a universal property of individuals and systems. Within this belief, all individuals and systems have a resistance to change in the status quo, and anyone who seeks to bring about change will experience resistance to their efforts. This belief is expressed in the popular phrase: "For every action, there is an equal and opposite reaction." Within family therapy, this idea appears in the concept of homeostasis. A homeostatic metaphor proposes that families are systems that view change as a threat and respond with attempts to maintain stability. The concept of homeostasis was originally introduced into physiology to explain the body's ability to regulate itself and maintain internal constancy in the face of external changes (Cannon, 1932). It was extended from physiological systems to cybernetic systems to explain a system's ability to maintain both stability and change (Ashby, 1952). Jackson (1957), in research on family dynamics and the etiology of schizophrenia, was the first to apply the concept to family systems. When he observed that changes (even improvements) in the identified patient often led to family destabilization, he concluded that the primary function of symptoms was to maintain the homeostasis of the family. This metaphor led to a focus on the ways in which families resist change and attempt to maintain stability while obscuring the ways in which families continually change. For example, Minuchin and Fishman (1981) state:

> When a family comes to treatment, it is in difficulty because it is stuck in the homeostatic phase. . . . One of the goals of therapy is, therefore, to move the family to a stage of creative turmoil, where what was given must be replaced by a search for new ways. . . . Therapy is the process of taking a family who are stuck along the developmental spiral and creating a crisis that will push the family in the direction of their own evolution. (pp. 26–27)

From a structural family therapy perspective, this induction of crises is done by challenging family symptoms, family structure, and family beliefs (Minuchin & Fishman, 1981). Within this perspective, a home-based team might initially go out to see Carolyn's family in the home to provoke a crisis that will bring the family into the clinic. However, an excursion with that intent orients the therapist to the family in a particular way. A focus on the family's homeostasis runs the risk of implying that the family has an investment in maintaining status quo. This can lead to a judgmental attitude that may provoke a family response easily viewed as resistance. Ransom (1982) points out that what families may be resisting in these situations is not change but the attitude and approach taken by the therapist. If we begin with an assumption that families are committed to stability, we are most likely to notice their efforts to maintain stability. Conversely, if we begin with an assumption that families are continually changing, we are more likely to notice openings for change. Again, what we see is what we get.

Homeostasis has been a useful conceptual tool in the history of family therapy. It has given rise to numerous powerful interventions and provides a clear organizational framework for intervention. However, like all metaphors, it has *real* effects, both positive and negative. One of the negative effects may include the invitation of an adversarial attitude toward families. The adoption of a homeostatic metaphor with its emphasis on stability may orient us to what family members are *not* doing rather than to what they are doing (highlighting deficits over resources). The emphasis on crisis induction and disruption can invite us into *working on* families rather than *working with* them (contributing to an antagonistic relationship in which we're trying to beat homeostasis and the family is trying to maintain it rather than a collaborative relationship in which we're working together against problems besieging the family). It may also contribute to an inadvertent disempowerment of the family's attempts to cope with problems.

In using a homeostatic metaphor, it could be possible to separate family members from a hypothesized force of homeostasis and ally with them against it. However, homeostasis has traditionally been located in the family and seen as something they are doing. When we become frustrated in our attempts to help families, locating the difficulty in them can provide us with easy answers. ("Oh, there they go being homeostatic again.") Our hypotheses then become statements of certainty rather than questions of curiosity and close down space for the emergence of new ideas. In addition, we run the risk of minimizing our own role and contribution to the family's reluctance. Though a homeostatic metaphor has been a fundamental concept in family systems theory, it is important to consider both the positive and negative consequences drawing on this metaphor in our work.

We Can Try to Outwit Resistance

Attempts to outwit resistance are most associated with the various strategic schools of family therapy. Michael Nichols (1984) points out that "tactics to outwit resistance are the very essence of strategic therapy; they are both its greatest contribution to the field and the object of its strongest criticism" (p. 466). The strategic schools assume that resistance is central to change efforts and have developed sophisticated strategies to minimize or overcome resistance through such techniques as reframing, prescribing, restraining, and repositioning. Although many of their techniques offer exquisite ways to get around people's opposition or defiance and negotiate the shoals of relational politics, they can also be experienced by families as disingenuous game playing by tricky therapists and provoke a continuation of such games.

In their attempt to outwit resistance, strategic therapists have often drawn on a "function of the symptom" metaphor. Related to homeostasis, this concept views symptoms as serving a protective function for a family. The adoption of this metaphor has been so pervasive in the field of family therapy that it has achieved the status of myth. It is important to remember that it is a concept we invented to support our work with families and to judge its value by its utility in that work. A functionalist metaphor has been useful in developing a better appreciation of a family's mix of desire for change and fear of the unknown and has provided a foundation for the development of a number of powerful interventions. In the previous clinical example, one could make a case that Maura's symptoms serve a function of keeping Carolyn focused on Maura and distracting Carolyn from other painful aspects of her own life. Developing an awareness of this possibility may help us to understand why attempts to help Carolyn provide better care for her daughter may not progress easily without addressing the function that we're assuming Maura's difficulties serve.

However, a functionalist metaphor is a slippery slope. We can easily slide from thinking about symptoms as serving a protective function to thinking about a family as needing the symptom. In moments of frustration, we can fall into attributions of intent and come to believe that a family may want a symptom to avoid change. This subtle blaming of families invites anger, suspicion, and defensiveness on their part which can then be interpreted as evidence of resistance and make collaboration difficult. In the clinical example, none of the helpers had ever discussed their ideas about the function of the symptom (or the related concept of secondary gain) with Carolyn, and yet their idea that her refusal to better support their treatment of Maura served a particular function within the family was subtly but strongly communicated to Carolyn. Her experience of the negative effects of a functional metaphor is captured in the following quote:

> "It's like they have this idea that I want Maura to not get better, like I enjoy taking half a day twice a week to drag all my kids into the city so they can watch me get berated by that doctor because Maura's not getting better. They have no clue what it's like living with Maura and trying to contain her."

In my own work, I have found it more useful to focus on the effects of problems (e.g., What effect does this situation have on family members and their relationships?) than on the function of problems. In the earlier example, a functionalist metaphor takes a significant toll on the relationship between Carolyn and helpers. This metaphor places us in a particular relationship with clients and has the potential to undermine the development of a stronger therapeutic relationship which we've seen from the research is the strongest contributing factor to therapy outcome. For this reason alone, I have grave concerns about a functionalist metaphor. Despite its potential conceptual utility, it has a quite limited relational utility.

A functionalist metaphor also orients us to locating the problem of resistance in the family and minimizing the contribution of family–helper interactions and the influence of the broader cultural and economic context that affects many families' lives. For example, Kagan and Schlosberg (1989) identify a number of patterns of resistance, including environmental dangers and hurdles and go on to say:

> Extremely scared and closed families need to keep the world out and nothing works better than bugs, lice, or offensive odors. The family worker entering such a home is likely to be repelled and frightened of becoming infected or bitten. . . . Environmental hurdles and dangers serve to protect the family from much greater risks. . . . [They] keep family workers out and maintain stability in the family. (pp. 62–63)

This quote highlights the danger of overextending the field's preoccupation with a functionalist metaphor. It may be true that workers are often hesitant about going into projects or homes with poor lighting, hazardous conditions, and cockroach or lice infestation, but framing inadequate housing as serving a protective function in the family rather than as an effect of poverty is a dangerous accusation. We risk adding therapeutic insult to economic injury and contributing to a process of self-blame for broader economic conditions.

Finally, attempts to outwit resistance have the potential to invite us into a focus on beating the resistance rather than meeting the client. These attempts have been critiqued as "techniquism" in which we become obsessed with high-tech interventions designed for a quick fix[2] (Nichols, 1987). This technological focus can be experienced by families as disingenuous ploys and invite resistance to the approach and technique.

We Can Try to Understand Resistance

The shift from beating resistance to understanding resistance appears in the conceptual evolution of the Milan Associates. They began in a strategic orientation, developing elaborate strategies to outwit family games with a strong focus on moves and countermoves (Palazzoli, Boscolo, Cecchin, & Prata, 1981). Over time, they shifted from managing resistance to understanding resistance (Cecchin, 1987; Tomm, 1984a, 1984b). The process of "positive connotation" shifted from a strategy to disrupt family stuckness to an attempt to fully appreciate the internal logic of a situation. When applied to resistance, the shift raises questions such as,

"How do family actions make sense? What is the internal logic of these actions? And, what particular dilemmas arise for family members in this behavior?" In this shift, a metaphor of understanding resistance invites the therapist into a relationship of curiosity (learning with) rather than intervention (doing to) with families. This shift in relational stance has a profound effect on the developing relationship. It is a response to resistance that does not exacerbate resistance.

Concerns have been raised about possible consequences of attempts to understand resistance. Minuchin, Lee, and Simon (1996) draw a distinction between interventionist and restrained therapies. They view interventionist therapies as those in which therapists actively use themselves to effect change in families through deliberate strategies crafted by the therapist and restrained therapies as those in which therapists, in an effort to be respectful and not impose their biases, restrain themselves from action. They question this noninterventionist stance and worry that the focus on understanding meaning precludes action toward change. Although this concern has legitimacy, the distinction between interventionist and restrained therapies is questionable. Our interactions unavoidably have effects on families, and curiosity can be profoundly interventive. Another way to punctuate this distinction would be to counterpose impositional interventionist therapies and invitational interventionist therapies. If we accept that all interactions have a potential for intervention, invitational interventions may provoke less resistance.

At the same time, there is a valid concern that therapists attempting to develop collaborative relationships with families who have not been well served by the mental health system may mistake the development of respectful collaborative relationships as an end in itself rather than a means to the end of change. There are therapists who have formed strong relationships with families that have been interesting and rewarding for the families in the short term but have not led to improvements in their lives. Developing an appreciative understanding of families is not an end in itself but, rather, a powerful means to the end of change. The interventive potential of curiosity is further explored in Chapter 5.

Attempts to understand resistance also moved beyond a focus on the client or family and sought to also understand our contributions as helpers to the development of treatment difficulties. In the process, the relevant unit of analysis for understanding resistance came to include the helping system as well as the family system. For example, Carol Anderson and Susan Stewart (1983) offered a working definition of resistance that includes family members, the therapist, and the therapist's agency or institution. In their definition of resistance, they include all those behaviors in the therapeutic system (family, therapist, and institution) that interact to prevent the therapeutic system from achieving the family's goals for therapy. Even though their understanding of resistance was embedded in homeostatic and functionalist metaphors (which were the dominant metaphors at that time), they were among the first to include helpers' contributions to resistance. Many people have argued for expanding our unit of analysis in attempts to understand resistance, but Evan Imber-Black's (1988) work on families and larger systems has given the clearest structure to this expansion. Broadening the unit of analysis shifts the description of resistance from an internal characteristic to an interactional process and forces us to consider our own contribution to difficulties that develop (Harkaway & Madsen, 1989; Madsen, 1992). We further examine engagement difficulties in an interactional context after exploring one final metaphor of handling resistance.

We Can Try to Dissolve Resistance

In 1988, Steve de Shazer heralded the "death of resistance" (de Shazer, 1988). He drew on cybernetic concepts to call attention to the ways in which families are continually changing. The concepts are *morphogenesis* and *morphostasis* (Maruyama, 1960). Morphogenesis (from the Greek *morphe*, form and *genesis*, generation) refers to a system's mechanisms for promoting change. Morphostasis (from the Greek *morphe*, form and *stasis*, stand still) refers to a system's mechanisms for maintaining stability and can more or less be used interchangeably with homeostasis. Decrying the field's preoccupation with homeostasis, de Shazer proposed that we focus on supporting and strengthening family's efforts at change rather than attacking their attempts to maintain stability. This effort leads to greater collaboration. In our work with families, we can emphasize homeostasis or morphogenesis. If we emphasize morphogenesis, we look for ways in which families are always changing and build on that. This leads to an expectation that change is not only possible but inevitable. de Shazer found the belief in resistance to be problematic because it implies that stagnation is inevitable.

de Shazer's decision to not believe in the idea of resistance is taken even further by Lorraine Wright and Anne Marie Levac (1992), who claim that noncompliance (they're writing in a medical arena) is not only a conceptual error but also a biological impossibility. They base their claim on Humberto Maturana's meta-theory of cognition. The details of his theory are quite esoteric but have useful applications for family therapy. One valuable idea is the claim that it is impossible to instruct others. As one person talks to another, the listener takes in that information in ways that are determined by the listener's individual structure. The speaker cannot control how that information is received. From this perspective, we can influence others but we can't predetermine how they will be influenced by us. We cannot put particular information into someone because we can't control how or in what form that information will be incorporated. In the prior clinical example, when Carolyn's physician lectures her about the need to kick Frank out of her apartment, she is trying to instruct Carolyn to do something. Within this perspective, such instruction is impossible. The physician cannot put that information into Carolyn and can't control how Carolyn will process it. Carolyn may learn a wide variety of things from the physician's attempts. She may learn that she should kick Frank out. She may learn that the physician doesn't have a clue what her life is like. She may learn that the physician is a frustrated professional who hates men (regardless of the physician's actual feelings about her job and men). Whatever Carolyn learns will be determined by her own history, life experiences, and perceptual structure. The physician cannot control what Carolyn will learn. This is not to suggest that we cannot impart ideas, just that we can't control how they will be received. For example, have you ever had clients at the end of your work with them thank you for a particular idea you never remember conveying and in fact would never have intended to convey?

Although we cannot instruct clients (based on these conceptual assumptions), we can invite clients to reflection. Wright and Levac (1992) suggest that inviting individuals and families to reflect can be accomplished by "creating a context for change, creating an environment in which persons change themselves and offering ideas, advice and suggestions that can serve as useful perturbations" (p. 916). Perturbation, in this context, refers to input that stimulates the person or family to reorganize around it. They suggest that interventions that work do so because they perturb individuals or families in ways that allow them to respond to problems more effectively. In this, the input that is offered fits the personal culture of the client or family.

The ideas in this book have been influenced by a metaphor of dissolving resistance, but there can be some potential negative consequences of this metaphor also. One is an unfortunate creation of an either/or situation in which families may be seen as either morphostatic (homeostatic) or morphogenic. The stance that resistance is just a unique way of cooperating can also be experienced as invalidating by therapists who are struggling with families. As a student told me, "Boy, for something that's not real, it's sure done a number on me." While the decision to not believe in resistance is a powerful approach for engaging reluctant families, the blanket declaration that there is no such thing as resistance can be as invalidating to other therapists as the concept of resistance can be to families. When difficulties arise, it can imply that if families are not resistant, the therapist must be inept. This implication can become problematic with students and other helpers and runs the risk of contributing to a polarization between practitioners informed by this metaphor and more traditionally oriented therapists. There is also a danger of invalidating family concerns. In our enthusiasm to support and strengthen family efforts at change, we may inadvertently minimize or trivialize clients' experience of problems. This has been described as solution-forced therapy (Nylund & Corsiglia, 1994).

As a foundation for examining our understandings of situations in which families are reluctant to engage in therapy, this section has traced a series of metaphors for handling resistance that in some ways parallels broader developments in the field of family therapy. In my own clinical work, I have been profoundly influenced by each of the metaphors at one time or another. Although I currently prefer to be more influenced by metaphors of understanding or dissolving resistance and less influenced by metaphors of interpreting, challenging, or outwitting resistance, I value the ways in which each metaphor has informed my thinking at various times. From here, let's consider how a cross-cultural metaphor can inform the process of engaging families.

THERAPY AS A
CROSS-CULTURAL NEGOTIATION

Each of the metaphors of resistance just described is embedded in broader cultural ideas that specify "appropriate" relationships between clients and helpers. This next section draws on a cross-cultural metaphor to examine resistance in the context of family–helper interactions and the broader cultural context in which those interactions are embedded. As discussed in Chapter 1, each family and helper can be seen as a distinct microculture with its own beliefs and preferred style of interacting. Therapy can be seen as a cross-cultural negotiation in which the two parties interact in a mutually influencing relationship. In this interaction, the actions of each party may be more understandable through each party's own lens than through the other's lens. Therapy proceeds better when both microcultures (helper and family) are on the same wavelength (i.e., hold similar beliefs about what the problem is, what should be done about it, and who should do what in addressing the problem or are aware and respectful of differences in those beliefs). Therapy can become problematic when therapists and clients hold different beliefs regarding problems, treatment, and roles of the client and therapist and those differences are covert and unacknowledged (Madsen, 1992). As helpers and families attempt to manage unacknowledged differences in beliefs, a variety of interactional patterns may emerge between them. In the situation described at the beginning of this chapter, Carolyn and the health care providers held differing beliefs about the severity and etiology of Maura's abscess, different ideas about what should be done about it, and different ideas about who should do what and how that should be decided. As each attempted to convince the other of the value of their respective beliefs, an escalating struggle arose. The more the medical personnel tried to get Carolyn to cooperate with their treatment plan, the more she felt insulted by their unwillingness to solicit her ideas and the more she then refused to go along with that situation. Her refusal to cooperate could be seen as a protest (albeit ineffective) of the unilateral definition of the relationship.

In the course of this interaction, each party's actions and intents may be misinterpreted through the other's lens. For example, the health care providers saw Carolyn as an inadequate mother who minimized her daughter's medical concerns and was "in denial" about possible sexual abuse by the uncle. Carolyn, on the other hand, saw the health care providers as stuffed shirts who were more interested in bossing her around than helping her daughter. These misinterpretations of each other invited attributions of malintent to the other (expressed in sentiments such as, "Can you imagine a mother who lets her house get that dirty," and "Those people don't care about my daughter, they just want to bust my chops.").

Another example of this polarized misinterpretation comes from a parent aide service that was extremely frustrated in attempts to provide services to a poor white, single-parent mother with five children on welfare. The treatment team sought a consultation after deciding that the mother, Jan, lacked the "appropriate empathy and the emotional maturity necessary to learn parenting skills." Jan had a short fuse and would often speak to her children in harsh tones laced with obscenities. Jan explained the context of her situation:

> "I don't like being a screaming asshole with my kids. But you spend two hours waiting in some damn line to get a pittance of a check from some twit sneering down her nose at you while your children run around like banshees embarrassing you and you might be running short on that empathy they keep talking about. Then we go outside and I got five kids flying in different directions across a busy street in a dangerous neighborhood. Those kids got to listen to me and know that I mean business."

The treatment team was extremely frustrated with Jan's resistance to their efforts. Jan wanted help and thought that some of the ideas offered to her were useful, but she added:

"I know some of them just ain't gonna work. I know my kids and they won't take those things seriously. They got some interesting ideas, but so do I. Those people don't seem too interested in any of my ideas, so why should I give them the satisfaction of looking like I'm interested in their ideas."

Within a cross-cultural perspective, the development of collaborative treatment relationships is a two-way street. Therapists as well as clients can be oppositional. From Jan's perspective, the parent aides were incredibly resistant to her attempts to get them to change their behavior with her. She kept trying to share some of her ideas about parenting and felt they just wouldn't listen to her. If Jan was to meet in a peer supervision group of clients dealing with "resistant helpers," what do you think she might be saying to them? How would she describe her helpers? What sort of consultation might she get from her colleagues to help her interpret, challenge, outwit, understand, or dissolve her helper's "resistance?" Questions such as these highlight who defines resistance. In viewing therapy as a cross-cultural negotiation, it is important to keep in mind that the parties are not in an equal relationship. Clients are generally more vulnerable and, despite attempts to flatten the hierarchy in therapeutic relationships, therapists have distinctly more power. The power discrepancy is particularly salient when clients come from nondominant cultural groups in which the power differences between clients and professionals parallel cultural power differences.

THE BROADER CONTEXT
OF FAMILY–HELPER INTERACTIONS

The cross-cultural negotiation between clients and therapists is also embedded in a broader social context and reflects the politics of that context. While increasing attention is being paid to gender and race dynamics in therapeutic interactions, there are also powerful class dynamics that may play out in treatment difficulties which have received less attention (Kliman & Madsen, 1998). Therapists are individuals but also represent a particular class background which may or may not fit for us individually. The profession of therapy is embedded in what has been called the professional middle class or professional–managerial class (Ehrenreich, 1989; Ehrenreich & Ehrenreich, 1979). This class includes doctors, lawyers, managers, academics, professionals, service providers, and others. Many of the families (though not all) who come to be referred to in community agencies as "difficult to engage" are poor or working class. Just as interactions between a male therapist and a female client or a white therapist and an African American client reflect and replicate cross-gender or cross-race interactions; so too, interactions between therapists (who are socially defined as professional middle class) and poor or working-class clients can represent a cross-class negotiation. It is important then to look at the effects of historical relationships between these classes as one organizing issue in therapeutic relationships.

There is a long history of tension between professionals and poor and working-class people that is often invisible to professionals but painfully apparent to the poor and working classes. The professional–managerial class emerged amidst the labor unrest of the 1900s and has had a rather inglorious history in regard to workers. As Ehrenreich (1989) puts it:

> Minds and mills did not have to be hotbeds of working class sedition; they could be run more smoothly by trained, "scientific" managers. Working class families did not have to be perpetual antagonists to capitalist society; they could be "Americanized" by teachers and social workers and eventually seduced by ad men and marketing experts. Almost every profession or would-be profession from sociology to home economics, had something to offer in the great task of "taming" the American working class. (p. 134)

Although the historical tension between the professional middle class and the working class may no longer be as strong as in the past, a common perception remains among many poor and working-class people that middle-class professionals don't really do anything that justifies their superior pay and status. Within the workplace, interactions between middle-class professionals and working-class people are often managerial. As one informant in Ehrenreich's study put it, "We're the ones who do the production. They're just here to make sure we do it like they want" (Ehrenreich, 1989, p. 138). Outside the workplace, working-class and poor people are most likely to encounter professionals as teachers, social workers, or physicians. Such relationships are frequently marked by helpful interactions, but the professionals often have the authority and power to make judgments about others and sometimes that judgment is not experienced as positive. Sennet and Cobb (1972) found that the anger and resentment engendered by this experience were seldom expressed to professionals. In this way, resistance to services can at times be seen as an act of protest against unexamined professional privilege.

For example, Jan's view of her welfare worker as "some twit sneering down her nose at me" reflects a historical class tension that is rarely directly communicated and when perceived by the welfare worker, may be interpreted as Jan's "bad attitude." Jan's resistance to the information provided by parent aides may be her protest against having her life defined by someone else's criteria. Unfortunately, this cultural protest and desire for self-determination often gets interpreted as pathological personal resistance to services. Viewing her actions within a broader context helps to make them more understandable and less personalized. This particular interaction transcends the involved individuals and has a significant historical and cultural context. Understanding this fact is an important first step in developing relationships across class lines.

If we return to the idea that collaboration is a two-way street in a cross-cultural negotiation, it makes sense that because therapists are in a leadership position in this exchange they have a greater responsibility for the development of a collaborative relationship. A collaborative relationship begins with us entering into clients' particular personal cultures rather than simply expecting clients to enter into ours. This endeavor ties back to the conceptual shift of working on client turf. How do we make our services relevant to clients rather than expecting clients to fit to our available services? One way to begin to do this is to attempt to understand how clients make sense of and perceive what we conceive to be problems in their lives.

EXAMINING THE STANCE
THAT CLIENTS HOLD TOWARD PROBLEMS

In a study of the interaction of patient, spouse, and physician beliefs in situations in which patient medical conditions had been chronically mismanaged, I found two common patterns of treatment difficulties (Madsen, 1992). I think an awareness of these patterns can support us in the process of engaging reluctant clients. Often, when people seek or are mandated for help with a particular problem, they hold a conceptual stance about that problem that reflects their relationship with it. There are a number of possible stances that clients may hold toward problems, and their stance significantly affects their ability to deal with problems. Consider the following three examples.

Jaime calls up and says, "I've been kind of depressed lately, it's interfering with the life I want to have. Can you help me do something about it?"

Roxanna calls for couple therapy saying, "Our relationship is going down the toilet. We're fighting all the time and it's escalated to violence. Last night we began throwing things at each other and a window got broken. I'm afraid one of us is going to get hurt and want someone to help us get things back to how things used to be."

Vanessa, who lives with her mother and two teenage daughters, calls for family therapy saying, "Our household has become a living nightmare. My girls are out all night. Nanna and I are spending all our time fighting with them and then we end up arguing with each other. My older daughter isn't eating right and the younger one just got out of the hospital after cutting herself when her boyfriend got her pregnant. This is the last straw and I need some help in straightening them out. Do you think you can help me do that?"

Although these three people face problems that differ widely in their severity, there are similarities in the stance each holds toward the problems in their lives. At the risk of oversimplifying their lives, we could characterize a common stance they each hold as follows: "This (the presenting concern) is a problem in my life, I have some influence over this problem, and I want to do something about it." This stance is useful because it provides a strong foundation from which to begin to address problems. It is also the stance preferred by most therapists and one that is easy to assume clients should have in relation to difficulties in their lives. However, clients often hold other stances about problems. I briefly outline two stances and then examine dealing with each in detail.

"This Is Not a Problem"

Sometimes people who come to therapy don't see themselves as having a problem. They may be mandated for treatment or be there under duress. In this situation, they have a very different relationship to their alleged problem and the process of therapy. Consider the following examples:

Fred, a bus driver has been referred by his employee assistance program after verbally abusing a man who didn't have correct change and then pushing him off the bus. When asked what happened, he replies, "Oh, it's nothing. We got into an argument because I didn't let him pull a fast one on me. What's the big deal?"

Roberta has been referred by her protective worker for help in parenting her three children under ten. She's had several neglect reports filed on her for leaving them alone while she went to a neighbor's apartment to get high. When asked her thoughts about the referral, she adamantly states, "My kids are fine. I don't have problems with drugs. Why don't you people leave me alone!"

Sammy has been referred for therapy after allegations that he sexually abused his four-year-old daughter. In the first session, he says, "Hey, this is really getting blown out of proportion. Besides, if she didn't climb up on my lap and excite me, this kind of stuff wouldn't happen."

In each of these situations, the referred client could be seen as holding a stance of "This is not a problem, and I don't need to do anything about it." A "no problem" stance evolves in the context of the interaction and often develops when the therapist persists in trying to define a problem that doesn't fit for the client. This situation has also been described as a "visitor relationship" in solution-focused terms (Berg, 1991; de Shazer, 1988). In this situation, the therapist and client build their relationship around different definitions of the problem and vastly different agendas for dealing with it. The way these differences are managed organize us into a particular relational stance with clients and can often lead to difficulties that constrain effective work. For example, we can end up trying to convince Fred that his violence *is* a big deal, or Roberta that her kids *are not* fine and that she *does* have a drug problem, or Sammy that concern about sexual abuse of a 4-year-old is *not* blown out of proportion. Unfortunately, our attempts to confront the "denial" often end up rigidifying a no-problem stance and threaten the therapeutic relationship. Such difficulties are often reflected in situations in which the presenting problem (according to the referral source) is substance misuse, violence, sexual abuse, neglect, and other situations characterized by "denial."[3]

"This Is a Problem, but I Have No Control Over It"

Other times, families may come to therapy with a clear and detailed sense of the problem but see themselves as not having any influence over it. Consider the following examples:

Ellen and her four burly teenage boys are referred for therapy by the court after the oldest son threw another young man through a hardware store window. In the first session, Ellen goes through a litany of complaints about each son and concludes with a shrug, "The court told me to come see you. I can't do anything with them. This is beyond me."

Maria calls a therapist and says, "Would you call my husband. He has a gambling problem and won't get any help for it. He won't listen to me and it's driving me crazy. Maybe if you talked to him. . . . "

Harold calls a therapist saying, "My son is a manic–depressive who was just discharged from the hospital. When he's depressed, he can become suicidal so we have to keep him at home. And when he's manic, he becomes uncontrollable and breaks everything in our house. We've become very scared of him because he's mentally ill and has no control over his behavior. I hear you do home-based work, will you come out to meet with him?"

In each of these examples, the caller could be seen as holding a stance of "This is a problem, but I can't do anything about it." I am referring to this stance as a no-control stance to highlight the client's perceived lack of influence in an out-of-control problem. This stance often manifests itself when parents call about out-of-control youths (mental illness, substance misuse, violence, and high-risk situations that include suicide, running away, risky sexual behavior, etc.) or when spouses call about their partner's substance abuse or other problematic behavior. In these situations, the person seeking help is often focused on trying to help someone else change (despite their lack of interest) instead of focusing on changes that could be made in their own life. These situations have also been described as a "complainant relationship" in solution-focused terms (Berg, 1991; de Shazer, 1988). Attempting to help clients in these situations can be frustrating, and the clients can often become labeled an "enabler or codependent." Therapists can feel as if clients are trying to hand over work that they need to do and respond by attempting to highlight a client's contribution to the situation or point out the influence they do have over the situation. The interaction that develops is usually quite frustrating to everyone involved and in the process the client's no-control stance is often rigidified.

In both of these situations, a no-problem and no-control stance can be seen as constraints that hinder clients from more effectively addressing the problems. We can shift from seeing the clients as the problem to seeing the stance as the problem. As helpers respond to these stances, the interactions that develop can further constrain attempts to address the problems. The next sections examine ways to avoid problematic interactions with clients who initially hold a stance of no problem or no control. I consider ways to shift our relationship with reluctant clients and engage them from a relational stance of an appreciative ally.

DEALING WITH A NO-PROBLEM STANCE

Bob is a 35-year-old white man who came to therapy saying he was not really sure why he was there, but perhaps could use some help in learning ways to meet women.[4] Further examination revealed that his driver's license had been suspended for driving while intoxicated, following an accident in which he drove into a parked car. The suspension time was reduced by the judge when Bob's lawyer said Bob would be starting therapy. Bob is divorced and lives alone. He works long hours as a phone solicitor and buys a six-pack each night on the way home which he drinks while watching rented porno flicks. He drinks at home to save money and contain his drinking but occasionally goes to a bar and then has difficulty getting to work the next day. His ex-wife divorced him after being repeatedly called to bail him out of jail for a variety of reasons. She has custody of their two girls (ages 7 and 5) and is furious with Bob because of his repeated tendency to miss scheduled visitations with his daughters and his neglect of them while they are in his care. Bob resents the way his ex-wife treats him around these lapses and wishes she would stop making a "mountain out of a molehill."

Bob's therapist, also a man, is concerned about Bob's drinking and his pattern of irresponsibility with his children. As he explores these concerns, Bob dismisses them in turn. Bob minimizes his drinking explaining, "I work hard and I need to unwind somehow. Besides, everyone drinks, don't they?" He says he feels bad about missing appointments with his kids but goes on to say, "Hey, they're kids, we can always reschedule. It's not like they're booked up or anything."

Near the end of the first session, Bob describes an incident in which he left his daughters sleeping in the car while he ran into a liquor store to buy some beer. He met two buddies who invited him across the street for a drink. Because his daughters were still asleep, he figured they were safe and ran into the bar across the street for a quick beer. When he emerged 45 minutes later, they were still asleep. He thought nothing of it until confronted by his wife who had received a call from a girlfriend who saw the sleeping children as she went into the liquor store. In response, the therapist tells Bob that he is concerned about his drinking and worries that Bob has an alcohol problem. He suggests Bob attend three Alcoholics Anonymous (AA) meetings during the next week. Bob rolls his eyes and says, "You sound like the broad in the alcohol class I went to for court; I thought a guy would understand this stuff." The therapist, annoyed by Bob's continued abdication of responsibility, decides to confront him more forcefully about his "denial." Bob wonders why the therapist is "making a mountain out of a molehill" and then listens with a disdainful smirk on his face. When Bob leaves at the end of the session, his therapist wonders whether he'll return again.

At the end of this session, Bob and his therapist are not well positioned for future work together. They have not jointly identified a goal on which to work, and Bob and his therapist have radically different ideas about the problem, what should be done about it, and who should do what. Bob defines the problem as getting the court off his back and perhaps getting some help in meeting women, whereas his therapist defines the problem as substance abuse and irresponsibility with his children. In their interaction, each attempts to get the other to work on his idea of the presenting problem and each becomes increasingly frustrated with the other's "noncompliance." The therapist wonders why Bob is "in denial" over his problems and Bob wonders why his therapist keeps harping on these issues. Paradoxically, the attempt of each participant to enlist the other's cooperation inadvertently backfires and rigidifies their respective stances.

The biggest danger in engaging a client who holds a no-problem stance is the temptation for the therapist to tell the client what to do or to confront the denial or resistance. A therapist who does this runs the risk of falling into an overresponsible/underresponsible pattern with the client. Bob's stance that his drinking isn't a problem invites a response from his therapist that attempts to highlight the effects of drinking on his life and "confront the denial." However, Bob's response is not, "Oh, I never thought about that! Thank you for pointing that out to me. I see I need to mend my ways?" No, he's much more likely to respond by further explaining why his drinking is not a problem and becoming increasingly annoyed with his therapist and less open to the therapist's ideas. In the process, his no-problem stance becomes increasingly rigidified. Paradoxically, the more the therapist confronts Bob's "denial," the more the therapist risks entrenching the "denial."

At the same time, holding back from confronting Bob's stance runs the risk of colluding with it. This situation creates an interesting dilemma for us as therapists. If we confront the stance, we run the risk of getting into a nonproductive struggle with clients that antagonizes them and inadvertently rigidifies their stance. If we hold back, we avoid an important discussion and are ineffectual in addressing the hold of that stance. One way out of this dilemma is to engage Bob outside the stance of "this is not a problem" and build on his experiences out there.

SUGGESTIONS FOR APPROACHING A NO-PROBLEM STANCE[5]

First, Do No Harm

We've examined how an overresponsible/underresponsible pattern constrains clients from addressing situations, rigidifies their position that "this is not a problem," and takes a toll on the therapeutic relationship.

An important first step is to anticipate and avoid being caught by such a pattern. The old medical maxim of "First, do no harm" could be translated here as "First, add no further constraints." However, the trap of an overresponsible/underresponsible pattern is easy to fall into. Let's examine some of the factors that can pull us into this pattern.

People who hold a stance of "this is not a problem" are often constrained from acknowledging difficulties in their lives by old habits, interactional patterns, and beliefs. We can assume they may want to live differently but are well practiced at avoiding responsibility for addressing a problem, often attributing responsibility to external factors and inviting others to take responsibility and attend to these difficulties for them. In response to the therapist's queries about the time that Bob left his children sleeping in the car while he ran into a bar, Bob declared, "Look, it's not a big deal. They were safe and sound. If my wife would put them down for naps when they need 'em, I wouldn't have to be finding ways to get them naps when I'm baby-sitting for her." In this example, Bob's actions are supported by cultural ideas and traditions that often encourage men to look to women to take responsibility for childrearing. We can find other examples of attributing responsibility to external factors in statements made by clients such as the following: "If I didn't work so hard for her and the kids, I wouldn't need to drink to relax." "If you want the violence to end, tell her to shut up." "If my wife gave me sex, I wouldn't have to look to my daughter for it." Statements like these represent personal lapses in relational responsibility, and they are also supported by cultural ideas and traditions that often encourage men to assume certain rights and entitlements in relationships and to not attend to the effects of their actions. It is important to recognize the cultural embeddedness of this pattern of not embracing relational responsibility to appreciate its strength and to avoid personalizing it. This is not simply something Bob is doing but a tendency that receives significant cultural support for Bob as a man in this culture.

In the face of such avoidance of relational responsibility, the therapist may be tempted to confront or challenge the client's explanation, to give advice or argue against his behavior, or to criticize or break down denial.[6] However, doing so (while giving us great moral satisfaction) runs the risk of perpetuating the problem. Confronting denial often invites defensiveness, promotes shame, and constrains the consideration of new ideas. Our clients may be better served by us not seeking to challenge denial but by successfully inviting clients to challenge those constraints that hinder them from responding to issues differently.

The history of past interactions with helpers and other family and community members also has a strong influence on the way in which an overresponsible/underresponsible pattern plays out. In Bob's situation, it is unlikely that this therapist is the first person to point out to Bob that his drinking and neglect of his children are problems. The history of previous interactions with significant others around this issue organizes Bob's anticipation of the therapist's interaction with him. Before the therapist opens his mouth, previous interactions prime Bob to anticipate that the therapist will (in Bob's words) "make a mountain out of a molehill." Bob enters prepared to defend himself from an anticipated onslaught of accusation and the therapist has the opportunity to comply with that anticipation or to try an alternate course.

Our own emotional reactions to such situations often encourage us to comply with the delivery of such an onslaught. Many situations in which a person takes a no-problem stance (violence, sexual abuse, drinking) pull for judgment. In Bob's situation, his therapist had two young children himself and was horrified at the way Bob treated his daughters. Our response is also influenced by broader professional and cultural ideas about how people who do things that offend our sensibilities should be treated. One common response to Bob leaving his children in the car would be to declare him an unfit parent and seek to cut off his visitations until he shows more responsibility. Berg (1994b) points out that this type of response is anchored in a Judeo-Christian ethic in which offenders should be confronted with their crimes, made to face up to them, and punished. We can become caught in an emotional response that seeks to punish neglectful or abusive parents in an attempt to protect their children. However, this approach can be exclusionary and shortsighted. It directs attention away from attempts at reconciliation and eventual inclusion. It also allows us to interact with clients in quite disrespectful ways in order to get them to act more respectfully.

In discussing his work with abusive men, Alan Jenkins (1996, p. 122) describes an "inner tyrant" that emerges when he hears denial and minimization in the face of abuse with serious consequences. He describes the ways in which that inner tyrant at times "wants to 'make him see sense,' or even 'knock some sense into him,' to 'make him see what it is like,' to 'break down his denial,' or failing that, to write him off as someone who is evil, bad, and uncaring." Jenkins is not alone in these feelings. They are common reactions to abuse that are inevitable and important to acknowledge. At the same time, these reactions may not be the most useful ones in bringing about change. We need to find ways to respectfully invite those who abuse to challenge such ways of being. This respect does not excuse clients of responsibility or minimize the effects of their actions. In fact, it is important that we act in ways that are always respectful both to those who abuse and those who are abused. As Jenkins (1996) puts it: "The issue of respect is critical. I am convinced that interventions which are disrespectful to either party inadvertently contribute to the maintenance and even exacerbation of abusive behavior" (p. 119).

Zehr (1990) draws a distinction in criminal justice between retributive and restorative views of justice that is also useful here. Within a retributive view of justice, "Crime is a violation of the state, defined by lawbreaking and guilt. Justice determines blame and administers pain in a context between the offender and the state directed by systemic rules" (p. 181). While retributive justice originates within the criminal justice system, its philosophy has spread to human services, especially in the treatment of problems such as substance misuse, violence, and physical and sexual abuse. Within a retributive philosophy, the therapist's role becomes one of confronting Bob with his offenses of drinking and neglect, breaking down his denial, and assigning appropriate consequences.

Within a restorative view of justice, "Crime is a violation of people and relationships. It creates obligations to make things right. Justice involves the victim, the offender, and the community in a search for solutions which promote repair, reconciliation, and reassurance" (p. 181). From this perspective, the therapist's job would be to help Bob develop and reconcile his relationship with his kids and make necessary amends to have an ongoing responsible relationship with them. This more inclusionary approach has been picked up in human services with family preservation and family-centered services. Retributive approaches end up costing more and in the long run exacerbate the fractures and disruptions in family relationships (Schwartz & Cellini, 1997). It is not a particularly useful approach. So what are we to do instead?

Make No Suggestions before Their Time

One way to avoid an overresponsible/underresponsible pattern when engaging clients who present with a stance of "this is not a problem," is to *initially* avoid giving suggestions or tasks. For example, telling Bob to go to AA or to reconsider how he treats his kids *at this point* runs several risks. The biggest risk is that he probably won't do it. Asking him to do something that he most likely will not do undermines credibility, runs the risk of shaming him, and undercuts the developing relationship. This is not to suggest that we ignore the issue and collude with an avoidance of important subjects but, rather, that we first establish a foundation for addressing those issues more effectively. One way for therapists to help themselves hold back from giving advice without authorization is to think of themselves as responding to continual invitations for overresponsibility and to decide whether they want to accept those invitations (and the consequences) or decline them.

Connecting with the Honorable Self

Alan Jenkins (1996) has a wonderful phrase, "Respectful therapy involves a process of knocking on doors and waiting to be invited in, rather than breaking them down, barging in, and then expecting to be welcomed with open arms" (p. 122). One way to get invited in is to elicit and connect with the client's "honorable self." This involves finding those qualities of clients that we can respect, appreciate, and value. If we view Bob as simply a neglectful alcoholic in denial, it becomes difficult to make a connection to him. It is more useful to begin with an assumption that Bob is more than that and then set about trying to prove that assumption to ourselves. This is not to say that we should ignore that he is neglectful with his children, that he may be abusing alcohol, or that he may be reluctant to address those issues. We need to find ways that people are more than their problems in order to connect with them without ignoring the presence of those problems in their lives.

In the previous example, Bob did come back for a second session. The therapist expressed his surprise:

THERAPIST: I'm glad to see you. I thought I was a bit hard on you last week and wasn't sure if I'd see you again or not. What made you decide to come back?

BOB: Oh I don't know. I made the appointment, so I thought I should keep it.

THERAPIST: So, you're a man of your word, eh?

BOB: Well yeah, I guess I am. If you say you're going to do something, you gotta do it.

At this point, the therapist has an important choice. He could either point out to Bob the discrepancy between claiming the identity of being a man of his word and his history of missing visits with his kids, getting in trouble with the law, and persistent substance misuse or continue to explore this aspect of him. The therapist chose the latter.

THERAPIST: So, it's important to you to stick to your word?

BOB: Yeah,

THERAPIST: Who else knows that about you?

BOB: Well, my boss knows he can count on me to finish the jobs I commit to. He tells me I'm the most reliable employee he's got.

Given Bob's history of unreliability with his children, the therapist could either begin to feel really sorry for Bob's boss in his difficulty finding reliable employees or continue to develop Bob's story of reliability and then examine what constrains him from being more reliable in other aspects of his life. Again, the therapist chose the latter.

As the therapist continues to elicit a story of Bob's reliability in a job that he doesn't particularly like, he inquires about how reliability became so important in Bob's life. Bob begins to tell a story of a domineering, critical father with very high expectations that Bob could never live up to. As the therapist listens empathically, he uncovers Bob's story of himself as a persistent "screw-up who could never get it right." The therapist becomes intrigued at how Bob has enacted a very different story at work and seeks to discover that. He learns about Bob's shyness (part of why he comes home to drink beer and watch porno flicks at night) and the difficulties Bob initially had as a phone solicitor. Despite the therapist's own negative feelings about phone solicitors (particularly the one who interrupted his dinner last night), the therapist develops a respect for Bob's courage to continue making phone calls to strangers, most of whom respond with outright disdain and rejection. He becomes intrigued at what Bob draws on to stay in such a difficult job and learns more about Bob's resilience in dealing with his father. In the process, the therapist begins to really appreciate Bob's resourcefulness and notices that Bob is talking in a more relaxed and open fashion. The therapist is not simply going through the motions of appreciating Bob. If he was, it would probably be experienced by Bob as patronizing and backfire. This is not a simple technique. In searching for an honorable self, the therapist begins with an assumption that it exists and then sets out to prove that to himself. In the process, his attitude toward Bob shifts.

Searching for an honorable self makes it easier to connect with clients and bypasses the resistance provoked by focusing on problems. The process of looking for an honorable self is perhaps best summed up by a client of mine who once said, "When I come to see you, I see myself reflected in your eyes. I like the me I see in your eyes better than the me I hold in my head." Part of our job is to see the honorable aspects of clients with enough intensity that those qualities are reflected back to them. Connecting to an honorable self makes it much easier to form a therapeutic relationship. It is easier for us to engage clients when we discover qualities that we appreciate, respect, and value about them, and it is much easier for them to connect with us when our interaction is inviting the enactment of those qualities rather than the enactment of shameful qualities.

Building on Exceptions to a No-Problem Stance

It's important to remember that the process of engaging clients who hold a no-problem stance is a means to opening space to examine that stance and perhaps shift their relationship to it. To avoid simply colluding with that stance, it is important that we keep the problem in mind as we go through the process. One way to do this is by looking for exceptions to the no-problem stance. Often the process of finding the honorable self yields such exceptions. But these initial exceptions are easy to miss. The trick is to listen carefully for them.

As Bob continues to describe his enactment of a "screw-up" story, he begins to talk with regret about how he screwed up his marriage and his worry that he'll now screw up his relationship with his daughters. This worry falls outside a no-problem stance. It is a small exception, but it offers momentum for a new direction than can be amplified. The therapist picks up on this exception and wonders what kind of relationship Bob would like to have with his children. He asks Bob to project forward into the future and talk about how he would like his daughters to describe their relationship with him looking back from their 21st birthdays. Bob describes a hypothetical relationship that is quite different from his current one and begins to get a bit teary-eyed. The therapist asks Bob if he would like to try to develop the relationship he would prefer to have with his children and finds himself moved by Bob's wordless nodding.

Developing a Collaborative Partnership

It is important to remember that a collaborative partnership is an interactional phenomena. As we have seen, both clients and therapists contribute to it. The development of a collaborative partnership begins with finding something that the client would be interested in working on with us. It begins by seeking to understand therapy's relevance to clients' lives rather than clients' relevance to helpers' treatment goals. Bob's agreement to work with his therapist on developing a better relationship with his daughters is the beginning of a relationship that will be relevant to his life. But, this is just the beginning. There is much work to be done in examining the knowledge and abilities that Bob brings to the task of developing the relationships he'd prefer and in together identifying and challenging the constraints to developing that relationship (which will probably include drinking and neglect). However, Bob and his therapist now have a foundation from which that work can proceed more rapidly.

As you read this story of Bob's second session, you may find yourself thinking about Bob in a new light. You may see him with more empathy and appreciation and view his relationship with his children and ex-wife with more hope. You may also find yourself concerned about the effect of his neglect on his daughters and ex-wife and wondering what will happen with his drinking. It is important to hold both stories. Bob is at a point of beginning to enact a different story about himself that will have quite different *real* effects on his children and his ex-wife. He also has a long history of living his life in a way that has taken a significant toll on those around him. We can focus on what Bob has done and our need for him to confess his crimes, or we can focus on how to help Bob develop a different story about himself and within that new story begin to interact with significant others in ways that include accepting responsibility for the effects of his actions, making necessary amends, and living differently in the future. In some ways, it comes down to a question of whether we primarily organize ourselves around the past and what Bob has done or around the future and what Bob needs to do to have a different relationship (which includes facing up to actions in the past). In this new future, it is important to not simply focus on the different story that Bob holds about himself but rather on the different story he enacts in his life and its effects on those around him. Important stories are enacted stories. This future focus is further discussed in Chapter 4.

The following five guidelines summarize these suggestions for engaging clients who hold a stance of "this is not a problem":

1. Anticipate and attempt to avoid an overresponsible/underresponsible sequence.
2. Avoid invitations to overresponsibility by making no suggestions without an invitation.
3. Get connected to clients by discovering their honorable qualities.
4. Look for exceptions to the stance of no control.
5. Build on those exceptions to develop a collaborative partnership.

SUGGESTIONS FOR APPROACHING A NO-CONTROL STANCE

At times, clients have a clear and detailed sense of the problem but see the situation as out of their control and beyond their influence. An example of this no-control stance comes from a white family who was court mandated for family therapy. The family consisted of Arnie (age 37) and Peg (age 35) and their sons Sam (age 14) and Jake (age 8). Arnie and Peg were looking for someone who would straighten out Sam who had been arrested for vandalizing his school and would not listen to them at home. The parents showed up with Jake for a noontime appointment, complaining that Sam was home sleeping and would not come. At the first appointment, I went out to meet them, walked them to my office, and began to introduce myself. My introduction was quickly interrupted by Arnie, the father, who launched into the following tirade.

ARNIE: We can't get Sam to do anything. If he doesn't want to do it, he doesn't do it. If he doesn't want to go to school, he doesn't go to school. If he wants to wreck the house, he wrecks the house. He does what he pleases. . . .

PEG: (*jumping in*) Sam's out of control. He needs a lot of structure and someone has got to do something quick.

BILL: That sounds worrisome. What have you tried at home?

PEG: There's nothing we *can* do. He won't respond to anything.

ARNIE: He's headed for jail. He really is. Let me give you an example. I painted his room for him and you know what my reward was? He vandalized my office at home. Can you believe that? The more you do for him, I don't know. I can't understand him.

BILL: What was your response to what he did to your office?

ARNIE: What do you expect me to do. He's not going to listen (*starts in again with a litany of complaints until Peg cuts him off*).

PEG: Maybe there's a program or something Sam could go to. Somebody needs to talk to him and figure out what's going on with him.

BILL: Let me ask you about that. What do you think is going on with him?

PEG: I have no idea. That's why we're coming to you. Would you be able to meet with him?

BILL: Well, that's a possibility. How could we get him here?

ARNIE: Maybe you could talk to his probation officer.

In this interaction, the parents clearly acknowledge that a problem exists (defining it as Sam) but do not see themselves as having any control or influence over that problem. At this point, therapists have an important choice. Confronting their stance, "This is a problem, but we have no control over it," risks a nonproductive struggle over whether they can influence their son. Holding back from confronting that stance avoids that struggle but risks colluding with a disempowering stance. Let's examine these two possibilities and search for a third alternative.

First, Do No Harm

In response to a no-control stance, a therapist is often faced with a dilemma of confronting that stance or holding back. Each choice has dangers. On the one hand, confronting that stance can lead to a criticize/defend pattern or a minimize/maximize pattern that may inadvertently rigidify the stance and further constrain the parents' attempts to help their son. On the other hand, holding back can lead to a passive supportive relationship that never challenges the stance. Let's examine the effects of each of these choices in turn.

In response to the parents' statements that they can't do anything about their out-of-control son, a therapist might inquire about their attempted solutions or encourage them with some suggestions of alternative responses. The questions about attempted solutions (which inadvertently highlight their inability to influence their son) or the suggestions of alternative responses may leave them feeling criticized and provoke defensiveness (e.g., Peg's response—"There's nothing we can do. He won't respond to anything."—or Arnie's response—"What do you expect me to do. He's not going to listen."). Their response can invite a counterresponse from the therapist of attempting to get them to see the control they do have over the situation which inadvertently provokes more defensiveness. The resulting pattern could be described as a criticize/defend pattern in which the parents' perception of criticism invites defensiveness and that defensiveness invites a response from the therapist that they further experience as criticism. As that pattern gains strength, it can easily lead to an escalating struggle over who should do what about this problem. The therapist's intention is not to criticize the parents, but they may experience the responses in that way. In the process, the parents are in a position of continually highlighting how little control they have and all the ways in which they can't influence this situation. In this way, the pattern rigidifies a no-control stance and further constrains them from helping their son.

A therapist could also respond to the parents by attempting to encourage them to get the son to come to the next session. The danger in this course is that the parents can experience such suggestions as minimizing the difficulties they're describing. From the parents' perspective, the therapist just doesn't "get it" and they feel compelled to emphasize the gravity of the situation and their inability to do anything about it. Paradoxically, their response invites a counterresponse from the therapist of further encouraging them to do something they've already said they cannot do. This resulting pattern could be described as a minimize/maximize pattern in which the parents feel their difficulties are being minimized and the therapist feels they're exaggerating the problem and tries to point out the ways in which it is manageable. Each action invites the other and as the pattern takes hold, each position becomes increasingly rigidified.

It's important to note here that the description of this situation as a minimize/maximize pattern does not refer to the therapist's intention. Although the therapist is in no way attempting to invalidate their experience, that may well be the effects of such actions. Likewise the parents' intent is not to exaggerate their difficulties but to highlight the seriousness of their situation. Both these patterns are often profoundly influenced by interactions with previous helpers and over time can take on a life of their own, pulling participants into them. These patterns also receive strong cultural support through the medicalization of deviance in which acting out is increasingly seen as a sign of a mental disorder in which something is inherently wrong with the child (attention-deficit/hyperactivity disorder [ADHD], oppositional defiant disorder, conduct disorder, etc.) which subtly conveys a message that if their child has one of these disorders, the parents are helpless to address it.

Unfortunately, both these patterns could have severe negative effects on the parents. As they participate in each pattern, their stance of no control becomes rigidified. As they enact this stance, they experience themselves as increasingly incompetent with their son and disconnected from each other and from the therapist. These patterns also have severe negative effects on the therapeutic relationship. The patterns can contribute to the development of a disempowering, adversarial relationship that promotes particular attention to dysfunction and pathology and invites criticism and judgment rather than understanding and appreciation. This is not a description of a solid foundation for future work together.

The decision to not challenge a stance of no control is also problematic. A therapist might decide to hold back from a nonproductive struggle and fall into a passive supportive relationship that subtly colludes with a no-control stance. As the parents come in and complain about their out-of-control son, the therapist listens supportively but doesn't attempt to challenge their stance or mobilize them as parents. Although this approach may provide some comfort to the parents, it doesn't help the situation to change. The goal here is not to simply avoid a problematic interactional pattern but to actively enter into an alternative interaction that establishes a stronger foundation for developing solutions to the problems they're describing. I've highlighted these potential dangers to help us apply the medical maxim of "first, do no harm." In encountering a no-control stance, the first step is to avoid adding further constraints by not becoming ensnared in a problematic interactional pattern with families or falling into passive collusion with a problematic stance that does not challenge it. From here let's examine another alternative.

Assuming a Positive Intent behind the Complaint[7]

A criticize/defend or minimize/maximize pattern between helpers and parents is often supported by the concern that helpers develop for children. We can be drawn into an alliance with children in which our concern for them and desire to be helpful make it difficult to listen to long parental harangues that can feel discomforting or even abusive. This is especially true in residential or school settings where helpers have significantly more contact with the children than with the parents and in which the context can sometimes pull for a subtle competition over who can best raise the child. At those times, we can fall into mistaking parental reactions as characterological and lose sight of their reactions as responses contained within an interactional context.

Although I had never met Sam, I had heard about him from teachers at his high school where he had a reputation as a kid with potential who came from a troubled home. As I listened to his father's diatribe, I wondered whether I'd be able to enlist the father's participation and found myself coming to think of him as part of the problem. I was becoming judgmental of him and wondered about referring Sam to a school-based counseling program at the high school where he could be seen individually. Sending kids such as Sam for counseling outside of their family can be a useful way to provide support for them that they may not be getting at home. However, Sam's network is the family he lives in and if we return to the assertion in the first chapter that our job is to support, not supplant, the functioning of clients' natural networks, we can see how it would be important to find a way to get better connected to the father in this family. The trick here is to be able simultaneously to acknowledge judgmental feelings, examine their potential negative effects on clients, and engage clients in a way that opens space for the development of an alternative relationship. One way to shift one's relationship to "difficult" clients in a situation like this is to assume there is a positive intent behind their complaints and search for it.

As a way to highlight this search, let's return to the clinical situation. I responded to the suggestion that I talk to the probation officer in the following way.

BILL: Well, I imagine he might have a lot to tell me about Sam. But, I got to believe that even if it doesn't feel like it right now, you guys know Sam better than anyone else. Can we back up a few steps and have you help me to get to know Sam better. What's he like?

ARNIE: (*quickly jumping in*). Stubborn, self-centered, selfish, destructive. He does what he feels like. Boy, he's gonna have trouble when he gets out to the working world.

BILL: What do you think will really happen when he gets out into the world?

ARNIE: I think he's headed for jail. I really do because you can't act that way in this society and get anywhere.

PEG: (*to Arnie scornfully*) You look so happy when you say jail.

ARNIE: Well, I think if he did go to jail, it might wake him up.

BILL: What's the wakeup call you'd like him to get?

ARNIE: He's got to learn that he can't keep running around destroying everything, not listening to anybody, doing whatever he pleases. . . .

BILL: You want more than that for him.

ARNIE: Yes!

BILL: What kind of man do you want him to be when he gets out into the world?

ARNIE: Well, I want him to be respectful, not like the little snot that he is. You wouldn't believe his mouth . . . .

BILL: (*quickly moving in to cut off Arnie's criticisms*). You want him to be a respectful man . . . and what else?

ARNIE: I want him to be able to earn things rather than steal them. I want him to appreciate all that we've done for him. If he has a girlfriend, I want him to treat her better than he's treated his mother . . . .

As Arnie begins to describe the man he wants his son to be, his hopes for him are liberally mixed with scathing attacks. I resist the temptation to point out to him that his attacks are not helpful and continue amplifying his hopes and gently redirecting him when he drifts back into attacks. With this help, Arnie gradually shifts from attacks to hopes. As this shift occurs, he softens a bit. I find myself admiring the kind of man Arnie hopes his son will become and appreciating the glimmer of connection between father and son that I'm beginning to see. I summarize those hopes, compliment Arnie on his desire to raise a son to be all that, and then ask Peg if any of her husband's hopes for their son were surprising to her.

PEG: Yeah, most of them. All I ever hear from him is his ranting about all the things Sam does wrong.

BILL: And, hearing about the hopes and concerns for Sam behind all that anger, what's the impact of that on you?

PEG: Well, it's strange. It's like Arnie cares more for Sam than I thought.

BILL: (*to Arnie*) It sounds like when those hopes get clouded by the kind of stuff he's been doing, it drives you crazy.

ARNIE: Yeah, I just see red and I go crazy.

As I begin to appreciate what I see as the positive intent behind Arnie's complaints about his son, I can feel less judgmental toward him. I am able to draw a distinction between the positive intent behind his tirades (which I can appreciate and respect) and the effect of those tirades on me and presumably on Sam. I begin to develop more empathy for Arnie's outbursts in the context of his disappointment that his son isn't living up to those hopes. Arnie experiences my newly developing appreciation of him in subtle ways and, as he begins to feel more heard and validated, eases in his attacks on Sam. As Arnie considers his hopes for Sam, he is able to step out from under his anger a bit and experience his anger and disappointment in a different way. He becomes a little less reactive and, although continuing to voice his disappointments in his son, he does so in a way that is less vehement.

My search for a positive intent behind the father's complaints has a number of beneficial effects on everyone involved. Arnie feels more understood and less criticized and responds with more openness. Peg feels a bit closer to her husband and views him in a somewhat different light. I feel more appreciative of the family and am more hopeful that I can engage the parents' participation. In the process, that positive intention is created and brought forth.

Developing Hope and Agency

After constructing a positive intent behind complaints, we can further shift our relationships with clients by searching for what has kept that positive intent alive. Clients who present a no-control stance often feel victimized by the problem they're describing and it can be very useful (and eyeopening) to ask what has sustained them in the face of the problem. The process of asking about what has sustained them opens space for the emergence of hope and agency (the sense that clients can take steps to bring hope to fruition). This is a joint process in which we are not simply discovering preexisting qualities but, rather, developing those qualities in the conversation with clients. Often hope and agency exist only as very faint glimmers that are extremely difficult to detect. In many ways, this process could be thought of as focusing on the little that is there rather than the much that is not. The goal becomes building a foundation that will help those faint glimmers to grow and expand.

The process begins with believing that the father's outrage points also toward his hope that things could be different for his son. (One could guess that if he didn't have hope that things could change, he wouldn't be so upset.) His outrage can be seen as a commitment to his son. For a man who is so disgusted with his son, it's admirable that he continues participating in attempts to help him. Commenting on this commitment is a good starting point. However, this comment is not a simple reframe. It is important to really "see" it and believe it. It works better as a deep conviction than as a facile reframe. From that foundation, we can ask questions to elicit hope and inquire about what factors have kept it alive.

I'll return to the clinical example. After developing a positive intent behind the father's complaints, I marveled at his hopes for his son and went on to inquire about how he had managed to hang onto those hopes in the face of all the difficulties in their life together.

BILL: You have a clear picture of what you want for your son.[8] Has that picture been easy to hang onto when he's pulling the stunts you've described or has it been really hard?

ARNIE: It's been a bear.

BILL: How have you been able to do that?

ARNIE: I have no idea.

BILL: Well, would it be OK with you if we slowed down a bit and tried to figure that out? Because I think it's pretty remarkable that you've been able to hang on to hope in the midst of all this and if we were able to learn how you've done that it might give us ideas about a foundation for helping your son.

ARNIE: OK.

I then ask a number of questions about how Arnie has not given up on his son even though he's spent the last 2 years "at the end of his rope." As Arnie, Peg, and I together learn about how they have coped with this situation for the last 2 years, they (organized by the questions asked) begin to describe a story of a beleaguered couple who are very committed to a frustrating son they just can't understand and who have managed to stay together despite the toll this situation has taken on their relationship. As they describe how they've managed this feat, they begin to describe themselves with such words as "loving, stubborn, persistent, and committed." These are not words that come easily to them but ones that they nonetheless embrace. As they experience and begin to enact a story of their life that holds more hope and agency, there is a noticeable shift in their posture. They are less slumped in their chairs, they have moved closer together, and they are looking at each other as if the movie they've stumbled into is completely different from the reviews they read beforehand. This foundation in which their own agency comes to the fore is a better one from which to help them challenge their victimization by the problem they've described. That challenge begins with an examination of exceptions to their experience of no control.

Building on Exceptions to a No-Control Stance

One pathway to helping clients who hold a no-control stance further develop hope and agency lies in their experience of life outside "no control." Our job can become amplifying and building on those moments when they experience alternatives to a sense of hopelessness and victimization by the problem. I'll return to Sam's family to illustrate this.

ARNIE: I think he's lucky to have us as parents. Most parents wouldn't have put up with all this.

BILL: I think he's lucky to have parents strong enough and committed enough to put up with him. He's really given you a ride for your money and yet you've managed to hold onto your hopes for him as he becomes a man. Have there been times when you've seen any glimmers of that man you hope he'll become in him now?

ARNIE: That's hard to say. I can't think of any.

PEG: Remember when he broke his friend's Gameboy and saved up to buy him another one. We didn't have to hound him a bit about that. But, of course, that was with a friend and not with us. . . .

ARNIE: Yeah, but that's how I'd want him to be with his friends when he grows up.

I ask a series of questions to get a full description of the incident and learn that Sam broke his friend's toy and told his parents about it. They suggested the friend would appreciate it if he replaced it but said it was up to him to decide how important the friendship was to him. They dropped the matter and were surprised when they later heard from the friend that Sam had saved up and bought him a new one. They were particularly impressed that he hadn't just gone out and stolen one. I proceed by asking them about their contribution to this exception to their usual experience of Sam.

BILL: You know, often parents influence their kids in ways they'd never imagine. What do you think you might have done in this situation to contribute to Sam being so responsible?

ARNIE: Nothing, though we didn't jump all over him.

The response of "not jumping all over Sam" is actually an interesting exception to the parents' usual interaction in which Sam misbehaves, they attempt to correct him, and he responds with more acting out. As this interaction develops into a repetitive pattern, it could be described as a correction and control/protest and rebellion sequence in which the parents' attempts to correct or control Sam invites a response from him of protest and rebellion which invites further correction and control from his parents, and on and on. In the course of that interaction, the parents, Arnie in particular, described themselves as feeling impotent and unable to exert any control over their son. In this exception, as Arnie stepped back, Sam responded differently. As we discuss the ways in which stepping back might affect Sam, the parents begin to experience themselves as perhaps having some influence in relation to him. As we examine those bits of influence, the parents shift from emphasizing their lack of control over Sam to wondering about the influence they might have.

This shift from control to influence is an important one. Although we have a strong cultural ethos that emphasizes being "in control" and the "master of one's fate," one could make a convincing case that we never have control over situations. However, we do have influence. This shift from "lack of control" to "emerging influence" provides a stronger foundation from which to work. It establishes a positive, forward-moving momentum that supports the elaboration of hope and agency. It promotes an empowering partnership and keeps our work anchored in what works within the client's personal culture rather than inviting the imposition of preferred solutions from within a professional culture.

Developing a Collaborative Partnership

At this point, my relationship with the parents has begun to change. They are beginning to see themselves as having some influence over the problem and there is a stronger connection in the therapeutic relationship. As they continue to examine instances of their influence, Arnie comments that Sam responds better to encouragement than correction, though with the disclaimer that "he doesn't give us many opportunities to do that." Sensing an opening, I respond to the father's statement that their son doesn't make it easy with the following remarks.

BILL: It sounds like when you folks get caught by this dance, it's much easier to fall into correcting him than encouraging him and every time you correct him he ends up acting out more which gets you correcting him more and on and on?

ARNIE: You got that right.

BILL: And it sounds like that's been a frustrating process for everyone. Like you'd rather be encouraging him to be the man you want him to be than correcting him from being the boy you don't want him to be and that he'd rather get your encouragement than your criticism.

ARNIE: Yes again.

BILL: Would you like some help not getting caught by that dance where he acts out and you criticize and he rebels and you criticize more and on and on in order to spend your time instead helping him become the man you hope for?

ARNIE: Sounds like a plan.

BILL: How about we meet again to develop a plan for that. Do you think Sam would be interested in a plan to get you off his back?

ARNIE: We can ask him and find out.

Whether Sam comes in or not, I am now in a much better situation with his parents. In fact, Sam did not come in for the next few sessions, and I worked with the parents to help them support each other in not getting caught by the pattern they had described and to develop a different way of interacting with their son. After a number of sessions, Sam entered the room in the middle of a session, saying he was in the neighborhood and needed bus fare from his parents. He expressed some curiosity about what people had been saying about him and accepted my invitation to stick around and find out.

In summary, we can shift from viewing the "reluctant family" as the problem to viewing the stance of "this is a problem, but we have no control over it" as the problem. We've seen how that stance constrains the family from more effectively taking action about the problem and exacts a toll on their relationships with each other. The series of guidelines that have been outlined could be summarized as follows:

1. Anticipate and attempt to avoid criticize/defend or minimize/maximize patterns.
2. Get connected to clients by assuming and searching for a positive intent behind the complaint.

3. Build a foundation of agency by jointly developing elements of hope and agency.
4. Use that foundation to elicit and examine exceptions to the stance of no control.
5. Develop a collaborative partnership to help them reclaim their lives from that stance.

SUMMARY

Although the two stances (no problem and no control) are quite different, there is significant overlap in the guidelines offered. In examining the common themes, we can extract three that provide useful generic guidelines for engaging all families:

1. *Get to know clients outside the influence of the problem.* Families are more than the problems that bring them to therapy. Discovering aspects of their experience outside the problems in their lives builds a strong foundation for a therapeutic relationship. It facilitates connection and bypasses the "resistance" that can be provoked when we confuse family identities with the problems in their lives.

2. *Honor before helping.* It is important to not attempt to help a family without an authorization to do so. One way to obtain such an authorization is to honor those aspects of families that are outside problems before attempting to help with those aspects of their lives taken up by problems.

3. *Keep the problem on the table.* Finally, in engaging families, it is important to remember that our engagement is a means to an end, not an end in itself. We have not entered into clients' lives simply because they are interesting and resourceful folks. We are there for a purpose and need to keep that purpose in mind. That purpose also needs to be continually negotiated with the family in order to maintain our authorization to be in their lives. The next chapter outlines a framework to organize our efforts toward that purpose through the development of collaborative therapy contracts.

NOTES

1. "Resistance" is put in quotation marks here to highlight that it is our construction rather than a real entity. I will not continue to use quotation marks around the word because it could become tedious, but I would encourage you as the reader to hold the concept in quotes in your head.

2. It is useful not to locate the problem of techniquism simply in individual practitioners. The search for a quick fix may protect us from the pain of family discomfort, but a "fix-it mentality" receives significant support from the contexts in which we work, particularly managed care.

3. "Denial" is another one of our therapeutic phrases that should be put in quotation marks. It often refers to clients not seeing what we view as the problem. Even though our determination that it is a problem may have a solid basis, it is important to own it as our determination.

4. Bob was seen by a therapist whom I supervised. Sections that reflect conversations between Bob and the therapist are taken from audiotapes of the sessions.

5. The ideas in this section have been strongly influenced by Alan Jenkins (1990, 1996) whose work with violent and abusive men I find to be profoundly humane and very effective. These suggestions are offered as a guideline, not as a recipe that should be followed step by step in the exact order.

6. In fact, this adversarial and confrontational relational stance underlies a number of common treatment modalities with offenders, batterers and substance abusers.

7. This description of my work with the family highlights work with the father because more work was required to engage his participation. The interview mainly focused on eliciting the father's participation; thus the work with the mother receives less attention here.

8. The father's clear picture emerged in the interview rather than being a preexisting picture I simply discovered. This process of jointly developing qualities through questions is further explored in Chapter 5.

4

❖———❖

Envisioning New Futures

Developing Collaborative Therapy
Contracts with Families

Many approaches to therapy consider goals important. This view has become even more intensified in an era of managed care, when continued funding for treatment is evaluated against the attainment of concrete, measurable goals. In this context, treatment goals are often seen as a necessary evil that have to be completed to obtain continued payment. However, one of the most common reasons that therapists feel stuck is related to unclear goals. Therapy goals provide a focus and an organizational framework for therapy. They can be used to both increase client motivation and ensure that our work is accountable to clients.

We can think about goal setting in therapy in many different ways. How we understand the function and process of goal setting has a significant effect on how therapy subsequently unfolds. Every action we take with clients is interventive and invites the enactment of life stories. The process through which we develop goals with clients invites them into a particular experience of themselves and supports the enactment of particular stories that organize that experience. The process of goal setting structures their experience of themselves, of us, and of our developing relationship. It also shapes our experience of clients, ourselves, and our relationship as well.

For example, a protective services worker develops a plan for an "underfunctioning, neglectful mother," which includes a vast array of ser-

126

vices for her children as well as parenting education and participation in an assertive training group for the mother. The worker goes out to the mother's home with the service plan and requires that she sign it. As the mother looks at the multitude of services being "offered" to her, she wonders how she'll ever find the time for them all and becomes overwhelmed and depressed. The worker senses that this mother will have trouble following through and wonders about her ability to parent. Over time, the worker increasingly steps in to do more and the mother experiences herself as increasingly incompetent and hopeless. The worker can't understand why the mother is so passive and wishes she would attend the assertiveness training group more regularly. What's going on here? The worker doesn't recognize how much the service plan highlighted only the mother's deficits and how the process of its development disempowered her. In fact, the worker's approach has inadvertently undermined the intention of the service plan.

Or, consider a defiant adolescent who is suspended from school and referred to a local mental health center after being found intoxicated in the school bathroom. At a case formulation meeting, the treatment team recommends weekly therapy and regular attendance at an AA meeting for teens to help this young man address his substance abuse problem. The therapist is not sure he can get the young man to go along with these recommendations but is shocked at the vehemence of his "resistance." The therapist describes to a colleague how he hates working with oppositional teenagers but doesn't grasp the degree to which the process of a treatment team developing treatment goals and then trying to mandate client cooperation places the client in a reactive position and invites potential "resistance." He also doesn't realize that the boy is an atheist for whom the idea of a higher power is an anathema and for whom the recommendation of participation in AA is another example of adults who "just don't get it." In this situation, the process of developing treatment goals constrains the development of a collaborative partnership that is sensitive to the unique culture of this particular client.

In both of these examples, the process of goal setting is anchored in practices of a medical model in which the "experts" diagnose problems and prescribe treatment, and clients receive and cooperate with those recommendations. Although this operational structure may work in some settings, it has the potential for difficulties when differences of opinion arise. We risk interacting with clients in ways that constrain rather than support effective work.

One solution to this problem would be to avoid setting goals and let the process of therapy unfold naturally. Unfortunately, this is not an option in many contexts. First, public agencies operate under unavoidable constraints from funding sources and managed care, and that reality needs to be accommodated. Second, goals that are collaboratively developed provide a focus for therapy that can increase its effectiveness and offer an accountability structure through which clients and therapists can mutually define and evaluate the preferred direction of therapy.

This chapter examines ways to develop therapy contracts with families that support the enactment of the core values and assumptions discussed so far. The chapter outlines an organizational framework to guide the process of therapy, offers a therapy contract outline that has been used in community agencies, and examines difficulties in the process of developing therapy contracts, especially with mandated clients and families in continual crises.

THERAPY AS A JOURNEY

A number of authors have drawn on a journey metaphor to describe therapy (Adams-Westcott & Isenbart, 1995; Durrant, 1993; White & Epston, 1990). Within this framework, therapy can be seen as a rite of passage in which clients (with our support) move from an old constraining identity to a new preferred one. The title of this chapter, "Envisioning New Futures," reflects a conceptual shift that is consistent with such a metaphor. In this shift, there is a movement away from trying to identify and correct old problems to supporting families in developing new lives. A journey metaphor is particularly useful for the organization of therapy and can be broken down into four steps, each of which is examined in detail:

1. Envisioning a new future.
2. Establishing a foundation of resourcefulness to get to a new future.
3. Anticipating constraints in the journey to a new future.
4. Developing collaborative therapy contracts with clients that draw on their strengths to manage the difficulties in the journey to preferred futures.

Envisioning a New Future

As described in the Introduction, the shift from fixing problems to envisioning new futures is a subtle but profound one. Traditionally, therapy has been concerned with problems that need to be resolved. There is a focus on what is wrong and what should be done about it. However, when we look for problems, we risk amplifying them. In the process, we may inadvertently help families become more entrenched in a problematic identity. (For example, think about the situation with Linda, described in Chapters 1 and 2.) A number of authors (e.g., de Shazer, 1991; Durrant, 1993; Waters & Lawrence, 1993) have emphasized the usefulness of helping families develop a proactive vision of the future toward which they can move. In this process, the focus shifts from what families are working on in therapy to where they are headed in their lives. Therapy begins by focusing on where families would like to be at the end of our engagement with them. In this way, the concept of "planned obsolescence" could become a beneficial force in human services. de Shazer's (1991) oft-asked question at the beginning of therapy, "How will we know when to stop meeting like this?," captures this effort.

Clinical Example: Planning Jon's Graduation

Jon is an 8-year-old boy whose father, David, and stepmother, Ruth, are splitting up for the fourth time. Ruth is tired of David's drinking, philandering, and irresponsible actions with his son and has ordered them both to leave the house. Jon lived with his father when the couple first split up, but when David lost his job and became homeless, he and Jon moved back in with Ruth and her two daughters. The family has a long history of involvement with protective services and has recently been referred due to concerns about David's neglectful parenting and significant tension between Jon and Ruth. The family has been referred for numerous services in the past and both David and Ruth are skeptical about the utility of services. David appears interested in help but has a history of not following through on recommendations.

The new therapist takes some time to get to know the family and then noticing David's high school ring and remembering from the conversation with the referral source that David had experienced great difficulty finishing high school engages him in a discussion about what high school he attended. They begin talking about the track team of which David had been a member and the difficulty of doing athletics and completing schoolwork at the same time. As the therapist asks David how he had balanced sports and schoolwork, David begins talking about the strong desire he had to finish school no matter what it took. In that context, the therapist asks David about his wishes and hopes for his son's future and David replies that he wants his son to finish high school and get a solid trade. They begin talking about David's high school graduation and the therapist asks David to imagine his son's high school graduation in 10 years. They discuss who might be there, how he'd feel about his son graduating, and what David would say to him. As David begins to generate a clear image of the future event, the therapist asks what needs to happen to get Jon to that point. Even though the therapist is only going to be involved with the family for a short time, he begins with a long-term vision and then focuses on what could happen in the next 3 months to increase the chances of that vision coming to fruition. This is analogous to strategic planning in which consultants help organizations develop a long-range plan even though they will not be there throughout that time to help the organization enact that plan.

Advantages of a Future Focus

There are a number of advantages to beginning with a future focus with families. A future-oriented discussion invites families to step out from under the weight of everyday problems and consider new possibilities. At the end of the session just described, David remarks on how fast the time went and mentions that this meeting felt different for him. As he thinks about his hopes and wishes for his son, he experiences anew his love for Jon and his desire to be the kind of father for Jon that he never had. As Ruth listens to David and talks about her own hopes for Jon, she remembers why she keeps taking Jon and his father back. She is committed to Jon, and although she is quite frustrated with David, she values Jon's love for him and doesn't want to disrupt that relationship. Over the course of the meeting, her furrowed brow relaxes and she begins to show traces of a smile. She begins to consider how she could support David's parenting without needing to continually rescue him. Meanwhile, Jon is watching the whole situation somewhat perplexed. He keeps waiting to be told what he's doing wrong and as that doesn't happen, he visibly relaxes into the session.

In this way, beginning with a future focus opens possibilities and yields more cooperation. The family is much more willing to continue meeting with the therapist to discuss what needs to happen in the next 3 months to increase the chances of Jon graduating high school. They agree to work on developing a stable living situation for Jon and clarifying how they will work together to care for him. David wants to work on becoming the father Jon would be proud to have at his imagined graduation and Ruth wants to support David's parenting without taking him back every time he struggles. Both parents are less skeptical of therapy and begin with enhanced motivation. In a program evaluation form filled out 6 months later, David notes the difference in this approach: "Before we had always talked about what others thought we were supposed to work on with Jon and how we still hadn't gotten there yet. Now, for the first time, we focused on where Jon was going and how we could help him get there. It gave us a new sense of him and the possibilities for all of us." These two questions "what are you working on" and "where are you headed in life" point to two very different directions in life (Durrant, 1993). While the first question keeps us within the realm of the problem and may constrain recognition of life outside of the problem, the second question orients us to life that may not include the problem and opens up expanded possibilities. This focus does not ignore the existence of problems but invites an examination of those problems from a perspective outside of the immediacy of them. In many ways, this is analogous to the way in which vacations sometimes offer us an opportunity to step outside the immediacy of our everyday lives and gain a quite different perspective on them.

A future vision also helps clients to cope with difficult times in the present. Waters and Lawrence (1993) note the work of Helen Markus and colleagues on the impact of one's sense of the future on current behavior (Markus & Nurius, 1986). They found that when faced with a crisis, individuals with a vision of the future coped much better in the present than those without such a vision. Though the work with Jon, David, and Ruth started out on a positive note, it certainly did not roll along smoothly. David's lapses in responsible parenting drove Ruth crazy and periodically led to pitched battles between her and David. However, throughout their struggles, periodic reminders that they were building a foundation for Jon's graduation made the situation more tolerable for everyone and allowed them to hang onto a "this too shall pass" attitude. A positive hopeful vision of the future supports improved current functioning.

A vision of oneself in the future provides clues about the path for getting there and in that sense acts as an incentive for present and future behavior. In that sense, a future focus is a profound intervention. It implicitly conveys that an alternative future (and present) is possible. The solution-focused miracle question is an example of a future orientation as interventive. In the miracle question, clients are asked, "Suppose one night there is a miracle while you are sleeping and the problem that brought you here is solved. What do you suppose you will notice different the next morning that will tell you that the problem is solved?" (Berg, 1994a, p. 97). A focus on the future eases us into times when desired behaviors are already happening. These emerging exceptions provide a template for further actions to move us closer to that preferred future.

Finally, future-oriented goals powerfully organize the process of therapy. The goal becomes a theme for therapy and offers a concrete way to keep therapists efficient and on track. It is also a way to make therapy more accountable to clients. It sets the stage for periodically reviewing the course of treatment with clients to assess our progress toward the projected end point and adjust if appropriate.

Questions to Envision New Futures

Following are some examples of questions that can be asked to help clients envision new futures:

> How will we know when to stop meeting like this? (de Shazer, 1991)
> At the end of our meetings, what would be different in your life that would tell you coming here had been worthwhile?
> What will others notice about you that is different from what's happening now?
> If we made a videotape of you now and then another one at the end, what differences would we see on the two videotapes? (O'Hanlon & Beadle, 1994; O'Hanlon & Wilk, 1987)
> How will you know that your daughter has gotten to the future you'd all like for her?
> What hopes do you have for your son on his 21st birthday? What kind of person would you like him to be? (*to the son*) What of that would you agree with? What will be different in your family at that point?
> What will be different when that is happening? How will that make things different for you? What will others notice about you then? If we had a videotape of that future, what would we see?

In each of these questions, it is important to develop with clients a concrete vision of the future. The strength of this process lies in the details that anchor it. The questions are designed to invite clients into an experience of the future and the depth of that experience depends on the elaboration of that picture.

What If Clients Can't Envision a Preferred Future?

Questions about envisioned futures are not always easy to answer. Many times, people's hopes for the future have been obscured by problems in the present. One of the most common initial answers to the questions eliciting an envisioned future is, "I have no idea what things would look like." It's important to realize the degree to which the ability to answer these questions is constrained not only by the immediacy of problems in people's lives but also by their expectation that they are supposed to talk about problems (that's why people usually go to therapy). This focus on the future may be quite unsettling. It is helpful to understand the magnitude of this shift and to be gently persistent in the questioning. The search for answers to these questions needs to be a collaborative process.

It can be helpful to first anchor clients in an experience from the past or present that stands out as memorable or especially valued for them. In the interview with David, the therapist's conversation about David's high school graduation provided a segue into questions about David's vision of Jon's graduation and future. If the therapist had directly asked about David's hopes for Jon's future, David might have had trouble responding because of the pervasiveness of problems in the present. The questions about David's graduation invited both David and the therapist out of the "problem-saturated" present and opened up space for a consideration of possible futures. A useful set of questions to accomplish this comes from Appreciative Inquiry (Cooperrider, 1990; Hammond, 1996):

- Think of a time when you felt most connected to your (partner, son, daughter, parent, etc.). What was happening? What were you doing? What was the other person doing? (Questions to get details.)
- What did you most value or appreciate about who you were and how you were acting?
- What of that would you like to bring more into your life and your future?

These questions anchor an investigation of possible futures in events that have worked previously and bring out positive, forward-moving energy. Because the answers are grounded in real experiences, they can be more easily built upon.

At other times when clients are having great difficulty responding to questions about the future, it may be helpful to shift into a discussion of the immediate problem and its effects on their hopes for a future. For example, I recently observed the top of a young man's head, while he avoided eye contact and stared at his shoelaces. As I asked him about his hopes for the future, he responded with vague mumblings that were variations on the theme of "I don't know, leave me alone." I asked him when his future had been stolen away from him. He gave me a puzzled look and I went on to explain that I figured he probably didn't just give away his hopes for the future and so they must have been stolen away from him. He shrugged and I continued, "Did he know other kids in high school whose hopes and dreams for their lives had also been stolen away?" His response was an imperceptible nod and I asked, "Does it seem fair to you that young people's hopes and lives are being taken away from them?" That aroused some interest and he began to talk about how it wasn't fair. His anger and sense of injustice was mobilizing and we began to slowly move into what his hopes might look like if he were to get them back. We began to talk about what he would like his current life (rather than his future) to look like and he began interacting with more energy. We moved into a discussion of this being his life and his ideas for his preferred life. The process elicited some motivation that could be harnessed for our work together.

Establishing a Foundation of Resourcefulness

If we begin by helping clients develop a vision of a preferred life or future, a logical next step is to establish a foundation for getting there. I used to paint houses for a living and found that the actual painting took up very little of my time. Most of the time was spent prepping the surface to be painted; scraping, plastering, sanding, and so on. When the surface was adequately prepared, the painting went smoothly. When it wasn't, I found myself continually going back and redoing work I thought had already been completed. Likewise, therapy can be thought of as a series of steps, each of which rests on the previous one. If we begin by laying a strong foundation, the subsequent steps will proceed more smoothly and efficiently.

A strong foundation begins with "developing family resourcefulness." That phrase is based on a social constructionist assumption that resources are not simply internal, innate qualities that families possess or lack but rather that resourcefulness develops in the course of social interactions. In this way, we as therapists do not go out and "discover" resourcefulness in clients but bring it forth in our interactions with them. Resourcefulness has been defined as the "capability to deal with a situation or meet difficulties" (*Random House Dictionary of the English Language,* 1987). The questions we ask families have the potential to elicit and elaborate their resourcefulness. Resourcefulness, as used here, includes the capacities, qualities, abilities, skills, wisdom, and knowledge that circulate among family members and their social networks. We need to move beyond the individual in thinking about resourcefulness. We need to investigate the capacities, skills, and knowledge that can be developed or accessed within a client's social network as well. It is important to identify who might be available as a community to support clients on their journey toward preferred futures. We need to look beyond the immediate family to friends, neighbors, and community contacts in establishing a foundation of resourcefulness.

We can also look at resourcefulness as influenced by gender, race, and class factors. For example, two affluent parents are frustrated with the lack of services provided for their special needs child in the local public school and opt to transfer her to a private school. Their access to the knowledge about the best private schools that specialize in learning disabilities as well as their financial resources are a source of support that help them meet and handle this situation. Their economic resources hold the potential to insulate them from the stresses of their child's education. Similarly, a poor woman who lives in a tough neighborhood has developed a certain wisdom about managing interactions with unsavory characters on the street. When accosted in dark alleyways, she describes acting crazy, talking loudly to herself, and breaking into a nonsensical stream of epithets as a way of maintaining her safety. She routinely negotiates a neighborhood that the first couple would be scared to enter. Her street-smart knowledge and coping strategies constitute aspects of resourcefulness.

As discussed in earlier chapters, establishing a foundation of resourcefulness invites connection, facilitates joining, and minimizes "resistance." This initial focus anchors a strong foundation for the work that follows. For example, imagine how the work with David might have gone differently if the therapist had begun by focusing on the conditions of David's homelessness rather than his efforts to graduate high school. Which sets a better foundation for a constructive conversation about David's parenting?

There are numerous examples of the advantages of beginning with a focus on resources. Sheinberg (1992) draws a distinction between stories of pride and stories of shame. In her work with families at the disclosure of incest, she makes a special attempt to elicit those things that family members feel proud about in their families before examining those things that invoke shame. Stories of pride become a foundation for an examination of stories of shame. Proud stories keep us and families anchored in a broader view of families and remind us all that families are more than the problems that bring them to therapy.

In a related fashion, Freeman, Epston, and Lobovits (1997) attempt to get to know children with whom they work apart from the problems in their lives in order to not let problems define clients, dominate the agenda, and set the tone for the therapeutic relationship. An example of this attempt comes out in their description of the following interaction between Jenny Freeman and a family concerned about their son Patrick:

Jenny noticed Patrick staring off into space with a sad face while members of the family busied themselves relating the various negative effects of his misbehavior both at home and at school. Jenny broke in, "I want to be respectful of your concern over the problem, but would it be okay with you if I took some time initially to get to know Patrick apart from the problem?" They were only too willing to tell about some of Patrick's interests and qualities. At the next session, Jenny asked Patrick what he remembered about the previous meeting. He recalled, "They said I'm smart and I can draw really well." Later Patrick confessed through the mouth of a puppet that he had a story about himself—that he was "real dumb." Needless to say, it took some time for things to change, but the foundation had been laid for Patrick to feel respected and learn to respect himself. (p. 35)

Similarly, I often begin by asking parents in an initial session, "I know you're really concerned about the problem you called me about, but I'd like to start this off somewhat differently if that would be okay with you." If it is acceptable to parents, I'll then ask, "What do you think I might come to most appreciate or respect about your daughter after I've gotten to know her a bit?" This type of question sets a different foundation for the rest of the meeting than beginning with the parents' litany of complaints about their child.

In each of these approaches, a foundation of competence is initially established. The importance of this foundation is crucial. Think, in your own life, about going to a party and how you might want to introduce yourself to strangers. How might the evening be different if the other person asked you about your failings or things that brought you pride? How would you experience yourself differently? How would you experience the other person differently? What might it be like the next time you encountered that person? Beginning with a focus on resourcefulness sets a foundation that makes subsequent therapeutic work significantly more efficient and effective.

Again, it is crucial in this discussion to avoid a dichotomy of clients being seen as either resourceful or pathological. We need to avoid simple solutions and allow ourselves to hold multiple views of clients simultaneously. It is important to help families develop a foundation of resourcefulness without minimizing their experience of difficulties. Therapy often begins with experiences of shame (we specialize in failure, after all) and may have difficulty moving beyond that. It is easy to get stuck in the experience of shame because it can become so engulfing. In an attempt to do something different we can begin with eliciting experiences of competence, connection, hopefulness, and pride and use these experiences as a foundation from which to examine difficulties. However, eliciting such experiences may not always work for particular clients or families. There are clients who may not be able to experience resourcefulness and pride until they feel the story of their difficulties and shame has been witnessed and understood. It is important to be responsive to client needs and avoid a rigid sequencing in eliciting stories of pride and shame. We can move back and forth between experiences of pride and shame; amplifying stories of pride, acknowledging stories of shame, and inquiring which fit better with families' preferred lives.

The process of establishing client resourcefulness also allows us to develop with families the competencies they can bring to bear on the problem. In the previous example, David and Jon loved to fish together. David knew a lot about fishing and thought Jon needed to learn the value of patience in his fishing. (Jon had a tendency to continually pull the hook out of the water to check on its status, rather than waiting for the fish to take the bait.) The therapist used David's regard for patience to help him become less reactive to Jon's misbehavior. David was very frustrated with having to tell Jon the same thing over and over again. It would drive David crazy and he would often end up storming out of the house. The therapist engaged David in a discussion of how important it was for David to "leave his hook in the water" and wondered what David needed to do for Jon to "take the bait."

In a similar vein, Ruth worked as an administrative assistant for two bosses. One was quite organized, and she described the other as a "space cadet." The therapist inquired how she managed to successfully balance their respective workloads and not let the disorganization of the one boss affect her work for the other. As she described her expertise at compartmentalizing their work demands and not getting caught up in the frenzy of disorganization, she suddenly realized that she could apply this expertise to her home life and compartmentalize the needs of her daughters from the demands posed by Jon and David. She reflected that this would allow her to not go crazy feeling like she was ignoring Jon or short-changing her daughters. This realization was not given to Ruth by the therapist but emerged for both Ruth and the therapist out of the conversation (organized to a large degree by the therapist's questions) and highlights the collaborative nature of eliciting client resourcefulness and bringing it to bear on problems.

Anticipating Constraints

After eliciting a vision of clients' preferred futures and bringing forth the knowledge and competencies that they can draw on in the journey, it is easy to engage clients in a discussion of what stands between their present and their preferred future. In this context, the issues that emerge are particularly relevant to clients. This process increases the chances that emerging goals will better reflect the family's agenda. This is important for two reasons. From a political perspective, it supports the value of self-determination. Unfortunately, we in the mental health profession can all too easily fall into drawing on our normative models to make decisions about how we think families should be living their lives and then work to enlist their compliance with that vision. This kind of therapeutic colonialism is disempowering and disrespectful of families. It supports a stance of missionary zeal in which our preoccupation with our own ideas may hinder our ability to recognize and value family wisdom. It also doesn't work.

From a pragmatic perspective, developing goals that reflect clients' agendas leads to much more effective therapy outcomes. Consistent research shows that clients are much more likely to pursue the goals that *they* have developed. Berg and Miller (1992) cite studies in the field of alcohol treatment that demonstrate that compliance with therapy increases dramatically when clients set and work toward goals they've developed (Hester & Miller, 1989; Miller, 1985). When goals are important to them, clients are more likely to be invested in their achievement. Their investment forms a stronger basis for a cooperative working relationship and enhances therapeutic efficacy.

To return to David and Jon, the therapist invited David to examine some of the likely potholes on the road to Jon's graduation. David identified his inconsistent presence with Jon as a possible one. When asked what got in the way of his being more present for Jon, David acknowledged that his drinking and carousing could be a problem in that respect. After some exploration about the effects of drinking and carousing on Jon, on David, and on their relationship, David decided to cut down on his carousing and not go out drinking, except occasionally when he would get a baby-sitter for Jon. If the therapist had begun by raising David's drinking as a problem, David most likely would have been reluctant to embrace it as a treatment goal. Their work together could easily have proceeded down a quite different path in which David acquired a label as "resistant" and "in denial." Framing immediate problems in the context of constraints to a preferred future increases the probability that addressing the problem will be relevant to the client. The problem becomes unwanted potholes on the client's road rather than a hoop set up by the therapist for the client to jump through. The process allows us to join with clients against constraints rather than fall into an adversarial role in which we're attempting to get them to do something. It supports partnership in that we sit with clients against constraints rather than against each other.

It's important to note that this division of the contracting process into three steps should not suggest that these steps proceed in a simple linear fashion. Sometimes we may begin with a focus on hopes and futures; sometimes on abilities, resources, and knowledges; and sometimes on an immediate pressing problem. It is important that the therapist take a leadership role in this process but be open to following the client's direction rather than imposing the therapist's own direction. The next section examines ways to codify these steps into a therapy contract.

Developing Collaborative Therapy Contracts

Once we have a good idea of the futures that clients would like to inhabit, the foundation of resourcefulness for getting there, and the anticipated difficulties on that journey, we are well-positioned to develop a contract with families to guide our work together. It is important to think of a therapy contract as a work in progress rather than as a finished product. The contract is a guideline that organizes the work that clients and therapists do together. The contract sets out a general direction for the work, but we need to retain the flexibility to make our work responsive to client needs.

Therapy contracting needs to be a collaborative process. The way in which we write therapy contracts and the process through which we develop them profoundly influences how we make sense of clients and how our relationships with them develop. The therapy contract outline that follows grew out of the same endeavor to rewrite forms as the assessment outline in Chapter 2, and it offers a way to promote the conceptual shifts described and invite collaboration. It has five components:

1. Agreed-upon focus of therapy
2. Short-term goals
3. Plan for therapy
4. Ways that improvement might first be noticed
5. Indications that goals have been achieved

Agreed-Upon Focus of Therapy

If we think about therapy as a journey from an old constraining identity to a new preferred one, the Agreed-Upon Focus of Therapy can be thought of as a brief, anticipatory summary of that journey. In the situation with Jon, David, and Ruth, the focus of treatment was summarized as follows:

> David and Ruth want to work together to build a foundation that will help Jon become a responsible young man who is able to complete high school, support himself, and get along with others. David, as the primary parent wants to become a more consistent figure in Jon's life and provide him with a stable home life. Ruth wants to support David in his parenting, while also building a life of her own outside of their relationship. Jon wants to get along better with Ruth and not feel compelled to defend his father in front of her.

Traditionally, licensing agencies require that treatment plans contain long-term goals, short-term goals, and plan and outcome measures to ensure accountability to funders. The Agreed-Upon Focus of Therapy contains long-term goals, though they are framed as something to move toward rather than something from which to move away. The long-term focus provides direction for the immediate work together and a context for subsequent short-term goals. It helps to make our work relevant to clients and organizes the therapy in a way that it becomes future focused and goal driven rather than problem driven. In this way, therapy fits to the context of clients' lives rather than attempting to fit clients to the context of therapy.

Short-Term Goals

Short-Term Goals refer to the immediate issues to be addressed in therapy that provide a foundation for the pursuit of a preferred long-term direction in a client's life. Short-Term Goals need to fit in the context of the agreed-upon focus of therapy and be developed collaboratively between therapist and client. We can distinguish between the content of goals and the process of developing goals. In the spirit of self-determination, it is important that clients have a leadership role in the development of the content of short-term goals. The journey that we are supporting them on is their journey and we need to ensure that our efforts do not inadvertently move from supporting them to supplanting them. In addition, when clients define the goals, they are more likely to pursue them. Therapy begins with increased motivation and we are more likely to reach goals that have been set when those goals are immediately relevant to clients' lives.

At the same time, therapists have a responsibility to play a leadership role in organizing the process of goal development. As discussed, the process of developing goals is profoundly interventive. Clients may set the direction they wish to pursue, but we as therapists bring particular skills to ensuring that their journey is constructive and empowering. The language in which we help clients to frame goals is very important. Goals need to strike a balance between capturing clients' imaginations and remaining concrete, specific, and achievable. An example of this is one of the treatment goals developed with David:

> David will draw on his love for and commitment to Jon to move from a *Miami Vice* lifestyle to a *Mr. Mom* lifestyle (i.e., find stable employment and housing, spend more time at home with Jon instead of out drinking and carousing, and provide more consistent parenting to Jon in the form of clear expectations, guidelines, and consequences, as well as special times for fun).

The language for this goal grew out of David's acknowledgment that his drinking and carousing could be a roadblock to his being more present for Jon. As the therapist sought to understand what David liked about his drinking and carousing days, David spoke admiringly about Sonny Crocket, the Don Johnson character from *Miami Vice* who drove flashy cars, was surrounded by beautiful women, and moved in chic and trendy circles. David and his therapist developed a contrast between a *Miami Vice* lifestyle and a *Mr. Mom* lifestyle (from a movie David liked in which Michael Keaton portrays a father staying at home and raising kids) and examined the pros and cons of each life. Although a *Miami Vice* lifestyle strongly appealed to David, he thought that it was ultimately unfair to his son and wanted to move into a *Mr. Mom* lifestyle for his son's welfare. In the conversation, David also began to appreciate the joy he found in just hanging out with his son. The simple phrase "moving from a *Miami Vice* lifestyle to a *Mr. Mom* lifestyle," captured a whole range of experiences for David and provided both him and his therapist with a succinct way of talking about those experiences. The language of the goal in parentheses (find stable employment and housing, etc.) was developed at the therapist's urging to concretize that shift (as well as to ensure that the therapy would be reimbursed). The goal, phrased in this way, captures David's playful, lyrical style while retaining concrete elements that can be measured and attained. We need to help clients develop goals that both touch them in powerful ways and can be framed concretely.

The process of helping clients frame goals in specific terms helps keep them focused on their preferred directions in life. Specifying with David the elements of a shift from a *Miami Vice* lifestyle to a *Mr. Mom* lifestyle invites him into an experience of that shift which provides a foundation for beginning to enact that shift. Vague goals (common examples are "We'll get along better" or "I'll have higher self-esteem") are hard to measure and difficult to achieve. There are a number of ways to invite descriptions of goals that are observable and concrete. One example that some therapists have used is "videotalk" in which clients are invited to describe a videotape of a nonproblematic future (e.g., "If we had a videotape of you two getting along better, what would be happening that is different?") (O'Hanlon & Beadle, 1994). The development of specific goals provides a more concrete vision toward which to move.

It is also important that we help clients develop goals that are achievable. Our overall focus on the future invites hope and a sense of movement. Goals that are too large or difficult to achieve can quickly sabotage that movement. We can help families develop achievable goals by encouraging them to focus on small steps and by breaking down large or vague goals into quantifiable entities through scaling questions (Berg, 1994a;

Berg & Miller, 1992). An example of scaling questions would be, "On a scale of 1 to 10, how much self-control would you like your son to have? How much would you say he has now? What would tell us that he had gone up one step?" Scaling questions help us to keep the focus on the direction of movement even when the degree of movement is small.

It is useful to help clients define goals that represent the beginning of new behaviors rather than the end of undesirable behaviors (Berg, 1994a; Berg & Miller, 1992). Positive, proactive goals that reflect the presence of something rather than the absence of something continue the momentum to a nonproblematic future and lead to more efficient therapy. It is difficult to *not* do something. In the process, we end up thinking about the activity we are trying to avoid. For example, a treatment goal of "I will not drink" keeps an image of alcohol squarely in front of us. It conjures up the forbidden alcohol, which we then attempt to ignore, making avoidance of it even more difficult. A treatment goal of ending an undesirable behavior keeps us embedded in the problem. A treatment goal of beginning a new behavior invites us outside the realm of the problem and opens up significantly more new possibilities. Asking a client what he or she might be doing instead of drinking leads us into a definition of a positive, proactive goal. For example, such a goal might be "I will exercise every night when I come home from work."

Numerous solution-focused therapists have highlighted the importance of language in inquiring about nonproblematic futures (Berg, 1994a; Durrant, 1993; O'Hanlon & Beadle, 1994; O'Hanlon & Weiner-Davis, 1989). If we begin with an assumption that goals will be reached, we increase the possibility of goal attainment. An example of such language would be: "What will you be doing *when* this is no longer a problem?" vs. "What would you be doing *if* this were no longer a problem." Presupposing goal achievement can help orient clients to an expectation of change. It is also important to emphasize client agency and action in these questions: "What will *you* be doing when this is no longer a problem?" vs. "What will *be happening to you* when this is no longer a problem?" Emphasizing client agency and action embeds the notion that clients *can* do something different, that *they* are the ones who need to do it, and that *doing* it is what will make the difference. Although the language is important, the true power of this phrasing relies on our faith and conviction that people can and will have better lives.

At the same time, it is useful to frame goals as involving lots of hard work. Berg and Miller (1992) emphasize that this realism protects client dignity and allows graceful acknowledgment of past failures if clients are unable to reach a goal. In this way, a win–win situation is created in which failure to reach goals can be seen as due to the difficulty of the endeavor (creating a stronger base from which to try again) and in which success leads to compliments for the hard work clients are doing. It also can help to avoid a minimize/maximize sequence in which clients point out how they can't quite meet the goal and therapists continue encouraging them to try a bit harder. Framing goals as involving lots of hard work validates clients' experience and can help us avoid the eye rolling often provoked by pious slogans such as "Just say no."

Each of these suggestions for our leadership in the process of goal settings (helping clients develop goals that capture their imagination and also remain concrete, specific and achievable; helping clients to define positive, proactive goals; using language that orients clients to an expectation of change; and validating the hard work that goes into addressing the issues in their lives) helps to enhance the interventive potential of goal setting.

Plan for Therapy

Goals have two components: what you are aiming for and what you are going to do to achieve it. The Plan for Therapy section of this outline highlights the latter by spelling out in concrete detail who will do what with whom for how long in order to accomplish the agreed-upon goals. The plan gives us a template against which to evaluate our work with clients. It allows us periodically to review what we've agreed to do and examine the degree to which the work we pursue together fits with our original intentions. In situations in which there is a discrepancy, a written plan allows us to evaluate together our reactions to that discrepancy. While therapy goals often specify actions to be undertaken by family members, it is important to include the efforts of various helpers as well. In the example of David, Ruth, and Jon, the plan for therapy included a number of specific things that the therapist would do to help David in job hunting. When, after several weeks, the therapist hadn't completed those activities, David was in a position to draw his attention to it and inquire why he hadn't done anything yet. The plan for therapy should hold helpers as well as family members accountable for the actions each agrees to take.

Ways That Improvement Might First Be Noticed

This section of a therapy contract orients therapists and clients to change. By inviting reflection on how changes might first appear, it promotes attention to the direction of change rather than the magnitude of change and reinforces a positive focus and sense of movement. The examination of Ways That Improvement Might First Be Noticed is interventive and increases the probably of noticing forward momentum. Framing it as ways that improvement *might* first be noticed alleviates discouragement that could arise in the event that changes are not noticed and opens up space for an investigation of other ways in which improvement might first be noticed.

This section also helps to break goal attainment into very concrete, measurable steps. For example, David's goal of moving from a *Miami Vice* lifestyle to a *Mr. Mom* lifestyle had some of the following ways that improvement might be first noticed:

- David would put together a resume.
- David would buy the Sunday paper and read the want ads.
- David would call two friends about potential living situations.
- David would notice what he particularly appreciates about the times he's home with Jon playing quietly.
- David would take a deep breath before responding to Jon next time he misbehaves.

These first indications helped David to stay on track toward the goals he had defined for himself and reassured him that changes were indeed happening even though they were beginning first steps. By focusing on the direction of change rather than the magnitude of change, it helped David stay hopeful, positive, and forward thinking.

Indications That Goals Have Been Achieved

This section helps to clarify a stopping point and make therapy more accountable to both clients and funders. It institutionalizes the question raised previously, "What needs to happen for us to stop meeting like this?" It is particularly useful for clients who have had chronic involvements with multiple providers. Often, services go on and on with no end in sight. A clearly demarcated stopping point gives structure to the work and provides clear distinguishing features against which to determine the necessity for continuing services. It also helps to make services more accountable to clients. We can measure events in clients' lives against the material in this section and use that comparison to make ongoing evaluations about whether to continue or end services. It is important in this process that these indications be mutually defined and mutually evaluated.

The indications that David's goal of moving from a *Miami Vice* lifestyle to a *Mr. Mom* lifestyle had been achieved included such things as:

- David and Jon will have a stable living situation.
- David will have stable employment, be home more often, and provide more consistent parenting.

- Jon will respond to David's limits and be spending more time hanging out with David rather than fighting with him.
- Jon will be asking to spend more time with his Dad.

The indicators for this goal (which was a goal for David) were jointly developed with David and had interesting effects on him. David later commented that the process of thinking about indicators helped to make the shift to a *Mr. Mom* lifestyle more concrete. It invited him to step into the experience of an .envisioned future. The next sections examine some of the difficulties in developing treatment goals with mandated clients, with clients whose lives are set amidst continual crises, and with funding organizations with radically different ideas about what should be done.

DEVELOPING THERAPY GOALS WITH MANDATED CLIENTS

Attempts to develop goals with mandated clients who have been required or "strongly urged" to attend therapy can be a frustrating endeavor for everyone involved. Mandated clients often do not define themselves as needing therapy and may have very strong reactions to being mandated to attend. Sometimes these reactions are immediately apparent, as in the situation in which a single father referred because of concerns about possible abuse of his child greets his female therapist at their first appointment with, "It's bureaucrats like you who give the Oklahoma City bombing a good name." Reactions such as this provoke strong responses on our part. For therapists, it is easy to get caught in a struggle with mandated clients over whether they really need to be there or not. We can become captured by our own indignation that they refuse to see the need for or value of our services and can get ensnared in an escalating struggle over whether or not they need to be in therapy that inadvertently adds further constraints.

Some clients may conceal their resentment of mandated services and present with a pseudo-compliant stance in which they hope that if they pretend to go along with us, we'll eventually take the hint and leave them alone. Their real feelings may remain concealed because they feel they can't risk sharing them with us. In these situations, therapy can take on an investigatory air in which therapists try to find out "what's really going on" and clients try to figure out what therapists are "really up to." This atmosphere takes a significant toll on the developing relationship.

In working with mandated clients, it's important to begin with an appreciation of the client's experience of having to attend a meeting about a problem he or she defines as not existing. A crucial question becomes, How do we begin a relationship with mandated clients in a way that acknowledges their humanity and in which they do not experience themselves being perceived as some "undeserving other"? This beginning is important for both ethical and pragmatic considerations. All clients deserve respect and respect serves as a foundation for efficient and cost-effective treatment.

One way to accomplish this is to recognize that mandated clients who attend an initial session could have decided to not meet with us. There is something that they want in meeting with us, even if it is to avoid the consequences of not meeting. The decision to meet is a proactive step that constitutes an opening for engagement. An adolescent comes to counseling so that his parents will let him back on the Internet. A husband meets with a substance abuse counselor so that his wife will let him back in the house again. The father who referred to the Oklahoma City bombing comes because he doesn't want to lose his children. In each of these examples, there is something positive that clients seek and that we can use as an opening to make ourselves relevant to them. The suggestions in Chapter 3 for engaging clients who present with a stance of "this is not a problem" constitute a foundation from which to begin goal negotiation with mandated clients.

It is crucial that goal negotiation with mandated clients be done in a collaborative fashion. Mandated clients, especially those involved with protective services, often receive "help" in an antagonistic context. An example of this comes from a conversation I once had with a trainer in child welfare who told me, "Quite frankly, Bill, I don't emphasize joining much in my work because in 95% of the cases it's going to be an adversarial relationship anyway." There are many examples of protective services organized around a partnership model, but this sentiment reflects an unfortunate preoccupation with motivating clients through force rather than through connection. It's a context that invites a particular response from clients and often gives rise to "resistance." In a mandated context, the development of a collaborative relationship is profoundly interventive. Mandated clients often expect clinicians to react to them in judgmental ways and may very well engage in ways that protect themselves from that anticipated onslaught. (For example, the Oklahoma City bombing remark, while provocative, is a good example of the phrase "the best defense is a strong offense.") Engaging with respect and connection can catch mandated clients off guard and open up space for the development of a new relationship. It is important to remember that a sympathetic stance does not mean condoning behavior, just that you are willing to hear the client's side of the story. Within this context, it becomes important to strike a balance between developing treatment goals as an ally rather than an adversary and engaging clients in a way that does not lead to a coalition against other providers. The process of negotiating treatment goals with a mandated client is highlighted in the following clinical example.

Cheryl's Strong Will

Cheryl is an African American single mother with two preschool children who are in a foster home in the custody of protective services after a charge of neglect was filed by a neighbor. Cheryl has been referred for therapy because of concerns about neglect of her children when she is partying, possible substance misuse, and her tendency to fly off the handle when she gets frustrated with her children. She comes to the first session with a hard glare on her face. After spending 15 minutes getting to know her, her white male therapist moves into the question,

THERAPIST: So, whose idea was it that you come here?

CHERYL: It sure wasn't *my* idea. This is *not* my idea of a fun time. My protective worker told me I gotta come here or they were going to take away my kids. She's always nosing about in my business. She ought to get a life of her own. (*Goes on for a while venting about her worker.*)

THERAPIST: Well, given that you don't like people in your business, I appreciate your willingness to come here and talk with me. How did you decide to come anyway, rather that blow it off?

CHERYL: I blow it off, I lose my kids. Seems pretty simple to me. I ain't gonna lose my kids. No way!

THERAPIST: So, they're pretty important to you.

CHERYL: Yeah, they're all I've got.

THERAPIST: So they're real important to you. What do you think your protective worker would say you need to do differently to get her out of your face?

CHERYL: I got no idea what she wants from me.

THERAPIST: Sometimes it's tough figuring out all the ideas that helpers have for you. What's your guess? What do you think it would take for protective services to close your case and get out of your life?

Cheryl takes a while, struggling to find an answer to this question. Despite her outrage at having protective services in her life, she has trouble imagining them ever leaving. Finally she comes up with an answer.

CHERYL: They want me to dump my boyfriend, be a miss prissy, and quit partying.

THERAPIST: So, if you did all that, they wouldn't be bothering you?

CHERYL: I don't know, maybe. They're so suspicious, they'd probably never be satisfied.

THERAPIST: That would be a lot to give up.

CHERYL: Damn straight.

THERAPIST: But your kids are important to you.

CHERYL: Yeah.

THERAPIST: Important enough to get protective services out of your life and get your kids back?

CHERYL: What are you up to?

THERAPIST: I'll tell you what I'm up to. Seems like protective services said you need to be in counseling because they're concerned about the kind of care your kids are getting. That's what they do. It's their job to be suspicious. Now I don't know you and so I'm in no position to say anything about what kind of parent you are. You strike me as someone who is very committed to her kids, otherwise you wouldn't be here. So, what I'm up to is trying to see if there's a way that I can help you get your kids back. Would that interest you?

CHERYL: Yeah, but how do I know I can trust you?

THERAPIST: You don't. I'd encourage you to not trust me unless it feels right to you.

CHERYL: (*Stares quietly at the therapist and then softly answers.*) Yeah, I don't know about trusting white folks, but you seem OK.

THERAPIST: Thank you. So tell me, why are your kids so important to you?

Cheryl goes on to talk about what makes each of her children special to her. The conversation invites Cheryl into an experience of connection with her children and competence as a mother that provides a stronger foundation for a subsequent conversation about what she needs to do to get her children back. The therapist sidesteps the invitation to tell her that partying is how she lost her kids in the first place. He focuses on a future of reunification and searches for Cheryl's honorable qualities by focusing on her competence as a mother.

THERAPIST: So, I'd like to ask you something. It's real clear you weren't too excited about this meeting and you could easily have blown it off.

And yet, you came because, as you say, your kids are your life. What does it tell you about yourself that you'd be willing to jump through all these hoops to hang on to them.

CHERYL: What kind of stupid question is that?

THERAPIST: It is kind of a weird isn't it, but what do you think?

CHERYL: It tells me that no matter what, I'm going to get them back. If I have to walk across fire, I'll do what it takes to get them back.

THERAPIST: Do your kids know how strong-willed you are?

CHERYL: Yeah, they take after me.

THERAPIST: So, that's a quality you've passed onto them. Is that a quality you're proud of?

CHERYL: If I didn't have a strong will, I'd be dead by now.

THERAPIST: So, you're someone who is really committed to her kids and has the will to put that commitment into action. How committed are you to getting them back? Like on a scale from one to ten?

CHERYL: I don't know. Eight or nine, I'm real committed to getting them back.

THERAPIST: Eight or nine? That's a lot of commitment. What do you think you need to do to get your kids back?

CHERYL: I gotta stop partying.

THERAPIST: That's a lot to ask, but it seems like you've got the commitment and willpower to do that. So, do you want help in getting them back?

CHERYL: You gonna help me with that?

THERAPIST: I'll give it a try if you want. But let me ask you something. Do you just want them back or do you want them back to stay? You know, like do you want to do it in a way that makes sure protective services won't be in your face anymore. Cause that's a bit harder.

CHERYL: Hey, if I'm gonna do this crap, I want to do it once and for all.

THERAPIST: All right, so let's start with putting together a picture of what life would look like with your kids back home to stay.

Cheryl begins developing a picture of life with her kids back at home and protective services out of her life. She and her therapist agree to continue meeting with a focus on helping Cheryl make the changes in her life necessary to get her children back and keep them back. They agree to work on Cheryl becoming a more consistent presence in their lives by staying at home six nights a week, by ensuring that her children have a baby-sitter the one night a week that she does go out, and by developing alternative ways of responding to the frustration provoked by little children. They also agree to continue to discuss her alcohol use, jointly evaluating the degree to which her drinking might constitute use or misuse.[1]

DEVELOPING THERAPY CONTRACTS AMIDST CONTINUAL CRISES

The challenges confronting multi-stressed families are often unremitting, and the process of developing therapy goals can at times feel like building a house in a hurricane. At each meeting we are greeted with a new imminent crisis and therapy goals seem to shift daily. In response, it is important to strike a balance between flexibility and focus. We need the flexibility to respond to family needs, coupled with a consistent focus to give the work direction. If we are simply responding to ever-changing family needs, we miss the opportunity to help family members shift out of a pattern of ongoing crises. However, the imminent crises in families' lives easily pull us into a fix-it mentality in which we feel compelled to immediately react. Even if we are able to resist the pull of immediate daily concerns, it can be difficult to effectively invite families to step outside of immediate crises.

If we return to the metaphor of therapy as a journey, therapy amidst continual crises becomes a tumultuous journey indeed. It is at these times that the four steps with which we began (envisioning a new future, establishing a foundation of resources, anticipating constraints, and developing a contract) become valuable in establishing and maintaining a focus amidst crises. However, envisioning a new future in the middle of a crisis may seem like an unaffordable luxury. A common response from families is, "I just need to get through this crisis and maybe then I can think about the future." However, *this* crisis often flows insidiously into the next one and families become caught in a pounding surf of unrelenting crises in which they are continually knocked off balance every time they attempt to get their footing.

For example, consider Katherine's situation. Her welfare benefits are being cut off, she's threatened with eviction, her 8-year-old son diagnosed with ADHD is suicidal, and her 16-year-old daughter has just announced that she's pregnant and wants to marry her boyfriend who is Puerto Rican. Katherine is worried that her extended Irish immigrant family will try to kill the boyfriend, that her son may kill himself, and that, if her kids survive, they will all be destitute and homeless. Her therapist questions whether the future can be considered at all while these pressing issues are unresolved. However, as the therapist inquires about how concerned each family member is about this situation, the 16-year-old daughter shrugs and says, "This is our life. It's always been like this." When crises become chronic, they tend to perpetuate themselves. Often families caught in this cycle acquire labels such as "crisis prone." These labels have the potential to further constrain family coping abilities by inviting an experience in which they feel blamed for the crises in their lives. Just as getting to know families outside the context of the problem that brings them to therapy is a useful way to begin, getting to know families outside the context of crisis opens up the potential for families to step outside crisis and develop a different relationship with crisis.

A future focus can be particularly useful in this endeavor. There is an apparent paradox here that if families don't take care of the present, there will be no future, but if they don't consider an alternative future, they will never escape the tyranny of present crises. While it is vitally important to respond to immediate dangers and safety concerns, taking the time to help families step outside the confines of immediate crises into a deeper appreciation of what they value in their lives is a powerful intervention. The process of establishing a space outside crisis can provide a refuge for families and help them to "keep their eye on the prize." Once we have an envisioned future, we can prioritize which constraints to address. However, it requires a leap of faith that inviting a family to step outside of immediate crises rather than simply reacting to them may be the most beneficial thing we can do for a family in the long run.

NEGOTIATING THERAPY CONTRACTS WITH FUNDING SOURCES

An often hidden but influential partner in the development of therapy contracts are the funding sources for treatment (managed care companies as well as departments of mental health, social services, public health, etc.). The framework for organizing therapy contracts outlined in this chapter can be quite incongruous with prevailing ideas that emphasize problem-focused goals with concrete, measurable outcomes. For example, how many managed care companies do you know who would embrace "moving from a *Miami Vice* lifestyle to a *Mr. Mom* lifestyle" as an acceptable goal? This section examines some of the dilemmas in negotiating such therapy contracts with funding sources that emphasize medically oriented, behavioral treatment plans.

There is a strong push these days for behaviorally specific goals that can be quantified (e.g., client will increase school attendance by 50%

within 30 days). There are three dangers in this push for behaviorally specific goals. First, we can become fixated on the content of goals or the outcome of the work and lose sight of the process of the work. Although specific goals can provide a concrete vision toward which to move, it is important that we not mistake the indicators of enacting a new future for the future itself. Returning to the example of David, Jon and Ruth, David's shift from a *Miami Vice* lifestyle to a *Mr. Mom* lifestyle may show itself through stable employment and housing, increased sobriety, and consistent parenting, but it is David's different experience of both himself and his interactions with others that will anchor him in living a different life. The work here is not simply about David getting a job but primarily about the way in which he experiences himself (and is experienced by others) as he goes about the process of getting a job. The work with David will not be successful if he simply gets a job but still organizes his life within an old story that no longer works for him. The specificity of goals is a means to an end, not an end in itself. We can use behaviorally specific goals as a tool to help clients envision and enact new futures, not simply to measure the development of new behaviors.

Second, therapy goals can do more than provide measurable outcomes. They have the potential to inspire. David's commitment to therapy was not captured by a desire to show a 50% increase in job-hunting behaviors but rather by the appreciation he developed for his commitment to Jon and his willingness to make sacrifices for him in the shift from a *Miami Vice* lifestyle to a *Mr. Mom* lifestyle. When we simply collapse goals into entities that can be measured, we lose the artistry, poetry, and magic of therapy—factors that make it a profound and moving enterprise.

Finally, as we become caught up in the outcome of the work, we can lose sight of its ownership. In the push to show results to reimbursers, we can get organized by fears such as, "What happens if my client only increases school attendance by 40% instead of 50%?," or "What if it takes longer than the 30 days we originally projected?" We can then become overly responsible for the accomplishment of the particular goal. We move out of *working with* clients and into *working on* clients. Handing the development of therapy goals over to number crunchers runs the risk of turning us into technicians who become interchangeable parts on an assembly line of therapy. It also runs the risk of colluding with forces that may not be in clients' best interests. So, how do we develop therapy contracts that inspire clients and keep us rooted in collaborative relationships while acknowledging the realities of how funding shapes the delivery of services?

We need to interact with reimbursers in the same way we've discussed engaging reluctant clients. We need to build relationships with them, preferably outside the context of struggles around fiscal or ideological differences. We need to think about how to make our efforts relevant to their interests. Fortunately a future focus, emphasis on resources, and collaborative partnerships are all extremely cost-effective. We need to search for funders' honorable selves by beginning with an assumption that reimbursers want the best for clients. And, we need to look for openings in their dominant stories about reimbursement that provide a basis for building on exceptions.

In the example with David, Jon, and Ruth, the therapist had an ongoing relationship with the protective worker whose department funded the service through an agency contract. The therapist worked hard to maintain this relationship. The protective worker viewed the therapist as a little odd but very competent. She was amused by the therapy contracts he developed with clients and he was willing to go over them with her to explain their logic. He framed his efforts with families as attempts to enlist family participation in creating safer environments for children and continually emphasized the degree to which he was attempting to responsibly help families get off her caseload in ways that ensured they would stay off. She also knew that he could be a fierce advocate for clients when needed. There are times that our accountability to clients may conflict with our responsiveness to reimbursers and we need to be very clear about our priorities.

SUMMARY

These first four chapters lay the foundation for our work with multi-stressed families. Together, they have highlighted the importance of the relational stance we take with clients and examined conceptual frameworks that support that stance in the processes of engagement, assessment and contracting. Chapter 3 examined some of the ways we can be pulled away from an allied stance in the process of engaging reluctant families and offered ideas about how to maintain that stance and work effectively with clients who initially present with a stance of "this is not a problem" or "this is a problem, but I have no control over it." Chapter 2 examined a conceptual model based on constraints in which clients can be viewed as separate from and more than the constraints in their lives. Particular importance was attached to the way in which we approach the assessment process. Finally, Chapter 4 has offered an organizational framework for therapy that shifts our focus away from problem solving. In this shift, we can organize therapy around four interrelated steps of helping clients to envision new futures, establish a foundation of resourcefulness, anticipate constraints, and develop a contract that draws on that foundation to address constraints on the road to preferred futures. The next five chapters examine clinical practices that help to keep us in a relational stance of an appreciative ally with families and other helpers, encourage a separation of persons and problems, and focus our vision and efforts toward possible futures.

NOTE

1. The therapist believed that Cheryl's drinking constituted heavy social drinking and although he would prefer that she might drink less, he was not concerned about her seriously misusing substances. He felt that when she was not responding defensively to the way in which others expressed their concerns about her drinking that she was able to think about and manage her alcohol use thoughtfully.

5

Invitational Interaction

An Anthropological Approach to "Intervening" with Families

In *The Wizard of Oz*, Dorothy and her rather nontraditional family (Scarecrow, Tinman, Cowardly Lion, and Toto) have two visits with a Wizard of a therapist. In their first session, the Wizard establishes his position in the therapeutic relationship. He appears in a billowing cloud of smoke and fire proclaiming, "I am Oz, the great and powerful. Who are you?" Dorothy's trembling response is "I am Dorothy, the small and meek." The Wizard briefly meets with them and then assigns a between-session task ("Bring me the broom of the Witch of the West") which, it could be argued, had a goal of helping them to experience themselves differently.

In the second session, Toto pulls aside the curtain and the Wizard is forced to come out from behind his socially sanctioned role. There's a subsequent shift in their interactions. Initially, the family is angry that he is not the all-knowing Wizard they had believed him to be. Dorothy asserts, "Oh, you're a very bad man." The Wizard, stepping out of his expert role, replies, "No my dear, I'm a very good man. I'm just a bad Wizard." He then goes on to use a series of rituals to acknowledge and highlight their competence (e.g., giving a diploma to Scarecrow, a heart to Tinman, and a medal to Cowardly Lion). Again, it could be argued that this intervention helps them to experience themselves differently. My intention in juxtaposing these two sessions is not to compare the techniques used. Between-session tasks and in-session rituals are both time-honored family therapy techniques. Instead, it is useful to consider how this therapist positions himself in each instance and how that positioning shapes the family's experience of themselves in the course of the interaction.

In the first session, the therapist positions himself as an expert. As the family begins to tell their story, he interrupts them, "Silence, the great Oz knows why you are here." He knows who they are, why they have come, and what they need to do. Therapy becomes a process of getting them to do it. However, in response, the family is meek, scared, and profoundly disempowered. Their response is summarized by the Cowardly Lion, who faints. In the second session, the Wizard comes out (or is pulled out) from behind the curtain and engages the family from a more collaborative position. He still has particular expertise, but he uses it differently. He elicits the family's own expertise and recasts it in a new light. In this interaction, family members experience themselves differently. Scarecrow enacts a story of intelligence, Tinman a story of compassion, and Cowardly Lion a story of courage. Their experience of self in these two sessions is profoundly different.

This whimsical example is intended to highlight that the way in which we interact with clients positions us in a particular relationship with them and affects their experience of self, of us, and of our relationship.[1] In both sessions, the Wizard is trying to help the family. However, the broader relational context within which that help is offered significantly affects its overall impact. If we acknowledge that every interaction with clients has the potential to invite the enactment of empowering or constraining life stories, we then have a responsibility to attend closely to the effects of our clinical practices. For example, consider again the words of a mother who spoke in Chapter 1 about the advantages of collaborative partnership between helpers and parents.

KAREN: I think what you're talking about is what I call breaking down the barriers and equalizing the relationship between professionals and parents. When you're sitting in a therapist's office and the therapist is sitting across from you in his or her professional attire and you're the person with the problems and you're feeling very ashamed about yourself in the first place, there's a definite hierarchy and it feels like this person sitting across from me has his or her life all together and I'm a mess, even though rationally we know that's not true. But, that's what it feels like and to have somebody be able to meet you on an equal footing and connecting as a human being, well it just changes everything.

BILL: How does that change things? If helpers connect with you as human beings rather than as the expert, how does that change things?

KAREN: I think it decreases the feelings of shame and helplessness. To me, it gets rid of the feeling of I'll never be able to live up to where this person is or I'll never be able to get it as together because no matter what I do, I'm always going to be one step below.

The first four chapters examined conceptual models or ways of thinking about families that position us differently with them. These next four chapters examine clinical practices or ways of interacting with families that invite connection, respectful curiosity, openness, and hope. This chapter begins with an examination of the controversy within the field about "intervening" and then explores a questioning process that positions us as co-researchers who are *working with* families rather than *working on* them.

WHAT DOES IT MEAN TO "INTERVENE"?

Family therapy has historically had a strong emphasis on intervention. Within mental health, family therapy represented not only a different conceptual model of clients and problems but also a significant shift in ways of interacting with clients. It began as a radical move away from the orthodoxy of psychoanalysis and contained a strong shift away from *understanding* problems as the goal of treatment toward *doing something* about problems in a short time (Ravella, 1994). In this way, family therapy has been quite interventionist. Cecchin, Lane, and Ray (1994) have described an interventionist model as one in which a "therapist organizes an action, suggestion or prescription for the purpose of having a predictable result" (p. 13). Often, that predictable result is informed by an implicit model of how families should function (e.g., what constitutes "appropriate" generational boundaries, or "differentiated" functioning or "healthy" negotiation of life cycle transition points). Our focus on rectifying family dysfunction can pull us into an instrumental orientation where we enter families with the certainty of a missionary rather than the curiosity of an anthropologist. When we begin specifying how things should be in clients' lives and prescribing a direction they should be following, we run the risk of losing sight of what direction fits best for them. At those times, we can get out ahead of clients and end up blocking their view of their preferred future (White, 1995). In addition, unless the predictable result we are seeking is explicitly negotiated with clients, they may experience us as *working on* them rather than *working with* them. That experience can be disempowering and constrain the development of a collaborative partnership. In this way, intervention as traditionally conceptualized becomes potentially problematic.

Numerous voices within family therapy have questioned an interventionist focus and proposed alternatives that emphasize collaborative conversations anchored in a "not knowing" stance (Anderson & Goolishian, 1988, 1992). A not-knowing stance refers to an attitude and belief that a "therapist does not have access to privileged information, can never fully understand another person, always needs to be in a state of being informed by the other, and always needs to learn more about what has been said or may not have been said" (Anderson, 1997, p. 134). The phrase "not knowing" has a rich lineage, but it is perhaps an unfortunate phrase that has often been interpreted as dismissing professional knowledge. Others have punctuated the issue of knowing versus not knowing as certainty versus curiosity, which may capture the distinction without provoking as many reservations (Amundson et al., 1993). For this discussion, I draw on the phrase "cultural curiosity" as introduced in Chapter 1 to refer to a continual attempt to actively elicit a client's particular meaning rather than assume we already know it or that it is the same as ours.

A striving for cultural curiosity is anchored in an acknowledgment that clients are the best experts on their experience and begins with an attempt to fully enter into and honor that experience. It includes a willingness to doubt what we think we know and a commitment to continually learn more about what clients have to say about their experience. This attitude is reflected in a Robert Louis Stevenson quote, "It is better to travel hopefully than to arrive." Although we cannot arrive at a complete grasp of another culture, we can always travel hopefully toward a better understanding. Weingarten (1995, 1997, 1998) has discussed a similar process that she refers to as "radical listening." She characterizes radical listening as the "shifting of my attention from what I think about what my clients are telling me to trying to understand what my clients think about what they are telling me" (Weingarten, 1998, p. 5). This shift could also be summarized as a movement from assigning *our* meaning to clients' actions to eliciting *their* meaning.

Whereas an attitude of cultural curiosity means continually questioning our assumptions, it does not mean disavowing our knowledge, playing dumb, or withholding ideas that might be useful to clients. Helpers often have important knowledge gleaned from working with families than can be helpful to other families. Curiosity guides us in interacting with families in ways that do not assume a preknowledge about them. It is an attitude that helps us not mistakenly believe we know who clients are or what their lives are about before we've entered into their world and really met them. This stance is an attempt to ensure that our knowledge is supplemental to client knowledge and *supports* rather than *supplants* client knowledge. We can begin by eliciting and elaborating client knowledge and then, if appropriate and if invited, share our knowledge adjunctively. I often have ideas that I share with clients. However, I consistently find that such offerings are most helpful when they are invited and when they stand in support of client knowledge.

Let's return to the issue of intervention. There has been a protracted debate within the field between proponents of interventionist approaches and those who would favor noninterventionism. Some of the concerns raised about noninterventionist approaches have suggested that they represent a retreat to abstract, academic understanding rather than the action focus that family therapy brought into the mental health field, that they rob us of flexibility in our responses through an ideological mandate that we can only act collaboratively, and that they ignore the reality that we have influence and a consequent responsibility to exercise it (Minuchin et al., 1996).

I think it would be helpful to shift the terrain of this debate. First, it is impossible for us to avoid influencing others. As Cecchin et al. (1994) state:

> When people interact, they inevitably influence each other, but not always with predictable results. Intervention, when thought about in this way, is unavoidable, because to interact means to intervene in the private space of the other. No matter how much we try, influence is unavoidable. . . . Although it seems true that we do, in fact, influence one another, we cannot predict the outcomes of our efforts. (p. 15)

If we acknowledge that interventions do not have predictable results, then every interaction with clients is an intervention. Everything we say or do and not say or do may influence clients. It is impossible to be noninterventionist. I think the issue is not whether we are interventionist or noninterventionist but what stance we hold as we intervene. In examining the stance we hold as we intervene, I have found it useful to draw a distinction between instructive interaction and invitational interaction.

FROM INSTRUCTIVE INTERACTION TO INVITATIONAL INTERACTION

Historically, much of the mental health field has operated from an attempt to change how individuals and families function. We developed a wide range of techniques to help bring about change. Many of those techniques have been anchored in a belief that we can get clients to see or do things. For example, we offer an insight, we teach skills, we set up enactments with particular outcomes in mind, we reframe behavior to promote an alternative perspective. In each of these situations, we can enter with a predictable outcome in mind. This belief has been referred to as instructive interaction or the belief that we can put predetermined information into a system or bring about a particular outcome. Many clinicians have found it useful to hold a belief that instructive interaction is a myth. From this perspective, we cannot impose new meanings on people but instead can only interact with them in ways that enable them to generate new meanings. This belief in the myth of instructive interaction may or may not be "true," but it can be extremely helpful in staying out of nonproductive struggles with clients and minimizing the degree of frustration in our work. We cannot determine the effects of our interventions. As Karl Tomm (1987b) has pointed out, the actual effects of our interventions are always determined by the client, not by the therapist. Our interventions may trigger responses, but they do not determine them. In this way, we cannot get clients to do or see things. However, as discussed in Chapter 3, although we cannot instruct clients in ways that we predetermine, we can invite clients to reflection (invitational interaction).

The following story sets a context for discussing this shift from instructive interaction to invitational interaction. A number of years ago I conducted a study on the interaction of beliefs held by patients, spouses, and physicians in situations of chronic medical noncompliance (Madsen, 1992). One of the couples I interviewed consisted of Pat, a 40-year-old white woman whose hypertension escalated out of control when she drank, and Jack, her 35-year-old white boyfriend with a long history of alcohol misuse. I showed up at their home; exchanged greetings; set myself up in their living room arranging tape recorder, microphone, and notes; and began the interview. About 5 minutes into the interview, Jack excused himself and went into the kitchen. He returned with two cans of beer, offered one to me and, when I declined, shrugged, polished off the first, and soon started on the second. I had a number of reactions. I was shocked and angry that he was drinking. I worried that it would "bias" the results of the interview and wondered whether I would be able to use this interview. I had worked hard over an extended period to find informants for the study and was upset that I might not be able to use this interview. However, though I was not happy about this situation, I didn't feel right asking Jack not to drink during the interview. This was their home and they had graciously let me into it. They were not being paid for the study and I did not have a relationship with them in which I had the permission or authorization to instruct them on what I might have considered "proper etiquette." I sat there in my discomfort unsure what to say. I decided to say nothing and continued the interview. Jack continued drinking throughout the interview, polishing off a six pack by the time we finished. In the interview, we focused (among other things) on potential consequences of various decisions that they might make about alcohol use (e.g., If Pat kept drinking and Jack stopped what would happen to her health and their relationship? If Jack kept drinking and Pat stopped what would happen to her health and their relationship? What would happen if they both kept drinking? What would happen if they both stopped drinking?).

In the course of the interview, the following story emerged. Pat felt caught between two pulls. Her original husband had abandoned the family (for which she blamed herself), and she was committed to establishing a two-parent family for her daughter. She believed that if she kept drinking, her hypertension would kill her and her daughter would be without a mother. She also believed that if she quit drinking, it would kill her relationship with Jack (because his first marriage had ended when his wife quit drinking). If she died, her daughter would lose a mother. If her relationship with Jack ended, her daughter would lose a "father." She was committed to her daughter's having a two-parent family and felt that in either choice she was doing her daughter a serious disservice. As I asked about the effects of this dilemma on Pat, she disclosed that it made her feel like a bad mother and made her terribly depressed. She felt caught in a bind that she couldn't escape and would subsequently become quite hopeless and end up drinking to numb the pain. As we talked about the effects of this dilemma on their relationship and their future together, the couple became reflective and slightly sad. I left the interview feeling appreciative of the power of this dilemma and its effects on Pat and Jack. Her continued drinking in the face of knowing its adverse effect on her health made sense to me and I found myself feeling connected to them.

Interestingly, in a 6-month follow-up interview with their physician, I found out that the couple quit drinking the next day and had maintained sobriety since then. In fact, seven of the nine patients interviewed in the study were now managing their chronic medical condition for the first time in 2 years. A number of the physicians attributed that change to the development of different perspectives that had come out of the interview process for both physicians and couples. As one informant from the study put it,

"I'm thinking about the difficulty I've had managing my medical condition in a whole different way. It makes sense to me now that I've had difficulty managing it and I'm not blaming myself for it. This shift has given me some room to go about dealing with my medical condition in a completely different way."

The changes in Pat and Jack's life were quite dramatic, yet I was not attempting to disrupt their drinking or to get Pat to better manage her hypertension. The interview with Pat and Jack occurred in the context of a research study. It was not an intervention designed to achieve a particular outcome and yet it had a profound influence on the couple. Although I did not have a particular outcome in mind, I did have some hoped-for effects. My primary intention was to gather information for my research study, but I assumed that the process of gathering that information would open up some new possibilities for Pat and Jack. My experience in this study was very much in line with others who have suggested that research can be a powerful family therapy intervention (McNamee, 1988; Wright, 1990).

Lorraine Wright (1990) developed a research intervention for families in which more traditional family therapy had proved unsuccessful. In this intervention, the therapist would explain that she had no further ideas for how to be helpful to the family and then offer the family an opportunity to participate in a research project (this occurred in the context of a family nursing unit that was an educational and research setting). Wright found that this shift was not simply an attempt to redefine family therapy but, rather, one that changed the context of her clinical work from therapy to research. She explained that this shift in context had a profound effect on the therapists involved in that it reduced their usual therapeutic impulse to inform, instruct, direct, or advise family members and contributed to the development of an investment in learning from the family rather than an investment in changing the family. She found that the families involved responded very positively and concluded with the belief that "we facilitate the greatest change in our clinical work when we focus on learning from our clients rather than believing that they are learning from us" (Wright, 1990, p. 484).

THERAPY AS CULTURAL ANTHROPOLOGY

The shift in emphasis described by Wright (1990) fits with an anthropological metaphor for the process of interacting with clients and families. In this metaphor, we can think of clients and their families as foreign cultures. We can think of ourselves as ethnographic researchers or cultural anthropologists who have been given the opportunity to enter into their life space and learn all that we can about the particularities of their culture. An example of this metaphor in action comes from the work of Marilyn O'Neill and Gaye Stockell (1991). They worked in an Australian day treatment center in which eight male consumers were dissatisfied with the system and expressed that dissatisfaction through a variety of destructive behaviors that included abusive language, violation of property, ongoing substance use, and a disregard for others at the center. These behaviors had managed to alienate many of the staff, who saw excluding the men from the center as the only viable course of action. O'Neill and Stockell proposed instead to run a group for the men. In their thinking about the group, they shifted from a more traditional psychosocial rehabilitation philosophy of teaching daily living skills to the men and instead viewed the men as experts in dealing with chronic mental illness. They sent letters to the men inviting them to explore their expertise in managing mental illness. In the group, they took an anthropological stance to elicit the men's *experience* of mental illness, the *effects* it had on their lives, and the ways in which they *coped* with it. As they listened to the men's experiences of the disempowering effects of mental illness, they resisted the temptation to give advice, offer ideas, or make judgments about their situations. The group consisted of eliciting and documenting the expertise the men had in managing chronic mental illness. The therapists' roles consisted of asking questions to guide the process. When asked to provide a name for the group, the men initially decided to call it "The Losers' Group." However, halfway through the group as participants' expertise in managing mental illness became more solidified, the men petitioned to change the group's name to "The Worthy of Discussion Group." By the end of the group the men were developing a different understanding of themselves and had made significant improvements in their lives (including daily living skills which were never directly addressed). O'Neill and Stockell (1991) summarized what they learned from the group:

> We believe that this [different] understanding developed from the opportunities provided in the group for the men to become experts on their experience. In talking about their experiences with others for whom the effects of mental illness has also been significant, the men's stories became validated . . .
>
> We observed changes were occurring for the men. We were also aware that these changes were not due to any teachings about problems and solutions, but from the discovery that their special knowledge, skills and qualities had enabled them to choose a preferred outcome for themselves. The men became responsible for choosing the directions that their lives should take. Our role in these groups was described succinctly by one of the participants: "You (therapists) have been asking us instead of telling us." (p. 205)

This example characterizes a shift from *teaching to* to *learning with* clients. There is a directional shift in information flow. Information does not go from the therapist to the client but, rather, develops in the space between client and therapist though the questioning process. This shift could be described as a collaborative co-research project. In it, our role can be viewed as stepping into clients' lives and inviting them to learn with us about their experience. The goal becomes organizing that collaborative research in a way that opens space for clients to experience themselves in an entirely new fashion.

THE PLACE OF VALUES AND KNOWLEDGE IN AN ANTHROPOLOGICAL ROLE

This shift from teaching to clients to learning with them does not mean that we abdicate our own values or knowledge. I am not advocating a kind of moral relativism in which we enter into family cultures uncritically and simply accept all aspects of how they operate. It is important to critically examine both our own and families' microcultures. We can seek to understand the development of particular beliefs and practices, the values that anchor them, and the effects they have. In the process of this work, there is a shift from adhering to universal values to attending to the particular effects of our ways of thinking and acting on others and being accountable for those effects. For example, we can shift from thinking about heroin use as something that is universally evil or bad to examining the effects of heroin use on a person's life and relationships with others. Although I might not tell a mother who is using heroin that she should just stop, I would seek to engage her in a discussion about her hopes for herself and her children and how she prefers to be as a person and a mother. Based on this, I would then likely explore with her how heroin use supports or constrains those hopes and preferred ways of being. I would also engage her in an extended discussion of the effects of heroin use on her children, with an effort to elicit her thoughts rather than impose mine. A preference for an invitational approach is a pragmatic as well as aesthetic decision. In my clinical experience, the pat phrase "Just Say No" does not work. Simply telling people to do something often does not work, and as we've seen in several examples in this chapter, inviting people to reflect on the consequences of their actions can yield powerful results.

Our job may not be to impose our values on others or attempt to get others to "see the light," but the values we hold profoundly influence the ways in which we interact with families and it is important that we openly acknowledge them. In this way, we can strike a balance between neither imposing our values on families nor compromising them. Rather than pretend we come to our work value-free, we can identify our values and be open about them. Values and the way in which they inform our actions can be an important topic of discussion in our work with families.

Within a cross-cultural metaphor, it is important to recognize and honor the assumptions that we bring from our own microculture into that negotiation. There are particular values that I hold strongly (e.g., anti-violence, pro-respect) that I communicate with families. However, it is important for me to acknowledge these as my values. They may or may not fit for particular families. If I try to force a fit, my attempts usually backfire. If I offer particular ideas or values as a piece of my culture that clients might find helpful, they are more likely to consider the ideas than if I try to "convert" them. At the same time, I will consistently act in accordance with my values. For example, I am offended when men talk to women partners in demeaning and degrading ways and I will raise questions with them about that way of talking. However, it is important to acknowledge that this attempt is anchored in my values and may or may not fit with their values. In this regard, the practice of transparency described in the first chapter in which we share the values, thoughts, and assumptions that organize our work helps to strike a balance between not imposing our values on families and not compromising them either.

Similarly, an anthropological stance does not entail an abandonment of our knowledge. Many ideas, observations, and distinctions may prove valuable for families. For example, the distinction between intent and effect in which our actions may have negative effects even though our intentions are positive is one that many couples have found helpful. Similarly, the distinction between "parenting to protect" and "parenting to prepare" is another useful idea (Parry & Doan, 1994). In "parenting to protect," a parent's job is to protect a child from bad things happening to them, whereas in "parenting to prepare" a parent's job is to prepare a child for living in a difficult world. Often (though not always), there is a developmental point at which parenting to prepare may be a more useful model for parenting. I have found this distinction very useful and have offered it to parents at times. However, my intention in sharing either of these distinctions with clients is to offer them ideas that might be useful rather than attempt to get clients to embrace the ideas. In a sense, I'm offering a piece of my professional cultural knowledge and heritage that might enrich their lives.

The timing of when we offer ideas to families is crucial. My preference is first to elicit their knowledge and bring forth ideas that are jointly constructed in the room. Following that process, if appropriate, I might offer additional supplemental knowledge that comes from my professional or personal microculture. However, it is crucial that we have an invitation for such an offering and that our ideas are conveyed in ways that honor, support, and complement the family's idiosyncratic micro-culture. The offering of our knowledge can support and enrich families or it can be experienced by families as invalidating and supplanting their particular wisdom and expertise. It is important to offer our knowledges in ways that are experienced by clients as empowering rather than inad-vertently disempowering. One way to do this is to make sure that the pro-cess by which we offer our knowledge is accountable to clients for its effects on them. We can do this by consistently and repeatedly checking in with them about how the process of therapy is going. As anthropolo-gists, the questions we ask are also not neutral or value-free. They come from somewhere and have particular effects on clients. The next section considers a questioning process to help us enact an anthropological meta-phor in our interactions with families.

QUESTIONS TO INVITE A NEW STORY

In our interactions with clients, the questions we ask and the way we ask them are profoundly important. Numerous authors have written about the interventive nature of questions (e.g., Campbell, Draper, & Huffington, 1988; de Shazer, 1994; Fleuridas, Nelson, & Rosenthal, 1986; Freedman & Combs, 1993, 1996a; Lipchik & de Shazer, 1986; O'Hanlon & Weiner-Davis, 1989; Penn, 1982, 1985; Penn & Sheinberg, 1991; Tomm, 1987a, 1987b, 1988; White, 1988, 1989, 1993; White & Epston, 1990). Our questions don't just gather information. They also generate experience. As Pat and Jack in my research study responded to the questions about possible futures, they experienced possible futures. As the men in the Australian day treatment center responded to questions about their expertise in managing mental illness, they experienced them-selves as having a particular expertise. Our questions invite clients into particular experiences of self. When that experience is profound, it may have a transformative effect on clients.

Chapter 4 used a journey metaphor as an organizational framework for therapy. In this metaphor, our role can be seen as helping clients to envision new futures, establish a foundation of resourcefulness to bring those futures to fruition, and address the constraints that preclude the development of those futures. This chapter and the next examine concrete ways to help clients examine and address the constraints in their lives. Constraints may consist of particular problems, interactions, beliefs, life stories, or situations. For example, a mother struggling with depression is concerned about her parenting of her children. Depression is a problem that constrains her from parenting more effectively by sapping her avail-able energy. She and her husband are caught in a minimize/maximize pattern in which she experiences her husband as minimizing the difficulties of parenting three young children and he experiences her as maximizing those difficulties. That pattern constrains effective parenting by impairing their ability to work together, disrupting their relationship, and rigidifying her stance that she can't manage the children. The couple hold a shared belief that only the mother should be responsible for the children's care and should always be there for them. That belief constrains them from organizing their parenting differently when she is struggling. The mother's life has been organized within a narrative of "never measuring up," which further constrains effective parenting by highlighting her inadequacy as a parent and "pruning from experience" her competence. Both the minimize/maximize pattern and the couple's shared beliefs about parenting are deeply embedded in broader cultural ideas about how men and women "should" act as parents and partners. These cultural specifications limit the available range of "acceptable" behaviors and experiences and additionally constrain parenting alternatives. Finally, their living situation of poverty, which includes a dangerous neighborhood and lack of access to day care, constrains more effective parenting by depriving the mother of moments of peace and quiet that she might otherwise have if the children could go out and play or if someone else could mind the children giving the mother a needed break.

Each of these constraints can be seen as separate from the persons affected by them. We can think about each of them (problems, interactions, beliefs, life stories, or situations) as distinct entities existing outside of people. The process of viewing people as separate from the constraints in their lives allows us to view the *constraint* as the problem rather than the *person* as the problem. This chapter draws on the narrative therapy concept of externalizing conversations to examine a way of thinking about constraints that helps clients more effectively address constraints.

FROM INTERNALIZING CONVERSATIONS TO EXTERNALIZING CONVERSATIONS

For the sake of simplicity, the various constraints examined earlier can be described as problems. In this way, we can think of problems as the things that stand between people and their preferred lives and futures. Externalizing conversations are "ways of talking about problems that make it possible for people to experience an identity that is distinct or separate from the problem" (Aboriginal Health Council, 1995, p. 18). Externalizing conversations begin with how we think about problems. For example, rather than thinking about a woman as *being* depressed or *having* a depressive disorder (which locates the problem inside of her), externalizing conversations would begin by thinking about Depression as a separate entity that exists outside of the woman and has negative effects on her life.[2] Based on an externalizing assumption, questions such as the following might be posed to that woman:

- In what contexts has Depression been more able to pull you down?
- What toll has Depression taken on your ability to pursue the life you'd prefer?
- How has Depression affected your relationship with your partner?
- What has Depression gotten you to do against your better judgment?
- How has Depression managed to do that?
- Do you know other women who struggle against Depression?
- Do you think Depression might act differently on women than on men?
- What cultural ideas might it draw on to gets its power over women?

The goal here is to use language to conceptually separate people from problems to help them get some distance from problems and take more effective steps to escape the influence of problems on them.

The process of externalizing conversations goes against the grain of how many of us were taught to think about problems. We are encouraged professionally and culturally to locate problems inside individuals (e.g., "She *is* a borderline" or "He *is* an alcoholic") or inside families (e.g., "They *are* an enmeshed family" or "They *are* a dysfunctional family"). This internalizing assumption organizes the kinds of questions we are likely to ask. For example, we might ask the following internalizing questions about depression:

- How long have you been depressed?
- When did you first become depressed?
- In what situations are you most depressed?
- When you are depressed, what kind of a parent are you?

In these internalizing questions, depression is assumed to be something that exists inside the individual. It is something they are or have. This assumption is anchored in and supported by individual psychology models that assume that personality and self represent the true essence of people (Gergen, 1991). Although internalizing conversations arise out of a genuine attempt to help people, they may inadvertently exacerbate the problem. The process of locating problems in individuals runs the risk of entrenching problematic identities. For example, a therapist refers to a woman who has experienced significant trauma as "my three o'clock PTSD [posttraumatic stress syndrome]," a man with nagging compulsions begins to describe himself as "an OCD [obsessive–compulsive disorder]," a man who misused alcohol 10 years ago remains (and always will be) a "recovering alcoholic." Such descriptions have profound effects on how professionals see clients and on how clients experience themselves. When problems are seen as an integral part of one's character or personality, they become more difficult to address because they are deeply embedded in one's being. Locating the problem within the individual may invite shame, blame, and defensiveness that further constrain attempts to address the problems. By viewing problems as outside people, externalizing creates a space between people and problems that alleviates the immobilizing effects of shame and blame and reduces defensiveness. In the process of externalizing, people are not the problem, people are in relationships with problems that have negative effects on them and others in their life.

The decision to view problems as external to people rather than as internal to them is a pragmatic decision. From a narrative perspective, problems are viewed as existing outside people as a linguistic device to reorganize our thinking in ways that counter shame and blame, minimize defensiveness, and promote client agency or the capacity to act on behalf of themselves in relation to problems. As clients perceive themselves in a relationship with a problem (rather than as a problem), they often experience more freedom and ability to address the problem.

Externalizing conversations are also based on substantially different assumptions than many preceding family therapy practices. For example, in structural family therapy, problems are seen as being maintained by dysfunctional family structures. This focus directs our attention to the family as the source of problems and the relevant unit of conceptualization. Externalizing practices would view family difficulties as an understandable effect of problems and focus more attention on the taken-for-granted cultural assumptions that support problems. In this way, difficulties with which families struggle are not seen as endemic to families but are viewed in a larger context.

As another example, much of strategic family therapy draws from a functionalist metaphor in which there is a search for the function of the symptom. As noted before, the influence of a functionalist metaphor is so strong within family therapy that it is often treated as a taken-for-granted truth. However, externalizing conversations are anchored in fundamentally different assumptions. Consider Talia, an 18-year-old woman diagnosed with Depression. She is the youngest of four children and the only one still living at home. Her parents profess that they want her to move out and establish her own household, but they both worry about her ability to do so. They quarrel often over her future, and her mother is particularly concerned about what would happen to Talia if she were on her own. We could approach this situation by examining the function of her depression and pose questions to ourselves such as the following:

- What protective function does Talia's depression serve for her parents' relationship?
- What might they have to face if she moves out?
- If she were to move out, what effect would that have on her siblings' relationships with their parents?

These questions can be contrasted with the following externalizing questions:

- What toll has Depression taken on Talia's life?
- As her mother and father watch Talia struggle with Depression, what effect does it have on their lives?
- What effect has Depression had on Talia's relationship with her mother? her father?
- What effect has Depression had on the parents' relationship with each other?
- If Depression has had a significant negative effect on their relationship, how have they been able to maintain a relationship with each other despite the toll it has taken?
- What does it say about their relationship that it can weather such a strong toll?

These two sets of questions are anchored in very different assumptions about Depression and each has powerful effects on the family, particularly the parents. The functional questions invite us to hypothesize about what Talia's parents might be avoiding in their focus on her depression. An idea such as "Talia's parents focus on her because they can't handle their own relational issues" may easily be experienced by the parents as judgmental and blaming. Their perception of judgment and blame from their helpers may constrain their openness to new ideas and provoke a response ("Why are you focusing on us? This is not about us. This is about our daughter.") that we in turn label as "resistance." The externalizing questions invite us to hypothesize about Depression's effects on various relationships in the family and how family members have managed to remain connected in spite of these disruptive effects. That focus may be experienced by the parents as more understanding and supportive and may contribute to a therapeutic climate that is less constraining and more liberating. In this way, the focus of our questions has profound effects on clients.

The difference between internalizing assumptions and externalizing assumptions has been highlighted to emphasize that externalizing conversations are much more than an interesting clinical technique. Many authors have described it as a way of thinking about or an attitude toward problems (Freedman & Combs, 1996a; Madigan, 1993; Madsen, 1999; Roth & Epston, 1996; Tomm, 1993; Zimmerman & Dickerson, 1996a). Externalizing conversations are based in a fundamental set of assumptions about problems and people that are often quite different from other approaches. A number of authors (e.g., Neal, 1996) have expressed concerns about the dangers of stripping the process of externalizing away from the assumptions in which it is embedded.

One central assumption within narrative therapy is that problems are anchored in and supported by cultural discourses or taken-for-granted cultural prescriptions about how we should act and within which we make sense of our lives. Cultural discourses refer to the cultural stories that provide a framework for making sense of our lives. Numerous authors who operate within a narrative metaphor view unmasking of cultural "truths" to be at the heart of this work; for example, see the special issue on narrative therapy in the Spring 1996 issue of *Journal of Systemic Therapies* (Zimmerman & Dickerson, 1996b).

A SIMPLE OUTLINE FOR
EXTERNALIZING CONVERSATIONS

Externalizing conversations are a powerful clinical practice that can initially seem difficult to apply in one's own work. In an attempt to make these ideas more accessible, this section outlines a simple framework for externalizing conversations that will subsequently be elaborated. Externalizing conversations can be organized into inquiry in three areas: experience, effects, and preferred coping. A clinical example provides a way to highlight this framework.

A couple is referred for therapy by their son's preschool because their verbal abusiveness with each other scares him. Both parents are concerned about their son. Their female therapist begins by developing with them a vision of the future they would prefer for their son and the kind of home they are trying to build for him. With help, the couple puts together a vision of a supportive home anchored in a loving couple relationship. The therapist asks them about the steps they've taken to build a loving

couple relationship and inquires about things that might get in the way of
continuing that process. As they begin to describe some of the constraints
to their preferred future, the therapist moves into an externalizing conversation.

Experience

The therapist begins by asking about their *experience* of constraints (e.g.,
"You said that the way your relationship is going now gets in the way of
the kind of home you want to build for your daughter. What's it like living in this relationship right now?"). In the process, she attempts to step
into their experience and develop as thorough an understanding as possible. As she hears the couple's response (e.g., "It's horrible, we're always
fighting."), she listens for constraining elements of their experience that
can be externalized as a separate entity (e.g., Fighting).

Effects

The therapist asks about the *effects* of those constraints (e.g., "What sort
of toll has the Fighting taken on each of you personally? What effects has
it had on your relationship?") and traces out the story of those effects in
great detail (e.g., Fighting gets the mother depressed and leaves the father
furious. They hardly talk to each other anymore. They feel out of control
and are worried sick about the effects of Fighting on their son.). As we
inquire about effects, it is helpful to include both the effects on individuals and the effects on relationships. Asking about effects helps us further
enter client experience but begins to shift the blame for those effects from
the person to the problem. We can imagine Fighting as a separate thing
that has moved in with them and overtaken their relationship. In this context, the mother's depression and the father's anger make sense. Effects
questions invite compassion and help to position us as appreciative allies
in clients' lives.

Preferred Coping

As the therapist hears the story of the effects of Fighting, she asks the couple questions about how they have coped with those effects in ways that
they prefer (e.g., "How have you stayed together as a couple? How is it
that Fighting hasn't completely destroyed your relationship? What personal and relationship qualities have you drawn on to stay connected to
each other despite the devastating effects of Fighting?"). Whereas questions about people's experience of problems and the effects of those problems often elicit readily available information, questions about preferred
ways of coping often introduce new information. People struggling with a

problem are typically more aware of the toll that a problem has taken on their life than on the ways in which they are coping with or resisting the effects of that problem. In the process of responding to questions about how they have coped with a problem, new ideas and experiences are often generated. As clients begin to examine their coping with a problem, they often follow their responses with remarks such as "Wow, I never thought about that before." In the process, they begin to experience themselves differently. We can then follow up with questions that extend and elaborate these new experiences.

In asking about how clients are coping with particular problems, it is important to anchor that conversation in their preferences. One way to cope with a problem is accommodation (e.g., "I cope with Fighting by locking myself in the bathroom and drinking."). Another way of coping with a problem is resisting the problem's effects (e.g., "I remember the kind of relationship I had with her when we married and I refuse to give that up. When I remind myself of the relationship we used to have, the anger eases a bit and that's when I realize how important she is to me and why I want to make this work."). If we have begun with a preferred future, we can use questions about clients' preferences to support coping that moves them toward those preferred futures. (Preference questions and their importance are discussed in more depth in Chapter 6.) The process of keeping our questioning anchored in preferred coping helps to ensure that we are on the same track with clients and that our assistance is helping them address constraints in a way that moves them closer to the futures they prefer.

This outline provides a simple framework for organizing externalizing conversations. We can seek to find out information about clients' *experience* of constraints and the *effects* of those constraints on them and on their relationships. Subsequently, as we learn about how they are *coping* with these effects, we can support them in developing a different relationship with those constraints and moving toward the futures they prefer. This outline provides a foundation from which to move into an in-depth examination of questions to help people shift their relationship to problems. The next section begins this focus with a detailed examination of questions that can help people experience themselves as separate from the problems in their life. Chapter 6 examines areas of inquiry that elaborate questions about effects and coping.

EXTERNALIZING QUESTIONS

The process of externalizing begins with how we listen to clients. As we ask clients about their experience, we can listen with an "externalizing ear" that translates their descriptions into externalized entities (Freeman et al., 1997). One way to begin this process is to transform adjectives into nouns. For example, in response to a man who says, "I'm afraid," we can inquire about how fear has made an appearance in his life, when fear seems stronger, what toll fear has taken on his life, and so on. The process begins with us thinking about these "characteristics" as external entities rather than as internal qualities. We can also move into externalizing conversations by asking questions such as, "How would you describe the problem that brought you here?", or "If we were to give this problem a name, what might we call it?"

Often, questions arise about what problem to externalize. As a number of authors have emphasized, the naming of a particular externalized problem is less important than the process of talking about problems in an externalizing fashion (Freeman et al., 1997; Monk, Winslade, Crocket, & Epston, 1997; Zimmerman & Dickerson, 1996a). The problem which is discussed in externalizing conversations often changes over the course of an interview. It can be helpful to not externalize the first problem, belief, experience, or pattern that emerges but first to develop a richer appreciation of the person's experience and to think in an externalizing fashion. Monk et al. (1997) suggest the usefulness of using the word "it" or "this problem" before assigning a specific label in the early part of an interview. The choice of what to externalize often depends on how the problem is discussed by the family, what effects the problem has on the family, and whether other institutionalized ways of thinking about the problem have influenced clients' thinking (Zimmerman & Dickerson, 1996a). I prefer to think about externalizing that which stands between people and the lives they would prefer to lead. In that regard, we can externalize problems, interactions, beliefs, lifestyles, life stories, and situations.

Beginning an Externalizing Process

When a family is united around a concrete definition of a problem (e.g., Depression, ADHD, Tantrums, etc.) it can be useful to begin by externalizing that problem. When we externalize a particular problem, the language we use is important. Externalizations that draw from or match clients' language will be more powerful and relevant to them. At the same time, because we are attempting to separate the problem from the person, we need to take care that our language invites distance rather than closeness between a person and a problem. For example, consider the different effects in talking to the parents of a boy struggling with Temper Tantrums between the questions "What toll have Tantrums taken on your relationship?" and "What toll have *his* Tantrums taken on your relationship?" That latter question which reinternalizes Tantrums runs the risk of being heard as blaming the boy for the deterioration of his parents' relationship. Possessive pronouns tend to internalize and run counter to a process of externalizing.

It can also be useful to develop externalizations that fit with clients' colloquial language rather than professional descriptions. For example, Matt was brought to therapy by his mother after a school counselor had diagnosed him with ADHD. We began talking about the effects of ADHD on Matt and his family. Matt's description of his experience included the sentence, "I feel itchy all over and can't sit still. It's like I've got the itchies." When asked if the Itchies were a better name for the problem, both Matt and his mother enthusiastically agreed. Whereas ADHD was a foreign term that held little meaning for Matt's family and implied a disease that was overwhelming, the Itchies felt more familiar and manageable. That term also captured their experience with the problem better and made subsequent discussions more relevant and meaningful to them. As we talked about times when the Itchies wreaked havoc with Matt and his family, instances began to emerge in which Matt was more in control of it. We were able to build on those times to help Matt better manage the Itchies and increase the proportion of his life outside of Itchy influence. Sometime later his mother, reflecting on the process, remarked, "When I heard the diagnosis ADHD, it scared me to death. I had no clue how to begin dealing with it and I feared I was going to have to turn my son over to the professionals. That felt horrible. When we talked about the Itchies, it was such a relief. I know the Itchies. I can deal with the Itchies."

At other times, families may be divided in their definition of a problem, which can lead to blaming and polarized escalations (e.g., "He's the problem; no, she's the problem.") In such situations, it can be useful to begin by externalizing an interactional pattern or relationship variable. For example, Fred is furious about his son Ray's difficulty getting a job, while Ray insists there'd be no problem if his father just got off his back. As we trace out a pattern in which Fred's "nagging" gets Ray to "blow him off" and Ray's "ignoring of his father" gets Fred even more "up in his face," I ask them each whether they like this dance. They come together in their mutual dislike for the dance (though they still blame each other for its existence). In response to a request for a good name for this dance, Fred replies, "The slower he goes, the faster I talk." Ray chimes in, "You mean, the faster you talk, the slower I go." We come to call the dance "that Fast/Slow Thing" and begin examining its effects on each of them and on their relationship. We could also have come up with "tension" as an effect of the pattern as something to be externalized.

When families are confronted by multiple problems, it may be useful to work toward an externalization of a lifestyle. A good example of this is the contrast between a *Miami Vice* lifestyle and a *Mr. Mom* lifestyle that developed in the conversation with David in Chapter 4. The two phrases came from a television show and a movie that David particularly liked and came to represent two different lifestyles that respectively contained carousing and irresponsibility and conscientiousness and commitment to his son. The phrases evolved in the conversation and were jointly constructed. As I inquired what might get in the way of David being more present for his son, he began reflecting on his "drinking and carousing." As I explored both the positive and negative effects of "drinking and carousing," David began to talk about his admiration for Sonny Crockett from *Miami Vice*. I replied, "So, are you in some ways talking about a *Miami Vice* lifestyle here?" David laughed appreciatingly and said, "That's it exactly." As he began to list the negative effects of a *Miami Vice* lifestyle on his son, I asked about alternative ways of being that would more benefit his son. He had earlier been telling me about a movie, *Mr. Mom*, which he had enjoyed and he replied, "I guess we'd be talking about a *Mr. Mom* lifestyle." We discussed what that lifestyle might look like and began contrasting the two lifestyles and their positive and negative effects on both David and Jon.

An important theme that cuts across various externalizing endeavors is the need to name the problem collaboratively with families. The Itchies, that Fast/Slow Thing, and the contrast between a *Miami Vice* lifestyle and a *Mr. Mom* lifestyle may be colorful phrases that worked well for these particular families, but they worked because they drew from the family's language and were collaboratively developed with them. They were not given to clients by the therapist and would not work as stock phrases applied across the board.

Although externalizing conversations may seem like an unusual way of talking about problems, clients often seem to enter into them quite naturally. Their level of comfort with it seems to correspond with our level of comfort. As we become more comfortable talking in this way, clients slip into it more easily. In this regard, it is helpful to use externalizing language from the beginning. Sometimes just talking in this way is sufficient to invite clients to enter into this way of talking about problems. At other times, it may be useful to directly explain the process. As an example, I often say to families something like the following:

> "Families that I work with have often found it helpful when we talk about problems in their lives as something separate from them and give it a name. A lot of times when we've done this, it seems to help figure out how to deal with the problem in ways that haven't emerged before. What would you think if we were to try that way of talking about problems and see how it works?"

If it doesn't work, we can move into other ways of talking about problems that are more congruent with a family's preferred style. It can also be helpful to refer to a particular space in the room when talking about a problem. For example (*looking to an empty chair in the room*), "If the problem was sitting right over there, what would it be thinking about our conversation now?" This helps to concretize the problem and give it more life in the room. At other times, when problems are particularly strong in their hold on clients, it may be useful to not give the problem so much life in the room until clients are experiencing a stronger sense of strength and agency.

Thinking about Culture in Externalizing

It is important to appreciate the cultural context of problems. Developing externalizations that are more easily anchored in cultural prescriptions helps to further separate problems from people and access taken-for-granted cultural beliefs that support those problems. For example, Marie, a young woman who came to therapy complaining of depression, began to talk about Self-Doubt. As we examined her experience with Self-Doubt, she described a persistent feeling of not living up to various expectations. She described profound expectations, such as "I'm not thin enough, I'm not attractive enough, I'm not making enough money to suit my middle-class parents and I'm not sexually satisfying enough to my boyfriend."

Talking about Expectations as the problem allowed us to locate the expectations in a context of traditional assumptions about how women should be. We talked about where her life would be headed if Expectations were to set the direction for her life. Maria thought Expectations would encourage her to "starve myself, get plastic surgery, get a job I hated to satisfy my parents, and become a sexual slave to my boyfriend." When asked if this seemed fair and whether Expectation's ideas for her life fit with Maria's ideas for her life, Maria resolutely declared no. From there, we began examining what direction Maria would prefer to set for her life.

Discussing the problem as Expectations rather than Self-Doubt and placing Expectations in a larger cultural context had significant effects on Marie. Whereas Self-Doubt held the potential to still locate the problem in Marie (she was the one who was doubting herself), Expectations more clearly located the problem outside her. Placing Expectations in a larger cultural context helped Marie escape from the additional burden of self-loathing. Earlier, she had rebuked herself, saying, "Only a real idiot would doubt themselves so much." As she began to blame Expectations rather than herself as the source of these difficulties, she began to develop a sense of her own agency in refusing to go along with Expectations. She came to appreciate her determination and stubbornness as qualities that helped her stand up to the Expectations.

Finally, acknowledging the cultural context of Expectations allowed Marie to develop a more charitable view of her boyfriend and parents as also falling under the influence of Expectations. As she put it, "They're just caught up in that middle-class success thing, and he's just worried that he's not gonna be a real man without some Barbie Doll on his arm." Marie's parents were invited in to a session that examined the ways in which Expectations drove a wedge in their relationship. Questions to bring out their hopes for her allowed her to hear the positive intent behind their complaints and helped her to reconnect with them. Her boyfriend refused to come to sessions, but Marie continued in that relationship. While she felt mixed about the relationship, she became significantly stronger in her interactions with him.

Disentangling Blame and Responsibility

At times concerns have been raised that externalizing conversations collude with clients' avoidance of responsibility. Some have asked whether in our attempts to minimize shame and blame, we've become lax in promoting personal responsibility. This has not been my experience. As clients are invited to think about problems as separate entities with whom they are in a relationship, they can also be invited to consider whether they prefer the relationship that has developed between them and the problem. (Preference questions, which are discussed in the next chapter, are particularly useful in this regard.) In the process, many clients describe both a freedom and accompanying responsibility to then begin to address the problem. As Tomm (1989) suggests, externalizing conversations work not only to *externalize* problems but also to *internalize* agency. When persons experience the ability to shift their relationship with a problem, many describe an accompanying responsibility to follow through on dealing with the problem. As a colleague recently said to me:

> "When I thought of Procrastination as characterological, it was a great excuse. As I now see my ability to push through it, I realize I can't postpone dealing with it any longer. Not only do I feel more able to do something about it, I feel like I need to do something about it. Thinking about it this way has been a welcome kick in the butt for me."

In our culture, there is a tight interconnection between blame and responsibility. Although it is important for people to take responsibility for addressing problems in their lives, blaming them for those problems has never seemed particularly helpful. In my experience, people do not change under the weight of shame and blame. The process of externalizing allows a separation of blame and responsibility. By thinking of problems as external entities that invite, coach, or trick us into particular responses, we can remove blame from individuals. People are not to blame for their difficulties; problems are to blame for their difficulties. Problems can be seen as inviting particular ways of being. However, externalizing conversations also allow space for clients to consider whether they might want to decline such invitations. Questions can be asked that represent irresistible invitations to responsibility.[3] We can promote responsibility by irresistibly inviting it rather than by demanding it. As Alan Jenkins (1996) has put it, "Respectful therapy involves a process of knocking on doors and waiting to be invited in, rather than breaking them down, barging in, and then expecting to be welcomed with open arms" (p. 122).

Attempting to force families to deal with the issues we think they're avoiding may actually be more likely to "let them off the hook." Our efforts to make clients be responsible may lead to nonproductive fights with families in which they end up focusing on our lack of manners rather than on what initially brought them to therapy. It's easier for everyone to stay focused on family concerns when we are allied together. In this way, invitational interaction can help to avoid nonproductive fights, minimize "resistance," and keep conversations focused.

EXAMINING THE RELATIONSHIP BETWEEN PERSONS AND PROBLEMS

Once a problem has been externalized, we can then begin to look at the relationship between that problem and the persons affected by it. We can juxtapose the relationship that a problem currently has with a family with the relationship that a family would prefer to have with the problem. In this examination of the relationship between problems and persons, we can shift from focusing on the person or the problem to focusing on the relationship between problems and persons. To quote Sallyann Roth and David Epston (1996): "It's not the person who is the problem; it's not even fully The Problem that is the problem. It is, to go the whole way, the relationship of the person with The Problem that is the problem!" (p. 151).

Focusing on a person's *relationship* with the problem rather than *the problem* has a number of advantages. Some problems cannot be eliminated. For example, many chronic medical conditions, such as hypertension or diabetes, cannot be defeated, but they can be managed, kept in their place, or taught better manners. This also holds true for neuropsychological problems, such as autism or developmental delays, that cannot be simply eliminated; for human emotions, such as fear, worry, anger that often emerge in everyday life; and for problems such as substance misuse that often make persistent reappearances in people's lives. Conveying the idea that such difficulties can be eliminated or expelled from our lives may set people up for disappointment and inadvertently support the problem. However, we can acknowledge that people are in an ongoing relationship with particular problems and help them to keep those problems in their place, or stay on top of those problems, or continue to lead the lives they'd prefer in the face of those problems.

In addition, some problems may have positive as well as negative effects. For example, the problem of Evaluation may have potential positive effects as well as disabling negative effects. In writing this book, I've been very aware of the voice of Evaluation. Sometimes, it speaks as a paralyzing tyrant with accusations that my ideas are trite, unclear, and irrelevant. At other times, Evaluation has offered thoughtful and provocative comments that have helped me to clarify and sharpen my thinking. Although I wouldn't want to respond to every criticism offered up by Evaluation, some have proven extremely useful. I wouldn't want to kick Evaluation out of my writing, but I might want to develop a relationship with it in which I consult with Evaluation rather than be held hostage by Evaluation. Similarly, with families, we can ask questions such as the following:

> When is Worry an old friend with good judgment who is looking out for you and when is it perhaps a bit overly cautious and needlessly concerned?
> Which of Worry's concerns would you like to take seriously and which would you like to just view with bemusement?
> When have you been in charge of what you take of Worry's advice and when has Worry been in charge of that? Which do you prefer?

In highlighting the potential positive effects of certain problems, I am not talking about problems serving a function for those persons involved with them. There's an important difference between acknowledging that problems are complex and may have positive as well as negative effects and contending that those problems then serve a function in someone's life. The original rationale in seeing the Problem as the problem was that it constituted a counterpractice designed to help us move away from internalizing metaphors (the problem is in the person), structural metaphors (the problem is in the family organization), and functional metaphors (the problem serves a function for the person or family). If we can clearly separate the problem from the person, a relationship metaphor that focuses on the relationship between the Problem and the person is useful. In this metaphor, the goal is to embrace a both/and position in which we can both help clients and families hang on to positive effects of problems and shift their relationship with the negative effects of the same problems.

SHIFTING OUR METAPHORS
FOR PERSON–PROBLEM RELATIONSHIPS

In examining the relationship between people and problems, it is important to consider the kinds of metaphors we use to describe that relationship. Many of the metaphors for approaching problems in narrative therapy have tended to foster an adversarial or aggressive relationship between people and problems. Often the goal of externalizing conversations has seemed to be an attempt to externalize and then expel or kill off a problem. For example, we have worked with clients to *silence* Critical Voices or *kick* Depression out of their lives or *beat* Worry. We have stood *against* problems, *exposing* their tactics and promoting *anti-problem* strategies. We have helped people line up teams to support them in their *battles* against problems. In each of these examples, the italicized words highlight a stance that demonizes problems and polarizes the relationship between problems and people. In an attempt to separate problems from persons, we have contributed to an "us and them" mentality that pits clients and therapists against problems and their cultural supports. Although this strategy has been an effective means toward the end of liberating people from the tyranny of particular problems, I fear that the way in which we have tried to accomplish this goal may have broader negative effects.

A number of authors have highlighted the ways in which aggressive metaphors in the externalizing process are anchored in a power over metaphor, expressing concern that such metaphors draw on and may encourage tendencies toward domination, competition, and aggressiveness (Freeman et al., 1997; Freeman & Lobovits, 1993; Roth & Epston, 1996; Stacey, 1997). Many of these authors have suggested a shift from confronting and struggling against problems to compromising and coexisting with problems. Militaristic metaphors such as beating, kicking, or thrashing a problem fit with patriarchal ways of being in the world and have the potential to replicate those ways of being at the same time that we are seeking alternatives to them. In our fervor to stand against social injustice, we risk becoming intoxicated with righteousness and replicating the very missionary stance we claim to oppose. Heather Elliot (personal communication, May 16, 1998) has commented that an oppositional approach to externalized problems replicates the Old Testament code of "an eye for an eye" in which we come to treat problems in the same way they have treated us. This way of being in the world becomes anchored in dualism and opposition. We end up standing in reaction to problems in ways that may inadvertently keep us organized around problems.

A central focus of this book has been a shift from attempting to fix problems to envisioning and building life outside of problems. In line with this focus, we can move to a stance that is explicitly pro-person rather than anti-problem. While this reflects a subtle language shift, it has powerful repercussions in helping us to move beyond what we oppose to what we stand for in our lives. As one example of this shift, consider the Dalai Lama's stance of compassion as a response to cultural genocide in Tibet. That response to a problem is anchored in a preferred way of being in the world rather than a reaction to the problem. Less aggressive metaphors for person–problem relationships may help to keep clients focused on *moving toward* preferred lives rather than *moving away* from problems.

A metaphor of opposition may also create problems for its adherents in their relationship with the broader field. As we divide the world into Us (those who stand with clients against problems) and Them (those who stand with problems against clients), we risk creating a club with very high standards for membership and contributing to a polarized and mutually disrespectful relationship between Us (those who work in this way) and Them (other helpers). The danger is the creation of a separatist movement that obscures the good intentions of other helpers and ultimately cuts itself off from potentially interested parties.

An oppositional metaphor of resistance also obscures other forms of resistance. An oppositional metaphor is anchored in patriarchal notions about how people resist the influence of problems. Stacey (1997) quotes Aptheker (1989) who critiques the patriarchal notion that resistance to injustice has always required oppositional politics and a struggle for power against those responsible for maintaining social injustices. Stacey suggests the usefulness of expanding metaphors of resistance beyond a protest metaphor and draws on feminist literature to celebrate small daily acts of resistance such as refusing to submit to other's pejorative definitions of oneself or continuing to endure in the face of problems. For example, a woman continuing to care for her children in the face of depression is an act of resistance to depression. Recognizing small daily acts as resistance to problems helps us to more clearly recognize life outside the problem.

Finally, our habitual use of oppositional metaphors in the relationships between problems and persons may not fit with families' preferred metaphors and may be experienced as impositional. For example, Elliot (1998) notes an interaction with a client in which she suggested "standing up to depression" and the client replied, "Couldn't I sit down with it instead. When I have a disagreement with someone, I'd prefer to sit down and have a cup of tea." In this way, it is crucially important to check out the effects of the metaphors we use with families. We can ask such questions as the following: "Is this way of talking about the problem working for you? If not, is there another more fitting way that we could talk about it?"

Our preferred relational metaphors are also deeply embedded in our broader culture. Tomm, Suzuki, and Suzuki (1990) in examining the application of externalizing conversations in Japan found that Western metaphors of confrontation and struggle against problems were "inconsistent with a basic Japanese orientation of compromise and coexistence with problems" (p. 104). Perhaps we can come into better harmony or balance with problems rather than banishing them. Tomm et al. (1990) contrast outer externalizations and inner externalizations. They use outer externalizations to describe conversations about problems that can be defeated, escaped, and left behind and in which themes of conflict, power, and control tend to prevail. They use inner externalizations to describe conversations in which problems are not necessarily viewed as negative or removable and are talked about as if some kind of ongoing coexistence may be necessary. They suggest that in situations of inner externalizations, a protest metaphor may work to the detriment of the person and work in favor of the problem. Freeman et al. (1997) suggest that we may want to fit our metaphors to the degree of oppressiveness of a problem, noting that we may want to use more aggressive metaphors with problems that had more serious effects (such as anorexia) and less aggressive metaphors with problems that are less immediately threatening.

Focusing on the relationship between people and problems opens new possibilities in externalizing conversations. It offers us more flexibility and helps us to better explore the complexity of those relationships. The next section examines some of the difficulties that can be encountered in the process of externalizing.

WHY ISN'T THIS AS SIMPLE AS IT SOUNDS?

When clinicians initially try externalizing conversations, they often run into difficulties. They may start with externalizing but can't seem to sustain the process. Clients don't "get it" and reject the idea of the problem as something separate from them. Or, despite seeing the problem as separate, clients seem so reluctant to let the problem go that we end up believing maybe it does serve a function for them. Let's examine each of these.

How Do I Keep This Going?

Many clinicians initially find externalizing conversations awkward to start and difficult to sustain. Externalizing conversations represent a very different way of thinking. They begin not with what we say but with how we think. Sometimes I have been asked, "But what if the problem really *is* in the person?" Seeing people as separate from problems is a conceptual device that organizes our work. The question is not "Where do problems *really* lie?" but, rather, "What are the *consequences* of thinking about problems as internal to clients or external from them?" Externalizing is not a technique but a conceptual stance that we take to organize our work in particular ways. As a new stance, it can take a while to fully enter into it. The initial outline for externalizing conversations that orients inquiry around the three areas of experience, effects, and coping provides a simple road map to focus our efforts. The earlier section on "Beginning an Externalizing Process" offers a number of concrete suggestions that may prove useful in starting this process.

It can also be useful to practice this way of thinking in our own lives. As a reader, you might find it useful to view issues that come up in your own life through this conceptual framework, posing questions about your experience of a problem, interaction, belief, or situation, the effects it has on you, and how you cope with it in ways that you prefer.[4] This way of thinking could be thought about as a new and unusual foreign culture. Entering it often requires an initial adjustment and, just as encountering any foreign culture, deeper immersion in it can be very useful.

What about When Clients Refuse to See Problems as Separate?

Sometimes, thinking about problems as separate is too distant from clients' experience. Some clients seem to cling to a notion that problems are an integral part of them. For example, Barry, a single-parent father who was devoted to his children and yet evaluated his parenting quite harshly, balked every time I raised questions about the voice of Evaluation (even though the phrase came from him). He would typically reply, "This is not something being said to me, this is me who is saying it. I'm a complete failure as a parent and I have to come to grips with that." Barry had previously been in a traditional therapy for many years and came out as a self-defined failure because "I'm passive–aggressive and refuse to deal with my core issues." Although Evaluation as an externalized problem did not suit him, he resonated with the idea of a Critical Part that spoke in a very harsh tone. As we talked about the Critical Part of him, Barry was able to talk about its voice, what it wanted for him, and the harshness with which it pursued those aims. We were able to talk about the relationship between Barry and this Critical Part and worked together to help him develop a different relationship with it.

Throughout the work with Barry, I continued to view (in my own head) that Critical Part as an externalized entity. Rather than attempting to impose such a view on Barry, I used a language that worked better for him. However, I held onto a conceptual framework (externalizing) that anchored me in a different relational stance with him. My view of Barry as someone who was under attack by this Critical Part that had perhaps good intentions for him but pursued them with vindictive zeal helped to position me in a more understanding and compassionate way than I think I might have if I had viewed him as passive–aggressively refusing to address core issues. Externalizing can be helpful as a conceptual device regardless of the language we ultimately use with clients.

What about When Clients See Problems as Separate, but Continue to Cling to Them?

Sometimes, people view problems in their lives as separate from them but have great difficulty shifting their relationship with those problems. They seem trapped in their existing relationship with problems and don't seem to want to leave that relationship. This can be particularly true with situations in which the problem–person relationship is an abusive one in which the problem's dictates for the person are oppressive and unjust. For example, Carla was besieged by Bulimia which exacted a significant toll on both her mental and physical health. She described feeling abused by Bulimia, believed she would always be subjected to its dictates, and showed little apparent interest in shifting her relationship to it. Although I never directly encouraged Carla to "leave" Bulimia, I certainly hoped that she would "file a restraining order" on it. As I became increasingly frustrated with her continued involvement in an abusive relationship with Bulimia, I began to think about the parallels to abusive interpersonal relationships.

As Goldner, Penn, Sheinberg, and Walker (1990; also Goldner, 1998) have pointed out in their examination of violence in couples, there is often a powerful bond between the partners in abusive relationships.

Usually, this bond is viewed by others as shameful, sick, and regressive. Often, the bond remains a secret hidden from the world. Paradoxically, attempts to separate the partners in such a relationship tend to strengthen this bond. As the bond goes underground and becomes more shameful and yet compelling, its secretive nature increases its binding power. In working with couples, they found that acknowledging the power of this bond without pathologizing the partners undercut the bond's power. In their work with women in violent relationships, they would listen for positive descriptions of the relationship and encourage that as part of the conversation. They found that when they were able to do that, the shameful bond had much less of a hold on women and they were freed up to more easily leave or alter the relationship (if they chose). It is fruitful to apply these insights from abusive interpersonal relationships to abusive problem–person relationships.

As I shifted from attempting to "separate" Carla and Bulima to becoming more curious about their relationship and listened for positive descriptions of aspects of it, I began to develop a better appreciation of the "bond" between them. As Carla put it, "Bulimia is the only thing I can count on. It's always there. It's the constant in my life." As I began exploring positive and negative aspects of her relationship with Bulimia, she was freed up to more openly examine that relationship. As we examined the cultural messages that supported her continuation in that relationship, Carla began to focus on ways in which she felt she was perhaps ready to move on. In this examination of positive and negative aspects of the relationship between a person and a problem, it is important to emphasize that I do not see the positive aspects of a relationship as akin to that problem serving a function for the person. Saying that people's relationships with problems are complicated and have positive and negative aspects is quite different from implying that those people somehow derive secondary benefits from or need that relationship. The first acknowledges the complexity of people's relationships with problems; the second has the tendency to blame them for the continuation of that relationship.

SUMMARY

This chapter begins an examination of clinical practices that are anchored in the relational stance, basic values, and conceptual assumptions outlined in Chapter 1. The current debates in the field between interventionist and noninterventionist approaches to therapy were recast as a question of what stance we take as we inevitably intervene in family life. Instructive and invitational approaches to intervention were examined.

Drawing on an anthropological metaphor for our roles as therapists, the power of questions to generate experience was examined. Externalizing conversations, in which people are helped to view themselves as separate from the problems in their lives, provides a basis to examine the current relationship they have with problems and envision the type of relationship they might prefer to have with those problems. The chapter concluded with an examination of the usefulness of shifting our focus from the problem as the focus of concern to the relationship between people and problems as the focus of concern. In examining the relationship between people and problems, we can identify three areas of questioning that can organize our thinking: experience, effects, and preferred coping. The next chapter enriches this organizational framework by examining Deconstructive Questions and Reauthoring Questions as a way to concretely help clients examine the relationships problems have with them and to develop the types of relationships they would prefer to have with problems.

NOTES

1. While this example may strike professionals as an exaggeration, a number of parents who have seen this clip have told me they think the first vignette accurately captures their worst fears about going to family therapy.

2. When a particular problem such as Depression is described as an externalized entity, it will be capitalized to set it off.

3. For fine examples of such questions, see Jenkins (1990).

4. Jill Freedman has a very nice exercise which consists of a series of internalizing questions to pose to oneself juxtaposed with a series of externalizing questions (Freedman & Combs, 1996a, pp. 49–50). I have found this exercise very helpful in developing an experiential understanding of the process of externalizing conversations.

6

——◦———

Helping Clients
Take Apart Old Problems
and Put Together New Lives

Chapter 5 offered an initial outline for externalizing conversations that directs our inquiry toward people's *experience* of problems, the *effects* of those problems on people's lives and relationships, and the ways in which people *cope* with and resist the effects of those problems. This chapter elaborates that first outline with a particular focus on effects and coping. It places those questions in a broader context and offers a more comprehensive outline with multiple concrete examples of questions. Once we have externalized a problem, we can juxtapose the *problem's influence* on the person with the *person's influence* on the problem. Questions about effects fall into a broader category of questions that attempt to map the influence of the problem on the person, their family, and community. Questions about preferred coping fall into a broader category of questions that attempt to map the influence of the person, their family and community on the problem. Michael White (1993, 1995) has referred to these two broader sets of questions, respectively, as deconstructive questions and reauthoring questions.

Deconstructive questions attempt to undermine the problem's influence on the person by *taking apart* unspoken assumptions and ideas that support the problem's influence. The story of the problem's influence on the person is often more evident and can be referred to as the *dominant story or plot*. This story is often deeply embedded in clients' lives and receives strong cultural support. Deconstructive questions do not directly challenge the problem's influence, but attempt to bring to light gaps or inconsistencies in the story of the problem's influence.

Reauthoring questions *put together* the person's influence on the problem. These questions seek to bring forth an *alternative story or counter-plot* of the client's coping with and resistance to the problem. The word "reauthoring" emphasizes the active construction of new stories of coping and resistance. The words "coping and resistance" are paired together to promote a broader view of resistance. As discussed in the last chapter, resistance to a problem includes more than opposing the problem. It also takes the form of responding to a problem, coping with a problem, containing a problem, or transcending a problem. Resistance is not just about opposition but takes the form of trying to make a better life. In this way, it is proactive and positively oriented. Resistance can be the pursuit of preferred lives.

The overall flow of externalizing conversations then consists of inviting a separation of people from problems (externalizing questions); taking apart the influence of problems on people, their families, and communities (deconstructive questions); and putting together the influence of people, their families, and communities on problems (reauthoring questions). The process could be diagrammed as follows:

Problem

Reauthoring Questions
Questions to "put together" the Alternative Story or Counter-Plot of the Person, Family, and Community influence on the Problem.

Deconstructive Questions
Questions to "take apart" the Dominant Story or Plot of the Problem's influence on the Person, Family, and Community.

Person

In examining the relationship between families and problems, community is included for two reasons. First, the toll that problems take on lives extends beyond individuals and families into their community. It is important to acknowledge the radiating effect that problems have on significant others in a person's life. Second, problems often have strong cultural support and people's attempts to develop a different relationship to problems are usually much more effective with the support of their community. Our work is much more powerful when we consider and draw on the power that people's communities (including our own) have to offer. Chapter 8 focuses particular attention on the importance of drawing on community in our work.

The remainder of this chapter examines broad areas to explore in deconstructive and reauthoring questioning. The ideas in this chapter have been profoundly influenced by the writings of numerous authors and build on their work (Dickerson & Zimmerman, 1992, 1995; Freedman & Combs, 1993, 1996a; Freeman et al., 1997; Monk et al., 1997; White, 1995, 1997; White & Epston, 1990; Zimmerman & Dickerson, 1993, 1994, 1996a). In practice, externalizing conversations seldom proceed in a stepwise process from deconstructing to reauthoring. Often there is an ongoing juxtaposition of the problem's influence on the family with the family's influence on the problem. However, for the purpose of clarification, deconstructive and reauthoring questions will be considered separately with specific examples of each to help concretize the exploration of these areas. The purpose of laying out specific examples of questions is to concretize the flow of the questioning process rather than provide a recipe of the exact questions to ask. Having a set of possible types of questions in mind can be useful, but seeing those questions as a step-by-step recipe results in an unnatural and awkward process. We need to attend to the person with whom we are talking as well as the questions that we ask. The power of externalizing conversations lies in the attitude we hold with clients (reflected in our voice tone, gestures, and stance). The overall flow of the conversation is more important than the specific questions. Although the questions are powerful and open up profound possibilities, they can come off as shallow, forced, and not especially helpful when approached as a technique or linguistic trick (Freedman & Combs, 1996a). The questions alone will not be as useful unless the person asking them really views people as separate from and more than the problems in their lives. We need to actively orient ourselves to what might be small openings to life outside the problem. In this way, examining the influence of the client and their community on the problem requires a leap of faith that there is life outside the problem and that there is always some degree of resistance to that problem's influence.

DEVELOPING A CONTAINING ENVIRONMENT

These questions require an interpersonal atmosphere that is contained enough that clients can successfully be invited into a reflective stance (i.e., be willing and able to consider such questions and respond to them thoughtfully and honestly). For many clinicians working with multi-stressed families, such containment may seem more often the exception than the rule.[1] Families can present as out of control, continually interrupting each other and being extremely reactive to each other. It can be useful for clinicians to observe the ways in which families interact as a way to gain valuable information, but it is notably less helpful for families to repeatedly experience themselves as out of control. Externalizing conversations both require and contribute to a safe, contained environment.

James and Melissa Griffith (1992, 1994) have distinguished emotional postures of tranquility and mobilization and examined the ways in which each opens or closes possibilities for therapeutic dialogue. Postures of tranquility include such states as listening, wondering, reflecting, affirming, understanding, and trusting. In emotional postures of tranquility, attention is focused inward, vigilance to threat is low, and there is a certain openness to new information. On the other hand, emotional postures of mobilization are a variation on the physiological "fight or flight" response and include states of guardedness, hyperarousal, shaming, blaming, attacking, defending, justifying, controlling, distancing, and ignoring. Vigilance is high and attention is focused outward in an effort to predict and control others' behavior. When people are primed to fight or flee, they are not well positioned to take in information or engage in creative problem solving.

Inviting multi-stressed families into an emotional posture of tranquility may strike many clinicians as a kind of oxymoron. These families are often seen as crisis prone, and their suspiciousness and reactivity are viewed as a family characteristic rather than an interactional process between families and helpers. Many families who have had multiple pathologizing encounters with helpers are justifiably vigilant as they interact with us. A relational stance of an appreciative ally helps to minimize the need for mobilization. When we begin by inviting families to envision new futures and preferred lives and then go on to establish a foundation of resourcefulness with them, we contribute to a containing environment that effectively invites clients into a reflective stance. The ideas discussed thus far in this book provide a foundation that allows these kinds of conversations.

The process of externalizing also contributes to a very different conversation. When people view themselves as having an identity separate from a problem, they are freed up to interact quite differently. This is true in their interactions both with us as helpers and with each other. At the same time, as we engage in externalizing conversations we can contribute to a containing environment in a number of ways. We can begin by getting agreement to a process in which one person is interviewed while others observe and then comment. As we interview an individual, we can pay particular attention to others' reactions, reading the feedback and engaging them before they react. We can also repeatedly compliment other family members for continuing to listen in the face of provocations.

A helper's role in an externalizing conversation requires active leadership. This is not a process of just listening to people's stories. It requires an active presence, setting a tone of respectful curiosity. The process of continually pulling for threads of competence, connection, vision, and hope requires focus and agility. If our job is to open space for people to have a different experience, then our work must begin with a belief that families can have these conversations. With this conviction in mind, let's move on to an examination of deconstructive and reauthoring questions.

DECONSTRUCTIVE QUESTIONS

The process of deconstructive questioning has been captured in a bumper sticker that states: "Subvert the dominant paradigm." In this instance, the dominant paradigm is the story of the problem's influence over the client or family. The goal in deconstructive questions is to undermine the problem by taking apart the taken-for-granted assumptions and ideas that support it. We can organize deconstructive questions around five broad areas:

- Learning about the problem's *influence* on clients and their community.
- Learning about the problem's *effect* on clients and their community.
- Learning about cultural and other *supports* that the problem draws from.
- Learning about the problem's *tactics* and strategies (or how it operates)
- Learning about clients' *preferences* (or opinions) about the problem's influence, effects, tactics, and supports.

Preference questions can be used to explore family opinions regarding the problem's influence, effects, tactics, and supports, examining whether they fit with client's preferred ways of being in the world and why or why not. Whereas questions about a problem's influence, effects, supports, and tactics can proceed in a stepwise fashion, preference questions are often interspersed throughout those other questions and can be powerful in helping the questioning process to become enriched and more personally meaningful to clients. Each of these areas is examined in turn.

Learning about the Problem's Influence

To learn about the problem's influence, we can begin by finding out about the current context of the problem—in particular, when, where, and around whom the problem is more or less likely to make an appearance.

Using this information as a foundation, we can then inquire about the history of the problem's influence over individuals and those around them. In the example of Matt and the Itchies (the word we jointly developed to describe attention problems) in the last chapter, we could begin by asking such questions as the following:

- When are the Itchies most likely to get a hold of you?
- In what situations do they have more power?
- Do they seem more powerful at home or at school?
- Are you more vulnerable to the Itchies in the morning when you have lots of energy or in the late afternoon when you're feeling tired?
- (to his mother) Are there particular situations in which you might expect the Itchies to grab hold of Matt?
- Are there particular people around whom the Itchies are more or less likely to show themselves?
- (to Matt again) How long have the Itchies been around in your life?
- How have the Itchies' influence changed over time? Has it gotten stronger, weaker, about the same?
- Can you tell me a bit about how the Itchies have come to take up more space in your life together?

Learning about the Effects of the Problem

Effects questions seek to understand the toll that a problem has taken on a family's life. We can explore a problem's effects on a person, on others, and on relationships in the present as well as in the past and anticipated future. Continuing with the example of the Itchies, we could ask a series of questions such as the following:

- It sounds as if the Itchies have taken up a lot of space in your household. What kind of toll have they taken on Matt's life? (It's useful to consider effects in various aspects of his life—at school, home, and play.)
- If the Itchies were to continue growing stronger in Matt's life, what effects do you think they would have come this time next year? How would that affect his education and his future?
- (to mother) I imagine that the Itchies have also taken a bit of a toll on your life. What's it been like for you having them in your house?
- How has that affected your emotional health, your physical health?

- How has it affected your relationship with each other? Have the Itchies brought you closer together or pushed you further apart? What effects have they had on other relationships?
- If the Itchies were to grow stronger in your family, what do you think might happen to relationships in your family over the next year?

Effects questions support the further externalization of problems. Clients' consideration of the effects that a particular problem is having on them increases the distance between the problem and them. People often find themselves annoyed with the problem and wanting to hold it at bay. Effects questions can also support connectedness between family members. Questions about the effects of a problem on relationships help to cast relational strains and tensions in a different light. Fred and Ray, the father and son in the last chapter who were caught in a pattern they described as "that Fast/Slow Thing," were invited to examine the effects it had on their relationship. Fred described it as "dragging their relationship right down the toilet." As he and his son talked, they moved from volatile reactivity to some degree of connection with and compassion for each other. As Fred put it later, "I feel like we moved from attacking each other to attacking that stupid Fast/Slow Thing."

There is often a hot potato of blame that gets tossed around in families (e.g., "It's not my fault we're in this mess. Well if you hadn't done that in the first place . . . "). Effects questions help families to shift from blaming each other to blaming the problem. This shift allows them to come together against the problem rather than against each other and contributes to a more containing experience in the room. When individuals are not feeling accused of being the problem, it's much easier for them to be less reactive and more reflective. In this way, effects questions help to promote a containing environment for the conversation.

Effects questions also support the development of empathy and connection between families and therapists. As we listen to the overwhelming stories that multi-stressed families have to tell about the devastation wrought by problems in their lives, we can fall into shell-shocked support ("Oh, you poor thing") or become instrumental and try to offer solutions or reassure clients that they have strengths and resources. When we move too quickly into trying to make things better, we can fall into the trap of "solution-forced" therapy (Nylund & Corsiglia, 1994). We can become ensnared in a minimize/maximize pattern in which clients experience our reassurance as minimizing their experience and respond by trying to get us to see how bad things really are. In the example with Fred and Ray, Fred was very clear he wasn't ready to change anything in his life until someone realized just how bad things were for him. Often, people have a strong need to vent. We have a common social work injunction: "Start where clients are at." Unfortunately, this useful phrase can sometimes become an excuse for going no further. Effects questions can offer clients an experience of someone understanding their pain without locating the cause of that pain inside them or someone else. The questions make the pain of a situation understandable in a way that removes blame. In this way, effects questions help us to stay connected to clients' experience and not move too quickly, while simultaneously shaping their experience of that pain in a different manner.

Effects questions can also be useful to explore anticipated future effects. These questions have the potential to heighten clients' resolve to reclaim their lives and relationships from problems. For example, with Fred and Ray, after tracing the effects of that Fast/Slow Thing on their relationship, I restated a summary of those effects and then asked the question, "If that Fast/Slow Thing continues to get stronger, what do you think will happen to your relationship?"

FRED: Kiss it good-bye. Just kiss it good-bye.

BILL: What do you think about that? Are you ready to have that Fast/ Slow Thing just kiss your relationship with your son good-bye?

FRED: No way. He's my son. We've gotten into some messed up stuff here, but I'm not willing to give up on him.

Gregory Bateson (1979) relates a quasi-scientific fable that if you take a frog and drop it in boiling water, it will jump out. However, if you put a frog in cold water and slowly heat up the water, the frog will accommodate to the increases in temperature, never jump out, and eventually boil to death. This story is an apt metaphor for the growing influence of problems in people's lives. As we live with the presence of problems, we accommodate to their debilitating effects. Anticipated future effects questions can be useful in exploring with families whether the water that is their life is getting hot.

Finally, effects questions can examine the effects of a problem on one's relationship with one's self. We can ask such questions as the following:

- What story might this problem tell you about who you are?
- If you lived out that story, what kind of future would it hold for you?
- What would it get you to notice and not notice about yourself?
- What important things would it keep others from noticing about you?

Preference Questions

Although questions about the problem's influence, effects, tactics, and support can proceed in a stepwise fashion, preference questions are usually interwoven with the other questions. Preference questions can help clients and us learn about whether these effects suit the person or not and provide a basis for further inquiry. For example, in response to Fred's statement that he would not want to let that Fast/Slow Thing just kiss good-bye his relationship with Ray, I asked, "Why is that? What is it about this relationship that makes it so important to you?" That question opened up a long-impassioned story about Fred's disappointing relationship with his own father, the effects that had on his life, and how important Fred felt it was for Ray to have a different experience with him. The follow-up to preference questions help to anchor conversations in clients' core values and best intentions. In this way, they enrich the questioning process and make it more relevant and personally meaningful to clients. Preference questions keep clients anchored in where they would like their lives to be headed and how their actions fit with their values and best intentions. The process further invites clients into a reflective stance. As Fred finished his impassioned story, he looked at his son and both had tears in their eyes.

Preference questions also provide an occasion for people to make their values and intentions known. To voice a preference out loud is to commit oneself to a direction in life. Preference questions create a context to make commitments. These questions invite people to clarify and elaborate their values. In this way, preference questions are helpful in mobilizing and aligning a person's emotional responses behind their preferred direction in life (Tomm, 1989, 1992). Fred's declaration of his values and best intentions in raising Ray in Ray's presence provided a platform for Fred to proclaim what he stood for and brought forth a particular pride in that aspect of his parenting. The rest of the examples of areas of deconstructive questions will have preference questions sprinkled throughout.

Learning about Cultural Supports for the Problem

Problems are embedded in a cultural context and often receive significant support from prevailing cultural ideas and practices. Marie's struggle against Depression and the effects of Expectations, described in the last chapter, are a good example of this support. Expectations' accusations that Marie was not thin enough, attractive enough, or sexually satisfying are all embedded in cultural assumptions about how women should be and look. Although many of these cultural specifications have come under increased scrutiny and are being challenged, they are still strong and complicated and still have a powerful hold. Exposing and critically examining cultural assumptions that support a problem help to further undermine the influence of that problem.

Our stance in raising such questions is important. Virginia Goldner (1992) draws a distinction between raising moral issues in therapy and being moralistic in therapy. She suggests that raising moral issues (asking people about the effects of how they act) is a mark of clinical integrity, whereas being moralistic (telling people how they should act) is a self-indulgent misuse of therapeutic power. This distinction is also useful in examining cultural supports for a particular problem. The goal in exposing cultural ideas that support a problem is not to substitute some other set of prescriptions of how to be in life (i.e., countercultural specifications rather than cultural specifications). Rather, the goal is to make visible the taken-for-granted assumptions that organize our lives so that clients can examine those assumptions and decide how they actually fit for clients' lives.

As an example of this process, let's examine some of the cultural supports for that Fast/Slow Thing in Fred and Ray's life together. (The work with Fred and Ray consisted of conjoint meetings with periodic individual meetings. This transcript is taken from an interview with Fred alone.)

FRED: I hate it that I end up lecturing him so much, but when I tell him to do something, he needs to do it.

BILL: And what's it like for you when he doesn't?

FRED: It drives me crazy.

BILL: I can understand that he should listen to you, but I'm thinking about shifting this a bit and asking about you rather than him at that moment. Would that be OK?

FRED: Yeah, I guess.

BILL: When he doesn't listen to you and it drives you crazy, how does that get you to think about yourself?

FRED: Like I'm an idiot. I feel like a jerk.

BILL: And this voice that's saying you're a jerk. What's it saying you should be able to get Ray to do?

FRED: I should be able to get him to listen to me. I should be in control of my son.

BILL: And this idea that you should be in control, do you know other men who hear that voice that they should be in control? What stands behind that voice?

FRED: Oh, you know, that stuff about men needing to be in control and all that.

We go on to explore Fred's thoughts regarding the gender discourse about men and control. He traces some of his experiences growing up with the idea that "a real man is always in control and doesn't take shit from anyone." After a bit, I bring the discussion back to his relationship with his son.

BILL: Do you think that Ray as a young man coming of age is influenced at all by that same idea that men should be in control and not take shit from anyone? What do you think that voice says to him when you get to lecturing him like you described?

FRED: (*laughing*) It probably says the same thing to him, you know like, "Are you going to let this old fart diss you like that?" It's a sneaky son-of-a-bitch, that voice of control.

BILL: So, if this voice had its way with your relationship, what would happen?

FRED: We'd be like two bulls butting heads. But that's what men do.

BILL: It may be what men can do. Is that how you want to spend your time with Ray? (Preference question)

From here we moved into a discussion that externalized the cultural idea that "real men are always in control," looked at the effects of that cultural idea on Fred's relationship with Ray, and examined how that fit with the relationship Fred would like to have with Ray. Fred began to get angry and declared that he was not going to let the "voice of male control" control him. We both laughed at the irony and moved on to talking about exceptions when their relationship had been more anchored in connection rather than in control battles. I asked which he preferred and which he thought Ray would prefer (he thought they'd both prefer connection). We ended with Fred expressing an interest in talking next time with Ray about how they could move from control battles to connection.

In this conversation, the problem moves from that Fast/Slow Thing to the cultural idea that "men should be in control." In response, we recycle through a deconstructive questioning process, learning about the new problem's influence, effects, supports, and tactics, as well as Fred's opinions and preferences regarding them. In this process, preference questions become particularly important to help me stay beside Fred and ensure that I'm seeking his ideas about the political questions I'm raising rather than simply advocating a particular political position.

It's important to emphasize that the goal in examining cultural supports for problems is not to forcibly strip away people's assumptions. To quote Zimmerman and Dickerson (1996a):

> Our intention is to explore the ideas that influence people, not to destroy them; to question them, not to leave persons without an anchor or without some sense of constancy in their lives. Our experience is that discourse can take us away from our experience, or get us to make sense of our experience only against some standard or norm. We believe that by questioning the discourse of influence, we allow people to consider their preferences more clearly, and to decide whether or not the ideas that influence them "fit" for them. (p. 69)

Here is where the idea of being in relationship with a cultural discourse can become particularly useful. The goal is not to sever that relationship but to develop a relationship that best "fits" for the client, as determined by the client. Examining the cultural supports that problems receive helps to put problems in a broader perspective and minimize self-blame. It also makes the difficulty of redefining our relationship to a particular problem more understandable.

Learning about the Tactics of the Problem

If we think about problems as separate from people, we can attribute intent, plans, and strategies to problems and examine the tactics that problems use to exert influence on people. As people are invited to consider a problem's strategies, they move into an observing position and shift their relationship with the problem. Clients, observing how a problem operates, often describe a certain distance from its influence. As they stand further outside the problem's influence in an observing position, they can develop a different perspective and experience of the problem. This shift in perspective and experience supports the development of agency in addressing the problem. For example, in Marie's struggle with Expectations, I asked the following questions:

BILL: You've described Expectations' ideas that you are not thin enough, attractive enough, wealthy enough, and sexually satisfying enough. You've also talked about how you don't appreciate those accusations and think they're, as you said, crap. When Expectations tries to lay that crap on you, do you have a sense of how it does that?

MARIE: No.

BILL: Does Expectations come up and tell you that it's going to try to lay that crap on you? Does it give you some warning?

MARIE: No, it'd be stupid to be that direct.

BILL: Why would being direct be stupid?

MARIE: Well, if it was direct I'd know what it was trying to do and then I'd tell it to just shove off.

BILL: So, would it be helpful for us to get a better sense of how Expectations tries to lay that crap on you?

MARIE: That's an intriguing idea. I like that idea.

BILL: So, if it had a voice, what would it be saying to you.[2] How does it build its case for this crap?

Marie began to describe how Expectations continually made comments that compared her to other women who passed by, particularly when she noticed them catching her boyfriend's eye. She described the critical voice of Expectations "running that line that they're prettier than me, dressed better than me, made up better than me, and all that crap." We began to talk about Expectations "running that line" on her and the support Expectations got in our culture. I asked Marie if she'd be willing to do some research on how Expectations "runs that line." She agreed and at the next session came in with detailed descriptions of Expectations' tactics. She also described how studying the tactics of Expectations took away much of its power. As she put it, "Now when Expectations tries to run that line on me, I can see it coming and I just laugh at it."

An important support in this process came from a woman friend who Marie told about the research project on Expectations. That woman became excited and joined Marie in an informal support group in which they shared their respective discoveries about Expectations. Marie proclaimed that Expectations didn't have a chance when they were working together. This again highlights the importance of people drawing on the power of supportive community in shifting their relationships with particular problems.

The process of examining problems' tactics and strategies often brings out clients' agency in coping with and resisting the influence of problems. For example, as Marie talked about Expectations' loss of influence over her, I asked if Expectations was losing its influence over her or if she was taking that influence away from Expectations. She paused thoughtfully, and we began to move into a discussion of her influence in relation to Expectations. In the process, a number of exceptions to Expectations' influence began to emerge. Those exceptions allowed us to move into the kinds of reauthoring questions that are examined next.

This section has outlined questions to examine the relationship that problems have with people, exploring areas of influence, effects, preferences, cultural supports, and tactics. The actual questioning process often does not follow this sequence in a step-by-step progression. It is useful to think about these areas as domains to be considered in a conversation that fits to clients' pace and style. Deconstructive questions take apart the influence of the problem on persons and set the stage for reauthoring questions. Sometimes we can spend little time taking apart the influence of problems on people and move quite quickly into reauthoring questions. At other times, when a problem has a significant hold on persons, it is important to take our time and more fully deconstruct the influence of the problem in order to open space for the emergence of the person's influence on the problem. As we have seen in Marie's situation, the process of taking apart the influence of the problem may open space for an easy transition into reauthoring questions.

REAUTHORING QUESTIONS

Problems are often deeply entrenched in people's lives. They may take up so much space that they begin to define our identities and convince us that there is little or no life outside the problem. However, despite the apparent strength of the problem's influence over our lives, there are always areas that fall outside the problem's influence. The goal is to look carefully for such exceptions and contradictions to the influence of the problem. Often these exceptions are small and quite easy to overlook. They go unnoticed because the problem is supported by a dominant story that "prunes from experience" those events that do not fall within it (White & Epston, 1990). The dominant story of the problem's influence promotes selective attention to some experiences at the expense of others. Those events that don't fit within the problem story go unnoticed and can be thought of as phenomenologically nonexistent for people living within the problem story. In this way, the stories about our lives powerfully shape our lives by directing selective attention toward some experiences and away from others. At the same time, no single story can adequately capture the complexity of our experience. There are always events that fall outside any story. Reauthoring questions build on these events to help clients develop and live out alternative stories. In the words of Monk (1997), "These 'pruned' lived experiences can be developed into a more favored story. In fact, we are keen to treat such prunings as cuttings that can be replanted, fertilized, nurtured and grown into fullness" (p. 14). Reauthoring is a process of collaboratively working with clients to "grow into fullness" new stories based on events that fall outside the problem's story.

The goal of reauthoring questions is to examine the influence clients and their community have on a problem in order to put together a new story of that influence and extend it. Whereas deconstructive questions further externalize the problem, reauthoring questions internalize client agency. Again, the goal is not to define for clients what relationship they should have with a problem but to support them in developing the relationship they would prefer. That preferred relationship may be to oppose the problem, or kick it out of their life, or cope with the problem, or contain the problem, or outgrow the problem, or draw on the problem as a consultant. In the spirit of self-determination, it is important that clients are the ones who define the relationship they seek to have with problems.

We can organize reauthoring questions around five broad areas:

- Opening space for alternative stories by examining life outside of the problem
- Clarifying client preferences and values
- Developing alternative stories in realms of action and meaning
- Examining new possibilities from alternative stories
- Developing support for the enactment of new stories

The remainder of this chapter examines the first four areas. The final area, developing support for the enactment of new stories, is examined in more detail in Chapters 7, 8, and 9.

The process of reauthoring begins with a search for a point in *time*, a point in *space*, or a point of *view* that falls outside what would have been expected within the context of the dominant, problematic story or plot. Points in time or space are moments or situations in which something different happened and/or clients experienced themselves differently. Points of view are others' perspectives on clients that fall outside clients' dominant stories. These points are usually referred to as exceptions, unique outcomes, or sparkling moments, and they provide the foundation for openings that can be developed into alternative stories or counter-plots.

These moments often emerge and are visible during deconstructive questioning. As we learn about a problem's influence over clients, we also learn about situations in which the problem's influence wanes and clients' influence grows. We can note when exceptions spontaneously arise and begin to build on them or we can actively elicit exceptions. As we notice exceptions with clients, it is useful to find out whether the exception is preferred by the client and if so why. Inquiries about clients' preferences help to ensure that the newly developing alternative stories fit with their preferred directions in life. These questions are important both as an accountability check (to ensure that our work is supporting clients moving in directions that they prefer in life rather than simply helping them move in directions that we would prefer for their lives) and as a way to solidify their commitment to those directions. Once we have elicited some exceptions that are in keeping with client preferences, we can begin to work with clients to elaborate these exceptions into an alternative story by coevolving a counter-plot that connects the various exceptions in a coherent fashion. The elaboration of a story of clients' influence on the problem occurs in realms of both action and meaning. As clients begin to develop and enact alternative stories, we can examine the possibilities that these alternative stories may hold for them and work with them to develop a community that will support the continued enactment of these new, preferred stories.

From here, two reauthoring situations are described, one from ongoing work with an individual and one from a consultation interview with a family. These examples are used to concretize the process of reauthoring, with multiple examples of questions. The first example provides a clear outline of a reauthoring process with an individual adult; the second extends it to work with families.

THE GIRL WHO COULD

Fran was a 31-year-old white secretary who was referred by her employee assistance plan after a run-in with her boss in which she became distraught and angry. She described herself as depressed, disorganized, and intimidated by her boss. She had trouble sleeping and couldn't focus at work. She was initially reluctant to come for help. In the first session, it was apparent that Depression had a strong hold on her. It had convinced her that she was worthless and unlikable, an accusation supported by an abusive father and a painful school history of being teased and taunted. She felt intimidated by Depression and was convinced she couldn't deal with it directly. She was also adamant against taking medication, which had been previously suggested. Depression's hold on Fran was very strong and the few exceptions to its influence that she noticed were quickly dismissed by her as inconsequential.

Fran was also an avid science fiction fan who read voraciously and was familiar with virtually every science fiction movie made. At our second session, she came in looking very tired after attending a 24-hour science fiction movie marathon. Even though she was exhausted, there was a sparkle in her eyes and an animation in her voice that contrasted sharply with the first session. In the first session, she had mentioned coping with the taunting and teasing as a child by watching hours and hours of science fiction movies on TV. At the time, I had thought about her fascination with science fiction as an escape from painful reality, but I now found myself wondering what science fiction might be an "entry into" rather than an "escape from." As I was contemplating this shift, Fran talked with anticipation and excitement about a science fiction conference that was coming to town. I asked her what she would be doing at the conference and she excited described a list of important responsibilities. As she spoke, I noticed her looking more alive and upbeat. I commented on this and asked her to describe the Fran I would have seen if I had attended past conferences. She described that Fran as "a big kid, a nut who has fun, wears outrageous costumes, and enjoys herself; a girl who is confident and not afraid of people, someone who is friendly and open." She described managing a crew that worked for the conference, and I asked how her crew would describe her. Their description matched hers with the addition of "in charge and inclusive, fair, kind and fun to work for." I had been writing furiously to capture these descriptions and as I read them back to her, I asked what she would think about a person such as the one she had just described. She replied that she would want to be her friend and we moved into a discussion of what she most valued about that description and why those things were particularly important to her.

I asked her what title she might give to this story of Fran that she was telling me and she replied, "The girl who could!"[3] I was very moved and found her a quite different person than the one that Depression had brought in the previous week. I commented on that and asked Fran what happened to Depression and its story of worthlessness at these conferences.

FRAN: Oh, it would never show up there. It's not that stupid. It knows it can't get me there.

BILL: What does it know about you there that holds it at bay?

FRAN: I have no idea. It's just not there.

BILL: So, is the conference sort of like a Depression-free zone?

FRAN: (*laughing*) Yeah, I like that. You know, it's like I live in a Sea of Depression and there are these Islands of Sanctuary where it can't get me. Some like the conference are bigger islands and some are very small. Some aren't even islands. They're like coral reefs where I can just keep my head above water.

BILL: Do you like it better when you're on the islands or out in the sea?

FRAN: The islands, definitely the islands.

BILL: What is it that you like better about the islands?

FRAN: I'll drown out in the sea. The sea will kill me. The islands sustain me.

We moved into a discussion about her choice for life and anchored it in her struggle against teasing and taunting throughout grade school and her determination to not get dragged down by it. Eventually, we returned to her metaphor of islands and coral reefs.

BILL: You talked about wanting to get more solid places to stand like islands. What do you think would need to happen to build some of those coral reefs into islands?

FRAN: I need to do what always happens to coral reefs, add sediment— the sediment are the people around me who will help me remember who I am and not get washed away by Depression.

This metaphor of Islands in a Sea of Depression organized our future work together. We mapped the terrain of the Islands of Sanctuary and added the sediment of people around her. The goal in this endeavor was to enlarge and solidify the land mass on which she stands in her life as a foundation for helping her develop a different relationship with the Sea of Depression. In this way, the work juxtaposed Depression's influence on Fran's life and Fran's influence on the life of Depression (her coping with and resistance to Depression's effects on her life).

All too often in our work as therapists, we focus on the sea of problems rather than the islands of competence. It is an ironic and tragic paradox that our attempts to help often result in us (and clients) learning more about problems' influence and less about clients' resistance and coping. Again, it is important to not ignore the influence of problems but to juxtapose the dominant story of the problem's influence with the counter-story of the client's agency.

THE FAMILY WITH A SOLID FRAME

A spontaneously emerging exception led to a reauthoring process in the first situation. In this second situation, the initial exception was elicited through questioning. The Smith family was a blended family with a long history of involvement with multiple helpers. The identified client was Joe, a 14-year-old boy who had spent the last 7 years in and out of residential treatment. He was his mother's only son, and she raised him alone after her first husband abandoned the family shortly after his birth. When Joe was 7, his mother remarried a divorced man with three older children. As the two families came together, significant tension arose and various children's behavior escalated out of control. For the past 7 years, the family had not been able to all live together. At the point of this consulta-

tion, the intact family consisted of stepfather Bob, mother Jane, and son
Joe. The three older children were living with their biological mother. The
family was referred to a home-based family therapy program upon the
son's latest discharge from a residential facility.

The family's dominant story emerges in the following excerpt from a
consultation interview:

BILL: What was your reaction to the idea of this consultation?

JANE: I thought it'd be an excellent idea because I have to say we're a very
complicated family. I mean we've been through so many counselors
and therapists, years and years of it, and nothing seems to help. This
is the last straw, right here, and there's gotta be some resolution.

BILL: OK, when you say that you're a very complicated family and you've
been through a lot of therapy, what's your experience of that been?
Do you feel like helpers who have been involved with your family
understand who you are as a family?

JANE: Yes, they say we're very complicated.

BILL: So, you've heard that from other people.

JANE: Yeah, in fact there was one counselor who said this family was
never going to make it.

BILL: Really?

JANE: Yeah, we had worked with her for years and years and she said,
"You're not going to be together much longer because none of you
are cooperating."

BILL: Cooperating with each other or cooperating with her?

JANE: With each other, with her, with the things we were supposed to be
doing. And, it wasn't just Joe who wasn't cooperating. It was Bob
and I.

BILL: What was your reaction to that?

JANE: I had to agree with her. I mean there was a time when I said to
myself, you know, I'm not much for this marriage either, because
things were getting to a point where I just couldn't stand it.

Although this exchange only involves Jane's voice, this story of "we
are a complicated, uncooperative family who can't make it together" was
held by all family members. Their dominant story had significantly hampered treatment progress over the past 7 years. It was a story that grew
out of and was supported by a number of previous family–helper interactions.

The following segment highlights the emergence of an exception elicited through questioning.

BILL: You talked before about the harder parts of being a family. If there are the easier parts of being a family and the harder parts of being a family, you guys have certainly had your share of the harder parts. How have you hung on to the connection?

JANE: Love, commitment.

BILL: But how do you explain that that love and commitment haven't been washed away with the difficulties?

JANE: Believe me, it's been washed away hundreds of times, but it's still there. I mean, I love Bob and I love Joe.

BILL: So it's taken some knocks, but somehow it hasn't been completely washed away?

JANE: No.

BILL: What does that tell you about yourselves as a family?

JANE: It just says come hell or high water no one's gonna stop us, and you know you can be as stubborn as you want, but I'm still gonna stick by you and I'll be here if you need me.

BILL: Whew . . . You've gotten a lot of help from lots of different people and you've had a lot of people tell you you're a very complicated family. If there was one thing that the professionals haven't understood about you as a family, what would you say it is?

JANE: I think they've seen everything.

BOB: I disagree. I think they've seen what's on the surface, but they haven't seen the family bond. They've missed the fact that the family bond is there. Otherwise, under no circumstances would this family have survived this long anyway. What they saw were the changes that they thought needed to be made, and they were very substantial changes. We made an effort to make the changes as best we could, considering who we are. If I attempted to present anymore of a change, based on their suggestion, I would stop being who I am.

BILL: You know it's interesting, I live in a house that's about ninety years old, and when my wife and I bought this house, it was in disrepair and there were a number of people looking at this house and what people were seeing was peeling wallpaper, this, that and the other thing. And what we saw was this house has got a solid foundation. These walls are sound and . . . .

JANE: It's got potential.

BILL: It's got potential, yeah and it sounds like what you're sort of describing is a number of people have seen the peeling wallpaper in the house that is your family, but they haven't . . . .

BOB: That's right, they seem to miss the frame. I mean they have valid points. There are a lot of shortcomings in my personality and there's a lot of shortcomings in Jane's personality, but what they failed to see were the offsetting benefits between Jane's personality and mine.

BILL: Well, that makes sense. To go back to that wallpaper, I know in our house that wallpaper was peeling and it looked hideous, but . . . .

JANE: You took it off and it was fine.

BOB: Yeah, when you peeled it all the way down the frame was still solid just like our family.

We went on to examine how they had developed this Solid Frame, who most appreciated that Solid Frame, in what situations they were most likely to see that Solid Frame, how that Solid Frame had been developed initially in the early years of their coming together as a family, and how it had weathered the ravages of the past 7 years.

This newly developing story, "We are a family with a solid frame that is going to stick together come hell or high water," opens up many more possibilities than the previous dominant story, "We are a complicated, uncooperative family who can't be helped." It provides a much stronger foundation for further work. For example, imagine the different possibilities for the parents in the "Solid Frame" family or in the "Uncooperative, Complicated" family to set and enforce consistent limits on their son.

If we refer to the social constructionist assumption that the self is constructed in social interaction rather than preexisting as an innate quality, we can see the ways in which new identities for the Girl Who Could and the Family with a Solid Frame are developed, constructed, or constituted in the course of the work. These two examples provide a foundation to explore the process of helping clients build new lives.

OPENING SPACE FOR NEW STORIES BY FINDING LIFE OUTSIDE THE PROBLEM

The process of reauthoring begins with focusing on events or experiences in clients' lives that contradict or fall outside the dominant story. These events often emerge spontaneously. The trick is to attend to them. The beginning of Fran's alternative story of the Girl Who Could is an example of an exception that could have been easily overlooked. I almost glossed over Fran's reporting of the movie marathon but was tipped off by the sparkle in her eyes that something important was occurring. That tip organized me to listen to her description of the science fiction convention in a different way. David Epston (1996) has described this way as listening with two ears, one attuned to the dominant story and the other attuned to exceptions. My attention to the possibility of exceptions opened up space for me to notice and inquire about them. This process is anchored in where we stand in our interactions with clients. If we actively look for exceptions, we are more likely to see them.

Discovering Times outside the Problem

If we haven't noticed an exception that spontaneously emerges, we can inquire about events or experiences from other times, other contexts, or other perspectives that fall outside the prevailing influence of the problem. We can focus on past successes or times when clients' experience of themselves was less organized by the dominant story. For example, in the family described previously, Joe had spent more time over the last 7 years living out of the home than in it. We could begin with a focus on why he couldn't live at home or we could begin with an inquiry into the times he had lived at home and how his family had remained connected when he wasn't living at home. This second line of inquiry opens up space for the emergence of experiences that don't quite fit within the story of "we are a complicated, uncooperative family who can't live together and can't be helped." Following are some examples of other questions that use exceptions in time to open up space for the emergence of new possibilities:

- Have there been times when Depression has taken less of a toll on your life?
- You mentioned that protective services closed your case 2 years ago, before reopening it recently. What was happening 2 years ago that got them to close it?
- How did you manage to get out of that abusive relationship?
- It sounds as if this pattern has wreaked havoc with your life together. Can you think of a time when it had less of a hold on your relationship?
- Since you've been together, when have the two of you felt the closest?

Discovering Space outside the Problem

People are different in different contexts. We can search for contexts or situations in which clients act differently or experience themselves differently as a foundation for the development of alternative stories about their lives. For example, Fran's description of herself at science fiction conferences was quite different from her presentation of self in the previous session. Her experience of self at those conferences is an opening for the development of a very different story. If we are on the lookout for contexts or situations in which people may experience themselves differently, we can inquire about those differences. Again, the trick is to be on the lookout for them. The following are examples of questions that might be used to inquire about space outside of the problem.

- In what situations does this problem have less influence on your son? What do you think he is doing differently at those times?
- You say this problem is strongest at work, where is it the weakest? What is different about that situation?
- How are you different when the two of you are not so caught by that pattern? How is your partner different? How is your relationship different at those times?

Discovering Perspectives outside the Problem

We can also elicit experiences outside the problem's influence by asking about the perspectives of others. For example, the question about how Fran's crew at the science fiction conference would describe Fran yielded further information to support the development of a new story. Here are examples of other such questions:

- (*in a situation in which a client says, my grandmother was the one person who I could always count on*) What was your grandmother's view of you? What did she particularly appreciate about you?
- As your son hears you talking about how you want to develop a different relationship with him than you had with your father, what do you think it tells him about you?
- I know you were not too keen to come here and meet with me. As I think about you doing that anyway, what do you think it tells me about this idea that you're an uncooperative family?

Hypothetical Experiences outside the Problem

Sometimes clients have great difficulty finding exceptions. At those times, it can be helpful to draw on the miracle question or coping questions from solution-focused therapy (de Shazer, 1988; Berg, 1994a). The miracle question, as described in Chapter 4, invites clients into imagined futures and provides a way to elicit hypothetical exceptions. The miracle question can be followed by asking the client to describe imagined changes in great detail, which can be followed by a questions such as, "What would need to happen to bring that about?" and "When have you noticed bits of that happening?" These questions provide an entry into potential life experiences outside the problem. When clients feel particularly hopeless and discouraged about their plight, coping questions that seek to elicit how clients manage their difficulties can be useful in opening up space for the development of alternative stories. The following example highlights this utility:

CLIENT: It's hopeless, I feel so beaten down that there's really no point in going on anymore.

THERAPIST: It sounds really overwhelming. How have you managed to cope with all this?

CLIENT: I don't think I am coping.

THERAPIST: I can imagine that feeling. But how is it that you continue to make it to work in the morning?

CLIENT: I have to get to work. I don't have a choice.

THERAPIST: Well, I imagine it must be very tempting to just blow it off sometimes and just stay in bed?

CLIENT: My job's important to me. Nobody notices it there, but I'm good at it and I need to get there to make sure it's done right.

THERAPIST: If people did notice how good you are at your job, what would they see?

CLIENT: They'd see that I'm very responsible and committed and I always get my work done no matter what stands in my way. I'm quite persistent.

These questions open space for an examination of responsibility, commitment, and persistence that may stand outside a prevailing experience of hopelessness and discouragement.

In searching for exceptions, it is important to start very small and look for subtle openings. The *direction* of the opening away from the problematic story and toward alternative possibilities is more important than the *magnitude* of the opening. It is also important not to become caught up in our own excitement about the possibilities these openings may hold. It is more useful to respond with curiosity than with cheerleading. However, a stance of curiosity does not constitute a position of neutrality. In my own work, I have a definite bias against the negative influence of problems and the constraining influence of problematic stories. My attempts to open space for the emergence of alternative stories consists of a series of active invitations to take up new possibilities. An example of this is shown in my use of the metaphor of an old house with Joe and his family. As Bob talks about the family bond that others have missed, the metaphor of an old house pops into my head. I share this with them with the intention of helping to anchor their appreciation of the family bond. (It's important to note that this metaphor was not a preexisting one that I brought into the session waiting to give to them. It was the first time I had thought of it and it emerged in the conversation. I used the metaphor to capture an idea that was developing in the room between us.) At the same time, I offered it with some concern that it was my metaphor and might move the therapy in a direction that more reflected my preferences than theirs. I was reassured by the fact that both Jane and Bob grabbed the metaphor and ran with it, completing my sentences. I also checked with them a bit later to ensure that this way of talking about their situation fit for them. It is important to ensure that the direction we are moving in therapy fits with preferred directions in clients' lives. The search for exceptions is not a process in which the therapist pulls the family out of an old "bad" story and into a new "good" story. Although I see myself as actively inviting families into the development of alternative stories, I think it is important to ensure that these stories reflect their preferences. White (1995) draws a clear distinction between reauthoring and reframing in this respect:

> In my view, this reauthoring process is not like the technique of reframing, in which the onus is on the therapist to develop a new and better story about the person's experience. Instead, it is a process that engages all persons actively in "meaning-making," and one in which there is a concerted effort on behalf of the therapist to privilege family members as the primary authors of these alternative stories. (p. 66)

This value for family members being the primary authors of their stories requires that the therapist "challenge his/her settled certainties. S/he can't know, in advance, what's 'right' for people—can't even know how the family 'should' look at the end of therapy" (White, 1995, p. 66). One way to ensure that we are making the therapy responsive to client preferences and honoring clients as the senior partners in this work is through preference questions (Epston & Roth, 1994; Freedman & Combs, 1996a).

CLARIFYING CLIENT
PREFERENCES AND VALUES

Preference questions, previously discussed in the section on deconstructive questions, are also useful in reauthoring questions. Preference questions help us examine whether developing steps in a new story fit with clients' preferred directions in life. The vignette with Fran has several examples of preference questions. One example is the following question: "Do you like it better on the islands than out in the sea?" Although I've assumed she would prefer the Islands of Sanctuary to the Sea of Depression, it's conceivable that I may be missing something. For instance, Fran might have answered, "I'm not sure. The Islands give me false hope that life could be different and get me to let down my guard. Then when I'm not looking, Depression really knocks me for a loop." In that case, working to help Fran expand the Islands' territory might not have been a preferred direction for her. In this way, preference questions provide us with useful feedback and help to keep our work accountable to clients.

Preference questions can be followed by questions that seek a rationale for that preference. Fran's explanation of her preference for islands led into a moving discussion of central concerns in her life. In this way, preference questions open space for discussions of clients' motivations and values and help our work become more meaningful to them. And, as discussed earlier, preference questions also solidify a commitment to preferred directions.

DEVELOPING ALTERNATIVE STORIES

Exceptions open space for the emergence of new stories, but they are not enough. We need to work with families to expand the elicited exceptions into a substantial and coherent alternative story. Freeman et al. (1997) draw on a nest-building analogy to describe this process.

> The process of restorying requires painstaking work. With the ingenuity and care of birds building a nest, we create the counterplot. The therapist collaborates with the family to gather and document past events, intentions, hopes, and dreams that stand in counterpoint to the problem-dominated story. Strand by strand, actions and ideas are woven into a narrative convincing enough to serve as an alternative to this problem-saturated story. (p. 98)

The development of a convincing narrative occurs simultaneously in realms of action and meaning. Michael White (1993, 1995), borrowing from Jerome Bruner (1986), proposes that stories have dual landscapes: the landscape of action and the landscape of consciousness or meaning.[4]

> The landscape of action is constituted by experiences of events that are linked together in sequences through time and according to specific plots. This provides us with the rudimentary structure of stories. . . . The landscape of meaning is derived through reflection on events in the landscape of action to determine what those events might say about the desires, preferences, qualities, characteristics, motives, purposes, wants, goals, values, beliefs, commitments, of various persons. (White, 1995, p. 31)

To return to the previous examples, as Fran (in the Girl Who Could) described the Fran I would have seen at science fiction conferences, she was moving in a landscape of action. She was telling me about the who, what, where, and when of that story. As she described her reaction to that description, she was moving in a landscape of meaning. In this landscape, she was describing what it meant for her to be that person. She connected to particular values and preferred ways of being. As Jane (in the Family with a Solid Frame) talked about the love and commitment that had been washed away hundreds of times but was still there, she was moving in a landscape of action. As she reflected on the meaning that story held for her family (e.g., that "come hell or high water no one's gonna stop us"), she was moving in a landscape of meaning. Reauthoring moves back and forth between the landscapes of action and meaning.

Freedman and Combs (1996a) have recast landscape of action and landscape of meaning or consciousness questions as story development questions and meaning questions:

> Through story development questions, people plot the action and content of their preferred stories. Through meaning questions, we invite people into a reflecting position from which they can regard different aspects of their stories, themselves, and their various relationships. These questions encourage people to consider and experience the implications of unique outcomes, preferred directions, and newly storied experiences. In naming the meanings of these experiences, they are constructing them. (p. 136)

Whether we are describing our work in terms of landscape-of-action questions and landscape-of-meaning questions or in terms of story development questions and meaning questions, the common thread is a distinction between realms of action and meaning. Following Freedman and Combs (1993, 1996a), I will refer to story development and meaning questions because I think these terms are closer to people's everyday experience. Story development questions consist of the common journalism questions of who, what, when, and where in order to expand alternative stories. Meaning questions focus on the meaning of the newly developing story in order to further embed that story. This is reflected in such questions as "How do you explain that you were able to do that?" and "What does it tell you about yourself that you did that?" Although it is initially helpful to discuss story development and meaning questions separately, the two realms are intertwined and are usually developed simultaneously.

In a realm of action, we can work with clients and families to develop alternative stories across time, space, and perspectives. We can inquire about the details of experiences in the past, present, and future; in varying contexts and situations; and from others' perspectives in order to expand a newly developing story. One way to think about this is as an expansion from a point in three dimensions (time, space, and perspectives). We begin with an exception that perhaps is just a small dot. The twinkle in Fran's eye after the movie marathon is an example of this small dot. Then, through our questions, we can work with clients to expand that dot into an expanding three-dimensional sphere across time, space, and perspectives. Examples of such expansion would be the elaborating of Fran's quite different description of herself at the science fiction conference (space), her recitation of others' description of her at that conference (perspectives), and descriptions of other times when that has happened (time). In this way, the alternative story becomes expanded across three dimensions.

As we are expanding the counter-plot of alternative stories with clients, we can also inquire about the meaning these new stories hold for them. Examples of such meaning questions are:

- What does it mean to you that you've been able to do this?
- What does it tell you about yourself?
- What qualities or characteristics does it show?
- Of those things, which are most important to you? Why? (Preference questions)
- How would you describe somebody who was able to do that?
- Does that description fit for you?
- In your struggles against depression, what important things have you learned about yourself? How has that knowledge affected your life?
- If you were to give a title to this story of your resistance to the effects of depression, what would you call it?

These questions seek to elicit the "desires, preferences, qualities, characteristics, motives, purposes, wants, goals, values, beliefs and com-

mitments of various persons" (White, 1995, p. 35). These are not easy
questions to answer and often involve a mental search to develop an
answer. The process of that mental search is very important. It is in that
process that questions *generate experience* as well as yield answers. In this
way, meaning questions invite people into an experiential reflection on
their lives.

It is important that these questions remain close to clients' experience. They are not abstract, intellectualized questions but ones that often
provoke strong emotional experiences for clients. The power of my question to Jane, "What does it tell you about yourselves as a family that your
love and commitment haven't been washed away?," lies in her experience
of herself and her family that is generated as she answers the question. As
she responds, she experiences her family in a different way that is full of
affect for her. Although we do not talk about her feelings, the process
invites a deep experience of those feelings which was reflected in the tears
in her eyes as well as a strong welling up for me.

Her answer to those questions also had radiating effects on her son's
experience of their family. Throughout much of that consultation, he had
sat looking bored and disinterested. As his parents began to describe,
enact and experience a story of "we are a family who will hang together
come hell or high water" rather than a story of "we are an uncooperative
complicated family that no one can help," he sat up in his chair and
began attending in a quite concentrated fashion. It was as if he was
watching a movie that had suddenly become very interesting. Meaning
questions are particularly powerful vehicles to invite a different affective
experience of ourselves, our world, and our relationships. The newly
developing alternative stories are not just conceptual phenomena. They
are lived experiences. In some ways, the word "stories" may be an unfortunate misnomer that connotes an abstract, intellectualized, affectless
experience. Although I will continue to use that phrase, my hope is that
readers will appreciate the experiential basis of those stories, which is
often quite affect-full.

INTEGRATING STORY DEVELOPMENT
AND MEANING QUESTIONS
TO SUPPORT THE DEVELOPMENT
OF ALTERNATIVE STORIES

Story development and meaning questions are often intertwined to support the development of new stories. To help develop an appreciation for
the way in which they complement each other, they are discussed jointly

here. I'll begin with a series of questions that could have followed from the consultation with the Family with a Solid Frame (in fact, a number of these questions were asked in that interview). By the end of the consultation, the family was describing and experiencing themselves in a powerfully different way. The following questions are examples that would continue the development of their alternative story of "we are a family with a solid frame who are going to hang together come hell or high water":

- How did you develop this Solid Frame? What steps did you take to accomplish that?
- What personal and relationship qualities did you draw on to develop that Solid Frame?
- What does it tell you about yourself? (Meaning question)
- Who would most appreciate those steps? (Story development across perspectives)
- What would it tell them about you? (Meaning question)
- In what situations has the Frame been stronger? (Story development across contexts)
- Bob, as you hear Jane talking about how she's gonna hang in there come hell or high water, does it remind you of times when you've felt that from her in the past? (Story development across time)
- What was happening then?
- What does it get you to remember about her in that time? (Meaning across time)
- Jane, as you think about the memory Bob's describing, how does it affect what we're talking about now? (Meaning question across time)
- As your family continues to take this foundation into the future, where will it lead you? (Story development across time)
- If this foundation continues to grow stronger, what will life look like next year?
- Does that fit with how you would like your life to look a year from now? In what ways? What about that feels particularly important to you? (Preference questions)
- As you reflect on the development of this foundation, what have you learned about yourself? How will that knowledge help you in the future? (Meaning question across time)
- If you were to give a title to the story of this accomplishment, what would it be? (Meaning question)

In the interplay between these questions, we can see how preference questions, story development questions, and meaning questions interact to enhance each other. The details of the new story help to concretely anchor it. As we seek answers to the questions of who, what, where, and when, it is important to get details with the "painstaking care of birds building a nest."

To further explain the integration of story development and meaning questions, I'll continue a description of the work with Fran. We charted the terrain of various Islands of Sanctuary across time, in different contexts and through others' perspectives. For example, in contrasting her story of competence (the Girl Who Could) with Depression's story of worthlessness (Nobody likes you and nothing you ever do is right), I inquired about times in the past where she had hung onto a sense of competence in the face of accusations of worthlessness. She described her struggle to hold onto a positive sense of herself in the face of teasing and taunting throughout grade school and her determination not to get dragged down by the unfairness of teasing and taunting. As I sought to learn more about that Determination, the questions I asked included some of the following:

- How did you develop that Determination?
- As you think about your Determination to not let yourself get dragged down by teasing and taunting, what does it tell you about yourself?
- What do you think your stance against unfairness tells me about the kind of person you are and what you stand for in your life?
- How do those qualities show themselves in your life these days?
- Who from that time in your life would most appreciate the way in which you've become someone who stands for fairness and justice?
- What do you think they saw in you then?
- What would they most appreciate about you now?
- If they were here now listening to this conversation, what would be their reaction?
- What's it like for you to think about that reaction? What would it be like for you if you told them that about your reaction to their reaction? How could you catch them up on this?

We also charted the terrain of Islands of Sanctuary across contexts. As we progressed, I asked Fran if the Girl Who Could was beginning to appear in places outside of the science fiction conferences. We discussed various interactions with friends and work colleagues and examined particulars such as "in what contexts, around which persons, at what times." As we began to examine emergent themes across different situations in which Fran was able to keep Depression at bay, Fran stated that the common theme seemed to be "I remember who I am. I'm around people who help me remember that. I like who I am. I'm an original. I'm definitely not a copy and that's okay. I don't have to fit in with everyone else and it's their problem if they have trouble with that."[5] Again this led into a series of questions such as the following:

- Do you prefer being an original or would you prefer to be a copy? Why? (preference question)
- What do you particularly appreciate about yourself as an original?
- What helps you stay anchored in your appreciation of yourself as an original and not fall into trying to be a copy of others' ideas for you?
- Do you think in our culture today, people get more encouraged to be originals or more encouraged to be copies?
- What do you think gets people to copy others' ideas for their lives rather than appreciating their own originality? (Cultural support for the problem)
- What does it tell you about yourself that you continue to be an original in the face of all that pressure to be a copy?

As we can see here, these last questions begin to appreciate the difficulties in Fran's life in a context of cultural ideas about who she should be and how she should behave. In my interactions with Fran, I found her to be bright, wonderfully creative, and definitely an original. The cultural response to her originality has at times created significant hardship and pain for her. To locate that hardship and pain in her (e.g., "this is really about her depression") adds insult to injury and runs the risk of blaming the target.

Finally, we charted the terrain of Islands of Sanctuary across perspectives. At one point, Fran described herself as a work of art and described how artists are their own worst critics. I asked Fran what she particularly appreciated about the work of art that was her and what friendly reviews she might get from others. As we traced various reviews and she reflected on them, the development of her self-appreciation became visible in the creeping smile on her face, the lilt in her voice, and the twinkle in her eyes. Again questions generate experience. After establishing a solid foundation of friendly reviews, I asked her what review Depression might offer up for the work of art that was her. She described a scathing review, laughed and decided she might like to keep that one around for amusement.

At the end of our five meetings together, Fran described having shrunk the influence of Depression in her life from an 8 or 9 (on a scale of 1–10) to a 1. Although she believed that Depression would always be a presence in her life, she had developed a different relationship with it. She no longer felt intimidated by it and was able to stop its accusations of worthlessness through her own development of a thought-stopping exercise.[6] Although Fran wanted to quiet what she described as "Depression's voice of accusation," she didn't want to lose touch with its "voice of sadness." She had experienced a lot of sadness in her life and believed that sadness "anchored her in kindness, made her a better friend, and gave her more depth." In containing Depression's voice of accusation, while listening to its voice of sadness, Fran shifted her relationship to Depression in a way that she found preferable. As she described it, stopping Depression's thoughts helped her to reconnect with her sadness and being in relationship with her sadness helped her to be less vulnerable to Depression's effects.

EXAMINING NEW POSSIBILITIES

The previous section examined the process of developing stories across time, picking a point in time, extending it back to a foundation in the past, and extending it forward to possibilities in the future. Future points in time are reiterated here to emphasize the ways in which our questions can invite the consideration of new futures. In this way, the questions we ask invite people into the experience of alternative futures. Questions to examine new possibilities help to further invite people into new futures and contributes to a sense of forward motion and accomplishment.

Examples of questions to examine new possibilities that were used with the Family with a Solid Frame would include the following:

- As your Solid Foundation continues to grow stronger, what will your life together look like next year?
- Does that fit with how you would like your life to look a year from now? In what ways? What about that feels particularly important to you? (Preference questions)
- How will some of those things you describe first begin to emerge?
- What will you learn about yourselves as that happens?
- If Joe carries this family bond as a foundation with him in his head, how will it affect his return to school?
- What will others see differently in him as that happens?

Examples of similar questions that were used with Fran include the following:

- What do you think will be some of the next steps you'll take in the emergence of the Girl Who Could?
- As you do that, what will you learn about yourself?
- Who outside of you will first notice that?
- What new possibilities will emerge as you do that?
- As your life becomes even more anchored in appreciating the original that is you, what new possibilities will unfold?

NOT BY WORDS ALONE: ACTION-ORIENTED METHODS TO INVITE THE ENACTMENT OF NEW STORIES

Narrative therapy strongly emphasizes language. However, this doesn't mean that narrative therapy is simply a therapy of words. Many of the families who come to be called multi-stressed families are often seen as "not very verbal," but this does not mean that they are not expressive. They are often quite expressive and we need to find ways to interact with them that meets them through the manner in which they express themselves. We can bring more action-oriented methods into this work. For example, a therapist working with an 18-year-old who was impulsive and unable to make any plans in his life began shooting pool with this young man and taught him how to shoot while thinking two shots ahead. In the process, the young man became a planful pool player who was enacting a different story about his life. The therapist was then able to help him expand Planfulness into other aspects of his life. If every interaction invites the enactment of particular life stories, how do we engage clients in ways that invite more liberating narratives? We can engage with clients in concrete activities that invite the daily enactment of different stories and then draw on preference questions and meaning questions to further embed those stories. In the same vein, the process of applying for welfare benefits, advocating for a school core evaluation, or dealing with children on a supervised visit are all opportunities for clients to enact different stories. The emphasis shifts our focus from the *outcome* to the *process* of our efforts.

Similarly, our attempts to expand and elaborate alternative stories do not have to rely on words. Many of the creative attempts to help families involve activities: playing with families, taking kids out for a soft drink, shooting hoops with an adolescents, and so on. These are often powerful experiences in which clients can actively enact different stories of identity. The fact that they occur outside the context of "therapists and patients" also has powerful effects. Once therapists step outside the traditionally defined role of therapist, it opens up the opportunity for clients to step outside the traditionally defined role of dysfunctional patient. This is especially powerful for clients with long histories of unsuccessful treatment. I spoke with a mother whose son after a long history of unsuccessful psychiatric hospitalizations was involved in a home-based program that had a series of activity groups (in which kids and families went to baseball games, camping trips, pizza parties, etc.). This mother found these activities more useful than any of their previous individual or family therapies because, as she put it, "It gave me an opportunity to see my kid as a regular kid and not a mental patient. In the process, I viewed him differently and he was able to be someone different."

SUMMARY

This chapter has examined a questioning process to juxtapose problems' influence on clients with clients' influence on problems. Deconstructive questions offer a way to take apart the dominant story or plot of a problem's influence and open space for reauthoring questions to put together an alternative story or counter-plot of the person's emerging influence on the problem. As we engage in a reauthoring process, it is important that we fit the process to clients' preferred modes of expression. Every interaction we have with clients is an opportunity for reauthoring. The process of helping clients to more fully enter into alternative stories and continue their elaboration is examined in the next three chapters. Chapter 7 focuses on ways to solidify alternative stories between sessions and to use our required paperwork to assist in this process. Chapter 8 examines ways to draw on clients' natural communities to witness and honor their enactment of preferred identities. And Chapter 9 examines ways to help the larger helping system become a more appreciative audience for the enactment of new lives.

NOTES

1. If such containment does seem more the exception than the rule in your work, it might be interesting to examine what is different in those exceptions. What are you doing differently? What is the family doing differently? From a bird's-eye perspective, what is different about the context? Do you like it better when those exceptions seem to be happening? Based on the differences you've noticed, how might you be able to extend those exceptions into more of your work? The same questioning process that we use with families can also be helpful in reflecting on our work.

2. This idea of Problems having voice and intention is more fully developed in *If Problems Talked: Narrative Therapy in Action* (Zimmerman & Dickerson, 1996a).

3. In response to Fran's use of the word "girl," I asked a number of questions trying to take apart some of the cultural assumptions behind it. Fran found the process interesting but for a variety of reasons preferred the word "girl" to "woman" or some other term and I went with her preference.

4. Bruner's original term was "landscape of consciousness." White has also used "landscape of meaning" and "landscape of identity." I primarily use "realm of meaning" and "realm of action" to align this section with previous chapters describing constraints in realms of meaning and action.

5. The examination of emergent themes across different situations is very much akin to the development of "grounded theory" in qualitative research and ethnographic interviews (Glaser & Strauss, 1967; Lincoln & Guba, 1985). In this way, this process very much fits with a cultural anthropological metaphor for therapy. interviewing process.

6. Fran had never been exposed to the cognitive therapy technique of "thought stopping," but her description of what she was doing to stop depression's accusations constituted one of the clearest descriptions of thought stopping I had ever heard. Her development of a thought-stopping technique highlights the value of eliciting clients' knowledges before imposing our own. Whereas teaching her thought stopping could have been a useful intervention, honoring her development of it had much more impact.

7

—◦◦◦—

Elaborating and Solidifying
New Lives

The previous chapter described a consultation with a family who moved from a story of "we are a complicated, uncooperative family that can't be helped" to a story of "we are a family with a strong frame that is going to stick together come hell or high water." The family and their therapist both found the consultation moving and helpful. However, a week later, the therapist went out to meet with the family and found that they had fallen back into their old pattern of bickering and hopelessness. At first the therapist thought that the consultation hadn't "worked." She wondered whether the family really was a "complicated uncooperative family that can't be helped" and found herself being taken over by hopelessness. However, let's reflect on this situation for a moment. For the past 7 years, this family had been caught up in that story of "we are a complicated, uncooperative family that can't be helped." That 7 years translates into 40,880 waking hours, many of which were spent embedded in that story. Is it any wonder that a new story that was experienced over the course of a 1-hour consultation might struggle a bit against an old story with a such an extensive history? The ability of alternative stories to emerge at all against such odds is testimony to the preferred fit they have for families.

The hold of dominant problem stories is extremely strong. People have been deeply embedded in them and the stories receive significant ongoing cultural support. In this example, the family's old story received strong support from broader cultural stories about what a successful

224

blended family looks like. They continually fell short when comparing themselves to *The Brady Bunch*. The strength of these old stories is particularly relevant for multi-stressed families faced with multiple, interrelated problems that have become deeply embedded in their lives and define their identities. Newly emerging stories often fade between sessions, being overshadowed by old stories and resulting in a sense of failure and demoralization. It becomes important to find ways to support the emergence of alternative stories in order to keep alive the hope and forward momentum that underlies this work.

In this example, I suggested to the therapist that if she noticed the family continuing in their old pattern of bickering in the next meeting, she could ask them if the bickering was the "peeling wallpaper" or the "solid frame" (going back to the metaphor developed in the consultation). When bickering did reappear and she asked them that question, the parents smiled and laughed about how they were so often captured by that old pattern. They began spending more and more time in their new story of hope and commitment and gently reminded each other to "strip the wallpaper" when bickering and hopelessness showed up in their interactions. The phrase "oh, go strip the wallpaper" became a powerful mechanism to reanchor them in their preferred story of "we are a family with a strong frame that is going to stick together come hell or high water." The power of that phrase lies in their ownership of it. It was a phrase they developed, not one given to them by a therapist. However, the family therapist created a context that allowed its emergence. This chapter examines ways to help clients and families elaborate and solidify newly emerging alternative stories, particularly through letters, progress notes, termination interviews, and reports.

SUPPORTING CLIENTS ON THEIR JOURNEY TOWARD A PREFERRED FUTURE

This book has drawn on a journey metaphor in which our role is to help clients move toward a preferred future. White (1995) has described this process as a migration of identity in which people move from an old constraining identity to a new preferred identity. This process can be thought of as similar to an immigrant passage that involves leaving the country of origin, passing across a transitional phase, and arriving in a new land and incorporating preferred parts of a new identity. Numerous therapists, drawing on the work of van Gennep (1908), have proposed a rite of passage metaphor to organize their work (Adams-Westcott & Isenbart, 1990, 1995; Durrant, 1993; Epston & White, 1995; Koback & Waters,

1984; Nichols & Jacques, 1995; Roberts, 1988; White, 1995). In this metaphor, there are three phases: a Separation Phase, in which people begin to separate from an old identity or status that no longer fits for them; a Liminal or Transitional Phase, in which people are migrating across identities move back and forth between dominant and alternative stories; and a Reincorporation Phase, in which people begin to incorporate a new identity into their life. From a narrative perspective, the process of externalizing supports movement through a Separation Phase, whereas deconstruction and reauthoring questions help clients move through a Transitional Phase.

This chapter examines a number of ways to support the passage to new identities between sessions and to help people begin to traverse a Reincorporation Phase by elaborating and solidifying new identities. The next two chapters continue this focus with particular attention on the role of community and the larger helping system. As we've seen, problems can be strong and have significant influence on people's lives. Often those problems receive powerful cultural support. In our efforts to help people develop preferred lives, it is helpful to assist them in identifying and drawing on members of their community to serve as a counterbalance. This process can be seen as the development of a community of support to help people develop new lives. As clients begin to enact alternative stories, that enactment solidifies the story. In our performance of preferred stories, we build our preferred selves. This is a much more powerful process when it occurs in the context of an appreciative community that witnesses, supports, and celebrates that performance.

This focus on the development of communities of support may be at odds with traditional conceptualizations of therapy, but many clients involved in it tend to become quite enthusiastic about the process. Traditionally, therapy has been seen as a private, protected space in which clients can disclose and work through painful issues. In this context, confidentiality has been an important protection against exposure and shame. This privacy becomes extremely important when problems are seen as internal to the individual or family. When people *are* their problems, it is understandable that they would not want others to know about their problems. However, as people experience themselves as separate from the problems in their lives and as having particular competencies in addressing those problems, there is less of a need for that privacy, protection, and confidentiality. In this context, therapy takes on a different connotation. In the words of Freedman and Combs (1996a) "When therapy becomes a context in which people constitute preferred selves, they have nothing to hide and much to show" (p. 237).

SUPPORTING THE DEVELOPMENT
OF NEW STORIES BETWEEN SESSIONS

There are a number of ways in which we can work with families to further develop newly emerging alternative stories between sessions. One
way is to simply ask families to notice exceptions to the old story as well
as events that support the new story and report on them in the next session. At that report, we can then ask a series of preference and meaning
questions about those events. For example, with the Solid Frame family,
we could ask the following:

- What did you notice about your solid frame this week?
- When you are more of a solid frame family, what do you particularly appreciate about yourselves?
- What does it tell you about the family you're becoming that more
  of this solid frame is emerging?
- Who else do you think would particularly appreciate those qualities?
- What further developments do you think you'll see as you continue this process?

We can also begin meetings by reviewing some of the ways in which alternative stories emerged in the previous session and ask families about both
their reactions to those new experiences and any examples of other new
experiences they have noticed since the last meeting.

If the aim of our work is to undermine problems' influence on families and support families' influence on problems, it behooves us to attend
to the power dynamics between problems and families (which are most
often played out between sessions). Just as ignoring other power differences in therapy (e.g., gender dynamics in couples) supports the status
quo, not attending to the power that problematic stories have over families inadvertently supports the problem's position. In this way, how we
begin sessions is quite important. If we think about a problem having a
strong voice, we can see that apparently innocent openings, such as
"How was your week?," can be an invitation for that problem's voice to
take over the session. For example, Fran (the Girl Who Could in Chapter
6) had talked about Depression's tactics of picking out half-truths and
twisting them to support its negative view of her. As she put it, Depression would "insert itself piece by piece, thought by thought into my life."
Simply asking her about her week runs the risk of providing a platform
for Depression's attack on her. I find it preferable to begin sessions with

questions that elicit movement away from the old plot and into the counter-plot. In this, I put my weight behind clients and against problems. At
the same time, it is important to do this transparently and in ways that
are not experienced by clients as minimizing their distress. For example, I
might say to a client the following:

> "We've been talking in here about times when you've been more in
> charge of your life and times when Depression has been more in
> charge of your life. My preference would be to learn a little about
> times this week when it's been more your life and use that as a basis
> to then examine times when Depression has tried to make it more his
> life. Would that be a good way to start for you or would it be better
> to begin by learning about times when Depression's been more in
> charge of your life?"

In this way, preference questions help us to stay beside clients and
avoid getting out in front of them. We can mark our position and then see
how that fits with clients' preferences. Clients often agree that it would be
better to start with highlighting their agency rather than a problem's
agency, but there have been times when a client has preferred to begin by
giving me a picture of just how horrible the week has been.

ELABORATING NEW STORIES
THROUGH LETTERS AND REPORTS

Another way to enhance the development of new stories between sessions
is therapeutic letters that are sent to clients to summarize sessions. David
Epston (1994) who is most closely identified with the practice of therapeutic letters, has summarized their purpose as follows:

> Conversation is, by its very nature, ephemeral. After a particularly
> meaningful session, a client walks out aglow with some provocative
> new thought, but a few blocks away, the exact words that had struck
> home as so profound may already be hard to recall. . . . But the words
> in a letter don't fade and disappear the way conversation does, they
> endure through time and space, bearing witness to the work of therapy
> and immortalizing it. (p. 31)

Another way to think about this would be to draw an analogy
between vacations and therapeutic sessions. Many of us have had the
experience of returning to work from a wonderful vacation and three
days later wondering whether the vacation had ever occurred. Thera-

peutic letters are an attempt to keep a vacation from problematic stories alive and to support a re-creation of ourselves in the context of
alternative stories.

The work with Fran (discussed in Chapter 6) involved two letters,
one after the second session and one after the fifth session. I include each
one here, followed by a discussion of their rationale.

Dear Fran,

*I was very touched by our meeting today. I was moved by
your description of yourself at the science fiction conferences.
Some of your words that I was able to jot down included "a big
kid, someone who is more confident to speak out for herself, a
nut, someone who has fun and wears costumes, someone who
enjoys herself and is not afraid of people she's with, someone who
is very friendly and open, stronger and in charge, fun to be with,
inclusive and very importantly, fair." What do you think of a person like that? Is that the kind of a person you value being? You
called yourself "THE GIRL WHO COULD" and from what you
said, it certainly sounded like a fitting title.*

*I appreciated your willingness to talk about Depression and
its attempts to steal away your confidence and self-worth. You
described its attempts to "insert itself piece by piece, thought by
thought into your life." You laid out a very clear description of
how it tries to pull you down by picking out half-truths and twisting them to support its negative thoughts about you. You gave me
one of the clearest pictures I've heard of how Depression gets a
hold on people. I realize that was a very difficult thing to do and
that you might have preferred to not talk about it. What does it
tell you about yourself that you are able to look Depression
squarely in the eye? What do you draw on to not simply run and
hide from it? What do you think Depression would make of the
fact that you can stand up and face it? Do you think it might get
worried about that? If you get a clearer sense of how it inserts
itself piece by piece into your life, do you think it might have a
harder time getting a hold on you?*

*I also appreciated your ability after talking about Depression
to reconnect with THE GIRL WHO COULD. You talked about
the islands of anti-depression zones and your idea of building
coral reefs into islands by adding sediment to them by gathering a
group of people around you. Who might be some of the people
that would stand with you against Depression? You mentioned
that you weren't sure if you could get rid of Depression or if you
needed to keep it in its place. As you draw more and more on
THE GIRL WHO COULD to keep Depression in its place, who*

*would best help you to REMEMBER her? I look forward to
meeting with you in two weeks.*

In appreciation of THE GIRL WHO COULD,

Bill Madsen

This letter flowed out of our second meeting. I routinely take notes
(with client permission) to organize my thinking.[1] Notes help therapists
to stay anchored in clients' own language as much as possible. We can
write down notable phrases that capture particular themes (e.g., "the Girl
Who Could"). The notes also help us to be more alert for the emergence
of exceptions and to better juxtapose old and newly emerging stories.
One way to do this is by drawing a vertical line down a page and noting
elements of the old story on the left and emerging threads of newer stories
on the right. The process of note taking can also support a elaboration of
alternative stories. For example, when I asked Fran to describe the Fran I
would have seen if I had attended past conferences, she used the words "a
big kid, a nut who has fun, wears outrageous costumes and enjoys herself, a girl who is confident and not afraid of people, someone who is
friendly and open." Writing those phrases down allowed me to then read
them back to see if I had gotten her words right and then ask her to
reflect on them. In this way, our notes help to underline a different story
about clients. It then becomes fairly easy to translate these notes into a
therapeutic letter.

The letter more or less followed the organization of the session. The
session began with me noticing the sparkle in Fran's eyes and eliciting a
picture of the Fran I would have seen at the science fiction conventions.
The letter began with reviewing her description of that picture. There are
a number of meaning and preference questions posed to Fran in the letter
that attempt to further elaborate the story of the Girl Who Could (e.g.,
What do you think of a person like that? Is that the kind of person you
value being?). After establishing a foundation of the Girl Who Could, I
inquired about the effects and tactics of Depression. As we talked about
Depression's effects, they became visible in the meeting. Fran became
more reserved and tentative, and her presence shrank in the room. The
second paragraph of the letter acknowledges the difficulty of talking
about Depression and attempts to reanchor that part of the conversation
in her experience of the Girl Who Could. The second paragraph ends
with meaning questions and future possibility questions that again
attempt to support a further elaboration of new possibilities. The final
paragraph honors Fran's ability to stay connected to the Girl Who Could

as she talked about Depression's influence. The word "remember" came from Fran, who talked about gathering a group of people around her to "help her remember the Girl Who Could as a foundation for holding Depression at bay."

In this way, letters can be used to juxtapose the influence of problems on clients with clients' influence on problems in an attempt to support the development of alternative experiences of self. It is helpful to use language that highlights client agency in its influence on problems. For example, the third paragraph of this letter begins with an expression of my appreciation for Fran's ability to reconnect with the Girl Who Could after talking about Depression. This language emphasizes Fran's participation in reconnecting with this alternative identity. As Michael White (1993) has described, a sense of agency "is derived from the experience of escaping 'passengerhood' in life and from the sense of being able to play an active role in the shaping of one's own life" (p. 53). The language we use in letters can actively support this process.

We can include questions to inquire about clients' preferences, the meaning of developing alternative stories, and future possibilities that may develop from these new directions. These questions invite reflection as the letter is read and further extend the original conversation from the session. By soliciting clients' thoughts through questions, their inclusion shifts the focus of the letter from instructive interaction (e.g., "Here is what happened in the meeting.") to invitational interaction (e.g., "What do you think about these things you said in the meeting?"). In the letters, these questions are not designed to yield particular answers but to generate experience. Their usefulness lies in the process of considering answers to them.

The closing of the letter "In appreciation of the Girl Who Could" reflects a deliberate choice of words. Often therapeutic letters have been signed in ways that support solidarity against a problem (e.g., Anti-anorexically yours or Yours in anti-depression). In line with the emphasis on a future-oriented direction (discussed in Chapter 4) and a stance that is pro-person rather than anti-problem (discussed in Chapter 5), my preference is to sign letters in support of preferred futures rather than in opposition to oppressive problems (e.g., In appreciation of the Girl Who Could, rather than Yours in anti-depression). I think this helps to keep clients and us anchored in what we are moving toward rather than that from which we are moving away. As discussed, a future-oriented direction keeps our "eye on the prize" and maintains a sense of forward momentum.

This letter had a profound effect on Fran. She carried it with her and read it multiple times. In her words,

"The letter reinforced for me that I know what I'm doing. It reinforces the self-worth that I can see and helps me realize it's not just imagined. It's not just me and my opinion, but there's evidence that the painting is as good as I think it is. You know artists are their own worst critics."

This response led into the discussion (described in Chapter 6) about Fran as a work of art, examining what she particularly valued about that work of art. In this way, therapeutic letters both solidify previous sessions and provide openings to continue elaborating alternative stories.

In addition to writing letters that summarize a particular session, we can also write letters that cover multiple sessions or the entire course of therapy. This second letter to Fran was written several weeks after our last session and reflects a summary of our work together. The letter was based on a termination interview format I often use to mark endings with clients. The format for this interview is based on work by Epston and White (1995) and is discussed in detail in the next section.

Dear Fran,

It's been a little while since we last met. I remember that you found the last letter summarizing one of our sessions helpful and thought I would write you a second. As I think back on our work together, I'm particularly struck by the success you had in putting Depression back in its place. You said that "Depression will always be there, it's a part of my life." However, you also told me that you had been able to shrink Depression's hold on you from an 8 or 9 down to a 1. Does that seem like an accomplishment to you? You had commented that the first letter "reinforced for me what I know about myself. It's not just me and my opinion, but evidence that the painting is as good as I think it is." My purpose in writing this letter now is to again reinforce for you what you know about yourself.

When I asked what you particularly valued about the piece of art that is you, you replied "It's mine. I'm an original and not a carbon copy of anyone else." We talked about others who also appreciate this work of art that is you and you mentioned a very long list of friends including Fred, Tom, Clarence, Jake, Paul, Keith, Peter, Bob, Wayne and others that I may have missed as I was trying to write them all down. You described a bit of what Fred's review of this piece of art that is you might have included and you used words like "funny, a good sense of humor, considerate, kind, smart and sharing things in common." If we were to think about you as a piece of art, what does it say to you that you would receive so many fine reviews? Is this information that Depression would want you to know about yourself? As you remember this information, what happens to the strength of Depression?

How has your containment of Depression gone? Has it made attempts to "insert itself piece by piece, thought by thought into your life again?" When we talked before about how you had shrunk its influence from an 8 or 9 to a 1, you mentioned a number of creative strategies. Do you remember them? I was particularly struck by your "promising yourself a future to look forward to." I think that's a wonderful phrase because in my work I often see Depression steal away people's sense of a future. What helps you to hang on to a future to look forward to?

I asked you what advice you would give to other persons struggling against Depression and thought you might find some of it useful to hear back. You included ideas such as: getting a hobby, doing physical activity such as dancing, going out with friends, even when you don't feel like it, carrying around pictures with pleasant memories and remembering what the pictures represent, getting a circle of friends to use as supports, never forgetting to eat, even when you're not hungry, and being active which breaks the hold of Depression. I have shared pieces of those ideas with other people who consult me and they've found it helpful. I hope that having an opportunity to hear your advice to others may be useful to you as well.

I am writing this as I'm preparing to go off to a family therapy conference (perhaps they are therapists' versions of your science fiction conferences). I will take with me the image of your courage to be an original. I wish you luck in continuing to be an original and continuing to appreciate the work of art that is you. If I can be of help in the future, please feel free to call me.

In appreciation of an original,

Bill Madsen

Again, this letter largely follows the flow of the conversation from our last session. Meaning and preference questions are included to further develop new experiences of self. The last two paragraphs grow out of a series of questions I had asked Fran about what advice she would offer to other people struggling against the effects of Depression and to therapists seeking to help people in that endeavor. This question captures her wisdom and expertise about building a life in the face of Depression. It elicits information that may be very useful for other clients and therapists but also has beneficial effects for Fran. It offers her an opportunity to reflect on her own advice (which she agreed was good advice). Questions soliciting her advice for others also shift her position in our relationship from a client to a consultant. Questions of this sort have been referred to as "consulting your consultant questions" (Epston, White, & "Ben," 1995). Helping clients to shift their position from a client receiving help to a consultant offering help can promote agency, be very empowering, and solidify new identities.

Another example of this shift in position comes from the consultation interview with the Family with a Solid Frame. At the end of the session in an attempt to help solidify the tentative beginnings of a new story, I said the following to them:

> "We have a number of people on our team here who provide training and consultation to mental health and social service workers. I think that you folks have a lot to teach mental health professionals about doing this work. I think you can serve as an inspiration for mental health professionals because it's very easy in this line of work to get focused on the peeling wallpaper and the yucky kitchen floors, to focus on what's wrong with families. Despite that, throughout all of your struggles, you have really managed to hang onto the knowledge that your foundation is solid. The story of how you've done that could be useful to helpers who are working with other families to do that. I'd like to ask if you would give us permission to use the videotape of this meeting as a training tape to help mental health workers learn from you about how to help families draw on their strengths and be about the business of supporting families rather than criticizing them."

When I asked for their reaction to this request, the 14-year-old boy looked shocked. He couldn't believe someone would be asking his family to teach professionals about helping families. However, as his parents both agreed that they would be glad to have others watch the tape if it would be helpful, Joe sat up in his chair and began to look particularly proud. His mother then went on to offer a number of incisive and helpful recommendations for helpers in working with families.

> "Well, we've been through a lot. Joe's home and things are gonna get better, but the things that we've been through and the things that people have said, it makes me believe that no wonder some of these families are failing because people come in with negative attitudes. They don't convey that this is a good family. They come in and say, 'You're doing this wrong and you're doing that wrong.' Sometimes if they focused on families doing something positive, it would be more helpful."

As she offered this advice, she looked stronger and more rooted in the family's solid frame. The invitation to share their wisdom had a powerful effect on her sense of self. Parenthetically, a number of helpers who have viewed this tape have found her comments very helpful. Honoring the wisdom and expertise that develops in families' attempts to move away from problematic stories and into alternative stories is a powerful way of solidifying those new stories.

The value of letters has been informally researched by David Epston and Michael White in which they asked clients how many sessions of therapy a letter was worth and what percentage of positive outcome from therapy could be attributed to the letters they received. Clients reported that a therapeutic letter was worth four to five sessions of therapy and attributed 40% to 90% of positive outcome to the letters (Freeman et al., 1997). In a similar study of 40 clients, David Nylund and John Thomas (1994) found that clients in an HMO (health maintenance organization) clinic rated therapeutic letters as being worth an average of 3.2 sessions with 52.8% of the positive outcome attributable to the letters alone. These figures suggest that letters have enormous therapeutic potential and can significantly enhance therapy.[2] Though therapeutic letters hold the promise of supercharging therapy, many clinicians under the pressure of inordinately high productivity demands complain that they could not begin to find the time to produce such letters. Given the potential for therapeutic letters to increase the efficacy and cost-effectiveness of therapy, it becomes important for funders (such as HMOs and state agencies) to become more informed about creative applications such as this and begin to incorporate it as a reimbursable activity. Articles such as Nylund and Thomas's (1994) on the economics of narrative therapy need to be seen by more than just clinicians.

At the same time, we can use required paperwork in a similar fashion. Most clinicians in agencies have to complete progress notes on each session. These notes could easily be altered into a format similar to the letters above and then shared with clients. Conceivably, the last 10 minutes of a session could be devoted to coconstructing a note that documents the session which could then be copied and given to a client to take home. Given the therapeutic efficacy that clients attach to letters, such an allocation of time would certainly be worth everyone's while. In addition, many clinicians are required to complete quarterly updates that summarize the work every 3 months. These reports, if handled in a manner similar to these letters, could be opportunities to have our paperwork actually support the work we do rather than be experienced as administrative nonsense that interferes with "the real work." Of course, it requires a shift in how we handle both what we write and the process through which we write it. This shift can be initially threatening to clinicians, but many who attempt it report significant changes in their work as well as their experience of report writing.

USING TERMINATION INTERVIEWS
TO SOLIDIFY NEW STORIES

The process of termination can also be used to solidify the development of alternative stories. However, it requires a shift in how we think about termination. Traditionally, our conceptualization of termination has been organized around a metaphor of loss in which the ending of therapy is a painful process that evokes other unresolved losses. Within this metaphor, the understanding of termination promotes attention to the client's grieving of the loss of the relationship and encourages the therapist to attend to the ways in which the client's handling of this loss is influenced by other unresolved losses. This metaphor runs the risk of emphasizing the therapeutic relationship over other influences in a client's life. Within this metaphor, the loss of this relationship has a powerful effect on clients. Although I do not wish to underestimate the importance of our presence in people's lives and acknowledge that there are often elements of loss in termination, it is important to acknowledge the limitations and potentially inadvertent negative effects encouraged by this metaphor. This metaphor supports an individualistic and private conception of self. It encourages a sense that the therapeutic relationship may be more important than other relationships. And, as a result, it may inadvertently constrain people from more actively drawing on their natural communities. These combined effects run the risk of deepening isolation and cutting people off from other relationships, thus accentuating a sense of loss.

Epston and White (1995) have proposed that termination could also be organized around a rite-of-passage metaphor. Within this metaphor, termination could be viewed as a ritual to celebrate and consolidate the development of new identities. Termination then becomes less about an ending with a focus on looking back and more about a transition with a focus on the future as well as a review of previous work. Epston and White (1995) have proposed a series of questions that can be posed to a client or family in a special meeting to elicit and document the changes made and the knowledges gained in the process of therapy. I have adapted these questions into a broader format that has been used in a number of different contexts. A termination interview consists of a specific interview that reviews the work a client or family has done and the progress made in therapy. The interview can be seen as a documentation of their journey through a migration of identity and can be used to solidify the integration of new identities. A termination interview can be organized around five broad areas of questions:

- Reviewing-the-journey questions
- Reauthoring questions

- Circulation questions
- Relapse prevention questions
- Sharing-client-wisdom questions[3]

A termination interview begins with an orientation to discover whether the client or family would be interested in taking some time to review the work they have done in the interest of better understanding and solidifying that work. The proposal for this venture can also be made ahead of time and discussed with a family. In my experience, clients and families are usually very interested in such a review. The second letter to Fran, the Girl Who Could, followed a termination interview such as this and is one example of the outcome of such a process. In the termination interview, I asked a number of questions to review her journey toward "keeping Depression in its place" and examined how she accomplished that shift (reauthoring questions). I asked who would most appreciate her work in containing Depression, catalogued their possible responses, and examined the impact of those possible responses on Fran (circulation questions). We anticipated how Depression might attempt to (in her words) "insert itself piece by piece, thought by thought into her life" again and revisited what from her initial strategies for containing it might prove useful in the future (relapse prevention questions). Finally, we concluded with what advice she might give to other persons who struggle with the effects of Depression (sharing-client-wisdom questions). The second letter, shown earlier, summarized her responses to these types of questions. The remainder of this section describes a format for termination interviews by outlining examples of questions that can be asked within each area and briefly examining the ways in which the interview was used with Fran, the Girl Who Could. The next section then examines this process in more depth using the example of a couple struggling with emotionally violent fights.

Reviewing-the-Journey Questions

Questions in this area attempt to establish a foundation for examining a client's journey in developing a different relationship with a particular problem. Questions might include the following:

- What were you most concerned about at the beginning of our work together?
- What problems were you struggling with?
- How much influence did they have over you? (on a scale of 1–10)
- How much influence would you say they have over you now? (on a scale of 1–10)
- When you compare the problems' influence at the beginning of our work together and now, what do you notice?

The first two questions are different ways of acquiring similar information. The second two questions (which are scaling questions) allow a
comparison of where clients were at the beginning of our work together
and where they are at the conclusion. In the interview with Fran, she
labeled Depression's hold on her as an 8 or 9 at the beginning and a 1
when we did the termination interview. The process of attaching numbers
to these points in time concretizes the magnitude of the shift and provides
a basis from which to inquire about clients' reactions to that shift. We
don't need to be wedded to numbers as a way to mark the transition, the
point is to highlight the significance of the shift in some way. In Fran's situation, she described the shift from 8 or 9 to 1 as very significant and we
were able to then move easily into an examination of how she made that
shift in a way that highlighted her agency in the process. My inquiry into
her reaction to that shift kept our conversation anchored in a "learning
with" process in which Fran and I were sorting this out together, rather
than a "teaching to" process in which I was pointing out the significance
of the shift to her. Keeping the conversation anchored in a "learning
with" process both increases the chance that we are working at the same
pace in the interview and intensifies the meaning of the process. It is
much more valuable for clients to be telling us that changes in their lives
are significant than for us to be trying to convince them.

In situations in which clients report very little change, we can stay
focused on the *direction* rather than the *magnitude* of change. Even if the
change is from a 9 to an 8, we can inquire about how clients have begun
to move their life in that direction and what they think about their movement in that direction. And, in situations in which clients report no
change or the problem getting stronger, we can use that response as a
foundation for an examination of their coping in the face of the problem's
strength. In such an examination, it is important to allow space to
acknowledge potential discouragement. This is not a process of putting a
positive spin on a bad situation but, rather, being open to elements of
coping and resilience amidst pain and suffering.

Reauthoring Questions

From the foundation established by reviewing-the-journey questions,
there is a natural segue into reauthoring questions such as the following:

- What steps did you take to bring about that change in the problem's influence over you?
- How did you do that?
- What personal and relationship qualities did you draw on to do
  that?

- What about your history would help me understand the development of those qualities?
- What do these achievements reflect about your life and relationships that is important for you to know about yourself?
- Who in your past life would be the least surprised to hear you had accomplished this?
- What have they observed about you that would support their belief in you?
- What would you conclude about someone who was able to accomplish this?
- What do these achievements tell you about the person you're becoming?
- With this new sense of yourself as a foundation, what changes will follow next?

These questions are familiar as story development questions and meaning questions across time, space, and perspectives, which were discussed in the last chapter. Going through these kinds of questions at the end of therapy offers a way to review the development of alternative stories and new relationships to problems. The questions are constructed to highlight clients' agency and actively amplify their participation in bringing about life changes. Clients are invited to reflect on the changes in their lives as well as their role in bringing about those changes. Many clients have described this reflective process as validating and promoting of self-appreciation. In the process, the enactment of alternative stories is further supported. In Fran's situation, the termination interview helped to solidify her emerging story about herself as the Girl Who Could by retracing the development of that alternative story.

Circulation Questions

The development of an audience that can witness and honor changes that clients have made strongly supports the solidification of those changes. Circulation questions help to identify and recruit such an audience. The following examples represent some questions to accomplish that:

- Now that you've accomplished these changes, who else should know about it?
- What difference do you think it would make in their attitude toward you if they had this news?
- Would it be better to go along with people's old ideas about you or catch them up on these new developments?

- What would be the impact of those people hearing about these developments?
- What would be the best way of letting them know about these accomplishments?

In our work together, Fran had developed a metaphor of her life as a work of art. She talked about her tendency to focus on the flaws in that work of art and lose sight of all that she valued. She thought that Depression was very good at using that tendency to reassert its influence over her. We talked about how art critics write reviews of art work and in the spirit of circulation questions, I asked her the following:

BILL: If you were to gather together art critics who know and appreciate this work of art that is you and they were to write a series of honest but friendly reviews of that art, what would they have to say?

FRAN: Well, I don't know any art critics, but I'll tell you what my friends would say.

From here, Fran went into a long list of different friends and what they particularly appreciated about her. As she went through the review that each would offer, I asked her opinion about that review. We then moved into talking about how she could let her friends know about this work of art that was Fran and have an opportunity to actually get the reviews she anticipated from them.

Relapse Prevention Questions

The problems and difficulties in people's lives can often make reappearances. The questions in this area of a termination interview can be used to anticipate such possible reappearances and develop contingency plans. The following are examples of questions to help in this process:

- If this problem were to attempt a resurgence, how would you first notice that?
- What might give you an indication that this problem was coming back?
- What might be the first sign of that indication? (continue to trace back)
- What have you learned about managing this problem in the past?
- What of that knowledge could you bring to addressing its attempted comeback?

While this category of questions is referred to as relapse prevention questions, it is more useful to think of these questions as questions about problem resurgence rather than personal relapse. Viewing the reemergence of difficulties as indicators of a problem's strength, rather than as evidence of a personal failing, better positions therapists as allies in helping clients address reemerging problems.

Questions of these sorts help to further solidify the wisdom and strategies that clients have developed in dealing with problems. If problems at a later date begin to reappear, clients are better positioned to see those emerging problems as things they can and have effectively managed in the past rather than as the beginning of an end to their new life. Therapists can remain available as consultants to clients to remind them of their expertise and the contingency plan they have developed. In the face of reemerging problems, it is more effective to remind clients of the foundation they've developed and the plan they've created than to attempt to develop a new plan amidst the onslaught of problems.

I used to work on a family crisis team and we attempted to shift our work with families who frequently contacted us from crisis intervention to crisis management. That shift worked best when we were able to develop early warning signs to anticipate crises with families and collaboratively develop contingency plans for dealing with those crises. In those situations, we were then positioned as consultants who reminded families of their plans for managing anticipated crises rather than as intervenors who became responsible for handling crises. In addition, the simple fact of having a contingency plan in place often provided enough reassurance for particular clients that they did not need to call us.

Likewise, the development of a contingency plan in termination interviews supports families in dealing with their worry or anxiety about the possible reemergence of problems. It is useful to help families develop plans that draw on their own natural networks. The goal in relapse prevention questions is not to anticipate our reinvolvement with families, but rather to help them function better on their own in the future. In this way, the existence of an early warning system and contingency plan solidifies existing knowledge and provides a stronger anchor should problems reemerge.

Sharing-Client-Wisdom Questions

As described before in the second letter to Fran and the videotape request with the Family with a Solid Frame, sharing-client-wisdom questions draw from what clients have learned about dealing with particular problems to solicit their advice for other people struggling against the effects of those problems as well as for therapists trying to help others in the process. Some examples of such questions would include the following:

- I periodically meet with other families struggling with the same type of problem you described. From what you now know, what advice would you suggest I might give to them?
- If they were to ask you about your success against this problem, what would you say to them?
- Much of what we learn about helping families comes from our work with families. Based on what you've learned in your accomplishments, what suggestions would you have for professionals in seeking to help families standing against this problem?

These questions have many beneficial effects. They elicit ideas that can be useful for the clients answering them. They bring forth wisdom and expertise that can prove useful for other clients and therapists. They have an empowering effect on clients and set a foundation for a more mutual and emotionally powerful ending. In the example with Fran, she offered some of the following advice for other persons struggling against the effects of Depression:

- Get a hobby or something, but stay active because action breaks the hold of Depression.
- Engage in regular physical activity especially if you don't want to and never forget to eat, even if you're not hungry.
- Get a circle of friends that you can use as a support. Find friends to talk with who will encourage you for yourself rather than try to get you to go along with others.
- Get pictures of pleasant memories and remember what those pictures represent and who you are in them.

These are useful ideas for persons struggling with Depression. However, the process of eliciting them was also important for Fran. As she spoke about these ideas, she reflected that they would be important advice for her to follow also. Many of these ideas could be offered to clients by friends or helpers (e.g., by family members or in a psychoeducational group for depression). However, they are much more meaningful and powerful when they are generated by clients rather than given to clients.

Fran also had a number of useful ideas for therapists supporting clients in their struggles with Depression. Among them were the following:

- Listen carefully but ask lots of questions so that clients don't feel like they're alone with Depression.
- Help clients come up with their own metaphors. Visualizing the idea of "islands of sanctuary in a sea of depression" gave me something to hold onto.
- Writing letters to clients is helpful. It lets clients know you're thinking about them and gives us something to hold onto when we run into problems.
- Believing in my courage to deal with Depression was probably the most helpful. I was scared of it and you weren't. Your belief in my courage gave me more courage.

When I have solicited advice such as this from clients, I have invariably found it interesting, useful, and moving. It has enriched my practice and for that I am grateful. However, given my ethical responsibilities for client welfare in my role as a therapist, I am particularly interested in the effects of this process on clients. Clients have been pleased (and at times surprised) to be asked about their thoughts and have responded eagerly. The process of consulting them shifts their status from a recipient of services to a more equal participant in the therapeutic relationship. It legitimizes and honors their knowledge and expertise and breaks down the barriers between professionals and clients. It decreases a "less than" experience of self for clients and invites increased participation in both therapy and their lives. Questions that solicit client expertise in these ways contribute to empowering processes (defined in Chapter 1 as "ways of thinking and acting as therapists that acknowledge, support and amplify clients' participation and influence in developing the lives they prefer") and enhance our work with clients.

This interview format can be used beyond termination rituals. For example, a couple that I saw was unsure whether to continue or take a break from therapy. As I asked them a number of questions from this format to review the status of our work together, they decided that they had made some progress in their relationship, hit a tough spot, and were unsure how to continue. The interview shifted our focus in therapy and they decided to continue. The format is also useful at other points of transition. For example, I met with a family with an adolescent girl who was returning home from a residential program. Rather than begin with an inquiry into why she had left home and gone into a residential program, I began with a focus on the family goal of making reunification work. Following the format outlined previously, I elicited and documented what changes they had made during the residential placement, what wisdom and capacities they had developed in that time, how they had accomplished those changes, who should now know about these changes, and what advice they would have for other families who were reuniting after a residential placement. They were particularly taken by the questions about their advice for others. As they responded to those questions, they reflected on the progress they had all made and the things they had learned. In this way, we began our work together anchored in their knowledge and expertise which was a much better foundation from which to examine their doubts and fears about living together again.

Many clients and families have remarked on the power of these types of interviews. Their significance can be amplified when they are marked through a document or symbol that concretizes them. For example, I often videotape such interviews (especially with children) and give clients the videotape. Letters such as the one sent to Fran can also be used to document the interview. We can also develop symbols or rites-of-passage rituals with clients that extend the interview. For example, the couple who recommitted to therapy rewrote their wedding vows to mark a new chapter in their relationship. The family whose daughter returned from residential placement sponsored a welcome-home party, inviting friends and family to mark not just her termination from the program but the beginning of a new life at home. At this party, her father, normally a shy and reserved man, gave a speech reflecting on their changes and honoring her return. This shift to reunion parties as a way to mark the transition out of residential programs has been elegantly developed and described by Nichols and Jacques (1995). We can also mark interviews such as these through daily institutional requirements such as termination summaries. The next section examines the use of termination summaries in more depth.

USING TERMINATION SUMMARIES
TO DOCUMENT NEW STORIES

In Fran's situation, a termination interview was captured in a final letter that was sent to her. One risk of encouraging such a project is the development of clinical practices whose effectiveness resides on the backs of overburdened clinicians. Clinical letters and documents that highlight shifts in identity are very effective and I would strongly encourage their use. However, without institutional accommodations that support clinicians in expanding their clinical activities (e.g., providing reimbursement for clinical letters), they will not be adapted on a widespread basis in the current climate. Again, it is important that funders begin to think "out of the box" and broaden their vision of how services are funded and hence delivered. One initial step toward integrating the documentation of termination interviews into current practices would be to modify existing paperwork requirements. Clinicians who work in community agencies are routinely required to write termination summaries. Traditionally, licensing agencies require that termination summaries contain the following required information:

- Presenting Problem and Diagnosis
- Treatment Goal and Plan
- Client Condition and Level of Functioning at Termination
- Reasons for Termination
- Follow-Up Recommendations

The format for termination interviews can be modified in ways that would support a documentation of the information from a termination interview. Based on the termination interview outline previously described, we could coauthor termination summaries with clients that are organized in the following fashion:

Initial Concerns
- Client/family's initial concern
- Level of concern (1–10)
- Effects of problem(s) on family members

Therapy Goals and Plan
- Agreed-upon focus of therapy
- Therapy plan (Who did what to address that focus)

Course of Therapy
- Current level of concern (1–10)
- Comparison of initial and current level of concern
- Client/family contribution to changes

Status at Termination
- Rationale for termination
- Early warning signs of possible problem resurgence
- Client/family plan to solidify progress and address possible problem resurgence

Follow-Up Recommendations
- Family/therapist recommendations for family
- Family recommendations for other families and therapists working on similar problems

To examine the ways in which a collaborative termination summary and a termination interview can be used to solidify the development of alternative stories, I'll offer an extended example with a couple whose relationship was taken over by violent fights.

FROM UNFAIR FIGHTING
TO LOVING FRIENDSHIP

After a brief description of the couple and our work together, I'll highlight the ways in which a termination interview and termination summary were used to solidify changes in the couple's life together. Manny (age 32) and Ellen (age 31) were a Latino couple with two children Raquel (age 11) and Juan (age 9). They were referred for couples counseling by Juan's pediatrician after Juan described his fear of their verbal fights in a checkup examination. Manny had dark complexion, spoke with a thick accent, and worked in an auto parts store. Ellen sold real estate and looked, dressed, and acted much more like an Anglo. They often had verbal fights over their children's education and future. Ellen wanted them to go to private school and get out of the neighborhood, while Manny saw that as economically unrealistic and wished Ellen had more pride in their culture. In their fights, Ellen would continually berate and criticize Manny for his lack of drive and ambition which he experienced as "being attacked by a whole nest of wasps buzzing around and stinging me until I finally swell up and explode." His explosions would result in brutal verbal assaults on her in which he would lash out with expletive-filled, disparaging phrases that would shock Ellen into stunned silence. She would withdraw into fear and hurt and not talk to Manny for several days. Her resentments would grow and after a few days, as she put it, "they would begin to leak out in really nasty little ways because I could never say them to him directly." Although their fights never became physical, Ellen was scared by them. Both Ellen and Manny were very concerned about the effects of the verbal fighting on their relationship and on the children. They cared deeply for each other and, although suspicious about therapy, were willing to accept the referral from the physician.

Our work together began with eliciting a picture of what initially drew them to each other and what kind of relationship and family they wanted to have together. They talked about their love for each other and the importance of the times in their lives when they were "close friends." We began to talk about "loving friendship" as a goal they wanted to move toward and examined the effects of Fighting (as they called it) on that Loving Friendship. Asking whether they were upset by the fact that they fought or the way in which they fought, I drew a distinction between Fighting that is anchored in loving friendship and Fighting that is anchored in violence.[4] I examined the pattern in which violence was embedded and their respective, though certainly not equal, contributions to that pattern (e.g., Manny's explosions and Ellen's stinging). As Goldner (1998) has emphasized, "to argue that partners mutually participate in an interactional process does not mean they are mutually responsible for it" (p. 266). There were distinct power differences between Ellen and Manny. While Ellen's "stinging" annoyed Manny, his "explosions" intimidated her. In talking about their different reactions, Manny reluctantly acknowledged that his verbal assaults on Ellen were of a qualitatively different nature than her berating criticisms.

I interviewed each in the presence of the other about the effects of their respective actions (a process that began with Manny hearing about Ellen's experience). As each was invited to step into the other's experience, they developed more empathy for each other and with practice began to be able to listen to each other better. I asked what pulled them away from Loving Friendship and into "exploding" and "stinging" and which they preferred. We moved back and forth between examining a life and potential future anchored in Violent Fights and their preferred life and future anchored in Loving Friendship. We also examined the broader cultural support for "exploding" and "stinging." As Colorado, Montgomery, and Tovar (1998) have pointed out, violence in Latino homes is contextualized by the violence Latino people experience from the North American dominant culture through pejorative messages from the privileged toward the poor, from citizens toward immigrants, and from white persons toward persons of color. We examined the humiliation that Manny and Ellen were each subjected to through daily experiences of racism. For example, Manny described experiences of people mocking his accent and thinking he was stupid because of his faltering English. He reflected on his original dream to make a better life in the United States and his shame that he hadn't been able to accomplish that. He described feeling out of control in his life and losing it when he got teased at the auto parts store for not being able to keep his "little woman" in line. Placing Manny's explosions in a broader cultural context of racism and internalized gender expectations does not excuse the explosions but helps us develop a fuller understanding of them so that our work against violence can be more effective.

Ellen's experiences of racism also affected their relationship. For example, she described losing a real estate deal after she introduced herself with her last name and explained her decision to try to pass as an Anglo in order to keep her job. When we examined Ellen's stinging attacks on Manny's "lack of drive and ambition" in the context of her response to discrimination and cultural expectations of upward mobility, it became less personalized and lost much of its sting for Manny.

Although Manny and Ellen still fought over schools and the neighborhood, the personal intensity of the fights eased considerably.

In juxtaposing lives of Violent Fighting and Loving Friendship, I also inquired about the cultural supports for Loving Friendship and learned about their values of respect and family that came from their families of origin and their culture. Manny and Ellen were committed to their children and building a home that bred respect. Over the course of our work together, Manny and Ellen began to draw on their values of respect and family to anchor their lives more and more in Loving Friendship. Our work together was interrupted after 5 months when Manny lost his job and their health insurance. Though I offered to continue with them at a significantly reduced fee, they were both very proud and wanted to stop rather than take a "handout." After a prolonged discussion about this, I respected their wishes and let them know I would be available if I could be of assistance to them in the future. I discussed with them the idea of a termination interview as a way to review our work together, solidify the changes they had made, and anticipate potential difficulties in the future. With this description as context, I'll move into a discussion of the termination interview and then offer the termination summary that flowed out of it.

The Termination Interview

In the interview, Manny and Ellen said they were initially most concerned about Unfair Fighting and the effect it had on their relationship and their children. They agreed that Unfair Fighting was taking up 90% of their life together at the beginning of counseling. At the point of the termination interview, Manny labeled it 30% and Ellen suggested it was more like 40–50%. When asked if they saw the shift from 90% to 40–50% as significant, they both strongly agreed. In this question, it is crucial to give priority to the determination of the person who is most affected by the problem, which in this case was Ellen as she was more affected by Manny's explosions in their relationship. Ellen described the shift as follows:

> "Huge. Before it was out of control and if we hadn't made this shift, our relationship would be over. It's not like we're completely out of the woods yet. We still have some big fights, but the fights are much different now. I'm not afraid of his anger and I don't feel emotionally abused by him."

The description of this shift provides a foundation from which to elicit a story of how the couple made this "huge" shift.

While acknowledging that they were still working on their relationship, I asked how they had made "huge" progress in only 5 months. Manny replied that he had begun to listen more to Ellen.

MANNY: When she used to criticize me all the time, I felt it just wasn't fair. Here I was working my ass off for her and my family and all I'd hear from her was how it wasn't enough. That was just really unfair, and we talked about there was just so much unfairness all around me and all throughout my life and I just couldn't take it. Then, as I listened to her talk about how the things I said beat her down and devastated her, I thought that's not fair either and I couldn't believe I was doing the same thing that upset me so. I felt horrible about that.

BILL: It sounds like hearing that from Ellen was really important for you. You said that it was hard to hear and I respect your ability to meet that head on and take it in. How were you able to do that? What does it tell you about yourself that you were able to do that?

MANNY: Oh, I don't know. She was right about what she was saying.

BILL: Ellen, what does it tell you about Manny that he was able to set aside his discomfort and really listen to what you were saying even through it was hard stuff?

ELLEN: Well, one part of me feels like he should listen because I've been trying to tell it to him for so long and it's about time. But another part feels like finally he's being a man. I don't mean like his buddies at the auto parts store who think they're so big because they can boss their women around. I mean like a real man who can stand for something.

BILL: And what does it tell you that he stands for?

ELLEN: That respect that we talked about.

From there we moved into a discussion of respect and family as two powerful values for each of them and how they were committed to building a family of respect even though their family got little respect out in the world. I asked Manny about Ellen's contribution to a relationship anchored in Loving Friendship and he described her persistence and her unwillingness to quit. She agreed she was stubborn and anchored her stubborness in a faith that things could be better. She offered a moving description of the way in which her spirituality kept her going.

I then asked about relationship qualities that helped them to anchor their life in Loving Friendship and they each talked about their sense of humor and ferocious pride. Ellen described Manny's pride for his culture (which had begun emerging more in the time we were meeting) and the effects for her of seeing his commitment to staying in the neighborhood as pride rather than laziness. Likewise, Manny developed more appreciation for the life Ellen wanted for their children and began to hear her comments about the neighborhood as concerns for their children rather than criticisms of him.

As I asked who should hear about these changes, both Manny and Ellen identified their mothers as people who would most appreciate their changes. Manny's deceased father had been quite abusive of both Manny and his mother, and Manny often was in a position of comforting his mother. She used to say to him, "Wives stick by their husbands no matter what. When you marry, treat your wife right because she will be the only one that you can always count on." Ellen, who was close with Manny's mother, thought his mother would be thrilled to hear about the husband Manny was becoming. Ellen also thought her mother should hear about the changes in their relationship. Ellen's mother had disapproved of their relationship and thought Manny was a loser. She had not come to their wedding which was a cruel blow for Ellen. When Ellen and Manny began to have problems, Ellen found herself wondering whether her mother was right and now felt it was important to catch her mother up on those changes. Ellen also talked about the importance of letting her best friend know. As she put it, "I've spent so much time complaining to her about Manny and it's only fair that she hear the other side."

This interview was done some time ago. Today, I would put much more emphasis on attempting to shift the conversation I was having with Manny and Ellen from a private conversation to a more public conversation. I would find it useful to involve their mothers and others in their community and place more emphasis on finding ways to have their journey honored in their community. One recent example of a community approach to violence in Latino families is reflected in the work of the Multicultural Narrative Team in Saratoga California (Colorado et al., 1998).

In an attempt to anticipate ways in which Unfair Fighting might begin to take up more space in their relationship, I asked Manny and Ellen to reflect on what might pull them away from a relationship anchored in Loving Friendship. Ellen observed that she would notice herself beginning to hang onto her resentments and not sharing them with Manny. We examined how that might begin to occur and what they both had learned about building an atmosphere in which Ellen would not be silenced. Ellen stated that she would need to remind herself that she had to be more straightforward with Manny for the sake of their relationship and family. Manny described the look Ellen got on her face when things were wrong and observed that he needed to make sure she knew he was listening to her. We discussed whether it would be hard to encourage her to express concerns that might feel like personal criticisms. Manny acknowledged that it would but maintained that he'd rather hear about them before they became big deals. We also examined what might pull Manny away from Loving Friendship and he admitted that when Ellen raised concerns with him, he sometimes heard the voice of his buddies at the auto parts store teasing him about being such a "wimp" around his wife. He acknowledged that those voices could pull him back into trying to assert his "authority" over Ellen and they both agreed the results would be disastrous. As he reflected on what had helped him move toward more Loving Friendship in the first place, he decided to put a picture of his mother in their bedroom as a reminder of the way his father had treated her and his deep desire to be different from that. Ellen decided she wanted to use her best friend as a sounding board to make sure she was not either holding onto resentments or minimizing the effects of Manny's outbursts on her.

I raised my concern about how Manny's unemployment might affect their relationship and we discussed Manny's plans for the future. I offered to also be available by phone to remind them of the foundation they had developed if problems began to creep back into their relationship. As they reiterated that foundation to me, Manny remarked that "I know we're on the same side, she's the one I want to spend my life with and sometimes I get scared that she's disgusted with me and she's ready to leave. When I remind myself that she wants to be with me, I can deal with that fear." Ellen added, "I have to remember that he knows the effects that his explosions had on me. He's not clueless. He may get angry from time to time, but I have faith that he's moving away from that crap. Knowing we're headed in a different direction gives me faith to deal with it." It's interesting that this shared vision of the future they are headed in provides comfort in getting through hard times. In this way, reanchoring clients in their own wisdom and resourcefulness helps shift their relationship to anticipated difficulties down the line.

When I asked them about their recommendations for other couples who might be working to reclaim their relationships from Fighting, they built on each others' ideas in a way that exemplified a Loving Friendship. The process invited the enactment of their newly developing couple identity. Their suggestions for other couples were very interesting and quite sophisticated and are outlined in the termination section that follows.

Termination Summary

Initial Concerns

Manny and Ellen sought counseling for help with "Unfair Fighting." While Unfair Fighting erupted over a number of different issues, the couple described the following fairly consistent pattern: Ellen would have concerns that she had trouble articulating and Manny had trouble hearing. As these concerns grew, Ellen would begin criticizing Manny in ways that he perceived as "stinging." Manny would not respond to her criticisms until he became infuriated and then verbally "explode." His strong explosions would shock Ellen into stunned silence. As her resentments began to build again and she felt silenced and unable to talk with Manny the pattern would repeat itself again. Manny and Ellen were both very concerned about the strength of Unfair Fighting and agreed it had taken up 90% of their relationship. Even though Unfair Fighting had never become physical, it took a significant toll on both Manny and Ellen who felt very cut off from each other and on the children who were quite fearful when it occurred. The couple sought counseling to address these concerns.

Therapy Goals and Plan

In reflecting on the foundation for their relationship, Manny and Ellen agreed that they loved each other and valued the times when they were close friends. The agreed-upon focus of therapy was to help them better anchor their relationship in Loving Friendship by reconnecting to the foundation they developed over the years and examining the forces and pressures that pulled them away from relating to each other in ways that reflect Loving Friendship. We met every other week for 5 months to accomplish this.

Course of Therapy

Our work in counseling together compared and contrasted their prior relationship overtaken by Unfair Fighting and their developing relationship anchored in Loving Friendship. We explored gendered beliefs and the couple's experiences of cultural violence as Latino people as a context for the violence in Unfair Fighting. The couple reported that considering the broader context helped to depersonalize the fighting between them and shift their perspective on each other. When we ended our work together, Manny and Ellen agreed that they had reduced the presence of Unfair Fighting in their relationship from 90% to 50%. They saw this as a "huge" shift in their relationship. Although they still have fights, they describe the fights as much different now. Manny's outbursts are much less explosive, Ellen is not afraid of his anger, and she no longer feels emotionally abused by him. The couple reports the following changes that contributed to this huge shift.

- Manny began to listen more to Ellen and think about the effects of his explosions on her. He felt his explosions were unfair and drew on his values for respect and family to develop more fair ways of relating to her.
- Ellen drew on her stubbornness and spirituality to convey her concerns to Manny in ways that were less "stinging" and more compassionate.
- The couple, drawing on their sense of humor and pride in family and culture began to shift from adversaries arguing about their children's schools and future to allies who shared a common vision but different paths.

Status at Termination[5]

Therapy is ending because Manny has been laid off from his job and the couple has lost their health insurance. They are unable to pay a full fee, and do not want to consider a sliding-scale fee. Manny and Ellen feel reasonably secure that they will be able to continue the changes they have made.

We anticipated ways in which the couple could be pulled away from a relationship anchored in Loving Friendship. Ellen stated that she would notice herself beginning to hang onto resentments and not sharing them with Manny, which could lead to them growing and leaking out as "stinging criticisms." Manny observed that when Ellen does share her concerns with him, cultural stereotypes about men being "king of the hill" and "in charge of their women" might encourage him to respond negatively to her criticisms and attempt to "assert his authority." We also discussed Manny's unemployment as a potential stressor on the relationship.

Their plan to solidify progress and address these potential concerns include:

- A plan to talk with their respective mothers to validate and support these changes.
- Ellen will continue to talk with her best friend as a way to ensure that she is not holding onto resentments and get other opinions about whether Manny's explosions are becoming a concern.
- Manny can tell by the "look in Ellen's face" when she's upset with him and has agreed to ask her how she's doing at those times to help develop a better atmosphere for sharing her concerns. Manny does not have friends he feels he could talk honestly about his explosions but has agreed to call the therapist and check in if either he or Ellen become concerned about his explosions.

Follow-Up Recommendations

At the conclusion of therapy, we discussed recommendations that Ellen and Manny would make to other couples struggling against the effects of Unfair Fighting on their family. The couple offered the following recommendations for other couples and agreed that the suggestions would be very useful for themselves as well:

- It is important to remember the difference between intent and effects. Someone may not mean to hurt another's feelings, but when they do it is important to acknowledge and apologize for the effects of their actions before trying to explain that they didn't mean it. It is also important for the hurt person to assume that the other had good intentions despite the bad effects.
- It is important for men, in particular, to put themselves in their wives' shoes and think about what the relationship is like from her perspective.
- It is important for couples to get away from the daily routine of children and life and find time to have fun. Having fun together reminds couples why they got together in the first place and keeps the relationship alive.

If Manny and Ellen decide to return to counseling, I would be very willing to meet with them.

COMMENTS ON
THE TERMINATION SUMMARY

I kept in touch with Manny and Ellen periodically for 6 months and they continued to keep their relationship anchored in Loving Friendship. Although they still had periodic fights, they were overall pleased with the direction of their relationship. They reported that they found the termination summary helpful and kept it in a drawer by their bed as a periodic reminder of "how far they had come." In situations such as this, my preference would be to write a summary letter rather than send a termination report. A letter is more personal and offers possibilities to pose questions that further extend the conversation. In an age of computers, it would be possible and not require significantly more energy to write a termination summary and from that cut and paste a letter that adds such questions. This example highlights again some ways in which our required paperwork can be used to better support our work. A termination summary written in this fashion can be more easily incorporated into our daily routine and may hold certain advantages in its legitimacy as an official document.

A termination summary written in this fashion also holds certain advantages for clients in its effects on other helpers. The report humanizes clients and invites a consideration of them as more than just another case. In addition, writing follow-up recommendations that reflect their wisdom and knowledge yields recommendations that are potentially more applicable and immediately useful to families in the future. If another helper were to read this report a year later, inquiring about how the couple is doing with their distinction between intent and effects, or how Manny is doing with his suggestion that men should step into their partner's shoes, or whether the two of them are finding time to remind each other of why they got together in the first place, offers the possibility of moving into a conversation with the couple that would have immediate relevance and significant effectiveness for them. In this way follow-up recommendations that draw from client experience have the potential to be much more useful.

Finally, the focus in termination summaries such as this represents a significant shift in how and for whom reports are written. Traditionally, termination reports document the work that professionals did with clients and are written to summarize our work for the benefit of another professional who might read it at some future date. The format of this alternate termination report documents the work that clients did in their life during the time of therapy and is written to summarize their work for their benefit. The proposal for writing termination summaries in this way reflects another example of an attempt to shift our work from *professional turf* to *family turf*.

SUMMARY

This chapter has highlighted a number of ways to elaborate and solidify alternative stories, particularly through letter writing and termination interviews. It examined subtle though powerful alterations in existing paperwork requirements that would allow therapists to more directly incorporate these practices into our daily work. This process further anchors helpers as an appreciative presence in clients' lives. However, these practices still keep clients primarily connected to professional communities. Despite our usefulness, it is important to move beyond our community and help clients to more actively draw on their own natural communities. The next chapter examines ways to accomplish this in detail.

NOTES

1. Even though clients rarely object to therapists taking notes, the process of asking their permission conveys respect and a willingness to make our actions accountable to them. If a client were to express reservations, I would seek to understand those hesitations, offer a rationale for my request, offer to let them keep the notes or a copy; and seek to find a way to work out an acceptable compromise. A number of clients *have* objected after I asked their permission, but we have always been able to work out an acceptable compromise and they have thanked me for involving them in the decision.

2. For those who are further interested in using letter writing as an adjunct to therapy, I'd refer them to Epston (1994), Freedman and Combs (1996a), Freeman, Epston and Lobovits (1997), White and Epston, (1990), and "Therapeutic Documents Revisited" in White (1995).

3. "Sharing-client-wisdom" questions represent the same category of questions as "consulting your consultant" questions (Epston & White, 1995; Epston, White, & "Ben," 1995). Referring to them as sharing-client-wisdom questions represents an attempt to develop more accessible language that also honors the original concepts.

4. Even though the violence in their relationship was primarily emotional and was never physical, I felt it was important to name it as violence and not minimize its effects. Much of my work with families and couples in which there is violence has been profoundly influenced by the work of Alan Jenkins (1990, 1996) and the Gender and Violence Project at the Ackerman Institute (Goldner 1992, 1998; Goldner et al., 1990).

5. Most licensing agencies require that termination summaries include a diagnosis and global assessment of functioning (GAF). Although I did not include that information in the copy of the report that I sent to Manny and Ellen, they were aware of it.

8

<hr />

Developing Communities
to Support New Lives

The African proverb "It takes a village to raise a child" could also be applied to the development of alternative stories. From a social constructionist perspective, narratives or life stories shape our lives. We live out the stories of our lives in our interactions with others, and those interactions solidify our narratives and further shape our lives. As we begin to enact a new story, the community that witnesses that enactment takes on great significance. The development of a village to witness and support the performance of new stories can be a crucial piece of our work with clients and families. This section examines ways to help clients develop supportive communities that nurture the enactment of alternative stories.

Often, the presence of problems in people's lives cuts them off from their social networks. Consider the following examples:

A family whose daughter is being discharged from a residential program is concerned about others' reactions to her return home. They don't know what to say to their friends and neighbors and dread dealing with the inevitable questions about where she's been for the past year. The girl, in turn, is convinced she'll never be able to return to her old school and is pleading with her parents to move to another town.

A young woman who has been in therapy for 3 months following her boyfriend's abrupt ending of their relationship confides to her therapist that he is the only one who knows her boyfriend left her. She feels ashamed and embarrassed that he left her, wonders what people will think, and is finding that there are fewer and fewer places she can go for fear of running into friends who might ask her about her boyfriend.

A woman calls a crisis line, saying a panic attack has forced her to leave work and come home. Even though she has a loving, supportive extended family she's embarrassed to let them know that she couldn't "tough it out." She desperately wants to talk with someone, but doesn't know to whom to turn.

In each of these examples, embarrassment, stigmatization, and shame contribute to the effects of other problems by separating people from potential sources of support. The resulting disconnection and isolation strengthen problems' influence. Factors such as embarrassment, stigmatization, and shame become a network of support for problems in people's lives—both enhancing the problems' influence and cutting people off from communities that could support them in developing a different relationship with those problems. When people are disconnected from others who have known and loved them over time, it becomes easier to be ensnared in the constraining problem story of who they are and lose sight of exceptions to that story. This process of disconnection often receives strong support from dominant cultural ideas about what it means to be a valued person (e.g., strong, independent, and achieving) which contributes to a "less than" experience for those who don't feel they live up to those ideals. Disconnection from others is also supported by our cultural habit of locating problems in individuals which contributes to a belief that "If I'm struggling with a problem in my life, there really must be something wrong with me, and I probably shouldn't let others know about it."

If problems gain influence when people are disconnected from others who love, care for, and support them, then efforts to reconnect people with a concerned community can powerfully support their influence on a problem. Recruitment of a "community of concern" can counteract the isolating effects of problems and help people stay in touch with alternative, preferred versions of who they are in their life (Madigan & Epston, 1995). This chapter examines ways to help clients develop communities that can witness and support the enactment of alternative stories and preferred futures. It begins with a description of *reconnection interviews*, which attempt to identify supportive others from across clients' lives (often from their past) and, through a questioning process, bring their presence into the room. The outline for such an interview is based on and has been profoundly influenced by Michael White (1997) and others who refer to them as re-membering interviews.[1]

Reconnection interviews provide a foundation for other mechanisms to help clients strengthen their relationship to a preferred community and draw on it for support. This chapter examines *letter-writing campaigns*, which more directly bring a community of support into someone's life; *self/mutual-help groups* which provide ongoing support to solidify new stories; and *leagues*, which help clients draw on the solidarity of communities of support to take action and directly address the broader cultural supports for problems.

RECONNECTION INTERVIEWS

Reconnection interviews entail a questioning process that helps people to connect to and internally hold the voices of an appreciative audience. The experience of others' presence often has a powerful effect on people as they confront particular problems. A quick example concerns a friend and associate of mine who was accused by a colleague of not being a "real psychologist" because of her unconventional ways of doing therapy. As she listened to this accusation, she thought of a group of associates from across the country whose work she admired and respected, and who in turn highly valued her work. These associates also approach therapy in unconventional ways and would probably also not be considered "real psychologists" by her colleague. Her reflection on her other unconventional associates brought fond memories, and she found herself smiling as she thanked her colleague for the compliment. The presence of a supportive community in her head helped her to stay in touch with a version of herself as a psychologist that she valued and changed her relationship with the accusation that she was not a "real psychologist."

Reconnection interviews are ways to help clients connect to and hold significant others in their heads in order to keep clients anchored in an experience of self outside the problem. Chapter 6 outlined questions to help develop alternative stories across perspectives. Similar questions are used in this process with an added intent of more actively bringing the presence of those perspectives into the room. The next section gives an example of a reconnection interview with a client and then discusses the ideas behind the practice.

Life Sucks and Yet You Survive

Maura, a single mother of three children (6, 4, and 3) was in her mid-20s, yet appeared to be in her late 40s. The careworn lines on her face and her smoker's hack reflected her hard life. Her parents divorced in the early 1980s after her father turned to drinking when his career as an air traffic controller was prematurely ended by Ronald Reagan's firing of all the air traffic controllers (PATCO) strikers in 1981. Her mother subsequently became an embittered recluse and Maura spent her adolescence living with an abusive uncle who constantly reminded her of her worthlessness. During that time, her father died of cirrhosis of the liver. She lost contact with her mother and escaped from her uncle's house into an equally abusive marriage with a con artist who quickly gave her three children and disappeared.

Maura's work as a waitress in a local diner was often interrupted by calls from the day-care center complaining about her two younger children's disheveled appearance, empty lunch bags, and out-of-control behavior. She'd respond to these calls by laying the phone on the diner counter and continuing on about her business. Clearly, the day-care center staff and Maura were not the best of friends. The staff had long since given up on rehabilitating Maura and Maura proudly proclaimed the fact that she was the only parent who had ever twice failed parent education classes. Her oldest son lived upstairs with a neighbor when he and his mother jointly decided to try some time apart. Numerous child neglect charges had been filed against Maura and her protective worker viewed her as a cantankerous old hag even though the worker was 2 years her senior. When I met Maura, she had been referred for family therapy as a last step to avoid placement of her two younger children. The protective worker was skeptical that things would ever change and saw the referral as a requisite step before placement. Maura's outlook on life was summarized in her oft-used phrase, "Life sucks and then you die." She had little use for therapists and wore her disdain for the mental health profession as a badge of caustic pride.

A brief review of the work with Maura and her family sets a context for describing the interview. Chapter 3 highlighted the usefulness of connecting with clients' honorable self (those qualities we can respect, appreciate, and value) when they present with a stance of "This is not a problem." Maura's relationship with the allegations of neglect is reflected in that stance. Influenced by Michael White (1997), my preference when working with parents when there is a concern about abuse or neglect is to begin by eliciting the parents' better judgment rather than attempting to correct their emotional abusiveness. After getting a thorough description of their better judgment and why it is important to them, we can then move into an examination of what pulls them away from it.[2] Beginning in this fashion sets a foundation that leads to more efficient work.

I began talking with Maura about her understanding of the referral. I asked about her experiences of parenting and told her that many parents I knew had found there to be times when we got stressed out and ended up responding to our kids in ways that didn't reflect how we'd best like to be with them. I wondered if anything like that had ever happened for her, and we got into a discussion of whether either of us knew parents for whom that hadn't happened. I asked her if she had ever found herself saying or doing anything with her children that went against her better judgment. When she acknowledged that she had, I asked her if it would be okay for us to spend some time getting to know more about that better judgment. I asked her a number of questions of what her parenting was like when it was "at its best," how she had developed those qualities, and what supported her in keeping her parenting anchored in them when things got tough with her children.

During this process, I was positioning myself as an appreciative ally in which I was inviting Maura to envision a preferred life that our work together could move toward rather than identifying a problem that I would attempt to get her to correct. The interview about her better judgment established a foundation of resourcefulness as the basis for the journey toward that preferred life. After getting a thorough description of her better judgment, why it was important to her, and how she kept herself anchored in it, we moved into a discussion of the things that pulled her away from it. One of the things she talked about was her attitude that "life sucks and then you die." We began to talk about the effects of that attitude and came to focus on Bitterness in particular.

We externalized Bitterness as an obstacle that constrained her from more solidly anchoring her parenting where she wanted it to be. Maura steadfastly maintained that Bitterness was a reasonable response to her history but didn't like that it so organized her life and feared the effect it would have on her children's development of a sense of hope for the future. As we began to search for exceptions to Bitterness, she movingly spoke about her commitment to her children. When asked how she maintained that commitment in the face of Bitterness, she replied, "I may be bitter, but I'm not giving up. Having a life of shit is no reason to stop trying." We began to talk about her determination (her word) and moved into juxtaposing a life of Bitterness and a life of Determination. We moved into the following conversation.

BILL: If you think back across your life, who would most appreciate your Determination to keep Bitterness in its place?

MAURA: My grandfather. He had been a labor organizer in the 1950s who stood up against the blacklisting of the McCarthy era. He believed the measure of a person was how that person held onto their beliefs when times got tough. I haven't thought about him for years. He used to tell me stories about Mother Jones (an anarchist labor organizer in the early 1900s) when I was a kid and never forgave my father for giving up after Reagan busted PATCO.

We talked for a bit about her relationship with her grandfather and their importance to each other in an attempt to bring his presence into the room. This foundation helped to anchor and concretize the discussion and contributed to the generation of alternative experiences of self. We began talking about the Mother Jones stories and what her grandfather might have hoped to pass on to Maura in telling them. Maura described her grandfather as someone who also had a right to be filled with bitterness and resignation but always found a way to hang onto hope and determination to fight for a better life for himself and others. Based on her description, we elaborated the juxtaposition of a life of Bitterness and a life of Determination to a life of Bitterness and Resignation and a life of Hope and Determination.

BILL: Do you think he saw those qualities of Hope and Determination in you?

MAURA: Yeah, I suppose he did.

BILL: Can you think of a time when he might have seen Hope and Determination particularly stand out in you?

Maura related a story of getting braces along with a friend and the two of them being teased mercilessly by some girls at school to the point of not wanting to go to school. She talked about finding comfort in the Mother Jones stories and how they helped her to keep going. As I asked more about how she responded to the teasing, she described standing up to the girls and telling them to leave her friend alone. After getting a lot of details in the story to anchor the experience, I asked her what her grandfather might have particularly appreciated about her determination to keep going despite the teasing and probably wanting to give up.

MAURA: (*pause*) Well, probably that Hope and Determination we were talking about.

BILL: He saw that in you then?

MAURA: Yeah.

BILL: What do you think it told him about you?

MAURA: Well, (*pause*) that I was a pretty strong kid.

BILL: That you were a pretty strong kid. What more do you think he would say about that? [This question is more an attempt to invite Maura into the experience of that strong kid than to simply get an answer.]

MAURA: I don't know. I think he was pretty proud of me.

BILL: He was proud of you. As you look back on yourself at that age through his eyes, what qualities stand out for you?

MAURA: Like from his perspective? (*pausing*) Well, I see a little girl who took a lot of shit but didn't let it get her down. She just kept on going. You know that's sort of the story of my life.

BILL: And, if your grandfather were here with us right now, listening in on this story of your life, what would his reaction be?

MAURA: It'd be mixed. He'd be angry that I've had to put up with so much shit and he'd be really proud that I haven't given up. You know, as I'm thinking about him, I realize how much I miss him and his stories.

BILL: And, if he heard how the message of those stories have continued on in you and had such an effect on your life, what would his reaction be?

MAURA: He'd feel like he'd done some good in the world. (*smiling*) He'd be really happy.

BILL: And, are Hope and Determination qualities that you also want to pass along to your children?

MAURA: I'm trying. Or at least sometimes, I'm trying. When I get caught up in my moods, I think, "Why bother," but it's what I'd like to pass on to them?

BILL: Would it be a good thing for your grandfather to learn that the Hope and Determination that he's passed onto you is continuing to be passed along to your kids?

Maura nodded and when I asked why, she recounted a story about the cutoff between her father and grandfather after her father's descent into alcoholism after the PATCO strike. She described her grandfather's disappointment with her father (as well as her own) and talked about how she was now seeing her father as being "beaten up" rather than "giving up." This made a big difference for her and she thought that if her grandfather could see his spirit living on in her and her feisty children, it would redeem his faith in the power of Hope and Determination. We talked about ways in which she might reconnect with her grandfather and catch him up on these events. She wrote to him and after he wrote back, they reestablished contact over the phone and eventually she moved out of the city up to where he was living so she and her kids could be closer to him.

If we look back on this story, we can pick out a distinct flow in the interview. This flow could be outlined as containing the following steps:

- Find a person in the client's past who would recognize and appreciate life outside the problematic story.
- Get details of that relationship and find a specific event that happened in the presence of that person that highlights an example of life then outside the current problematic story.
- Learn the story of that event—who, what, where, when.
- Learn about the meaning of that event.
- Link to the present and future, attempting to bring that person's presence more into the client's current life.

In the interview with Maura, the question, "Who across your life would most appreciate your determination to keep Bitterness and Resignation in its place?," helped to identify her grandfather as such a person. Our discussion of their relationship and its importance to each of them helped to anchor the subsequent conversation. We discussed a particular event in which her grandfather's appreciation of her Hope and Determination shone through and I asked a lot of who, what, where, and when questions to develop a detailed story around that event that was consistent with the developing alternative story of Hope and Determination. Meaning questions about that event (questions such as the following: What did he appreciate about you? What qualities did he see in you that you might have missed? As you look at your life through his eyes, what stands out for you? What would his reaction to this conversation be? What effect does that have on you?) helped to further enrich the developing story of Hope and Determination. Questions that brought her grandfather's presence more into Maura's life helped her develop a negotiating team in her head as she bargained with Bitterness and Resignation. His presence (as well as other important members of a supportive community) helped to inoculate her from some of the effects of Bitterness and Resignation and helped her develop a life more anchored in Hope and Determination in the face of adversity.

This outline is one way to proceed with a reconnection interview. It is offered to exemplify the flow of such a conversation and highlight the thinking behind my questions. It is not offered as a recipe. It is extremely important to have these be conversations *with* clients rather than have them be an interview that we are doing *to* them. Interviews such as these can be useful in helping clients to develop an actual community of support. For example, Maura not only began carrying her grandfather around in her head, but she recontacted him and eventually moved to live close to him. They are also useful to help clients develop a virtual community of support. They can be held with clients about departed family members, important historical figures, or spiritual figures such as a higher power. For example, I also talked with Maura about what she thought

Mother Jones would appreciate about her struggle with Bitterness. This led into a moving conversation about the integrity of her existential stance of "carrying on in the face of adversity." Although this might sound like an intellectualized, academic topic, Maura's experience of it was an affect-full examination of what she stood for in her life and how that could be witnessed and honored by a historical figure with whom she had come to have a deep personal relationship. After that conversation, Maura went out and got a picture of Mother Jones that she began carrying around with her. She would periodically consult the picture and found Mother Jones's presence in her life to be very empowering.

The process of helping people develop and connect to communities of support has been a more recent development within my own work, but one that I and clients have found extremely useful. Reconnection interviews are just one example of a wide variety of practices to help clients develop and draw on a community of support. These interviews provide a basis for helping communities become a stronger presence in people's lives. The next sections examine ways to further extend this process.

LETTER-WRITING CAMPAIGNS
AS A VEHICLE TO DEVELOP COMMUNITY

There is a scene in Mark Twain's book *The Adventures of Tom Sawyer* in which Tom Sawyer and two friends surreptitiously attend their own funeral. The local townspeople thought the boys had died on the river and conducted a funeral which the three boys observed from the gallery. The following section describes the service:

> As the service proceeded, the clergyman drew such pictures of the *graces, the winning ways, and the rare promise* of the lost lads, that every soul there, thinking he recognized these pictures, felt a pang in remembering that he had persistently blinded himself to them, always before, and had as persistently seen faults and flaws in the poor boys. The minister related *many a touching incident* in the lives of the departed, too, which illustrated their *sweet, generous natures,* and people could easily see, now, how *noble and beautiful* those episodes were, and remembered with grief that at the time they occurred they had seemed rank rascalities, well deserving of the cowhide. The congregation became more and more moved, as the pathetic tale went on, till at last the whole company broke down and joined the weeping mourners in a chorus of anguished sobs, the preacher himself giving way to his feelings, and crying in the pulpit. (Twain, 1876/1980, pp. 116–117; emphasis added)

At this point, Tom Sawyer, Huck Finn, and a third friend emerged from the gallery and "were smothered with kisses and poured out thanksgivings" (p. 117). The dominant story about Tom and his friends up to this point had been a story of scalawags, ne'er do wells, and scoundrels. That story promoted selective attention to their "faults and flaws" (p. 117) but obscured "the graces, the winning ways, and the rare promise of the lost lads" (p. 116). However, during the funeral, an alternative story began to emerge. The congregation began to remember Tom and his friends quite differently and were profoundly moved. In the process, their experience of Tom and his friends shifted. Judging by the "kisses and poured out thanksgivings" (p. 117) there was also a shift in relationships. That shift continued with Tom's family being "very loving and attentive to his wants" (p. 119) the next day and children in school later in the week "making much of him" (p. 122) and showing "eloquent admiration for him" (p. 123). Twain also describes changes in Tom's behavior with Tom subsequently relating differently at home and school. In the process, Tom both constructs himself and is viewed quite differently within his community. Although there is no direct mention of the effects of the funeral on Tom's experience of self, we might imagine that witnessing the emergence of this alternate story could significantly influence his self identity. In the book, these memories of Tom fade and his actions are again shaped by and viewed within the old story, but imagine what might have helped to keep these new memories about Tom alive in his life.

Stephen Madigan (1997; Madigan & Epston, 1995) has developed letter-writing campaigns as a way of reconstructing memories to further support the elaboration of emerging alternative stories. He has likened letter-writing campaigns to a eulogy or obituary made on behalf of the client while the client is still living (similar to Tom Sawyer's experience). In this project, important members in a client's life are asked to assist in a process in which they send letters to the client outlining memories of their relationship together outside of the problem's influence. Madigan (1997) describes the process as "re-remembering" to emphasize the way in which it brings forth other remembrances. One goal of letter-writing campaigns is to help clients incorporate aspects of themselves that have been obscured by the problematic story (e.g., Tom Sawyer's "grace, winning ways and rare promise"). The process of collecting, reading, and rereading letters elicits other experiences and relationships that support the continued enactment of alternative stories (e.g., Tom behaving and experiencing himself in ways that are more in keeping with the funeral sermon). A second goal of letter-writing campaigns is to reconnect people to their natural networks or communities from which problems have disconnected them (e.g., Tom's discovery being greeted with kisses and poured out thanksgivings and the continued changes in relationships with important others from whom he had been previously estranged). Thus, letter-writing campaigns have a twin goal of reconstituting both memory and community to support emerging alternative stories.

Letter-writing campaigns often develop out of interviews to reconnect people to preferred communities and can extend their impact by providing tangible momentos that solidify the presence of important others in clients' lives. Madigan (1997) provides a thorough description of the process of letter-writing campaigns. In brief, therapists can begin by asking clients to identify others who would view them differently from the problem's description of them. We can then juxtapose the problem's description and these alternate descriptions, and inquire about clients' reactions to each and the possibilities each might hold for clients. As we elicit client preferences, we can generate a list of people who would stand in support of their preferred stories and construct a letter of invitation to elicit letters highlighting memories of their relationship as it has been more anchored in the client's preferred story. As letters come in, we can engage in a process of reading and reflecting on the letters that arrive. Sessions can also elicit emergent themes across letters in an attempt to weave together a richer counter-plot. As I have repeatedly emphasized throughout this book, guidelines such as these provide a rough framework for approaching the spirit of the work rather than a recipe to be applied in a stepwise fashion. There are many ways to adapt practices such as letter-writing campaigns and the following section highlights one such example.

DIANA'S BOOK:
A LETTER-WRITING CAMPAIGN IN ACTION

One of the programs with which I consult is an intensive family intervention program with a community support component designed to help young people draw on local resources to avoid hospitalization or transition back into the community. I had talked with the program director about letter-writing campaigns and, unbeknownst to me, one community support worker, Anya, picked up on the idea and ran with it. When I first heard about Anya's implementation of a letter-writing campaign with a client, she and the client were fully immersed in it and I was fascinated by the ways in which this particular client had creatively taken ownership of the process. After the completion of the project, I interviewed the client and Anya. The remainder of this section is their story of their work together on a letter-writing campaign.

Description of the Situation

Diana is a 17-year-old girl who once again lives with her mother, stepfather, and 15-year-old brother after spending a significant time placed in various programs. By Diana's report, problems in her life began in seventh grade with "substance abuse and always getting kicked out of school." By the end of eighth grade, Diana had moved out of the house to live with a friend. Diana is a wonderfully engaging young woman who was actually voted Queen of Suspension in her junior high yearbook. (Fittingly, she was suspended from school on the day of yearbook pictures and the yearbook ran the title under a blank picture.) Diana entered her first treatment program at age 14. Over the next 20 months, there were a variety of attempts to help Diana turn her life around and return home, including 13 placements in hospitals, halfway houses, and residential treatment programs. Diana has described her experience of services as "mixed."

When originally designed, Anya's program offered long-term intensive support with a focus on utilizing clients' natural networks and community resources. Anya officially worked with Diana for 1½ years and continues to be informally involved in her life. At first, Diana wanted nothing to do with Anya. Diana had "endured" more than 20 workers and had no interest in meeting another one. She was convinced that no matter what attempts were made, she would inevitably end up back in another residential program and flatly refused to participate in the community support program. However, when Diana met Anya, she changed her mind, attributing that change to Anya's willingness to be "honest and real."

When I met with Anya and Diana to discuss their work together, Diana described the differences in her life.

> "Things are really different now. I care and trust people. I didn't use to care. I have a good relationship with my mother. I have a job. I get along with my brother and I especially get along with my stepfather, which is a real big shift."

Diana described the shift from a life of "drinking, drugging and not caring or trusting" to her new life as an important one. Undoubtedly, many things contributed to these changes, but Diana attributes much of the difference to her work with Anya. A significant piece of their work together revolved around the letter-writing campaign that provided a framework for that work. Both Diana and Anya maintain that the letter-writing campaign and the book Diana developed to hold those letters have played a significant role in these changes in her life.

Diana's Description
of the Letter-Writing Campaign

The following description of the letter-writing campaign was written by Diana earlier in the process:

"Anya first told me about the letter-writing campaign in December 1997. She explained that Ellie (the program director) had mentioned a new idea which involved a client choosing certain people and having those people write a letter to that client, and for the letter to be kept in a special book. My first thought was that nobody would write a letter, my second thought was that if they did write a letter, it wouldn't be honest. When we began talking about the idea of having people that I pick write a letter to me, I started to feel a little more comfortable. We talked over a period of days and slowly made progress.

"The first step toward starting the book was to decide who I was going to ask to write the letters. For me, this was hard because I wanted to pick people with whom I have a special relationship, and also people who will be 'real' when they write to me. I started to make my first list at the end of December 1997. On my list was, Kira, a teenager who helped my transition home from residential, my psychiatrist, my therapist, a friend from the store I worked at, my Department of Mental Health worker, and my brother. After making my list we set out to a store to make sure we got the perfect binder and protection sheets. I chose a green binder, because that is the color of the store I work at. The next thing I did was pick out protection sheets, Anya picked up a package of 25 and I said, 'NO WAY.' I never thought I could use 25 sheets!! I was wrong!! I then brought the binder with the sheets in it to my work and put the biggest store logo directly in the center of the binder. We were both ready to start this letter writing.

"I was very nervous to ask anybody. I felt like they were going to reject me, but with the help of Anya I took that chance. The first person I asked was Kira. Anya described what the letter writing was about and what should be in the letter. She explained that only the positive things about me could be in the letters, and that we would pick a place and people would read them to me. I was very nervous to hear what Kira had to say. We made a date when Kira would have the letter written and then we made the plan to meet. Kira picked me up from school and we met Anya at the mall. Kira and I took a picture at the photo booth to also put in my new book. When we finally got heading toward a place to sit, Kira realized she lost the letter. In a panic we all headed toward the parking lot and found the letter on someone's windshield after it had been run over. The tire track still stands on the envelope today!! We then headed to the pizza store and sat down. My heart was racing I was so anxious. Kira began to read the letter to me and I relaxed. I listened to every word she read and I stored the letter in my mind. Her letter was written on two pieces of stationary, very neatly written. The first line was very striking. She said, 'Stevie Wonder once wrote a song, "I just called to say I love you," well, today Diana I am just writing to say, "I love you."' I was very surprised to hear this. She was being so honest, something at first I thought nobody was going to do. After she read it, we sat and talked about it for awhile. It was a whole new experience to be hearing such good things about myself. When we were done, we went to play the arcade game we would always play and I saved the tickets we won in the book. It was the first of the letters and I had survived.

"The second person who I asked to write a letter for my book was Dr. Ford, my psychiatrist. He was very excited when we asked him to write a letter and explained to him what it was about. He read his letter to me before one of our scheduled appointments. I was very nervous about this letter because I didn't know what to expect from my doctor. I didn't know if he would talk about my meds and stuff or if he would be 'real.' Dr. Ford's letter was great. He talked about how I was when he first met me and how I am now. He said I was always moving all around the room and that I never stayed still and now I am a lot more relaxed with him. Dr. Ford also gave me a prayer and read it to me after the letter. I'm not much into prayers, but I sat and listened to everything that he read to me. Then the next appointment we had, he gave me a copy of a prayer for teens that he had revised and written over the summer. The prayers were very colorful and bright. After we were done with everything, Anya took a picture of him. I wouldn't be in the picture because my hair was messy, so Dr. Ford pulled up and put his arm around that which was supposed to be me. Now, I was done with my second letter and my book was beginning to build up!"

Comments on Diana's Description

This description brings home Diana's tentative mixture of excitement and trepidation. The chance that she describes taking in asking others to join her in this process is nerve-wracking and yet an important step for her. As the process invites particular remembrances of Diana outside the old story of "drinking, drugging and not caring or trusting," it also invites Diana to live out a life more anchored in caring and trusting. The chance she takes in reaching out to others helps her to develop a community of support. It is important to carefully consider who to include in such a project and to frame the invitations clearly. For example, Diana initially decided not to include her mother or stepfather. At the time, Diana and her mother had a conflictual relationship and her stepfather had little involvement with her. Diana's mother was very worried about losing Diana and reluctant to rock the boat by saying anything that might upset her. As Diana put it,

> "My mother knew the old story about me, but couldn't see the changes I was making. If she had written honestly, she would have to write the old stuff and she was too protective to do that. So, I was afraid she would just write something like 'You're a great kid' and end there. I wanted people to be real in the book. I wanted my mother and stepfather to be a part of the book, but I didn't want to force them to be in it."

Diana subsequently left the book out for mother to examine. The book provided an opportunity for her mother to see Diana through other people's eyes and invited her mother to consider Diana's newly developing identity. The book then became a way for Diana to communicate with her mother and stepfather and set a foundation for bringing them together. They later made up an award certificate to celebrate her 90 days of sobriety, and she put that in the book. In this way, letter-writing campaigns both support the development of community and provide a way to draw on one's community.

Diana's explanation that the letters should contain only positive things deserves some comment. In my experience with letter-writing campaigns, the letters have been uniformly positive, but I would not want to draw the distinction between positive and negative stories. This is not a process of pointing out strengths and minimizing difficulties. It is more a process of inviting descriptions of clients outside the dominant problem story. Letter-writing campaigns don't seek to simply replace negative stories with positives ones but attempt to support the development of preferred lives by soliciting others' remembrances of events and experiences outside of old constraining stories.

Diana made some interesting choices in her development of a letter-writing campaign. One choice was to include both helpers and people from her natural community. As a "systems kid," much of Diana's community has been helpers. She began primarily by asking helpers for letters but then began getting letters from friends and nonprofessional contacts. The process of the letter-writing campaign both mirrored her transition back into the community and supported that move.

A second interesting choice was Diana's decision to meet personally with each letter writer. Often in letter-writing campaigns, a letter of invitation may be sent out by the therapist (examples of such letters are contained in Madigan & Epston, 1995) to solicit a number of letters which can be sent to the client's home or the therapist's office depending on the client's preference. Typically, the therapist and client read and discuss the letters and may periodically invite the letter writers into the office. Diana insisted on contacting each letter writer individually (initially with Anya's assistance). She asked each letter writer to meet with her personally, to read the letter to her, and then to put it in her book. Typically, Diana and each letter writer would have a snack or meal together and then take a photograph together to include with other momentos that might be appropriate (tickets, poems, prayers, etc.). In this way, each letter was given in a ritual that was witnessed and facilitated by Anya. That ritual strengthened the symbolic value of the letters. The process was time-consuming and labor intensive but provided an ongoing framework for Anya's work with Diana.[3]

The repetition of the process contributed to its depth. For Diana, the value of meeting personally with the letter writers was immeasurable. In her words, "Deep down, it was important for me to hear the letter for the first time in the person's voice." The personal contact enriched the letter's ability to bring each letter writer's presence into Diana's life. It also deepened their subsequent relationships, as we'll see shortly. Diana has graciously offered to share several of her letters here. I've included her first letter from Kira and a later letter that particularly touched her.

Two Letters

As Diana described earlier, the first person she approached for a letter was Kira. Kira was an 18-year-old college freshman whom Anya knew. Anya approached Kira and asked her to serve as a mentor with Diana. Kira loved the idea and enthusiastically became very involved with Diana, receiving significant ongoing support from Anya. Diana lacked a community in her life and her journey through residential programs had strongly embedded her in the helping community. Anya's work with Diana initially focused on helping Diana begin to build a more natural community by hooking Diana up with Kira. Anya explains her rationale:

> "I thought if Diana could make good connections with other teens in the community, it would make more of a difference in her whole life than anything I could do to break her pattern of drinking, drugging, and not feeling good about herself. To quote Diana, 'It would be more real.' If my work is community support, it makes no sense for me to replicate the pattern of professionals providing services that

leave kids and families feeling like they hadn't made real connections in the community. It felt like a better use of my time to help Diana connect up with a community and be in the background while that happened."

Kira became an important presence in Diana's life. She helped Diana transition from a reliance on the professional helping system for community to the development of her own "real" community. Kira's letter is captured as follows:

Dear Diana,

I know that Stevie Wonder once sang "I just called to say I love you," Well today I am writing to say, "I love you." I have enjoyed our afternoons together so much. Never in my young life have I ever met someone as intelligent, funny, sensitive and energetic as you are. Whether we are playing the driving game at the arcade (which, by the way, I will someday be able to kick your butt at) or just hanging out, driving around, I always have a fabulous time when we're together. Thank you so much for enriching my life by teaching me how to play and be fun at the same time as showing me how to be strong and survive. Diana, you are a survivor, one of the strongest people that I've ever met, and I admire and respect your wonderful ability to keep going in the face of obstacles and set backs. You are a fabulous mixture of 16-year old girl and 80-year-old woman, and I adore this uniqueness that makes you you.

This winter break has been weird for me. I've come back home after four months away at school only to find that I don't relate to some of my friends well anymore or that we no longer have anything in common. And yet, with you, I always feel that I can talk and be myself and that you will accept me no matter what. That is a wonderful gift you have, Diana, an amazing quality for making people feel at home and welcome. The other day, when you left after Jessie and I drove you to Falmouth, my sister turned to me and said, "Diana's cool." Now my little sister is one of the most judgmental people I know, and for her to accept you so warmly, after so brief an interaction, is a testament to all your outstanding social and emotional qualities.

I am so proud to know you, and I am so proud of your fine achievements lately in relation to drugs and alcohol. Your sobriety makes all who know and love you extremely happy, and I'm sure that it gives you confidence in your strength of will. I can't wait for you to go to college and show everyone what strength and spirit you have. I'm sure that they'll be floored by you!

You are a wonderful friend and charming person (I would love to be able to find somewhere where no one knows you and smiles and waves when they see you, but I'm sure that place does not exist) and a credit to you yourself. Diana, you have made yourself the magnificent person you are—your intelligence, charm and energy has molded the girl we all love. You should—you simply have to—take pride in all that you are, and all that you have made yourself. Few people I know are as incredibly loveable and intelligent and sensitive as you are, and I only hope that you realize how special you are. I am honored to be your friend.

Love,

Kira

As described earlier by Diana, this letter was an important one for her. She was nervous about beginning the process and feared rejection. Asking for help from others in this way was a big step for Diana. The first letter from Kira gave her the courage to continue the process.

The second letter included here is from Diana's friend Abby. Abby was a coworker who had heard about Diana's book of letters and was excited when Diana asked her to write a letter. Along with the letter, Abby included a poem by her boyfriend, Dale, who had died in a car accident while Abby was driving. Shortly before his death, Dale wrote a poem about his struggle with substance abuse and gave it to Abby. When Abby passed the poem along, Diana felt it must have been written specifically for her because it so captured her experience. Here is the letter. (The poem is not included.)

Dear Diana,

I feel lucky to know you. You have this amazing ability to always sparkle and your positivity rubs off on everyone around you. You possess such a wonderful spirit and your ability as a "survivor" is powerful.

Diana, you have a wonderful heart. You look out for others, including me, and I respect that. When you asked me to be part of your letter album, I knew exactly what to do. I went to my most treasured shoebox and pulled out Dale's poem. He told me that one day I would know who to read it to. Well, that was six years ago and nobody but myself has read it. Dale died next to me in a car accident one month after I got this poem. His strength and memory I know and trust I will now pass onto you. I have chosen not only to read his poem, but to give it to you.

Stay strong, be true to yourself and remember you are never too far from people who love you.

Love,

Abby

The giving of the letter and poem had a profound effect on Diana, Abby, and their relationship. They went to a coffeehouse where Abby read the letter and poem and put them in the book. They cried and then talked for hours. Diana opened up and began sharing things in her life with Abby that many people had never known. The process brought their relationship to a completely different level. In Diana's words, "Our whole relationship changed and we got very close. We don't work together anymore, but we see each other all the time."

The process also had numerous benefits for Abby. Previously, she had held the pain of Dale's death all to herself. When she gave the poem to Diana, it allowed her to let go of that pain and begin to move on. Sharing the poem and then her feelings about Dale's death with someone else left her feeling much less alone in her life and more a part of a community. In Diana's words,

> "When Abby gave me the poem, it allowed her to let go of the pain and move on. No one had seen it and now others know about it and she's no longer alone. Now his poem helps others."

These two instances highlight the ways in which letter-writing campaigns have a strong impact on the letter writers as well as the recipient of the letters. In this way, letter-writing campaigns become community interventions with a potentially wide-ranging impact.

Further Effects of the Letter-Writing Campaign

These two letters and the many others that accompanied them had a profound effect on Diana. She had assumed that nobody would respond and that any possible responses would not be real. As a result, Diana was "blown away" by the letters she received. As she viewed herself through the eyes of the letter writers, she liked what she saw. Diana and Anya went over each letter, reviewing and talking about them. The process progressively amplified the impact of each letter. The consistency with which various people viewed Diana from outside the problem of "drinking, drugging and not caring" brought home for her the ways in which she was more than those problems and supported her in the development of a life outside drugs and programs. As Diana put it:

> "This book is like everything to me. When I'm having a bad day, I just whip it out and read it. I remember where I was the day I got the particular letter I'm reading and it makes me feel better and keeps me going. It makes it easier to go on and I'm not alone with those troubles."

The process also had significant effects on Diana's relationships with the persons who wrote letters for her. As she put it:

> "The relationships changed between me and the people who got the letters. We got much closer. It just changed. Especially with the professionals. They weren't just my counselor or my worker anymore. They told me how they felt and became much more real for me."

In the course of the interview about her letter-writing campaign, Diana began to reflect on the impact the process of writing letters had on others. She thought that it was "awesome, just awesome to know that I've been such a big deal in so many people's lives."

Diana's words movingly convey the effects of letter-writing campaigns. However, in a human service world concerned with measurable outcomes and concrete results, consider the following: For the first 20 months of Diana's involvement with the mental health system, she was in 13 programs (including hospitals, detox centers, and residential programs) and had (by her estimate) more than 20 different workers. For the second 20 months, beginning with Anya's involvement with her, Diana lived at home with no readmissions and significantly fewer workers in her life. Although that time was not consistently rosy and trouble-free, the savings in treatment costs were enormous.

Diana kept her letters in a book that she was thrilled to show to others. That book also provided a concrete way of documenting her progress. In Anya's words:

> "It gave the folks at the Department of Mental Health an opportunity to see the kind of work that was happening, exactly what Diana was doing, the kind of relationships she was building, what was happening in the workplace for her. It was much better than progress notes or quarterly updates. This was really what was happening as opposed to 'Diana's been home for 11 weeks now and she attends this meeting and that meeting and she's compliant with this and attending family therapy this many times a week' and on and on."

Extensions of the Letter-Writing Campaign

In their work together, Anya and Diana used the letter-writing campaign as a foundation to further extend that work. They developed *lists* to help anchor Diana in an internalized supportive community. When Diana had a rough day, Anya would ask her, "Whose wild about you, cutie?" and have Diana list all the people who cared about her. Diana's list of people continually changed and grew. Others learned about this list and began joining in. After a while, Diana had a wide network of people rooting for her and reminding her that they were "wild about her." Eventually, Diana began to pose the question to herself.

> "I always had trouble sleeping and I would think about Anya saying, 'Cutie, whose wild about you? Let's make the list.' And, I'd take twenty minutes and make the list and it just reminded me that people cared and that I wasn't alone in this. And that made me feel good and I could then go to sleep."

In another extension of the letter-writing campaign, Diana was asked to do an *in-service training* for Anya's agency on letter-writing campaigns. The staff found the training valuable and it had a number of powerful effects. The staff served as witnesses to Diana's description of what the process meant for her and Diana came away feeling very proud of herself. The process also affected the program staff. Ellie, the director, reported that,

> "People were bowled over by the intimacy, the caring, the level of the descriptions of what knowing Diana evoked in letter writers. I was struck by how deeply personal it was. I was so touched and it made me feel very connected to my original dream of what working in this field would be like. It put me in touch with why I wanted to do this work."

Ellie went on to describe the broader effects of the training on the staff of the program.

> "Part of the culture of this program is that we become very involved in people's lives and establish very deep connections. At times we question our level of involvement with families and wonder whether we're maintaining enough "professional distance." We can get worried about what other programs might think of our work. But, seeing the effect of the letter-writing campaign on Diana in the training gave us more confidence in trusting our relationships with clients and taking the lead from them."

The *interview* about the letter-writing campaign with Diana and Anya also extended the letter-writing campaign. A portion of the interview consisted of sharing-client-wisdom questions, as described in Chapter 7. Here is some of Diana's wisdom, which she wanted to share with other youths and helpers.

BILL: So, your book has had a pretty profound effect on a number of people now. What do you think about that?

DIANA: Wow, it's good. If I can help some other kids that are stuck in residential, that's very cool. That's why I'm doing this today cause if other therapists are gonna hear about it and can get some ideas from it about how to help can help kids, that would be great.

BILL: If you were to talk to other kids who were trying to begin to care and trust again and pull their lives together, what advice would you offer them?

DIANA: To listen. To be patient. Patience is a hard one, to not be stubborn. Listening is a big one cause us kids in residential think we know everything. I'm telling ya . . .

BILL: Anything else?

DIANA: No, listening's the big one.

BILL: And what advice would you have for helpers?

DIANA: Be honest. Don't fake like you're something you're not. And, don't check your watch every five minutes. That's the worst!

BILL: And if professionals were honest and not faking like they're something they're not, what difference would that make?

DIANA: It would make kids want to be honest with them and open up.

There is valuable advice in Diana's suggestions, and the process of inviting her to share that wisdom with others also places her in a different position in her life. Diana has moved from a recipient of services to a valuable consultant for young people and helpers alike. Each of these extensions of the letter-writing campaign further embeds Diana's new experience of herself and more deeply connects her to a concerned community.

Once again, it's important to emphasize that letter-writing campaigns are not a simple technique to be applied across situations. They are not a magic bullet but, as Anya put it, "a useful tool." They organize a way of working with clients that can help position ourselves as appreciative allies. This section concludes with a portion of the interview that hopefully captures the spirit of this kind of work. Diana had asked the program director, Ellie, to write her a letter and described her preparation for the meeting in which Ellie was going to give her the letter.

DIANA: You need to know, Ellie cries over anything. So, before we met, while Ellie was in another meeting, me and some of the other therapists all got boxes of tissues. We collected boxes from all the other offices in the program. There must have been 15 boxes of tissues. We put them all over her office. We taped them to the walls, put them behind the plants, under the seats, everywhere. We just filled her office with tissue boxes. She walked in and just started laughing so hard. To this day, there's a box of tissues still taped to the back of her door. It's empty now, but it's still taped there.

BILL: I've seen that box. You know that's a wonderful story. I go into Ellie's office periodically to talk about the program and often when I go in there for a serious conversation, she'll close the door. And now if I go in there for a serious conversation about the program, Ellie will close the door and I'll look at this box of tissues on the back of the door and I'll have a whole different reaction to the conversation we're about to have. Knowing this story, and seeing the tissue box on the back of the door will help to anchor me in what is important in this work. Thank you for that.

DIANA: It's like what Anya's always saying. The most important thing is relationships.

SELF/MUTUAL-HELP GROUPS
AS COMMUNITIES OF SUPPORT

Another potential community to help solidify new stories can be self/mutual-help groups. The self-help movement is a growing alternative to professionally defined and delivered mental health services. An estimated 7 million Americans attended a self-help group in 1992 and researchers have predicted a 9% growth rate every year (Monaghan-Blout, 1999). This is a powerful community resource that is often overlooked. Beginning with Alcoholics Anonymous in 1935, self-help groups have proliferated to now encompass a wide range of problems and life situations. Although there are many different types of self-help groups operating from various philosophies, virtually all are based on a foundation of free membership and peer leadership.

A number of researchers have suggested that a more appropriate name for self-help groups would be mutual-help groups because members are both givers and receivers of help (e.g., Maton, 1993; Rappaport,

1993; Rappaport et al., 1985). They express a concern that the word "self-help" connotes a type of individualism that does not fit with the mutuality and shared responsibility that characterize such groups. However, as Rappaport (1993) points out, many leaders of the organizations representing various self-help groups prefer to be called members of self-help groups (usually for practical reasons of public communication because "self-help group" is widely understood in the popular media to refer to such organizations). For that reason, I (following the lead of others) refer to these groups as self/mutual-help groups.

The Power of Self/Mutual–Help Groups

The presence of mutuality in self/mutual-help groups in which people both give and receive support has been seen as a particularly powerful factor in their effectiveness (Maton, 1988, 1989, 1995). As previously described in the sharing-client-wisdom questions in Chapter 7 (as well as in Diana's reaction to the in-service training she provided in the last section of this chapter), inviting people who have typically spent a significant portion of their life being receivers of help into a position of also being a giver of help can be a powerful experience. The mutuality that comes out of self-help groups can have a significant impact on people's identity.

People who join mutual-help organizations are often looking for an alternative or addition to professional services. In finding a community of people with similar life experiences, they may encounter a powerful group of witnesses to support the development of a new life. Julian Rappaport (1993), a community psychologist, has referred to self/mutual-help groups as "normative narrative communities where identity transformation takes place." He observed that people typically referred to as "chronic mental patients" who belonged to a particular mutual-help organization often told very different stories about themselves than did their peers who continued to be treated solely under professional care. The professional patient stories often revolved around viewing themselves as dependent recipients of services who were sick and requiring of medication with little to offer others. In contrast, stories told by the organization's members emphasized a view of themselves as part of a "caring and sharing" community of givers as well as receivers, with hope and a sense of their own capacity for positive change. In addition, members often described their lives in terms of "before and after" their involvement in the organization, suggesting the organization's strong influence in the development of these alternative stories of identity.[4] Rappaport noticed marked similarities across members' stories and suggests that the existence of a shared community narrative provides a context for the transformation of personal life stories. As highlighted throughout this book, individual life stories are embedded in broader cultural narratives. The transformation of individual life stories is enriched by a supportive alternative culture. This book has repeatedly drawn on a rite of passage metaphor in which people experiencing problems pass through a *separation stage* during which they begin to move away from an old identity, a *liminal or transitional stage* during which they begin to develop alternative identities, and a *reincorporation stage* during which they solidify an alternative, preferred identity. Self/mutual-help groups are powerful communities in witnessing and supporting the solidification of new stories. In addition, they also provide support for the ongoing maintenance of alternative stories. The remainder of this section examines Parents Anonymous (PA) as one example of the promise of mutual-help organizations.

What Is Parents Anonymous?

Parents Anonymous is a highly effective treatment and prevention program for child abuse and neglect. It has operated as a resource for parents in crisis and those experiencing stresses in parenting since 1970.[5] Currently, PA reaches more than 60,000 parents a year across the nation through a network of groups (Watson, 1995). Although many members have experienced difficulties in parenting, not everyone who participates in these groups has abused children. The only requirement to join a group is concern about and desire to improve one's parenting.

PA groups are led by a parent chairperson and a professional volunteer facilitator who acts as a consultant to the group, providing support to the parent chair and serving as a liaison to group members who may need assistance in connecting with external services (Monaghan-Blout, 1999). PA's organizational literature describes the groups as "a place to find other parents who truly understand how you're feeling, someone to talk to, a caring shoulder to lean on, people who will listen, a place to share practical advice, a community to call during the week when you need to talk." Despite the name, PA is not a 12-Step program. It is not based on the internalizing assumptions that characterize many 12-Step programs (e.g., the internalizing assumption in AA that I *am* an alcoholic rather than an externalizing assumption that I am in a relationship with alcohol that has taken a severe toll on my life and I might benefit from changing that relationship).[6] The program emphasizes the ways in which parents are more than the problems that bring them to the group and doesn't prescribe a particular approach to parenting. Members determine the content of meetings and parents are encouraged to use each other as supports between meetings. Although PA groups honor confidentiality, they see children's welfare as the highest priority. They particularly emphasize the process through which they address issues of children's safety. Consider the following description from Karen, a parent group leader:

> "Our policy is never to take control out of the parent's hands if we can possibly avoid it. As a group, we talk to the parent about our concerns about both the parent and the child. We encourage the parent to seek additional help voluntarily, whether at school or in other agencies or with protective services. We call protective services when necessary, but we encourage parents to make the call themselves. The group will support them in any way we can, such as someone being there with them while they make a call or going down to the agency office with them and just offering lots of support. But the parent is in charge of what support they get from the group. In the process, we really focus on the strength of the parent and see them as asking for help which requires a lot of courage."

In this way, the group's process of filing reports to protective services is anchored in a focus on resourcefulness, a commitment to empowering processes, and a preference for partnership and reflects a stance of an appreciative ally, as discussed in Chapter 1.

In an ethnographic study of mothers who had traumatic histories in their own lives and who subsequently developed better ways of parenting their children, numerous participants identified PA as the most important resource available to them in their efforts to become a different kind of parent (Monaghan-Blout, 1999). These mothers revealed that their involvement with PA led to profound changes in self-esteem and self-acceptance, improved interpersonal skills, and the emergence of a sense of hope and agency. An examination of PA's contributions to the changes in their lives supports Rappaport's description of self/mutual-help groups as "normative narrative communities where identity transformation takes place." The mothers in Monaghan-Blout's study identified three interconnected characteristics of PA groups that led to positive changes: (1) the power of a shared goal of becoming a different kind of parent, (2) the reciprocal nature of a peer helping process which both offered a sense of belonging and multiple ways of learning, and (3) the guarantee of acceptance and expectation of honesty. Each of these characteristics is intimately tied to the development of a supportive community. The characteristics both contribute to the development of community and derive from it.

Supporting the Development of Alternative Stories through Self/Mutual-Help Groups

Mutual-help organizations are one of a number of potential communities of membership available to people. In joining a mutual-help organization, members may not be deciding to obtain treatment so much as seeking to answer identity questions and may be rejecting the identity offered to them by professional treatment as "recipients of services" (Rappaport, 1993). This framework for understanding self/mutual-help groups raises interesting questions about the identities available to people as "patients" in mental health settings and as "members" of a self/mutual-help group. Referring again to an interview with the two women (Karen and Naomi) involved with PA (first discussed in Chapter 1) about their experiences with the mental health system provides a closer look at this phenomenon. We can contrast Naomi's experience of therapy in one clinic and her participation in PA groups.

NAOMI: In that clinic, I felt like they had this very stereotyped view of me. They seemed to see me as an abusive parent, probably an alcoholic. That's the message that I got. All they saw were problems. But that's not all that I was. I needed help, but the way it was offered stunted my growth.

BILL: How did that stunt your growth?

NAOMI: I would leave sessions crying because there was a lot of shame. I kept hearing that I was a bad mother. I would feel all this guilt and shame, and in turn not be a good mother. I had this image portrayed of what a good parent was supposed to be doing and I obviously wasn't doing that, so there was something clearly lacking in me. And the whole focus was on what I wasn't doing rather than what I was doing. It was almost impossible to focus on the good parts of my parenting and I'd come home and all I could see was the way in which I wasn't parenting well. All I could see was the negative, and so my parenting skills were really affected.

The interactions in these sessions invited an experience of self that was anchored in guilt, shame, and negativity for Naomi. The process invited the enactment of a life story that subsequently affected her parenting and, by extension, her daughter. It is doubtful that Naomi's therapist set out to provoke guilt and shame, yet the broader socially constructed expectation of therapy as a place where patients seek professionals' expert knowledge puts the two parties in a particular relationship and generates particular experiences of self for each. Contrast Naomi's experience of therapy with her experience of PA groups.

NAOMI: What made PA work for me was that the focus was not put on what I was doing as a *parent* but what was going on for *me* at the time that I was mistreating my kids. It was not a shame-based thing like, "OK, you slapped your child," but instead a focus on "What's going on for you? How are you feeling? What was going through your mind at the time?" Focusing on me first allowed me to better focus on my child. You know it's hard listening to a kid going, "I need, I need, I need" when inside you're also saying, "I need, I need, I need." I got what I needed through the group and therefore I was capable of giving to my child what she needed. I remember after meetings, it was like a flower blossoming. I would come out feeling so full and feeling good about myself and then I was more able to give to my child.

In this second situation, Naomi's experience with PA supported her emerging alternative story of being more than an "abusive parent." That transformation of identity was nurtured by her experience of self in the groups. This commentary is not simply a critique of therapy but an invitation to consider the identity choices available for participants in the process. How do we find ways to support therapy as an empowering experience that can be claimed with pride? Many of the ideas and practices in this book offer ways to elicit, elaborate, and solidify alternative experiences and stories. However, it is useful to examine some of the limitations of the broader context in which professional help is embedded.

Chapter 1 examined a number of the ways in which the current organization of services may have inadvertent disempowering effects on clients. For an alternative to that structure, consider the following comments from Naomi and Karen.

NAOMI: In PA groups, everyone is there on an equal footing. In our groups, we do check-ins and the leaders also check in. I've found that so rewarding because I learn from that. I learn that I'm OK and we're all in this together and nobody is perfect. And so, I'm more honest. I feel human and on a level with everybody else in the group and not less than human because I have problems and they're just there to help me. I find that in a group it's easier to have that happen. We're like spokes on a wheel and we work as a group. We all bring strengths and weaknesses to the group.

KAREN: Including the group leaders. You know, it's really different in a group like that. This question of us all being more equal is a cool question. I've always wanted to ask a therapist this question. Are you taught, is it protocol, is it like a boundary that you're not allowed to cross over to tell a client that you might have struggled with the same issue yourself because then it becomes your therapy and not the client's or something? To me, it's always been more helpful to hear, to have a person in a helping position tell me that they have struggled with a problem too and to let me know what helped them and no therapist I saw would ever do that with me.

Karen's question about professional boundaries is an interesting one. Although I would argue that clear professional boundaries are important and simple advice from professionals is often not particularly helpful, Naomi and Karen raise thought-provoking questions about the broader constraining effects of rigidly defined roles between service providers and service recipients. Much of the power of self/mutual-help groups is due to the reciprocity of group experience and the mutuality of both receiving and giving help. In this way, self/mutual-help groups hold the potential to be powerful contexts for the solidification of alternative stories. The hierarchical nature of professional services (despite our best intentions to flatten hierarchies) may contribute to a one-down relationship and inadvertently reinforce pathologizing identities. If the goal of our work is to help people step away from old constraining identities and support the development of new alternative identities, self/mutual-help groups may be particularly useful in this process.

Implications for Professional Help

What are the lessons to be drawn from the apparent power of self/mutual-help groups? One potential lesson would be that helpers could benefit from drawing more on the power of self/mutual-help groups. However, I believe we can learn even more from these groups. Self/mutual-help groups have often been viewed as an important adjunct to professional treatment modalities. Salzer, McFadden, and Rappaport (1994) found that although professionals, regardless of their discipline or work context, tended to see self-help groups in a positive light, they always viewed professional groups as more helpful than self-help groups. This finding is in direct contrast to the experience of the mothers in Monaghan-Blout's (1999) study in which numerous mothers identified PA as the most important resource in their efforts at change. This contrast raises an interesting question about whose judgment should be privileged regarding the question of what "help" is helpful.

Perhaps professional "treatment" could be seen as adjunctive to self/mutual-help groups rather than vice versa. Unfortunately, we as professionals generally know significantly more about professional services that we do about self/mutual-help groups. Yet, professional services (especially in an era of managed care) are a poor substitute for ongoing community. If we are to be truly supportive of the growth of alternative stories of identity, we need to better support the "village" it takes to raise those stories. This shift requires a rethinking of professional assumptions and has important implications for how we think about both self/mutual-help groups and our own practices. Referring back to the cross-cultural metaphor used throughout this book, we may benefit from examining the effectiveness of self/mutual-help groups within their own cultural context rather than within our professional cultural context. Such a shift would privilege members' views of how participation in groups has affected their lives and their identities rather than trying to measure them based on outcome data that professionals deem relevant.

We can also rethink the roles of mutual-help organizations in the design and delivery of professional services. One way to do this is to include consumer groups more in the design of services and involve them more in the training of professionals. Consumer groups such as PA have been and could be more widely used as valuable, *paid* consultants to state agencies seeking to develop child abuse treatment and prevention programs. Their members could also provide valuable training to students and agency staff. When I have interviewed or shown videotapes of consumers talking about their experiences of service delivery, staff and students have consistently found the process valuable and moving.

Self/mutual-help groups can also serve as an accountability check in our ongoing work with clients. They can provide clients with a reference group with which to reality-test their reactions to our services. For example, Naomi earlier described her negative experience in a mental health clinic in which she felt stereotyped as "abusive, probably an alcoholic." In asking how she managed to hold onto a broader view of herself, she credited PA meetings.

NAOMI: PA really helped there. I would go to PA meetings and talk about what happened. I'd hear from other people what they saw in me and that was enough to keep me alive in another view of my parenting. I didn't cave into the clinic's view because I had this whole group saying, "Well, this is how we see you." And the feedback wasn't all perfect. The group saw that I needed help in parenting, but they also saw the good in my parenting. They kept me motivated and empowered me to say, "This help doesn't fit." Before I couldn't say that because I desperately needed help and had no other input. I was pretty much at the mercy of any social worker or any agency to help me out. But PA empowered me to say, "You're wrong in how you see me. That's not what's going on here." And so I left that agency.

BILL: Was that hard to do?

NAOMI: Yes, it was very hard because I really questioned whether I was "in denial," or whether the clinic saw something real that I didn't. I didn't trust my own judgment, but in the end the experience was just so devastating to me that I had to get out. There was just no working with them.

Naomi later received services from another helper and initially had concerns about this second worker also. She brought her concerns to her PA group and described her experience:

"I brought it to the table and said, 'This is what's going on with me.' After the first experience, I was really leery. I wanted help, but I was pretty scared to trust someone. So again, I listened to the group and they were able to help me keep open and continue."

In this way, self/mutual-help groups can also serve as a place for clients to reflect on their experience of our efforts and receive some assistance in making sense of what they find helpful or not helpful. When clients have a reference group that can provide them with reality testing, they can examine our services more critically and respond rather than simply react to our efforts. At times, this idea can be threatening to professionals and may disrupt what has become, for helpers, a comfortable distribution of power in therapeutic relationships. However, it seems to have broader positive effects for clients. When people have input from multiple sources, they can choose what best fits for them. Similarly, when people don't feel trapped in a particular relationship and have the possibility of leaving it, they are often able to be more fully in that relationship. From here, the next section examines mutual-help organizations that help clients to take action to directly address the broader supports for problems in their lives.

ARCHIVES AND LEAGUES

A further extension in developing communities of support is the idea of *leagues*. At the end of the termination interview outline described in Chapter 7, the sharing-client-wisdom questions sought to elicit client suggestions for other persons struggling with similar problems. These questions grew out of earlier efforts by David Epston in New Zealand. During the early 1980s, he began collecting clients' experiences, ideas, and wisdom about such problems as tempers, night fears, truancy, asthma, anorexia, and bulimia (Madigan & Epston, 1995). He developed *archives* that contained various letters, artwork, and audiotapes and began to share them with other clients in an attempt to circulate a new form of expert knowledge. As these archives grew, he began to bring together a network of clients, primarily in New Zealand, with the purpose of supporting and consulting to each other. He called these networks leagues. In Vancouver, Canada, Stephen Madigan, who was working with a number of women struggling with anorexia and bulimia, supported the development of the Vancouver Anti-Anorexia/Anti-Bulimia League (Grieves, 1997, 1998; Grieves & Madigan, 1996; Madigan & Epston, 1995).

The Vancouver Anti-Anorexia/Anti-Bulimia League began as a loose confederation of individuals who had come together to nourish hope and support each other in resisting the influence of anorexia, bulimia, and compulsive eating. In an expansion of agency from a personal to collective level, the group promoted the sharing of people's immediate knowledge about anorexia, bulimia, and compulsive eating to stand in solidarity with each other against those problems (hence the anti-language; e.g., anti-anorexia). By their definition, the Vancouver League functions as follows:

> A gathering of persons who have a desire to protest the societal practices that promote comparison, perfection, an unrealistic "body ideal," and anorexia/bulimia/compulsive eating. The aim of the group is to provide an alternative perspective on disordered eating to those who are in the grips of the problem, as well to those who are in positions of helping or supporting those who are struggling. (Grieves & Madigan, 1996)

In 1994, the Vancouver League obtained nonprofit status and since then has continued to broaden its activities to include preventive education and community awareness that includes professional consultation and education, media interviews, letter writing, public education in schools, and distribution of a magazine called *ReVive*. In the process, the league has moved from support to action. Through action, league members are not only addressing the broader cultural supports for anorexia, bulimia and compulsive eating but also supporting each other in living out very different personal life stories in the process. As Lorraine Grieves (1997) has put it, "the League is not a therapy group, but involvement can be very therapeutic" (p. 83).[7] In leagues, the role of professional helpers moves further to a supportive, adjunctive position. In this position, professional helpers are more embedded in a stance of an ally.

This description of leagues represents one of many powerful community projects through which participants engage in actions that profoundly shift their relationship to problems while addressing the cultural supports for those problems. The *Dulwich Centre Journal* (formerly the *Dulwich Centre Newsletter*) in Adelaide, Australia, has described many innovative community projects.[8]

SUMMARY

Problems do not stand alone in their influence on people's lives. They are embedded in a network of interactions, beliefs, and cultural assumptions that leave people disconnected from the communities that otherwise might provide concern and support for them. As emphasized in Chapters 5 and 6, externalizing and deconstructive questioning benefit from attempts to bring to light the cultural support for problems in order to help clients disconnect from (or change their relationship to) the network of support for old problems. As people move from the grip of old problems to the hope of new futures, they can receive powerful support in this process by reconnecting to a preferred community of support. This chapter has highlighted a number of ways to help clients develop preferred communities of support and draw on them to move toward envisioned futures and alternative lives.

The examples here represent just a few of the possibilities available in effectively drawing on natural networks. Reconnecting interviews hold the potential to bring the imagined presence of important others into the room. Letter-writing campaigns can help to concretize that presence and further develop people's communities. Self/mutual-help groups offer opportunities for people to share respective expertise and actively embed themselves in alternative communities of support. And, leagues provide opportunities to take action in the expansion of new lives.

NOTES

1. In this book, I use the phrase "reconnection interviews" in place of the original phrase "re-membering interviews." While the concept of "re-membering" is embedded in a rich theoretical context, it can be confusing outside that context, and "reconnection" is offered as an attempt to develop more accessible language that also honors the original concept of "re-membering."

2. I would only begin this way if I know the children's immediate safety needs have been addressed. If not, I would begin by taking the necessary steps to ensure that everyone is safe.

3. It is important to note that Anya in her role as a community support worker had the flexibility and organizational support to "hang out" and spend a vast quantity of time with Diana. This example highlights the importance of our availability to fit "services" to client needs rather than simply offering a menu of predetermined categorical services to which clients must fit. This again underscores the crucial importance of working on client turf rather than on professional turf.

4. The power of these shifts-in-identity stories is also reflected in more tradi-

tional outcome measures. For example, during the 32 months prior to the date the member joined the mutual-help organization, members and nonmembers spent a similar number of days in the hospital (174 vs. 179). However, during the next 32 months, after members joined the mutual-help organization, they spent significantly less time in the hospital than did their nonmember counterparts (49 days vs. 123 days). This contrast in hospital stays represents a dramatic cost savings. The details of this study are briefly described in Rappaport (1993) and in greater detail in Kennedy (1989).

5. My experience with PA has been primarily with Parents Anonymous of Massachusetts. For those interested in finding out more about PA or locating the existence of a PA group in your area, contact (909) 621-6184 or look in the local white pages of the phone book under Parents Anonymous.

6. Twelve-Step programs such as AA have provided powerful supportive communities for people seeking to transform their lives. I want to acknowledge their usefulness for many people. At the same time, alternate approaches based on externalizing assumptions raise interesting possibilities for addressing substance misuse dilemmas. For further exploration of such approaches, consider Sanders (1997, 1998).

7. People interested in contacting the Vancouver Anti-Anorexia Anti-Bulimia League can reach the organization at VAAABL #207-1168 Hamilton Street Vancouver, BC, Canada V6B 2S2. The phone number is (604) 688-7860. The fax number is (604) 688-7865.

8. The *Dulwich Centre Journal* can be hard to find. Subscription information in North America is available c/o Sarah Hughes, P.O. Box 34185, Station D, Vancouver, BC, Canada V6J 4N1. A phone number is (888) 245-4411.

9

⟫⟪

The Larger Helping System
as an Appreciative Audience
for New Lives

This book has explored the usefulness of helping families develop a vision of preferred futures, address the constraints to those futures, and draw on a community of support to stand with them in the development of new lives. For families involved with multiple helping systems, professionals are often a very important part of that community of support. In working with families involved with multiple helpers, it can be useful to think about helpers (including ourselves) as audiences for the performance of preferred stories. If interactions between clients and helpers have the potential to invite the enactment of particular stories, our responses to a family's newly developing story can help to expand or suppress that story. Our recognition and appreciation of clients' enactment of alternative stories can open space for the continued elaboration of that story. Likewise, when those newly developing alternative stories are in their early fragile states, our skepticism can have a chilling effect on their development and inadvertently support the dominant story's reassertion of itself. When our help is anchored in strength-based, collaborative partnership, we are well positioned as an appreciative ally in the elaboration and solidification of preferred lives. However, sometimes we, as helpers, are constrained from better serving in this capacity by problematic interactional patterns, the stories we hold about families, and the stories families hold about us.

This chapter offers a way of thinking about situations in which the help offered to families is no longer experienced by them as helpful. I have previously referred to these situations as "stuck treatment"[1] (Harkaway & Madsen, 1989; Madsen, 1992). This chapter examines common problematic interactional patterns that can develop between families and helpers and explores ways to anticipate and step out of those patterns. It also considers situations in which the work with families has become chronically stuck, with a particular focus on helpers' stories about families in those situations. Some of this chapter overlaps with Chapter 3 on engaging families. However, the primary focus here is on working with other helpers to develop an appreciative professional audience that supports families' enactment of alternative stories and preferred lives. In examining the ways in which helpers can become stuck with families, it is important to include ourselves to avoid the hubris that somehow we (unlike other helpers) are immune to the grip of constraining patterns and stories. The section on working with other helpers examines ideas for engaging other helpers, offers suggestions for the ongoing involvement of other helpers in our work, and explores ways to invite other helpers to reflect on potential constraining effects of their stories about clients. Finally, the chapter concludes with an examination of ways to proceed with families when other helpers' constraining stories about them seem rigidly fixed and show little flexibility.

    This section begins by reviewing some of the basic assumptions that inform this conceptualization of stuck treatment. It is useful to draw on a cross-cultural metaphor in examining stuck treatment. Families and helpers can each be viewed as distinct microcultures with particular beliefs, preferred styles of interacting, and different rules of engagement. Therapeutic services can be seen as a cross-cultural negotiation in which families and helpers interact in a mutually influencing relationship. It's useful to think about engaging families with the curiosity of an anthropologist rather than the certainty of a missionary. Because the activities of any foreign culture become more understandable through the lens of that culture, viewing therapy from both the family's and the worker's perspective allows a different understanding of the difficulties that may emerge. Within this framework, it is more useful to view stuck treatment as an interactional process rather than an individual or family characteristic. In examining stuck treatment as an interactional process, the concept of constraints shifts the organizing question from "What caused this work to become stuck?" to "What might be constraining the family and helpers from working together more effectively?" Again, we can identify constraints in realms of action (problematic family–helper interactional patterns) and meaning (problematic stories held by families or helpers about the other).

INTERACTIONAL CONSTRAINTS
IN STUCK TREATMENT

Chapter 2 drew on Karl Tomm's (1991) organizational schema of "pathologizing interpersonal patterns" to examine interactional patterns in families. This schema is also useful for examining recurring patterns that develop between families and helpers. The remainder of this section examines a variety of common problematic patterns that can develop between helpers and families.

Overly Harsh/Overly Protective Pattern

At age 12, Samantha told her therapist that her 14-year-old brother, Freddie, had exposed himself to her and her younger sister 1 year prior. The therapist, who had been seeing Samantha individually for depression, viewed her as a lost child and had concerns about her parents' rather lax parenting style. Somewhere in the transfer of information from the girl to the therapist to protective services, the report became quite alarming. A protective services worker accompanied by two policemen went to Freddie's school. During a break between classes, the police went up to the boy in the hallway, read him his rights, handcuffed him, and took him away to a foster home. The protective services worker informed Freddie's parents of his placement and demanded that the boy not have any contact with his sisters.

Freddie's parents were shocked, particularly his mother, Ethyl. Ethyl had a mix of reactions. She was simultaneously horrified for her daughters, furious at the thought that her son had potentially exposed himself to her daughters, incredibly guilty that she didn't know about it, and completely dumbfounded. As she later put it, "This was not the son I knew and loved. There must be some mistake, my son would never have done something like that." Her main reaction though was outrage at the way Freddie had been treated by protective services. She thought the public arrest was humiliating and unnecessary. She saw her son as victimized by protective services and was furious with them. When the protective services worker met with Ethyl to enlist her help in holding Freddie accountable for his actions, Ethyl responded with outrage at how her son had been treated and offered numerous excuses for his behavior. The worker felt the mother was colluding with her son's denial, which confirmed for her that she needed to actively intervene to protect the sisters. The protective services worker demanded that Freddie not have any contact with his sisters and charged the parents with neglect. Ethyl, in turn, threatened a lawsuit and made numerous calls to newspapers and state legislators. Freddie refused to follow any rules in the foster home, got in trouble in his new community, and was asked to leave the foster home. He went through a series of foster homes and was finally placed in a residential program because of his deteriorating behavior and unwillingness to take responsibility. A number of family therapists attempted to work with the family and were subsequently fired by the parents when they refused to participate in the lawsuit the parents continued to threaten.

One way to describe the pattern between Ethyl and the protective services worker would be as an overly harsh/overly protective pattern in which the protective services worker's "harsh" actions of sending out the police to place him invited "protectiveness" from Ethyl and Ethyl's protectiveness of her son (which focused her attention on his victimization and obscured his victimizing) confirmed for the worker the need for more extreme measures. In the process, the protective services worker's and Ethyl's stereotypes of each other were confirmed and each continued her part of the pattern with increased righteousness.

The pattern constrained the adults in Freddie's life (school, protective services, and parents) from working together to help him acknowledge his actions, accept responsibility for the effects of those actions, and make himself accountable. As the family–helper system became increasingly polarized, their respective stances rigidified and became more black and white with increasingly less room for complexity or gray areas. The source of conflict became framed as either Freddie was an abuser or he was a victim of the system. As might be imagined, this pattern also drove a wedge in helping relationships. Ethyl and the protective services worker came to distrust each other, and neither would return phone calls from the other. In time, the pattern became self-perpetuating in that each new therapist was greeted with a demand that he or she sign on to a lawsuit against protective services before the family would be willing to discuss other issues. When new therapists expressed hesitation to do that, they were immediately cast as the enemy. Finally, the pattern took a toll on individual helpers and family members. Helpers attempting to work with the family often described feeling frustrated and angry at Ethyl's "unreasonableness" and yet also feeling incompetent because of their inability to shift her stance. Ethyl, for her part, feared that she was developing an ulcer. In this way, problematic family–helper interactional patterns can have significant negative effects on therapeutic relationships and individual participants as well as on services.

Viewing the interactional pattern (rather than the individuals) as the problem helps to mitigate these effects and points to directions for anticipating and perhaps avoiding them. An example of this possibility comes from a therapist who anticipated this interaction when reading the referral he got for the family. When he met with the parents, Ethyl demanded he support her suit, and the therapist replied that he needed to look into his organization's rules about that sort of thing before giving her an answer. He was very curious about Ethyl's rationale for the suit and listened empathically to her story of Freddie's victimization. As he listened, he commented on Ethyl's sense of fairness and justice. In this response, he was deliberately stepping out of the pattern that had engulfed multiple helpers. As he began interacting with Ethyl outside this pattern, she responded in kind. Her demand that he sign onto the lawsuit faded away. The therapist did not begin by talking about Freddie's responsibility in the situation but built on Ethyl's sense of fairness and justice to eventually ask about her daughters' perspective on the situation. From that basis, Ethyl began to talk about the effects of Freddie exposing himself to her daughters and became adamant that he "do the right thing" and get help for "his problem." Ethyl's shift supported Freddie to eventually accept more responsibility for his actions. That shift was facilitated by the therapist engaging Ethyl outside the problematic pattern.

Overresponsible/Underresponsible Pattern

We have seen multiple examples of overresponsible/underresponsible patterns throughout this book. This pattern often occurs in situations in which a client is seen as being in denial or as minimizing his or her problems. In this situation, the client stance of "this is not a problem" (substance misuse, violence, physical, sexual and emotional abuse, etc.) invites a counterresponse of confronting the "denial." Unfortunately, in situations in which this pattern has a previous history, confronting denial may paradoxically rigidify denial. The extended example in Chapter 3 of engaging Bob, a "neglectful" parent who struggled with alcohol, highlights a way of breaking this pattern. Anticipating an overresponsible/underresponsible pattern allows us to respond differently when we are invited into overresponsibility. As we sidestep that invitation, we can look for small exceptions in which clients begin to take some degree of responsibility and build on that opening.

Minimize/Maximize Pattern

Evelyn was a competent and committed Irish foster mother whose pride in her work was captured in the special place reserved on her mantelpiece for the Foster Mother of the Year award she received 2 years ago. She had taken in a large number of difficult kids and considered herself an underrecognized expert on child development. Rashad was a 12-year-old African American boy who had been in several foster placements after his parents abandoned him. His therapist and protective services worker saw past his tough, street-kid demeanor and viewed him as a misunderstood child with great potential. However, this view of Rashad was not shared in the general community. He had been repeatedly suspended from school for his bad attitude, interracial fights, and continual taunting of female teachers. He had been in Evelyn's home for 2 months and she was at her wit's end. She was fed up with his verbal harassment of her daughter and another foster girl and became scared when knives in the house began to disappear. She saw Rashad as a seriously disturbed boy who had conned the other helpers and insisted that he should be placed in a residential program before someone got hurt. The therapist and protective services worker remained convinced that Rashad could make it at Evelyn's if she would just give him a chance. They worried that her rejection of this boy was tinged with racism but weren't sure how to raise that issue with her. The more they spoke about Rashad's potential as a youngster, the more Evelyn pointed out his misbehavior. She began keeping a log of his misdeeds which she would give to Rashad's therapist each week. The therapist and the protective services worker spent increasing amounts of time on the phone strategizing about how to deal with Evelyn and found themselves wondering how she ever got that foster parent award.

This situation could be described as a minimize/maximize pattern in which Evelyn perceived the workers' efforts to convince her that Rashad could make it as minimizing her concerns about him. Her feeling that they just didn't get it invited a response of trying to highlight the alarming nature of Rashad's behavior. The workers in turn, became increasingly frustrated at her continual emphasis on his misbehavior, and so they continued trying to get her to see that the placement could work if Evelyn would just give Rashad a chance. Again, this pattern constrained Evelyn and the helpers from working together more effectively. Just as the two helpers were in a position of attempting to prove to Evelyn that Rashad could make it, Evelyn was in a position of attempting to prove to them that he couldn't. The pattern rigidified her negative view of Rashad and undercut both Evelyn's sense of competence and her connection with the helpers.

Again, awareness of this pattern helped to disrupt it. In a supervision meeting, the therapist was invited to examine this pattern from Evelyn's perspective and reflect on how she might respond to it. The therapist decided that Evelyn, who took great pride in her skills as a foster mother, might feel pretty embarrassed to be unable to manage a kid whom the helpers were describing as a creampuff. The therapist went out to meet with Evelyn, confessing that maybe she had missed something and asking Evelyn to fill her in about the concerns about Rashad. As the therapist listened, she went out of her way to validate Evelyn's concerns and wondered out loud how Evelyn had coped with all that she was describing. As the therapist continued asking questions and acknowledging Evelyn's expertise with Rashad, Evelyn began to soften. "Oh, he's not so bad," she said, "You just have to have a little tolerance with him." Evelyn went on to express concerns that Rashad was getting scapegoated in school because he was black (which was a much better foundation for a discussion about racism with Evelyn). The two began talking about how Rashad coped with prejudice at school and how he might perceive a white foster mother, which eventually led into a discussion about Evelyn's reactions to having an African American young man in her home. Evelyn raised a number of questions about some of Rashad's demeanor that she didn't understand, and the therapist subsequently engaged the two in a mutual exploration of their respective cultures.

In each of these examples, the pattern was disrupted when the helpers stepped away from their part in the pattern and challenged their own stereotypes in order to do something different. In each, the helpers engaged the other with empathy, curiosity, and validation. However, empathic listening is not enough. The workers were also actively on the lookout for exceptions to the pattern and when they saw glimpses, they stepped into them and expanded them.

Other Family–Helper Patterns

We could trace out a number of other common family–helper patterns that undercut collaborative partnership. Some brief examples follow. A *Demanding Disclosure/Secrecy and Withholding Pattern* can be seen in a situation in which a home-based worker enters a home and senses in her gut that the children are not safe. The more she attempts to get a disclosure of possible abuse, the more the family seals over and withdraws. The family's response convinces her that she needs to get a disclosure and yet her attempts to obtain a disclosure inadvertently invite silence. While we could view this family as "in denial" and needing to disclose for the children's safety, the interactional pattern paradoxically rigidifies that "denial" and constrains the exchange of information. As the worker acknowledges to herself her inability to take action without a disclosure, realizes the futility of demanding a disclosure, and sees the importance of her continued presence in the family's home, she backs off and attempts to stay connected to various family members. Eventually, when she is seen as a presence who is connected to all members of the family and can be trusted, the mother begins to confide her concerns.

A *Correction and Control/Protest and Rebellion Pattern* can develop in residential programs when the staff's attempts to manage an acting-out adolescent invite increased defiance and that defiance invites further correction. As staff examine their own expectation that they will be "in control," they back off and shift from attempting to control adolescents to supporting them in developing a sense of having more control over their behavior and emotions.[2]

A *Reduced Expectations/Reduced Performance Pattern* is shown in a situation in which a mental health case manager holds little hope for the chronic mental patients on his caseload and counsels them to accept their limitations. They in turn respond with increasingly less adaptability and competence, which confirms his lowered expectations. As the case manager shifts and begins to think about the effects of mental illness on their lives, he increasingly notices their resistance to it. As he shifts to supporting them in their resistance to the effects of mental illness, they begin to show increased competence and adaptability.[3]

Another pattern is *Withholding Information/Reactive Suspiciousness* in which a medical team holds back the bad news because they worry about a patient's reacting inappropriately. The patient in return responds with suspiciousness and paranoia that they're lying to him which paradoxically confirms the team's decision to titrate medical information. As a medical social worker helps the team shift to acknowledge his suspicions, he is initially furious but calms down and thanks the team for being honest with him.

A *Criticize/Defend Pattern* can develop between a parent aide team and a parent when the way in which the team offers parenting education classes is perceived by a mother as a criticism of her current parenting and she responds defensively and points out how their ideas just won't work. This situation has often been described as a "yes, but" game that is played by the client. If we view it instead as an interactional process, it is possible to shift our emotional response to the situation and move to honoring and supporting client knowledge before offering our own if invited. That situation can degenerate into an *Attacking/Counterattacking Pattern* in which the perceived criticism is responded to under the ethos of "the best defense is a strong offense." We can find this pattern often developing between parents and foster parents who are in competition. Again, shifting out of that pattern into a stance of validation begins to disrupt the pattern.

In each of these types of situations, the futility of the situation becomes readily apparent when viewed through the lens of a recurring pattern. However, when we are in the midst of a situation, the pattern is not so obvious. The invitations of these patterns can be very strong and can easily suck us into them. Holding a template of possible patterns can help us to become more easily aware of them as they're developing.

THE BROADER CONTEXT OF PROBLEMATIC FAMILY–HELPER PATTERNS

All the patterns examined here reflect a final problematic family–helper pattern that could be described as an instruct/resist pattern. In this pattern, a helper attempts to get a client to see something deemed important in a way that invites client resistance. That "resistance" in turn, invites more strenuous or sophisticated attempts to "instruct" on the helper's part. The attempts to confront denial, get a disclosure, manage acting-out behavior, get a client to acknowledge his or her limitations, manage a client's reaction to our formulation, or provide skills to clients are all in some ways attempts to put information into a system that may resist it.

These family–helper patterns do not develop in isolation. They receive significant support from professional ideas and practices that we take for granted as well as broader cultural discourses. The ways in which we are traditionally taught to interact with clients and many of our standard practices have the potential to encourage instruction of clients, which the clients may perceive as attempts to convert or colonize them. For example, from a behavioral perspective, we attempt to shape behavior in a predetermined direction. From a psychodynamic perspective, we attempt to offer an insight (at the "appropriate" moment). From a structural–strategic perspective, we set up an enactment or offer a reframe with a particular outcome in mind. In each of these perspectives, the way in which the helper–family relationship is defined privileges the helper's knowledge and experience.

Families' relationships with helpers are culturally defined as complimentary: helpers offer help and families receive it (Imber-Black, 1991). This relationship prescription is reflected in our language, through the common use of phrases such as case and case manager and recipient and provider. It is also reflected in the differential boundaries that exist in which families may be required to share much more information with the helping system than the helping system is required to share with the family and in which families are expected to provide open entry into their system while entry into helping systems is often regulated by formal and complex processes (Imber-Black, 1988). In addition, families are often expected to accommodate to the peculiar language of professional jargon. As an example, a student who recently sat through her first hospital case conference described feeling completely lost amid the professional jargon. When she later told her supervisor, her supervisor apologized and offered to clarify anything the student did not understand. Unfortunately, no such conversation was held with the single-parent mother who had also attended her first hospital case conference. Who is accommodating to whom here? The movement from a professional-centered service delivery system to a family-centered helping system would be an important step in disrupting problematic family–helper interactional patterns. One small step in this process would be to begin referring to clients as "the people for whom we work."

It is important to also place the professional discourses that influence stuck treatment in a broader cultural context. This situation is embedded in broader cultural ideas about getting help and professional expertise. Clients often come expecting to "get the answers" from those who are being paid to provide the answers. When the "answers" don't fit (as is often the case), the cultural discourse of getting help structures a setup for frustration and failure. Viewing these interactions in a broader cultural context helps us to not blame individuals participants and supports a deeper appreciation of the difficulties of stepping away from these patterns. The next section examines beliefs that may interfere with effective work with families.

CONSTRAINING BELIEFS
IN STUCK TREATMENT

These patterns give rise to and are supported by beliefs held by helpers and families. Families seeking help (or having help foisted on them) often enter the helping relationship with beliefs about helpers and the meaning of receiving help. As Imber-Black (1988) has pointed out, these beliefs may grow out of intergenerational legacies or out of critical incidents that developed between the family and helpers in the past. Critical incidents are the important interactions between a family and a particular helper that provide a lesson about helpers and constitute a template for making sense of future interactions with them. These critical incidents could be positive (e.g. "That therapist was the first person in my life who really listened to me. Therapy has changed my life.") or negative (e.g., the experience of Ethyl, the mother in the overly harsh/overly protective pattern described earlier). The lessons from these critical incidents provide a framework for anticipating and making sense of future interactions with helpers. For example, after the protective service worker placed Ethyl's son in a foster home, Ethyl expected that every subsequent helper was out to get her son and entered her interactions with them with considerable suspiciousness. These templates can become a self-fulfilling prophecy that promotes selective attention to disconnection, frustration, and pathologizing interactions and selective inattention to moments of connection, help, and support. Clients also hold beliefs about the meaning of getting help. These beliefs are embedded in and influenced by intergenerational and cultural stories. For example, one family may believe that receiving services is a mark of shame, a belief supported by our culture's emphasis on individualism and achievement. Another family may believe that they will always need help and cannot function without helpers, a belief that can be supported by the helping system's tendency to prescribe more helpers as a solution to additional problems.

Helpers hold beliefs about families, their ability to change, and the meaning of their involvement with helping systems. These beliefs are influenced by current theories passed off as essential truths about human nature (e.g., "Adolescence is a time of separation and we need to help this boy individuate from his mother."), from prejudices about categories of families such as poor or minorities (e.g., "Welfare recipients lack initiative."), from reports written by other helpers or information shared at case conferences (e.g., "The Millers are an enmeshed family with weak generational boundaries and a poorly functioning executive subsystem."), and from previous experiences with similar clients or families (e.g., "Alcoholics always deny.").

These beliefs are embedded in broader cultural assumptions about families receiving services. As Imber-Black (1991) has pointed out, helping systems tend to reflect cultural norms that support traditional and nuclear family forms, even though the families we serve often do not conform to such forms. Based on unexamined assumptions about "normal" families, helping systems may see deficiency and pathology in families that deviate from those norms and thus begin services with unacknowledged prejudices and stereotypes. For example, single-parent families are seen as less functional than two-parent families with emotionally absent fathers. Adults living with their parents are seen as emotionally immature. Grandmothers who head families are often ignored or seen as intrusive. Gay partners become invisible.

Our interactions with mothers in families often reflect the broader double-binding cultural messages that they receive. We expect mothers to be involved in services, while we only hope to engage fathers. We discuss weak generational boundaries in single-parent, female-headed families and then make referrals to a big brother organization for a male role model. We rely on mothers as the information conduit between the family and multiple helpers and at the same time criticize them for over-involvement. Helpers in a team meeting focus on a mother's inability to parent her son who has been in six placements but neglect to include that the six placements haven't been able to contain him either. Again, these practices are not simply tendencies of individuals but reflect widespread cultural assumptions.

The current cultural disdain for people receiving services (the "undeserving poor") insidiously creeps into our attitudes toward the people we serve. For example, a father seeking services for heroin addiction after being incarcerated describes having to prove that he is deserving of services. A social services worker who has noncategorical funds available for family emergencies adamantly declares that she is not going to give anything more to the Smith family until the Smiths show her some progress. A team of professionals file a neglect charge against a mother who consistently misses the case conferences for which they have scheduled her.

One upshot of these beliefs is that when treatment difficulties arise, we, as helpers, are encouraged to look "out there" in the client system for an explanation of the problem. As families and helpers become increasingly caught by problematic interactional patterns, these patterns take an increasing toll on their experience of themselves, each other, and their relationship. Over time, repeated treatment failures give rise to a pervasive atmosphere of negativity in which participants begin to lose hope for the possibility of change and interact in ways that protect them from a sense of failure, blame, and shame. The development of a protective stance may be reflected in a number of ways. Ethyl's demand that helpers sign on to a lawsuit against protective services is one example. A worker's resigned response, "I'll refer them, but what's the use; it won't make a difference," is another. This hopelessness is understandable in the context of repeated frustrations. Ethyl is unwilling to invest her time and energy in another worker who is not going to fully back her. The resigned worker has felt burned one time too many by clients that she hoped for and is not interested in "setting herself up for disappointment" again. In this situation, a shift occurs from attempting to get and give help to getting out from under feelings of shame, blame, and failure. These reactions (hopelessness, frustration, disappointment, etc.) can then be seen as a problem and fruitfully externalized in order to help helpers and families develop a different relationship to them.

UNSTICKING OURSELVES

When our help to the clients for whom we work is not experienced as helpful, we can benefit by an awareness of the pitfalls of these constraining patterns and beliefs. They are most helpful as a roadmap of potential potholes that we might seek to avoid. However, these patterns and beliefs are very powerful, and it is easy to become ensnared in them. When that happens, the following questions can be helpful to "unstick" us (Madsen, 1998):

- What is this interaction like from the client's perspective?
- How would I react to this situation if I were in this family's shoes?
- What could I do as the therapist to make this situation worse?
- What in fact might I be doing to make the situation worse?
- What is the positive intent behind their behavior that I find frustrating?
- How can I come to respect and appreciate that?
- What strengths and resources haven't I discovered yet about this family?
- What don't I know about this family that would change my opinion of them?
- What could I learn from this family?

These questions can help us to identify constraints to more effective work with families and keep us anchored in the relational stance we would prefer to hold. They can be useful as questions to pose to ourselves. We can also turn to our colleagues or supervisors for help in extricating ourselves from stuck situations by having them ask us questions similar to these.

The next section shifts the focus from ways in which we can become stuck to ways of working with other helpers to help them become appreciative audiences for clients' enactment of new stories. It begins with an examination of the process of engaging other helpers, discusses informal, ongoing ways to shift their relationship to constraining patterns and beliefs, and concludes with an examination of ways to work with families when helpers' pathologizing beliefs about them appear to be fixed and rigidly held.

ENGAGING OTHER HELPERS

Before meeting families for the first time, my preference is to obtain very little information from other helpers. I want to approach families with a fresh perspective and avoid a situation in which I falsely believe that I know who they are before I've met them. However, after meeting with families, it is useful to get their permission to contact other involved helpers to hear their thoughts, avoid duplicating services, and increase the chance that we're operating on similar wavelengths. It is important to take the process of getting a family's permission seriously and not to assume that we have the right to talk to other helpers simply because we're involved in the family's life. We can frame the request to talk to other helpers as our need. As an example, the information release form I use contains the following introduction:

"I have found that I'm able to be most helpful to individuals, couples, and families when I can coordinate my efforts with other services you may be receiving or have received from other helpers. To do that, I'm requesting your permission to talk to other professionals in order to get their ideas about how I can be more helpful to you. I will be glad to share with you the ideas I receive if you would like."

As indicated in the last line of this introduction, I explicitly tell clients and families that I am willing to share any information that comes out of conversations with other helpers. Professional conversations about clients occur as attempts to be helpful to them and it is important that those conversations be accountable to the people they are designed to help. Our conversations about families can have a tendency to slide into a kind of professional gossip in which helpers exchange information and opinions in ways that can be experienced by the family as demeaning or judgmental, and it is important to guard against that. If we have an agreement to make conversations with other helpers transparent to the family, it is important to let other helpers know that. At times, the existence of such an agreement can cause discomfort or provoke dismay on the part of other helpers and may constrain the type and amount of information we get. However, it keeps us from being pulled into secretive coalitions that exclude families and supports the enactment of the values discussed throughout this book.

When talking with other helpers, the additional effort taken to develop a relationship saves time down the line. Just as it is useful to get to know families outside the problem, getting to know other helpers outside the immediate context of working with a particular family helps to build a foundation that can be drawn on later. This attempt does not require long phone conversations and can be done in brief moments. As an example, a home-based program that I used to supervise developed a WINS program (a take-off on a state acronym—CHINS—Child in Need of Service, referring to youths who become involved with social services without being a protective case). When a team member saw a protective services worker who was looking particularly burned out, he or she would file a WINS (Worker in Need of Service) on the worker. This was an in-house, informal procedure that led to such things as bringing pastry to the next meeting with that person or sending the person a thank-you card for his or her work with a particular family. This same team made a point of feeding workers who came to our office for meetings and routinely kept track of and asked about other helpers' hobbies or children. Although the intention behind these activities was to contribute to a more caring helping environment, the team members also gained significant relational legitimacy that supported their recommendations in times of crisis. This example highlights the importance of the attitude with which we approach other helpers.

It's helpful to learn about the organizational context in which a helper works. That context organizes the family–helper relationship and influences the helper's view of the family. For example, the organizational mandates for a protective services worker, a parole officer, and an outpatient therapist encourage them to attend to different elements in their interactions with families. Where we stand organizes what we see. The knowledge of where helpers stand as they comment on a family provides a context for understanding their observations. As we move into asking about clients, it can be fruitful to begin with questions that invite other helpers to paint a rich picture of the client as a human being. For example, we could ask questions such as, "Can you help me get a sense of what these folks are like? What do they do for fun? What do you like about them? What would it be like to meet them on the street rather than in a therapeutic context? What do you think I might particularly appreciate about them?" These questions anchor what we learn about a client or family in an acknowledgment of their humanity. It helps to protect against the possibility of an objectifying discussion of a "case." And, in an abridged transfer of information, it helps both us and other helpers move from an exchange of thin conclusions to the development of thicker descriptions.

Chapter 2 highlighted the importance of learning about client beliefs in the areas of problem, treatment, and roles (Harkaway & Madsen, 1989; Madsen, 1992). These areas are also useful to explore when asking helpers about their work with a family. In learning about helpers' beliefs about the problem, it is useful to inquire about who they are seeing and how they came to be involved with the client or family. We can ask about what they are most concerned, who else is concerned about what problems, what the client is most concerned about, and how they and the client would each explain the problem. In learning more about their beliefs about the problem, we can seek to understand their ideas about how it came to be a problem, whether they think the client can affect the problem, and whether there are special meanings (for the client or the helper) associated with the problem. While the cultural norm for helper–family relationships is a complementary one, helper relationships are usually experienced as symmetrical relationships among equals. As a result, it is important that the questions that we ask other helpers be asked in a conversational way rather than as an interview of the helper. Most of these questions can be asked straightforwardly. However, inquiry about special meanings is something to be on the lookout for rather than asking about directly as it has the potential to be quite offputting.

As we seek to learn about helpers' beliefs about treatment, we can

solicit their opinion whether something can be done about the problem
that most concerns them and their ideas on what would be the best thing
to do? Again, we can inquire both about their beliefs and how they think
their client would respond to those questions. Asking how they imagine
clients might respond both gives us significant information about their
relationship with a client and has interventive potential. Inviting other
helpers to examine a client's experience has the potential to shift their
perspective on that client.

Finally, we can look at beliefs about roles—in particular, the helper's
beliefs about the family's role and the roles of the various helpers. We can
consider the ways in which these beliefs are shaped by organizational
mandates. Again, it is useful to learn about helpers' beliefs about roles as
well as helpers' perception of client beliefs about roles. As we're learning
about beliefs about roles, we can attend to differences that might emerge
between helpers and families and then examine perspectives on how those
differences are managed. If there are differences, are they acknowledged,
ignored, or suppressed? Are they managed overtly or covertly? If the differences are overt, do they lead to open discussion, escalating polarization, quiet submission on the client's part, or pseudocompliance in which
a client appears to agree and then doesn't follow through on helpers' recommendations?

After getting a sense of how helpers understand a family's situation,
it is fruitful to learn about their experience of working with the client or
family. What have they particularly liked about the client? What has been
hard, frustrating, or difficult? How do they cope with that? What do they
think we might come to appreciate about this family? What has worked
and not worked in their work together? Based on that, what suggestions
would they offer to others? Chapter 2 contained a section examining the
family's previous experience with helpers. Similarly, it can be useful to
explore helpers' previous experience with others in our role or agency.
This is reflected in such questions as "Have you made referrals to or
worked with people from our agency in the past? What's that been like
for you? Based on your previous experiences with our agency, do you
have any concerns that I should be aware of?" These questions open
space for open discussion of stereotypes and hidden conflicts that may
affect the work together. In these questions, one could even speak to some
of the concerns that might arise. The question itself signals that those
issues can be discussed and contributes to easing potential interagency
tension. Simply asking these questions opens space for the development
of different relationships.

Finally, it makes sense to learn about other helpers' hopes for our
work with the family, discuss what ongoing contact we should have with
each other, and arrive at some agreement on how to work cooperatively

together. Throughout all of this, we can focus on forming a relationship with other helpers, developing an appreciation for their experience of the client or family, and discovering what we can learn from them. This process is informed by an anthropological metaphor. Just as in our interactions with clients, we can think about this interaction as a crosscultural negotiation. We can enter helpers' microcultures from a stance of cultural curiosity and try to learn as much as possible. In this learning, we can be particularly interested in the helper's interactions with families and the story he or she holds about them, with an eye toward the degree to which that story and those interactions open up or constrain the development of new possibilities.

CAUTIONARY NOTES IN WORKING WITH OTHER HELPERS

The problematic interactional patterns that we've discussed between families and helpers can also play out among helpers. There are a number of possible patterns that we could get caught by, but I want to highlight two in particular. The first is a minimize/maximize pattern in which our attempt to highlight family strengths and the enactment of alternative stories is perceived by other helpers as minimizing family difficulties, which invites attempts on their part to highlight the seriousness of those difficulties. This is a common experience for many workers operating from a strength-based perspective. As they meet with a family and actively look for their strengths and resources, they find what their perspective highlights. In their attempts to open space for an expansion of family resourcefulness, they enthusiastically share their views with other helpers who, perhaps organized by another perspective, have a very different experience of the same family. In their interactions, the other helpers experience the strength-based workers as naïve optimists who minimize pathology and the strength-based helpers experience the other helpers as blinded by their own pathologizing formulations. The resulting polarization ends up confirming each one's stereotypes about the other and inadvertently rigidifying their respective perspectives.

A second potential problematic pattern in working with other helpers is an instruct/resist pattern in which our attempts to share our perspective is experienced by other helpers as us relating to them from a missionary stance as if the story we hold about a family is the correct one and we are trying to convert others to it. Influenced by the work of Evan Imber-Black (1988, 1991), I used to provide meta-consultations to families and larger systems. These consultations attempted to intervene into problematic interactions between families and various helpers. Often there was a sense in such a consultation that because consultants stood outside that system of care, they held a privileged view of the interactions within the system. This view was captured in a common phrase of that time, "meta is better."

One day, a family therapy team requested a consultation for a family and its helpers, including a protective services worker, parole officer, guidance counselor, and three therapists. The family therapist requesting the consultation was concerned about a series of escalating conflicts that had developed between the family members and various helpers and wanted a consultation to address the problematic interactions between the family and helpers. That therapist contacted the participants and arranged the meeting time. Later on I found out that the therapist was particularly concerned that the protective services worker had a pathologizing and negative view of the family. The therapist's concern emerged in a context of a long history of conflicts between the family therapy team and the protective services unit. The family therapy team viewed the protective services unit as pathology detectives who were completely blind to resources and the protective service unit viewed the family therapy team as misguided Pollyannas who in their attempts to be strength focused, often ended up putting children at risk. These respective views developed in the context of a minimize/maximize interactional pattern in which the protective services unit was always trying to get the family therapy team to see real difficulties in the families with which they worked and the family therapy team was always trying to get the protective services unit to see family strengths. The polarization that developed became clear when the protective services worker arrived at the consultation accompanied by her supervisor and their own consultant, a noted child psychiatrist who was an expert on developmental psychopathology. The protective services worker viewed me as an expert coming into set her straight and responded with her own expert.

I thanked them for their concern about the family and interviewed everyone about their various perspectives in order to help me learn how I might be able to be more helpful to the family therapy team. That consultation was an important learning experience. It is not only our work with families that needs to be anchored in strength-based, collaborative partnership. Our work with other helpers is more efficient and effective when it stands on the foundation discussed in Chapter 1. The attitude we bring to our work with other helpers is as important as the attitude we bring to our work with families. Even when we are in conflict with other helpers, it is important to respect their knowledge, honor their intent (even if we are troubled by their effects), and find ways to view them as part of the solution rather than part of the problem.

Years ago, many residential programs worked primarily with children and did little work with families. In those days, programs would often experience situations in which the child showed great progress and then "relapsed" when he or she went home. Sometimes staff would become angry at the parents and see them as resisting or undermining the program's work. In a number of instances, programs learned that you can't view children acontextually and came to believe in the value of including families in residential work from the beginning. When they involved families, the work often became more effective. Similarly, in working with families with multiple helpers, it is dangerous to work acontextually with the family and not recognize the importance of including other helpers in the work from the beginning. Just as residential programs learned that ongoing family relationships would continue long after the placement ended, so too there needs to be an appreciation that the relationships families have with various helpers may continue long after short-term services end. In both situations, care must be taken to strengthen the constructive aspects of both intrafamilial relationships and ongoing family–helper relationships.

Family therapy is undergoing a shift from working with families because they are part of the problem to working with families because they are an important part of the solution. It is important that we approach our work with other helpers in a similar fashion. In some quarters of the child welfare field, there has been a distinct shift from child protection to family preservation. In this shift, the thinking has moved from protecting children from unsafe families to preserving families in an effort to make them safe for children. Similarly, in strength-based work, it is important that we come to see ourselves as engaging not in family protection but, rather, in family–larger system preservation. In this shift, the goal is not to protect families from "bad" helpers but to preserve family–helper ties in an effort to make helping systems more responsive to families.

DEVELOPING AN APPRECIATIVE AUDIENCE FOR THE ENACTMENT OF NEW STORIES

If we acknowledge the importance of the receiving context in which families enact and construct new lives, the development of an appreciative professional audience becomes very important. This next section examines ways of doing that in our ongoing work.

Sherry was an African American single parent whose two daughters (ages 4 and 3) had been placed in foster care after a cocaine habit began to interfere with Sherry's parenting. She thought she had been rescued from an inner-city abusive home by James, a promising Carribean American man who was on the fast track to success. They married and moved out of the neighborhood to a semirural community that was predominantly white. He had gotten a high-tech job and she followed him to build a new life. There was a lot of conflict between Sherry's husband and her family and her family was infuriated that she was abandoning them for this uppity, lighter-skinned man. They cut her off and she moved into a life of supporting her husband in his new environment. As part of his new career, he began partying heavily and Sherry joined in with him after their younger daughter stopped breast-feeding.[4] During a downturn in the economy, James was laid off and their shared cocaine habit siphoned off their financial and emotional reserves. In desperation, James accepted a high-tech job in California with the idea that he would reestablish himself and then bring the family out to join him. Feeling abandoned by her husband and ashamed to talk to her family, Sherry found solace in cocaine. James continued to send her small amounts of money, but he was very critical of her habit and cut her off when her children were taken away from her by protective services. After a downward spiral, Sherry quit cocaine and began to consider whether she could get her children back. Her protective services worker, a white 34-year-old woman named Rose, saw Sherry as a passive and inadequate mother whose badly neglected children were now doing much better in a foster home. Rose was anticipating moving toward freeing up the children for adoption when her supervisor recommended a referral to a home-based family reunification team. Rose was extremely skeptical about this idea but went along and made the referral. A brief description of the work with Sherry sets the stage for an examination of the work with Rose.

Working with Sherry

Two therapists, supported by a larger team worked with Sherry. One therapist predominantly worked with Sherry while the other met with the children. The second therapist also met informally with the foster mother to build support for Sherry's reentering her daughters' lives. Sherry wanted her children back but was convinced that she was "cursed" and "everything she touched turned to shit." She was ashamed of the course her life had taken since she left her family and recoiled at the thought of looking to them for help. She was committed to her children yet feared her curse would ruin their lives also. Her therapist accepted her experience of a curse and began by examining that curse, the relationship she currently had with it, and the relationship she would prefer to have with it. The team saw a good bit of truth in the idea that a now impoverished

African American single mother in a predominantly white community might experience her life as cursed. In the course of the work, Sherry began describing effects of the curse of racism in her life. While she was dark-skinned, her children were very light-skinned and she described being subjected to assumptions that she was their nanny in the predominantly white community. Her therapist (who was white) found her own thinking shifting from the curse of parental inadequacy to the broader curse of racism. In examining how Sherry coped with the curse of racism, the therapist and Sherry both began to learn about hitherto unacknowledged strengths and resources. The therapist inquired what of those resources she would like to pass on to her daughters to support them in dealing with racism and used that as a foundation to support her parental functioning. This work helped to shift Sherry's experience of self from a unworthy victim of a powerful curse that she somehow deserved and couldn't escape, to a resilient fighter who was overcoming cocaine addiction and confronting institutional racism to build a better life for herself and her children.

The work with Sherry and her daughters began by shifting the issue of reunification from physical reunification (where the girls would live) to emotional reunification (the reestablishment and strengthening of emotional connections). It is often useful to begin with emotional reunification as a foundation for subsequent physical reunification. These girls would benefit from having their mother as a constructive presence in their lives whether they live with her or apart from her. Strengthening affective ties both increases the chances of successful reunification and can be an end in itself. Although it may not always make sense for families to be physically reunited, the reunification of severed emotional ties helps to reconnect children to a community of support. Even if a particular parent on the whole is not a constructive presence in a child's life, a strong bond usually exists between them and it is in everyone's best interest to acknowledge that and support the constructive aspects of those ties. In Sherry's situation, she began interacting quite differently with her children and eventually got back in touch with her family, made amends, and was able to draw on them for support. In this process, Rose became an important source of support for her. With this as context, we can now examine the work with Rose that helped her to become an appreciative audience for Sherry's enactment of a different story.

Working with Rose

Rose was a veteran protective services worker who was committed to reunification when feasible but whose concern for children inspired outrage at the system's willingness to let kids languish in foster care. She thought Sherry lacked the basic capacity to parent and doubted that her early sobriety would continue. She worried that a protracted reunification attempt that failed would have dire consequences for the girls. Rose's story that Sherry was incapable of parenting and unable to maintain sobriety opened little space for Sherry to develop and enact an alternative story. It is extremely important to attend to protective concerns. At the same time, the hope for change lies in our assumption that clients have and can further develop parenting skills. We are then oriented to proving that assumption rather than beginning with a belief that they can't parent and becoming oriented to information that will confirm that belief.

In their initial contacts with Rose, the team sought to enter into Rose's phenomenological world with curiosity. They appreciated the intent behind her skepticism and joined with her concern about the effects of youngsters lingering in the system. The team and Rose had worked together in the past and shared a relationship of mutual respect that served as a foundation for their work together. After connecting with her concern for the children, the team raised questions about the potential consequences, respectively, of attempting a reunification attempt that would subsequently fail and not attempting a reunification attempt that would have succeeded. As Rose contemplated the possibilities of the girls in adolescence trying to reconnect with their mother, or of Sherry coming out of her passivity at the last minute to challenge the adoption with ensuing legal entanglements, she decided that reunification was worth a shot. Although a reunification attempt would have probably proceeded anyway given the department's orientation at that time, getting Rose's buy-in was crucial to its success. The team viewed Rose's openness to trying reunification despite her doubts as a sign of her willingness to go the extra mile for these children. They talked with her about this and inquired how she had stayed so committed to children and families over the years. Whereas this brief description of the conversation has the potential to come across as a crude attempt to manipulate Rose into a particular viewpoint, that was not their intent. The team's inquiry into Rose's commitment was genuine. They talked about it because they were moved by it. They noticed it because they were always looking for moments of competence, connection, and hopefulness. Their intention was to open space for the emergence of more hope in Rose's work with Sherry.

Once Rose signed on to this endeavor, the team moved into a discussion of what would decrease the chances of a failed reunification attempt, which had been Rose's biggest concern. Framing it as an attempt to be responsive to her concerns and to learn more about what was working, the team asked Rose to monitor any changes and give them feedback on what improvements she noticed. This request helped to orient Rose to change and shifted the context of her observations from attending to events that would solidify her existing story of a passive, incapable mother to attending to exceptions that would open space for the emergence of an alternative story.

In this situation, Rose could be described as holding a stance of "Sherry's parenting is a problem, but we can't do anything about it." The way in which the team approached this stance in many ways follows the recommendations for approaching a no-control stance with clients in Chapter 3. The team resisted the temptation to attempt to prove to Rose that Sherry could do it, thus avoiding a minimize/maximize pattern. They assumed and looked for a positive intent behind Rose's complaint that Sherry couldn't parent and connected with her around her concern for the kids languishing in care. They opened up space for Rose to rediscover elements of hope in her work with Sherry and helped Rose begin to orient to exceptions that could then be expanded.

Shifting the Context
of Family–Helper Interactions

After establishing a foundation of trust and an openness to exceptions in Rose's view of Sherry, the team focused on ways to shift the context of Rose's interactions with Sherry. The intention in this shift was to help Sherry move from being an audience for the dominant problem story to becoming an audience for alternative stories. They began by attempting to shift the context of supervised visits. As part of the initial reunification efforts, Sherry was granted supervised visits with her daughters at the protective services office. These visits needed to be monitored and Rose, in an attempt to not intrude on Sherry, monitored the visits through a one-way mirror. In those visits, the children were timid and hesitant to interact with Sherry. Sherry in response became increasingly tentative in her interactions with her daughters and she ended up sitting quietly in a corner while the girls played by themselves across the room. Rose was concerned about Sherry's lack of involvement with the girls and the supervised visits confirmed Rose's view of Sherry as a passive, incapable mother.

The team wondered whether Sherry's tentativeness was a reaction to fear of evaluation and judgment. In talking with Rose, the team took a both/and approach, both acknowledging Rose's view and offering an alternative perspective. The team invited Rose into a consideration of what it might be like for Sherry, struggling to prove herself, to have an unseen worker watching and recording her every move. One team member reflected about her own anxiety when she first received live supervision through a one-way mirror and how she viewed her supervisor (whom she knew respected her work) as a monster during those first few sessions. As the conversation continued, Rose spoke about her anxiety when she was told she had to take a licensing examination after being on the job for many years. They all reminisced for a while about their various experiences with performance anxiety and Rose seemed to consider Sherry's response to the supervised visits in a different light. In this conversation, the team members sought to invite Rose into a different perspective from which to interpret Sherry's actions. They did not attempt to instruct Rose in how to view Sherry and did not attempt to suggest that their view of Sherry was more correct. Their goal was to put another view about Sherry alongside Rose's view. They were not attempting to put a "correct" view on top of or in front of Rose's "incorrect" perception.

At the end of the conversation, Rose announced that performance anxiety or not, she still had to determine Sherry's competence as a parent and the whole group needed to find a way to deal with that. A meeting was called with Rose, the team, and Sherry to discuss this dilemma and the following plan emerged based on the organization of live supervision sessions in family therapy training. Sherry, Rose, and the team did a presession in which the primary therapist interviewed Sherry about the effects of fear and evaluation and the ways in which she resisted and coped with those effects as preparation for the supervised visit. Then Sherry visited with her children while the team and Rose observed behind the mirror. The children, as usual, shied away from Sherry, but the focus behind the mirror this time was on Sherry's small steps toward engaging them rather than on her tentativeness. At a prearranged time, Sherry took a break and came back behind the mirror to witness the primary therapist interview Rose and other members of the team about their observations of Sherry's steps away from the influence of fear and evaluation and toward her children. After Sherry's response to that interview, she went back into the room with her children for another period. While her girls were still shy, Sherry continued to quietly engage them. At the end of the visit, Sherry again came back behind the mirror and was asked some reauthoring questions by her therapist to elaborate the emerging story of competent parenting and her resistance to fear and evaluation. She again listened to and commented on various reflections on others' experience with fear and evaluation. During the time Sherry was behind the mirror, another team member watched the children. Because of time constraints, there were only two such meetings. However, the meetings had profound effects on both Sherry and Rose. Sherry described feeling supported rather than evaluated by the helpers in her life and began to wonder whether her family might be another group who could move from criticism to support. Rose remarked on the courage it took Sherry to go through with those meetings and began to view her in a different light.

This is a rather elaborate example of the effort to develop a community of support among other helpers in a client's life, but it highlights the basic idea of shifting the context from attending to the dominant story to attending to exceptions. This shift can be encouraged through phone conversations and informal meetings as well as in formal settings such as case conferences and team meetings. In the process, it is important that we engage other helpers from a stance of curiosity, entering into and seeking to appreciate their phenomenological realities. We need to be open to what we can learn from them and take a both/and approach that lays our observations alongside theirs rather than seeking to replace their viewpoint with ours.

SHIFTING FAMILY RELATIONSHIPS WITH HELPERS

The process of shifting relationships between helpers and families also requires work with families. The story that a family holds about a helper affects that helper's ability to become an appreciative audience for the enactment of alternative stories. In the previous example, Sherry was convinced that Rose had a personal vendetta against her and Sherry wanted nothing to do with Rose. As Sherry put it, "She's a nosy, white bitch who's out to get me. What kind of woman takes children away from their mamas for a living anyhow?" When Sherry was asked what it was like for her to work with someone who she thought wanted to take her children away, her reply was, "Its horrible. It's that curse again. See I *am* cursed." Rather than confronting her stance and attempting to point out that Rose did not have a vendetta against her, the team sought to enter into that story, examine its effects on Sherry, and her reaction to those effects. From that understanding, they then searched for exceptions that could become the basis for a different relationship.

In this process, it is important to validate clients' experience of their relationship with other helpers without being pulled into a coalition with clients against other helpers. It can be useful to remind ourselves that other helpers may describe their experience of the relationship with a client quite differently and remember the importance of holding multiple stories simultaneously.

As we begin to look for events outside a narrowly defined, problematic relationship that can lead to the development of more constructive relationships, we can pose questions such as the following about the constraining context of the relationship:

- What do you think gets in the way of her being able to see these changes you've worked so hard to make?
- If she met you outside her current professional role with your family, what would she most appreciate about the changes you've made?
- How would she see you differently?
- What does he need to know about you to do his job better?
- What does he most like about your family?
- What is he most troubled by?
- What does he need to know about you to view you differently?
- What about her role do you think she most likes/dislikes?
- What would you like or dislike about being in a role like that?

In the course of questions such as this, Sherry began to see Rose's job as ensuring that her kids were safe. Although Sherry still objected to being the object of that inquiry, she begrudgingly acknowledged that Rose's role put them in a potentially conflictual relationship. From there, she was willing to move into a discussion of the fact that she was stuck with Rose in her life for now and needed to find some way of more constructively dealing with that fact.

SHIFTING FAMILY RELATIONSHIPS
TO PATHOLOGIZING HELPER STORIES

There are also times when helpers' constraining stories about clients seem quite strong and our invitations for those helpers to reflect on them are rebuffed. Without an authorization, we are ill positioned to question those stories and run the risk of becoming embroiled in a problematic interactional pattern that may inadvertently rigidify their story. Although it is important to make clear our perspective and not diminish it for fear of disagreement, the most helpful work we may be able to do in such a situation is working with the family to examine their relationship with the effects of pathologizing helper stories.

For example, an outpatient therapist I supervised described a case conference with multiple helpers in which a worker from another agency announced, "We can put in all the services we want, but eventually this client's borderline illness is going to rear its ugly head and destroy any and all progress that she's made." Despite various questions about the development of that idea and repeated invitations to consider other viewpoints, this helper was adamant that the mother's impulse control was destined to eventually break down and saw his job as preparing her family for that inevitability. In this situation, the other helper was not malintended. He cared about the mother, was concerned about the children's welfare, and wanted to be helpful to the family. However, the story he held about their situation offered no hope for change. The outpatient therapist, who saw the mother individually, made various attempts to enter the phenomenological logic of the other helper's perspective but found no openness to alternative viewpoints. Although she was concerned about his *perspective*, she did not view *him* as the problem. She saw him as falling under the influence of a particular set of beliefs and was worried about the real effect of those beliefs on the mother and her family. The mother was no longer using heroin, no longer physically abusive to her children, and actively working to contain her temper and emotional outbursts in her family. She had made significant strides but at times wondered whether she could continue to hold it together and valued the outpatient therapist's faith in her. The outpatient therapist feared that the hopelessness in the other helper's story would support a reemergence of the mother's old dominant story of herself as a "washout." However, the therapist resisted the temptation to try to protect the mother from the other helper's story about her and, instead, asked a number of questions about his perspective and its effects when the issue came up in a conversation with the mother. Some of the questions the therapist asked included:

- How do you think Jim [the other helper] would describe you?
- What words would he use?
- What's your reaction to that description?
- What of that description feels on target for you? What of it feels off target for you?
- Is that description more a story of who you've been or who you're becoming?
- What changes in the person you're becoming do you think he might have missed?
- If he saw those changes, how might he describe you differently?
- Would you prefer to update him on some of those changes or just keep yourself anchored in them?

These questions implicitly cast the other helper's perspective as a story rather than as objective truth and supported a separation between the mother and that story of her identity. She could then examine the effects of that story on her life and family and consider the kind of relationship she would like to have with that story (e.g., Which aspects of that story fit for her? Which didn't? Did aspects of that story raise new questions or thoughts for her? How did she hang onto aspects of that

story that felt useful to her and not get overly organized by those that
didn't feel useful?).

In this situation, the mother decided that the other helper was quite
pessimistic about her chances of continued improvement. She thought
that his pessimism was not helpful to her children and decided to talk
with both him and her protective services worker about those concerns.
She found some of his ideas about parenting useful and was willing to
continue meeting with him but did not want him to meet individually
with her children because of her concern that his pessimism had the
potential to disempower her in their eyes. While he interpreted her concerns as a manifestation of her "borderline illness," her protective services worker shared her concerns and saw her actions as a giant step forward in advocating for her children. More important, the mother's
actions helped to further elaborate her alternative story of an increasingly
protective and competent mother.

There are some cautions to be considered in raising questions with
clients about a particular helper's perspective and its effects on them.
From a psychodynamic perspective, there might be concern about "splitting." Splitting is one of those taken-for-granted psychological truths used
to refer to a tendency to view others as either representations of rewarding, good objects or representations of withholding, bad objects. Within
this framework, splitting serves a defensive function of keeping contradictory primitive affective states separate from each other (Masterson,
1976). While I understand this phenomenon from a quite different conceptual framework, I think the concern deserves attention. When multiple
helpers are involved with a family, often different perspectives about them
are directly or indirectly shared with them. As the family and helpers seek
to negotiate this maze of perspectives, conflicts between family members
and respective helpers can develop. Often, drawing on the concept of
"splitting," this conflict is attributed to a client's pathology. It could also
be seen as an attribute of the situation and reflective of our cultural difficulty of holding multiple perspectives. In asking for a commentary on
helpers' perspectives, it is important that we clarify that we are questioning the *stories* held by individuals not the *individuals* themselves. In this
endeavor, we are not seeking to undercut "false truths" about a client and
promote our own preferred truth but, rather, creating space for multiple
perspectives. In laying out multiple perspectives, we can then evaluate
them in terms of the real effects that they have on people rather than in
terms of their "validity."

In holding a both/and position, it becomes important to examine
both multiple perspectives and multiple effects (positive and negative) of
those perspectives. In response to the therapist's questions about Jim's
description of her, the mother's first response was, "On his good days or

his bad days?" She knew he had different perspectives and they had different effects on her. She was worried about his pessimism and its effects on her children but embraced his "pragmatic good advice," which she believed he wouldn't offer if he didn't think she could use it. In this way, the mother's perspective on Jim was broader than that held by the rest of the helping system. One way to avoid contributing to a "separation of contradictory affective states" is to inquire about multiple effects of a perspective (e.g., What do you like about that description? What do you not like so much?). Usually, people who are described as engaging in "splitting" are considered unable to hold contradictory affective states (hence the splitting). However, in my experience, they are usually able to answer such questions and find the questions useful in helping them to acknowledge multiple reactions to situations.

A second danger is that such questions can put a client in a loyalty bind between other helpers and us. In asking these kinds of questions, it is important that we take a stance of respectful curiosity and avoid implicitly implying how we think a client should answer. It is important to also include ourselves and our perspectives in such questions. If we are going to ask about the effects of other helper's stories on clients, we need to include what they find useful and not particularly useful in our stories. This effort helps to avoid an invitation to gossip about other helpers and promotes our own accountability to clients. We need to make sure we are not pulling for a response of "You understand me and they don't" but, rather, raising a question of "Are there ways in which *I* might not fully understand you?" In this way, we are helping clients to reflect on the types of relationships they have with helpers (ourselves included) and the types of relationships they would prefer to have with the people who work for them.

One helpful idea with parents who are trying to make sense of varying professional views of their child is to list the various helpers on a sheet of newsprint and have the parents generate a series of adjectives that they think the various helpers (including ourselves) would use to describe their child as well as their own adjectives. After generating a rather exhaustive list, we can ask the parents to assume that perhaps each of these descriptions contains some truth in them and reflects aspects of their child. This introduction can then be followed by a series of questions such as the following:

- What of these qualities do you particularly value in your daughter?
- What qualities strike you as bitter truths that you might reluctantly accept?
- What qualities would you prefer to have your daughter bring out more in her life?

- What qualities would you prefer to have your daughter hold back more in her life?
- When do you notice those preferred qualities coming out? What is happening then? Who is around? What is going on?

This exercise invites parents to examine various descriptions of their child's identity, offers an opportunity to inquire about the effects of those descriptions, and opens up possibilities for reauthoring. From here we can enter into a discussion of preferred identities and recruit supports for their attempts to move toward that.

At times, the notion that families could determine their relationship with helpers may be a foreign idea for clients who are used to having helpers define the relationship. For example, I saw a family whose son was being medicated by a psychopharmacologist who was notorious for giving "off-the-wall" advice to parents. The mother complained about him and described feeling stuck because he was the only psycho-pharmacologist in the area who took Medicaid. While she saw him as an excellent doctor who was good with her son, she was annoyed by how he related to her and distrusted the parenting directives he gave her. As she put it, "He's good with my son's plumbing, but has no social skills. Who is he to tell me how to raise my son?" At the same time, she felt compelled to follow his advice because "after all, he is the doctor." In an effort to open other possibilities, I told her a story about a plumber I hired when I was renovating my house. He was a great plumber who kept giving me unwanted advice on some painting I was doing. I talked about how hard it had been to find a plumber and my struggle to stay clear about valuing his significant plumbing skills and not taking his bad advice about painting too seriously. I then asked, "If you thought about the doctor as a plumber whom you had hired to do some work with your son, what work would fall within his purview and what work would fall outside of it?" My intention in the story was not to suggest what sort of relationship she should have with the doctor but to open space for a consideration of the idea that she could play a role in defining that relationship. She began to talk about things she appreciated about the doctor's work with her son, things she felt she needed to ask him to stop doing, and things she thought she could tolerate. She later thanked me and said the image of a plumber helped her to see the doctor as someone who was working for her rather than an authority figure to whom she must submit. When clients are freed up to consider the kinds of relationships they would prefer to have with helpers, they are more able to consider the kind of relationships they would prefer to have with helpers' stories about them. In this way, they are much better positioned to determine who they would want to have as an appreciative audience for the enactment of alternative stories and how they might want to deal with helpers who constitute a skeptical audience.

SUMMARY

As we help families step into new stories of their lives, the professional helping community becomes an important audience for the enactment of such stories. The reception these new stories receive from a professional audience profoundly affects the direction of their development. When the helping community relates as an appreciative audience, attending to elements of competence and connection and conveying an attitude of hopefulness, we increase the likelihood of elaborating and solidifying alternative stories. When we respond to new possibilities with skepticism and mistrust, we risk inadvertently supporting the old problem story in reasserting itself.

Though helpers don't intend to undercut clients' attempt to develop new lives, they can inadvertently have that effect when they are pulled into the old story by problematic family–helper interactional patterns or by beliefs that promote selective attention to pathology and dysfunction rather than movement in the direction of clients' preferred futures. This chapter examined a number of ways in which our attempts to be helpful can be constrained and offered concrete suggestions to help us reanchor our own work in a preferred stance and help other workers become an appreciative audience for the enactment of alternative stories.

As we work with other helpers, it is crucial that we ground that work in the same stance that informs our work with clients. Much of this book has emphasized the importance of maintaining connections with clients and not becoming caught by a tendency to view them as some "undeserving other." Similarly, in our interactions with other helpers, it is crucial that our passion for helping clients does not pull us into a disconnected relationship with other helpers in which we come to see them as some "uncaring other" whose actions are harmful to clients. While professional actions may have negative effects on clients, it is important that we retain a distinction between intent and effects and honor others' positive intentions while inviting them to examine their inadvertent effects. Ultimately, for this work to be effective, the spirit that suffuses our work with clients must also be brought into our work with other helpers. To accomplish that, we need to embed ourselves in organizational contexts that fully support the spirit of this work. The next chapter concludes this book by discussing ways to develop such contexts.

NOTES

1. Although the word treatment in this context is problematic because it implies something we are doing to families rather than with families, I will continue using it because it is a common term for this phenomenon and because, as I'll describe, the taken-for-granted ideas behind the concept of treatment contribute to this process of stuckness.

2. This shift is easier said than done in everyday life. For a helpful discussion of this shift and ways to support it in residential programs, I'd refer readers to *Residential Treatment: A Cooperative, Competency-Based Approach to Therapy and Program Design* (Durrant, 1993).

3. As previously discussed, a shift of this sort is well described in O'Neill and Stockell (1991).

4. We could view Sherry beginning to party at this time as evidence of her inadequacy as a parent, or we could view her postponing of partying until after the drugs could be transmitted to her daughter through breast-feeding as evidence of a concern for and commitment to her daughter. The question is not which is true but, rather, which provides a more solid foundation for work with Sherry. Are attempts to help her in her parenting best served by beginning the work with an examination of her parental inadequacy or an examination of her concern for and commitment to her children?

10

⇒•⇐

Envisioning New Futures, Revisioning Human Services

In an attempt to help families envision and develop new futures and preferred lives, this book has repeatedly emphasized the importance of how we approach clients (and other helpers) and has suggested the usefulness of positioning ourselves as appreciative allies in clients' lives. The conceptual frameworks and clinical practices offered in this book reflect powerful ways of working with families. However, the full enactment of these ideas requires attention to the context of clinicians' work. The way in which workers are treated in agencies is reflected in how they subsequently interact with families. A relational stance of an appreciative ally is enhanced by institutional structures that build an appreciative organizational culture. In the spirit of envisioning new futures, this concluding chapter begins a revisioning of the organization of human services.

In the last 10 years, we have witnessed a concerted effort to promote accountability and quality assurance in human services. Although the intent of continually improving our efforts to help families is extremely important, I am concerned that many of these efforts may be more focused on accountability to funders than on accountability to consumers. In addition, many of accountability mechanisms have tended to emphasize extensive documentation to ensure quality of care. If one accepts a central thesis of this book that the foundation of our work with clients lies in the conveyance of connection, respect, curiosity, and hopefulness, then the most powerful way to ensure quality services may well lie in the development of organizational structures and cultures that institutionalize those qualities.

FROM MULTI-STRESSED FAMILIES
TO MULTI-STRESSED WORKERS

A relational stance of an appreciative ally is important, but it can be difficult to maintain. This book has highlighted a number of ways in which
clinicians can be pulled away from such a stance. As an example, consider
the following two stories:

> A clinician comes into a family therapy seminar in a community
> agency and breaks into tears. "I can't stand it," she says catching her
> breath, "I'm so frustrated and angry that I keep trying to do a job
> that just can't be done. I'm cutting corners left and right in order to
> get done all that I'm responsible for and I'm scared to death that I'm
> going to be caught and held responsible for what I'm not doing." She
> concludes by apologizing for breaking down.

> A worker, contacted to assess training needs for his program,
> despairingly replies, "Unfortunately, the idea of getting any training
> right now feels self-abusive. If I focus on what my work *could* look
> like, I won't be able to tolerate what it *has* to look like right now.
> There is no room to apply new ideas and learning about them just
> feels like a set-up to me. I'm hanging on by a thread here."

Clearly, when one's experience of work is similar to these stories,
holding on to connection, respect, curiosity, and hopefulness with clients
becomes difficult. The workers in these two stories are experienced, competent helpers who are passionately dedicated to their work. Their stories, although distressing, are not unusual. In the process of providing
training and consultation to community agencies and public-sector workers, I encounter stories like these everyday. The common themes are of
overwhelming frustration, severe emotional strain, exhaustion, and
demoralization. These elements have often been collectively described as
"burnout" and attributed to the difficult nature of the work and seen as
an effect of prolonged exposure to clients' suffering and misery. However,
in a phenomenological study of child protective workers (one of the most
likely groups to be candidates for "burnout"), Joyce White (1996) found
that although all the participants described their jobs as extremely difficult, frustrating, and overwhelming, they did not attribute their distress
to clients but, rather, to organizational problems such as high caseloads,
inadequate resources, too much paperwork, and wasted time in transpor-
tation. As one worker put it:

> I think that, although my clients often wear me down, I am somehow
> inspired by them. . . . I have no idea how they manage to live their

lives. . . . Some of my clients . . . have to manage with so little. So little money, so little support, that I'm stunned, really, at their strength and their creativity. I think that in this era of cutbacks it's probably gotten a lot worse for them. . . . I find my clients funny, lovable, different, amusing. Sometimes I've had clients that I consider brilliant. . . . I very rarely actually get depressed by my clients themselves. (White, 1996, p. 133)

Their relationships with clients and colleagues actually buffered these workers from the disconnection and alienation that developed out of organizational difficulties. Many clinicians would agree that dealing with the organization of the work is much more difficult than direct client contact. Clinicians describe having too much to do with not enough time and too few resources, being overwhelmed with paperwork, and feeling exasperated with bureaucratic dilemmas and continually shifting mandates. As evidenced previously, the relationships developed with clients have the potential to buffer workers against these organizational stresses. In this way, therapeutic relationships anchored in connection, respect, curiosity, and hopefulness both anchor quality care and provide an effective bulwark against contextual forces that inadvertently undermine quality care.

Many of the ideas expressed in this book are anchored in family-centered services and collaborative approaches to therapy (a rubric that includes narrative, solution-focused, and collaborative language systems therapies). These approaches represent a radical shift in service delivery and share a common set of assumptions that I have characterized as a belief in resourcefulness, a commitment to empowering processes, a preference for working in partnership, and an attitude of cultural curiosity. Based on these four assumptions, therapy can become more effective, efficient, and humane (for those people called helpers as well as those people called clients). Clinicians who have embraced ideas such as these have found their work transformed and their lives enriched.

However, this way of working is difficult in isolation. There are many pressures that organize clinicians into a working-on rather than a working-with approach to clients (e.g., managed care demands for measurable results, accountability standards that emphasize extensive documentation, paperwork licensing requirements anchored in a medical model, and outcome measures that may have little relevance to families' actual lives). Just as clients benefit from a supportive community standing behind them, the development of an allied stance with clients requires acknowledgment and support. Community agencies committed to this stance can support it by developing organizational cultures that embed clinicians in an atmosphere of connection, respect, curiosity, and hopefulness. The development of such an organizational culture can be a daunting prospect. Administrators and managers are also under significant pressures that organize their work and their relationships with the people they supervise. However, the process of developing organizational cultures of connection, respect, curiosity, and hopefulness holds the promise of beneficial effects for clients, workers, and administrators alike. As a beginning step toward this goal, the next sections examine ways to shift clinical discussion formats, clinical and administrative paperwork outlines, and quality assurance practices to help institutionalize this atmosphere.

REVISIONING CLINICAL DISCUSSIONS

As a result of a workshop about parent involvement, a protective worker insists that a mother attend a team meeting about her son's future. At the meeting, team members go around and describe their respective observations about the mother's difficulties in relating to her son. As the process continues, the worker becomes very concerned about the mother's reaction to this intense scrutiny of her incompetence as a parent but doesn't know how to interrupt the process and begins to wonder whether this idea of parents being present at professional meetings is a huge mistake.

There has been an important increase in parent participation in professional meetings. However, we need to move beyond parents being *present* at meetings to parents being a *presence* in meetings. An initial step in this direction would be to revise the ways in which we discuss clients in meetings they do not attend. Many clinical formats include a focus on strengths and resources, but that portion of the presentation often becomes an addendum rather than the foundation for the discussion. We can institutionalize a belief in resourcefulness by reordering our priorities in clinical discussions. Efforts to help families envision new futures and draw on their resourcefulness to bring those futures to fruition can be best supported by following a parallel process in clinical discussions. Those discussions can begin with questions about what a clinician appreciates and respects about a family, where that family would like their life together to be headed, and what clinical work so far has effectively supported that happening. In this way, the team is positioned as an appreciative ally to the clinician who is seeking help. Clinical discussions that are focused on eliciting competence, connection, vision, and hope support clinicians in bringing those elements to their work with families.

Workers who have reordered clinical discussions in this way describe a profound shift in their experience of those discussions. For example, consider one worker's response to such a format,

"It felt great to build on what I was doing right than to have people tell me what I should be doing instead and then try to correct their misperceptions. I'm walking out of this meeting with much more energy and confidence, and I think I will carry that into my work with the family. It's got a momentum of its own now."

At the same time, old habits die hard. A second important step to enhancing clients' presence in meetings designed to help them is to increase our sensitivity to the possible negative effects of taken-for-granted ways of talking about clients. One way to do this is to include "client voices" in clinical discussions by having someone on the team listen to the discussion in the role of the client being discussed and subsequently interview the person in that role about his or her experience of the discussion (Madsen, 1996).

This process can be facilitated in a number of ways. I have often begun with a discussion about the rationale for doing it, emphasizing the usefulness of therapeutic practices being accountable to the clients they are designed to help and seeing whether participants would be willing to engage in a process of holding their work accountable to clients. A typical format for the discussion itself is as follows:

- A clinician is interviewed about a family or presents the family to the rest of the group which listens and then asks questions of clarification.
- The group conducts a reflecting team discussion about the material presented.
- The clinician reflects on the team discussion.
- The person who is listening as the "client voice" is (in role) interviewed by the group about his or her experience of the discussion.
- The group debriefs.

Questions for the person listening in the role of the "client voice" often include examples such as the following:

- What was this process like for you?
- What reactions did you have to it?
- Did it feel respectful and empowering?
- Were there new things you learned about yourself in the process?
- Were there parts of our discussion that did not feel helpful?
- What could we have done differently?
- How could we have had the discussion in a way that raised difficult issues, and yet felt respectful?

Many participants have found the process helpful. In addition to valuable direct feedback from the person in the client voice role, clinicians have found it useful to both listen as the "client voice" and receive feedback from the "client voice." Feedback from the "client voice" has often been direct, politely confrontive, and quite profound for participants. This format has been used in workshops, student seminars, ongoing consultation groups, and agency team meetings. The power of the format grows over time. As more participants spend time in the "client voice" role, the voice becomes a stronger presence in the room.

The process has also had interesting ripple effects. A student in a seminar utilizing a "client voice" process began raising questions at his practicum site about how clients would regard their clinical discussions. An outpatient therapist referred to the use of this process in team meetings to open a conversation with her individual supervisor about how they could talk differently about clients in supervision. A mental health case manager who learned about this process in a workshop suggested it for a larger systems meeting that a mother could not attend. As the "client voice" becomes stronger in clinical discussions, participants seem to become emboldened to respectfully advocate for clients in other settings.

This process has raised a number of considerations. It is important that participants fully agree to participate and authorize the "client voice" to give them candid feedback. It's also important that team members who are discussing a client have permission to be inadvertently offensive in their comments as long as they are willing to receive feedback about and address the effects of those comments. It also helps when there is a foundation of trust in the group. At times, the person in the "client voice" role has spoken bluntly and passionately, and this process works best when it is done lovingly and in a way that honors people's best intentions. There are times that using a "client voice" might be less useful, that is, when a clinician wants to examine difficult personal reactions to a client or family and the conversation is more focused on the therapist than on the family (William Lax, personal communication, March 25, 1996).

The process has also raised interesting questions about who to include as the client voice. Generally, when I have used this process, teams have either tended to pick a perspective they find particularly interesting or sought out the most marginalized voice in a clinical situation. Often this voice is not a family member. Some of the more interesting "voices" have been those of "impossible, pathologizing collaterals." While we have generally listened to one voice (in the interest of time), it is possible to enroll several voices. For example, Harlene Anderson (1997) described a similar process using multiple voices which she refers to as an "As If" exercise. Interestingly, this format can also be used in management discussions about workers and academic discussions about students.

The format can have a lasting impact on participants. One student reported that as a result of this process, she now carries two voices in her head when she does therapy. She experiences a "supervisory voice" reminding her to be a good diagnostician and conduct a thorough assessment and a "client voice" reminding her to be an authentic human being and develop a strong relational connection. By her report, the two voices usually complement each other. This is an intriguing comment. Although it is a fairly common experience to internalize a "supervisory voice," the additional internalization of a "client voice" holds significant potential to shift how we think, talk, and act with clients. These two shifts of revising how we organize discussions about clients and making those discussions accountable to the people they are designed to benefit provide a foundation for developing better habits in our ways of talking about clients and support the development of a respectful atmosphere. The next section examines ways to shift the context of writing about clients.

REVISIONING CLINICAL PAPERWORK

A licensing auditor was examining records in an agency as part of an important site review. As he reviewed the record of a teenage boy diagnosed with bipolar disorder, he noticed, much to his dismay, one of the treatment goals was that the boy would raise his reading level (the boy was barely able to read). In a conversation with the program director, he criticized that goal saying it had nothing to do with the boy's bipolar disorder and hence was inappropriate for a mental health organization. He went on to give examples of appropriate goals: helping the boy become medication compliant, helping the family to accept and understand the boy's disorder, or helping the boy develop a better awareness of his disorder in order to manage it more effectively. The director replied that the goal was in the chart because the mother had requested it believing the boy had to learn how to read in order to support himself in the future. As part of the program review, the auditor met with the mother. When he asked about how the program had helped her family, she immediately responded, "They've helped us help him learn to read. That's been the most important thing anyone has ever done for him."

If we want to support clinicians in making their work relevant and important to clients, we need to develop ways of documenting that work that support this endeavor. These days, there is a lot of talk about involving consumers in treatment planning and utilizing treatment planning to "drive" the treatment. However, if the definition of what constitutes an acceptable goal remains unexamined, we may inadvertently drive treatment in a direction counter to our preferred values. Alternatively, we may simply go through the motions in completing paperwork and then do the "real" work outside that process, creating additional work and contributing to a lack of accountability in our work. Much of the paperwork we use in the field is based on a medical model and organizes our thinking in particular ways. It decontextualizes and medicalizes people's lives. Carole Warshaw (1995) a physician who was originally trained in internal medicine and later completed a residency in psychiatry, reflects on the effects of the medical model in examining problems in living:

> The medical model in fact is designed to extract information from the context of the patient's life that gives it meaning to her or to him and transform it into medical events that have meaning for the clinician. It reduces information to categories that can be readily handled and controlled, transforms symptoms into disorders that can be treated or managed, and dismisses anything that does not fit the diagnosis or treatments that are known and available to that particular clinician or specialty. Thus, there is no place for psychosocial problems and no way to form a general assessment that links the person and her context to the symptoms she presents with, making intervention difficult to conceptualize within a framework that only recognizes pathology within the body. There is no room for the patient to say: "This is what is important to me." (p. 75)

When our paperwork requirements direct attention away from those issues that are important to families, we risk developing *form-centered services* rather than *family-centered services*. It is important that we develop paperwork that supports and enhances our work rather than simply documents it. This book has extensively reviewed alternate approaches to both the content and process of assessments, treatment contracts, and termination summaries. I won't revisit those discussions here but would refer readers to Chapters 2, 4, and 7 for concrete ideas about ways to maintain compliance with licensing regulations and institutionally reinforce a commitment to the four basic conceptual assumptions highlighted throughout the book.

REVISIONING ADMINISTRATIVE PAPERWORK

In a meeting to discuss the implementation of new agency forms, a clinician fidgets in her chair and finally bursts out, "What do you mean I'm going to have to begin with people by filling out fourteen pages of information that is completely irrelevant to their lives? What are you crazy? That's what they're going to be asking me.

> They'll look at me and say, 'What has this got to do with me?' How am I supposed to make a connection to a complete stranger when we're spending all our time filling out forms?"

Over the last few years, there has been a proliferation of forms in many agencies. We can distinguish between administrative forms (e.g., forms such as patient information form, agreement to accept services, limits of confidentiality, explanations of clients rights and responsibilities, release of information forms, and audiotape or videotape release forms) and clinical forms (e.g., assessments, treatment contracts, progress notes, quarterly updates, and termination summaries). Many of the administrative forms exist to register clients, maintain compliance with licensing standards, or initiate reimbursement mechanisms. These forms are often viewed as annoying but necessary evils. However, if we refer back to the repeated assertion that everything we do with clients has the potential to invite the enactment of particular life stories and influences the therapeutic relationship, we are well served by attending to clients' experience of completing forms. The process of filling out initial forms can be seen as an engagement ritual. Do we want clients' initial contact with an agency to be channeled through a set of forms? How can we structure the process of completing forms so that it acknowledges, supports, and amplifies people's participation and influence in their lives? How can we develop forms and organize the process in ways that help to humanize initial contact and encourage respectful connection?

One way to attend to the process of completing forms lies in how we explain particular forms. For example, the process of completing release-of-information forms is often approached very matter-of-factly. Professionals can come to assume that conversations with other professionals about clients are a right rather than a privilege granted by clients and can approach the requisite signing of a release form as a bureaucratic inconvenience. However, clients may experience the form as notice of our intention to engage in professional gossip and feel objectified and disempowered or have any number of reactions. As a hedge against unwittingly contributing to negative experiences of self, consider the introduction to the release-of-information form that was previously discussed in Chapter 9:

> "I have found that I'm able to be most helpful to individuals, couples and families when I can coordinate my efforts with other services you may be receiving or have received from other helpers. To do that, I'm requesting your permission to talk to other professionals in order to get their ideas about how I can be more helpful to you. I will be glad to share with you the ideas I receive if you would like."

This introduction contextualizes the request to contact other helpers and opens more space for a conversation about the purpose of such communication and the conditions that clients may wish to attach to their permission. One way to encourage a different response to paperwork is to build such contextualizing introductions directly into our forms. Doing so institutionalizes the practice. However, when using more traditional forms, clinicians can verbally contextualize them. The important point is to attend to clients' experience of filling out forms and attempt to organize that process in ways that highlight rather than constrain clients' participation and influence in their lives.

REVISIONING QUALITY ASSURANCE

My vision of managerial teams would be that they would support workers, that they would say to the workers, "Look, you do 99% of the work here. You are the backbone, you are the workhorses of the agency. We will do everything we can to support you, respect you, honor you. We will provide the support to help you do the work."
—Comment from a protective services worker in White (1996)

If quality of care is anchored in the development of relationships built on a foundation of connection, respect, curiosity, and hopefulness, how do we develop organizational structures and cultures that institutionalize these qualities, both in how clinicians are encouraged to relate to clients and how supervisors and administrators are encouraged to relate to clinicians? The following ideas represent some initial thoughts designed to stimulate thinking "outside the box" rather than to provide definitive answers.

One organizing criterion for evaluating agency policies and procedures would be to subject them to the following questions:

- Does this policy or procedure promote attention to resourcefulness in clients and workers?
- Does this policy or procedure support and enhance clients' and workers' influence and participation in the development of their lives and work?
- Does this policy or procedure encourage a working-with rather than a working-on approach to both clients and workers?
- Does this policy or procedure encourage clinicians and supervisors respectively to attempt to better understand families' and clinicians' phenomenological realities?

These questions help to anchor institutions in the four conceptual assumptions outlined in Chapter 1 (a belief in resourcefulness, a commitment to empowering processes, a preference for partnership, and an attitude of cultural curiosity). In posing these questions, I am not suggesting that managers abandon their organizational responsibilities to hold workers accountable for job-related performance but, rather, recommending a reconsideration of how that is done. Accountability needs to be a joint venture and managers need to be accountable for how they hold workers accountable. How do we develop institutional practices that are deliberately crafted to build the organizational cultures we seek? As an example, let's examine alternative possibilities for approaching outcome measures, utilization review and quality assurance procedures, and mechanisms to elicit consumer input.

Outcome Measures

In a discussion with a funder about possible outcome measures for a new program, the director suggests interviewing families about the changes in their lives and what contributed to them. The funder shakes her head and says, "No, that's a subjective measure. We need something objective. How about GAF?"[1]

With an ever-present push for documenting success, the field is continually searching for valid and reliable objective measures through which to assess treatment outcome. In an instrumental era, programs that can concretely measure outcomes receive increased legitimacy among funders. However, it's conceivable that such legitimacy may come at the expense of clients. Currently, many programs measure family improvement or outcome by researcher-generated criteria that may or may not be relevant to families' lives. Perhaps we should collaborate more with families in the development of outcome measures that feel most relevant to their lives. Who is the best judge of what constitutes important changes in their lives? Who is best positioned to decide what services are most helpful? What is the message in asking a family to complete a form or questionnaire that feels irrelevant to them in order to assess whether we've been helpful?

Although "objective" measures may not adequately capture the complexity of families' lives, there is a danger that without such measures our efforts will not be considered sound enough to be taken seriously. This danger poses an interesting contradiction between what we might need to do for continued funding and what might be in families' best

interest. If we need to utilize "objective" measures, we can at least pair
these with coresearch projects that are collaboratively undertaken with
families. The following two brief ideas are intended to stimulate thinking
about potential coresearch projects with families that can assess outcome
while enhancing effectiveness.

One way to begin coresearch projects with families would be to ask
them at the beginning of contact, "How would we know that what we're
doing here is helpful?" At the end of services, we could go back and evaluate
our progress in light of those early comments. We could also inquire about
ways in which their early opinions might have changed over time. In this
way, the outcome measure is immediately relevant to families and the process of completing the outcome measure supports therapeutic work. The
termination interview outlined in Chapter 7 offers a second model of a
coresearch project that has the potential to develop a thick description of
therapy outcomes. Emergent themes across interviews could be drawn out
to develop grounded theory about contributions to positive outcome. Both
of these projects offer ways to develop outcome measures that support
rather than detract from or are irrelevant to the work.

Utilization Review
and Quality Assurance Mechanisms

> The morning after a sensationalist news story about two young chil-
> dren who were found alone in a filthy house, a protective worker
> comes in late to a monthly off-site seminar on forging collaborative
> partnerships with families. She apologizes and explains, "As I was
> heading out to come here, my supervisor came up to me and said, 'I
> think it's great you're going to that seminar, I just want to make sure
> it doesn't interfere with your work. After the news story last night,
> we're doing a random audit of records and heads are going to role if
> things aren't up to snuff.' "

Public-sector agencies are under intense scrutiny from both funders
and the public. Part of that scrutiny is reflected in agency utilization
review/quality assurance teams (UR/QA) that meet to review clinical
records or charts. These reviews typically focus on whether paperwork is
completed and meets certain regulatory requirements. Those regulatory
requirements are traditionally based on a medical model and promote
selective attention to certain aspects of records and inattention to others.
UR/QA processes are a regulatory requirement that can also be used to
support the ideas presented throughout this book. For example, in addition to the required questions on a UR/QA form, we could add the following questions:

- Are individual, family, and broader contextual issues adequately considered?
- Does this record promote sufficient attention to clients' strengths and resources?
- Does this record convey a tone of respect for the client or family?

Admittedly, the inclusion of these questions adds more work to an overburdened system. However, excluding them runs the risk of ceding quality assurance to disconnected bureaucratic requirements rather than keeping it anchored in the foundation of connection, respect, curiosity, and hopefulness that has consistently been shown to enhance therapeutic effectiveness (based on extensive psychotherapy outcome research described in Chapter 1 as well as client and clinician reports).

In addition to broadening the scope of UR/QA, we can shift the way in which the process is organized. I used to chair a UR/QA team in a mental health clinic. In that context, we were bound by licensing regulations and the combined tyranny of too many records and too little time. Despite our attempts to humanize the process, a common anticipatory response on many clinicians' part was a fear of "flunking UR." If clinicians' interactions with families around issues in families' lives invite the enactment of particular stories about their lives, administrators' interactions with clinicians around issues in clinicians' work can also invite the enactment of particular stories about their work. Based on this assumption, a number of questions can be raised about our administrative practices. What would be the consequences of also acknowledging, celebrating, and honoring what is present in clinicians' work rather than simply searching for what is missing in the documentation of that work? What would be the radiating effect of administrators who are reviewing paperwork searching for what they can learn from clinicians' work? What might grow out of clinicians being asked such a question? How can UR/QA teams be developed as an appreciative audience rather than a critical audience? And finally, how could administrators, supervisors, and clinicians find ways to openly discuss and share their dilemmas between embracing family-centered philosophy and responding to licensing regulations that often operate from a very different set of assumptions? Each of these questions reflects an important shift from fixing problems to growing competence. The ways in which organizations treat their employees are directly reflected in how workers treat clients. If organizations want workers to anchor their work in a stance of an appreciative ally, they need to develop a culture that supports it.

Consistently responding to workers from a stance of an appreciative ally is a difficult endeavor for administrators who themselves are under similar organizational pressures. As an ex-administrator who often was pulled into reacting to staff in ways that were inconsistent with how I would prefer to respond, I realize this all too well. Again, I am not suggesting that managers abdicate organizational responsibilities but rather highlighting the usefulness of approaching those responsibilities in ways that are consonant with the spirit of this book. Many of the ideas for engaging reluctant clients who hold a stance of "this is not a problem" or "this is a problem, but I have no control over it" are applicable for administrators in their interactions with "reluctant" staff.

Eliciting Client Input

One of the best ways to ensure quality is through feedback from clients we serve. They are the best judge of the effects of our efforts. For example, consider the research cited in Chapter 1 that clients' perception of therapist attitudes are a better predictor of psychotherapy outcome than clinicians' perceptions (Bachelor, 1991; Free et al., 1985). We can seek consumer input to improve services through a variety of mechanisms.

Many programs that receive public funding are required to conduct consumer satisfaction surveys. Such surveys provide a powerful way to elicit consumer feedback about our efforts to help them and yield a potential gold mine of valuable information to ensure quality of care. They provide a way to evaluate our services against the four questions used earlier to assess the effects of policies and procedures and offer opportunities to institutionalize connection, respect, curiosity, and hopefulness. In consumer satisfaction surveys, we can ask questions such as the following:

- Did you feel that your strengths, resources, and wisdom were acknowledged and honored by our staff? If so, in what ways?
- Were you encouraged to be an active participant in our work with you? Did we ask for your feedback throughout the process? Did our staff treat you with respect?
- Were you treated as an important partner in our work with you? If so, in what ways?
- Did you feel that staff members made an effort to understand the uniqueness of your life and family?

Questions such as these convey a message about agency priorities and subtly organize clinicians' interactions with families. These questions also invite clients to reflect on their lives and have interventive potential. In this way, they both support the work and contribute to an appreciative organizational culture.

We can also draw on family input to evaluate existing programs.

One example of such an evaluation is reflected in Chris Petr's (1999) development of the Family-Centered Behavior Scale (FCBS), a tool that draws on family input to assess the quality of agencies' partnerships with families. Tools such as this can be easily integrated into existing program evaluation mechanisms. We can, in addition, put more effort into the development of consumer advisory boards and develop ways to help them hold agencies truly accountable. We can also make human rights committees more than a regulatory requirement and give them a role in the governance of agencies. Finally, we can involve parents in developing proposals for funding (paying them as we would any important consultant) and, at a state level, in developing requests for proposals from agencies. Efforts such as these require a shift in professional identity that can be threatening but ultimately productive.

THE LAST WORDS

One of the underlying assumptions of this chapter has been that a powerful way to continually improve services lies in hearing about how families have made changes in their lives and eliciting their thoughts about how we can best support them in that process. One way to gather such information is through follow-up interviews that elicit client wisdom. (It is often helpful to have someone other than the existing helpers conduct such interviews.) These follow-up interviews can serve a dual function of informing training and quality assurance endeavors and helping to solidify new stories in clients' lives. They can include questions such as the following:

- What changes have you made in your life?
- How have you made those changes?
- What does it tell you about yourselves that you have made these changes?
- How can you continue to solidify and build on those changes?
- What advice would you have for other families struggling with similar problems?
- What advice would you have for therapists trying to help families struggling with similar problems?

These kinds of interviews have enriched my own thinking about therapy and the organization of services, and this book contains numerous quotations from clients that have grown out of such interviews. In the spirit of honoring client voices, this book concludes with an interview of a mother about changes she made in her parenting and the advice she has for other parents and helpers.

Anna, a working-poor, white mother, was referred to an agency for help in parenting her daughter who had been explosive with daily temper outbursts and routine physical attacks of Anna. Those explosions had taken a significant toll on Anna, her daughter, and their relationship. Over a period of 6 months, Anna had significantly shifted her relationship to her daughter and her daughter's temper outbursts had diminished significantly. Anna described her concern about her daughter's difficulties going from a 10 to a 2. She talked about the ways in which her daughter "pushed my buttons" and described the ways in which she had worked to "disable those buttons." Some of the steps she described taking to disable those buttons included the following:

- *Taking ownership of her parenting.* Anna described her realization that she was the primary caretaker and the need to go with her gut rather than have her parenting organized by a preoccupation with others' criticism of her parenting.
- *Focusing on her daughter.* Anna described how important her daughter was to her and the kind of life she hoped for her daughter. When she was able to stay focused on what her daughter meant to her and the hopes she held for her daughter, it was easier to disable those buttons.
- *Allowing herself time out.* Anna spoke eloquently about the need to take care of herself in order to ensure that she was responding rather than to reacting to particular situations.

Her advice for other parents seeking to disable their buttons included three elements:

- Be open to what your children have to teach you.
- Let your children know they matter and are important.
- Don't let others rule your parenting and don't parent out of fear.

Finally, her advice for helpers was simple.

"Don't sit in judgment. When helpers don't sit in judgment, the defensiveness goes away. Clients don't feel the need to sit there and defend every little thing they just said or did. When I talk to these guys (the two helpers in the interview), I can say anything and not think, 'Oh my God, I can't believe I just said this to them. What's gonna happen now? What are they gonna think or do?' When I'm not caught up by that, I can be more open and they can be more helpful. That's my only suggestion, but it's a big one."

The next day, I did a training for a group of human service workers who were overwhelmed after a tragic incident that was followed by a paperwork crackdown to ensure that they were doing their jobs "correctly." The workers described feeling almost paralyzed in their work and distressed that it was becoming less and less "their" work. I told them about this interview (without using names) and described Anna's efforts to take ownership of her parenting and shift her relationship to those critical voices in her head. The workers were very moved by her efforts and thought the story would help them reclaim their work from bureaucratic reactivity. They asked me to thank Anna for her inspiration.

Hearing about Anna's story had a powerful effect on these workers. Hearing back from them had a powerful effect on Anna. The process of relating the story had a powerful effect on me. I think it is right to close this book with a reflection on Anna's words of wisdom. Her advice to parents seeking to disable buttons they don't want pushed strikes me as sound advice for parents, clinicians, supervisors, and administrators.

- Be open to what the people with whom you work (children, clients, or clinicians) have to teach you.
- Convey to them that they matter and are important.
- Take ownership of your work (whether parenting, therapy, or supervision/administration) and don't work out of fear.

Perhaps we are not all that different from each other and the privilege of sharing this journey is ultimately what this work is all about.

NOTE

1. Global Assessment of Functioning (GAF), a 100-point scale on Axis V of DSM-IV (the prevalent classification system of "mental disorders"), is used to report the clinician's judgment of a client's overall level of functioning and is seen as useful in planning treatment and measuring its impact and in predicting outcome (American Psychiatric Association, 1994).

References

Aboriginal Health Council. (1995). Reclaiming our stories, reclaiming our lives. *Dulwich Centre Newsletter, 1*, 1–40.

Adams-Westcott, J., & Isenbart, D. (1990). Using rituals to empower family members who have experienced child sexual abuse. In M. Durrant & C. White (Eds.), *Ideas for Therapy with Sexual Abuse*. Adelaide, Australia: Dulwich Centre Publications.

Adams-Westcott, J., & Isenbart, D. (1995). A journey of change through connection. In S. Friedman (Ed.), *The Reflecting Team in Action: Collaborative Practice in Family Therapy*. New York: Guilford Press.

American Psychiatric Association. (1994). *Diagnostic and Statistical Manual of Mental Disorders* (4th ed.). Washington, DC: Author.

Amundson, J., Stewart, K., & Valentine, L. (1993). Temptations of power and certainty. *Journal of Marital and Family Therapy, 19*, 111–123.

Anderson, C. M., & Stewart, S. (1983). *Mastering Resistance: A Practical Guide to Family Therapy*. New York: Guilford Press.

Anderson, H. (1997). *Conversation, Language, and Possibilities*. New York: Basic Books.

Anderson, H., & Goolishian, H. (1988). Human systems as linguistic systems: Evolving ideas about the implications for theory and practice. *Family Process, 27*, 371–393.

Anderson, H., & Goolishian, H. (1992). The client is the expert: A not-knowing approach to therapy. In S. McNamee & K. J. Gergen (Eds.), *Therapy as Social Construction*. Newbury Park, CA: Sage.

Anderson, H., Goolishian, H., & Winderman, L. (1986). Problem determined systems: Towards transformation in family therapy. *Journal of Strategic and Systemic Therapies, 5*, 1–13.

Aponte, H. (1992). Training the person of the therapist in structural family therapy. *Journal of Marital and Family Therapy, 18*, 269–281.

Aptheker, B. (1989). *Tapestries of Life: Women's Work, Women's Consciousness, and the Meaning of Daily Experience*. Amherst: University of Massachusetts Press.

Ashby, W. R. (1952). *Design for a Brain*. London: Chapman & Hall.

Bachelor, A. (1991). Comparison and relationship to outcome of diverse dimensions of the helping alliance as seen by client and therapist. *Psychotherapy, 28*, 534–549.

Bateson, G. (1979). *Mind and Nature: A Necessary Unity*. New York: Dutton.

Bepko, C., & Krestan, J. (1990). *Too Good for Her Own Good: Breaking Free from the Burden of Female Responsibility*. New York: Harper & Row.

Berg, I. K. (1991). Of visitors, complaints, and customers: Is there really such a thing as resistance? *Family Therapy Networker, 13*, 21.

Berg, I. K. (1994a). *Family Based Services: A Solution-Focused Approach*. New York: Norton.

Berg, I. K. (1994b). *It's Her Fault* [Audiotape]. Milwaukee, WI: Brief Family Therapy Center.

Berg, I. K., & Miller, S. D. (1992). *Working with the Problem Drinker: A Solution-Focused Approach*. New York: Norton.

Berry, M. (1992). An evaluation of family preservation services: Fitting agency services to family needs. *Social Work, 37*, 314–321.

Blount, A. (1987). *Systemic Approaches to Management in Clinical Settings*. Conference presentation at American Association for Marriage and Family Therapy Annual Conference, Chicago, IL.

Blount, A. (1991). *The Two Worlds of Mental Health Services*. Conference presentation at American Association for Marriage and Family Therapy Annual Conference, Dallas, TX.

Bordin, E. S. (1979). The generalizability of the psychoanalytic concept of working alliance. *Psychotherapy, 16*, 252–260.

Bruner, J. (1986). *Actual Minds, Possible Worlds*. Cambridge, MA: Harvard University Press.

Bruner, J. (1990). *Acts of Meaning*. Cambridge, MA: Harvard University Press.

Burish, T. G., & Bradley, L. A. (1983). Coping with chronic disease: Definitions and issues. In T. G. Burish & L. A. Bradley (Eds.), *Coping with Chronic Disease: Research and Application*. New York: Academic Press.

Burr, V. (1995). *An Introduction to Social Constructionism*. London: Routledge.

Cade, B., & O'Hanlon, W. H. (1993). *A Brief Guide to Brief Therapy*. New York: Norton.

Campbell, D., Draper, R., & Huffington, C. (1988). *Teaching Systemic Thinking*. London: D. C. Associates.

Cannon, W. B. (1932). *Wisdom of the Body*. New York: Norton.

Cecchin, G. (1987). Hypothesizing, circularity, and neutrality revisited: An invitation to curiosity. *Family Process, 26*, 405–413.

Cecchin, G., Lane, G., & Ray, W. A. (1994). Influence, effect, and emerging systems. *Journal of Systemic Therapies, 13*, 13–21.

Colorado, A., Montgomery, P., & Tovar, J. (1998). Creating respectful relationships in the name of the Latino family: A community approach to domestic violence. *Dulwich Centre Newsletter, 1*, 2–33.

Connor-Greene, P. A. (1993). The therapeutic context: Preconditions for change in psychotherapy. *Psychotherapy, 30*, 375–382.

Cooperrider, D. L. (1990). Positive image, positive action: The affirmative basis of organizing. In S. Srivastva & D. L. Cooperrider (Eds.), *Appreciative Management and Leadership: The Power of Positive Thought and Action in Organizations*. San Francisco: Jossey-Bass.

Denton, W. H. (1989). DSM-III-R and the family therapist: Ethical considerations. *Journal of Marital and Family Therapy, 15*, 367–377.

Denton, W. H. (1990). A family systems analysis of DSM-III-R. *Journal of Marital and Family Therapy, 16*, 113–126.

de Shazer, S. (1988). *Clues: Investigating Solutions in Brief Therapy*. New York: Norton.

de Shazer, S. (1991). *Putting Difference to Work*. New York: Norton.

de Shazer, S. (1994). *Words Were Originally Magic*. New York: Norton.

Dickerson, V. C., & Zimmerman, J. (1992). Families with adolescents: Escaping problem lifestyles. *Family Process, 31*, 341–353.

Dickerson, V. C., & Zimmerman, J. (1995). A constructionist exercise in anti-pathologizing. *Journal of Systemic Therapies, 14*, 33–45.

Dore, M. M., & Alexander, L. B. (1996). Preserving families at risk of child abuse and neglect: The role of the helping alliance. *Child Abuse and Neglect, 20*, 349–361.

Duncan, B. L., Hubble, M. A., & Miller, S. D. (1997). *Psychotherapy with "Impossible" Cases: The Efficient Treatment of Therapy Veterans*. New York: Norton.

Duncan, B. L., Solovey, A. D., & Rusk, G. S. (1992). *Changing the Rules: A Client-Directed Approach to Therapy*. New York: Guilford Press.

Durrant, M. (1993). *Residential Treatment: A Cooperative, Competency-Based Approach to Therapy and Program Design*. New York: Norton.

Ehrenreich, B. (1989). *Fear of Falling: The Inner Life of the Middle Class*. New York: HarperCollins.

Ehrenreich, B., & Ehrenreich, J. (1979). The professional-managerial class. In P. Walker (Ed.), *Between Labor and Capital: The Professional Managerial Class*. Boston: South End Press.

Elliot, H. (1998). En-gendering distinctions. In S. Madigan & I. Law (Eds.), *Praxis: Situating Discourse, Femininism and Politics in Narrative Therapies*. Vancouver, BC, Canada: Yaletown Family Therapy.

Epston, D. (1994). Extending the conversation. *Family Therapy Networker, 18*, 31–37, 62–63.

Epston, D. (1996, November). *Questions for a narrative practice*. Presentation at Family Institute of Cambridge, Watertown, MA.

Epston, D., & Roth, S. (1994). *Framework for a White/Epston Type Interview* [Handout].

Epston, D., & White, M. (1995). Termination as a rite of passage: Questioning strategies for a therapy of inclusion. In R. A. Neimeyer & M. J. Mahoney (Eds.), *Constructivism in Psychotherapy*. Washington, DC: American Psychological Association.

Epston, D., White, M., & "Ben." (1995). Consulting your consultants: A means to the co-construction of alternative knowledges. In S. Friedman (Ed.), *The Reflecting Team in Action: Collaborative Practice in Family Therapy.* New York: Guilford Press.

Fenichel, O. (1954). Psychoanalysis of character. In *The Collected Papers of Otto Fenichel* (Vol. 2). New York: Norton.

Fleuridas, C., Nelson, T. S., & Rosenthal, D. M. (1986). The evolution of circular questions: Training family therapists. *Journal of Marital and Family Therapy, 12,* 113–127.

Foucault, M. (1980). *Power/Knowledge: Selected Interviews and Other Writings, 1972–1977.* New York: Pantheon Books.

Frank, J. D. (1982). Therapeutic components shared by all psychotherapies. In J. H. Harvey & M. M. Parks (Eds.), *Psychotherapy Research and Behavior Change. The Master Lecture Series* (Vol. 1). Washington, DC: American Psychological Association.

Free, N. K., Green, B. L., Grace, M. C., Chernus, L. A., & Whitman, R. M. (1985). Empathy and outcome in brief focal dynamic therapy. *American Journal of Psychiatry, 142,* 917–921.

Freedman, J., & Combs, G. (1993). Invitations to new stories: Using questions to explore alternative possibilities. In S. Gilligan & R. Price (Eds.), *Therapeutic Conversations.* New York: Norton.

Freedman, J., & Combs, G. (1996a). *Narrative Therapy: The Social Construction of Preferred Realities.* New York: Norton.

Freedman, J., & Combs, G. (1996b). Gender stories. *Journal of Systemic Therapies, 15,* 31–46.

Freeman, J. C., Epston, D., & Lobovits, D. (1997). *Playful Approaches to Serious Problems: Narrative Therapy with Children and Their Families.* New York: Norton.

Freeman, J. C., & Lobovits, D. (1993). The turtle with wings. In S. Friedman (Ed.), *The New Language of Change: Constructive Collaboration in Psychotherapy.* New York: Guilford Press.

Freud, S. (1949). *An Outline of Psycho-Analysis.* New York: Norton.

Geertz, C. (1973). *The Interpretation of Cultures.* New York: Basic Books.

Gergen, K. (1985). The social constructionist movement in modern psychology. *American Psychologist, 40,* 266–275.

Gergen, K. (1990). Therapeutic professions and the diffusion of deficit. *Journal of Mind and Behavior, 11,* 353–367.

Gergen, K. J. (1991). *The Saturated Self: Dilemmas of Identity in Contemporary Life.* New York: Basic Books.

Glaser, B. G., & Strauss, A. L. (1967). *The Discovery of Grounded Theory.* Chicago: Aldine.

Goldner, V. (1992). Making room for both/and. *Family Therapy Networker, 16,* 55–61.

Goldner, V. (1998). The treatment of violence and victimization in intimate relationships. *Family Process, 37,* 263–286.

Goldner, V., Penn, P., Sheinberg, M., & Walker, G. (1990). Love and violence: Gender paradoxes in volatile attachments. *Family Process, 29,* 343–364.

Grieves, L. (1997). From beginning to start: The Vancouver Anti-Anorexia/Anti-Bulimia League. *Gecko, 2,* 78–88.

Grieves, L. (1998). From beginning to start: The Vancouver Anti-Anorexia/Anti-Bulimia League. In S. Madigan & I. Law (Eds.), *Praxis: Situating Discourse, Feminism and Politics in Narrative Therapies.* Vancouver, BC, Canada: Yaletown Family Therapy.

Grieves, L., & Madigan, S. (1996). Re-sounding voices: Tales from the Vancouver Anti-Anorexia/Anti-Bulimia League. *AFTA Newsletter, 64,* 27–29.

Griffith, J. L., & Griffith, M. E. (1992). Owning one's epistemological stance in therapy. *Dulwich Centre Newsletter, 1,* 5–11.

Griffith, J. L., & Griffith, M. E. (1994). *The Body Speaks: Therapeutic Dialogues for Mind–Body Problems.* New York: Basic Books.

Hall, R. (1996). Partnership accountability. In C. McLean, M. Carey, & C. White (Eds.), *Men's Ways of Being.* Boulder, CO: Westview Press.

Hammond, S. A. (1996). *The Thin Book of Appreciative Inquiry.* Plano, TX: CSS.

Hare-Mustin, R. (1994). Discourses in the mirrored room: A postmodern analysis of therapy. *Family Process, 33,* 19–35.

Harkaway, J. E., & Madsen, W. C. (1989). A systemic approach to medical non-compliance: The case of chronic obesity. *Family Systems Medicine, 7,* 42–53.

Hartley, D. (1985). Research on the therapeutic alliance in psychotherapy. *American Psychiatric Association Annual Review, 4,* 532–549.

Hartman, A. (1992). In search of subjugated knowledge. *Social Work, 37,* 483–484.

Hester, R., & Miller, W. (1989). *Handbook of Alcoholism Treatment Approaches: Effective Alternatives.* New York: Pergamon Press.

Imber-Black, E. (1986). Toward a resource model in systemic family therapy. In M. A. Karpel (Ed.), *Family Resources: The Hidden Partner in Family Therapy.* New York: Guilford Press.

Imber-Black, E. (1988). *Families and Larger Systems: A Family Therapists's Guide through the Labyrinth.* New York: Guilford Press.

Imber-Black, E. (1991). The family-larger system perspective. *Family Systems Medicine, 9,* 371–396.

Jackson, D. D. (1957). The question of family homeostasis. *Psychiatric Quarterly Supplement, 31,* 79–90.

Jenkins, A. (1990). *Invitations to Responsibility: The Therapeutic Engagement of Men Who Are Violent and Abusive.* Adelaide, Australia: Dulwich Centre Publications.

Jenkins, A. (1996). Moving towards respect: A quest for balance. In C. McLean, M. Carey, & C. White (Eds.), *Men's Ways of Being.* New York: Westview Press.

Johnson, J. (1973). *Foucault Live: Collected Interviews, 1961–1984.* New York: Semiotext(e).

Kagan, R., & Schlosberg, S. (1989). *Families in Perpetual Crisis.* New York: Norton.

Kaplan, L., & Girard, J. L. (1994). *Strengthening High-Risk Families: A Handbook for Practitioners.* New York: Lexington Books.

Karpel, M. A. (Ed.). (1986). *Family Resources: The Hidden Partner in Family Therapy.* New York: Guilford Press.

Kennedy, M. (1989). *Psychiatric Hospitalizations of Growers.* Paper presented at the Second Biennial Conference on Community Research and Action, Tempe AZ.

Kinney, J., Haapala, D., & Booth, C. (1991). *Keeping Families Together: The Homebuilders Model.* New York: Aldine de Gruyter.

Kliman, J., & Madsen, W. C. (1998). Social class and the family life cycle. In B. Carter & M. McGoldrick (Eds.), *The Changing Family Life Cycle* (3rd ed.). Boston: Allyn & Bacon.

Kliman, J., & Trimble, D. (1983). Network therapy. In B. Wolman & G. Stricker (Eds.), *Handbook of Family and Marital Therapy.* New York: Plenum Press.

Koback, R. R., & Waters, D. B. (1984). Family therapy as a rite of passage: Play's the thing. *Family Process, 23,* 89–100.

Kuehl, B. P., Newfield, N. A., & Joanning, H. (1990). A client-based description of family therapy. *Journal of Family Psychology, 3,* 310–321.

Lambert, M. J. (1992). Implications of outcome research for psychotherapy integration. In J. C. Norcrocss & M. R. Goldfried (Eds.), *Handbook of Psychotherapy Integration.* New York: Basic Books.

Lambert, M. J., Shapiro, D. A., & Bergin, A. E. (1986). The effectiveness of psychotherapy. In S. L. Garfield & A. E. Bergin (Eds.), *Handbook of Psychotherapy and Behavior Change* (3rd ed.). New York: Wiley.

Lincoln, Y. S., & Guba, E. G. (1985). *Naturalistic Inquiry.* Newbury Park, CA: Sage.

Lipchik, E., & de Shazer, S. (1986). The purposeful interview. *Journal of Strategic and Systemic Therapies, 5,* 88–99.

Madigan, S. (1993). Questions about questions: Situating the therapist's curiosity in front of the family. In S. Gilligan & R. Price (Eds.), *Therapeutic Conversations.* New York: Norton.

Madigan, S. (1997). Re-considering memory: Re-remembering lost identities back toward re-remembered selves. In C. Smith & D. Nylund (Eds.), *Narrative Therapies with Children and Adolescents.* New York: Guilford Press.

Madigan, S., & Epston, D. (1995). From "spy-chiatric gaze" to communities of concern: From professional monologue to dialogue. In S. Friedman (Ed.), *The Reflecting Team in Action: Collaborative Practice in Family Therapy.* New York: Guilford Press.

Madsen, W. C. (1992). Problematic treatment: Interaction of patient, spouse and physician beliefs in medical noncompliance. *Family Systems Medicine, 10,* 365–383.

Madsen, W. C. (1996). Integrating a "client voice" in clinical training. *American Family Therapy Academy Newsletter, 64,* 24–26.

Madsen, W. C. (1998). Attitude as intervention. In T. Nelson & T. Trepper (Eds.), *101 More Interventions in Family Therapy.* New York: Haworth Press.

Madsen, W. C. (1999). Inviting new stories: Narrative ideas in family-centered services. *Journal of Systemic Therapies, 18,* 1–22.

Markus, H., & Nurius, P. (1986). Possible selves. *American Psychologist, 41,* 954–969.

Maruyama, M. (1960). Morphogenesis and morphostasis. *Methods, 12,* 251–296.

Masterson, J. F. (1976). *Psychotherapy of the Borderline Adult: A Developmental Approach.* New York: Brunner/Mazel.

Maton, K. (1988). Social support, organizational characteristics, psychological well-being, and group appraisal in three self-help group populations. *American Journal of Community Psychology, 16,* 53–77.

Maton, K. I. (1989). Towards an ecological understanding of mutual-help groups: The social ecology of "fit." *American Journal of Community Psychology, 17,* 729–753.

Maton, K. I. (1993). Moving beyond the individual level of analysis in mutual help group research: An ecological paradigm. *Journal of Applied Behavioral Science, 29,* 272–286.

Maton, K. I. (1995). Organizational characteristics of empowering community settings: A multiple case study approach. *American Journal of Community Psychology, 23,* 631–656.

McNamee, S. (1988). Accepting research as social intervention: Implications of a systemic epistemology. *Communication Quarterly, 36,* 50–68.

Miller, W. (1985). Motivation for treatment: A review with special emphasis on alcoholism. *Psychological Bulletin, 98,* 84–107.

Minuchin, S., & Fishman, C. (1981). *Family Therapy Techniques.* Cambridge, MA: Harvard University Press.

Minuchin, S., Lee, W. Y., & Simon, G. M. (1996). *Mastering Family Therapy: Journeys of Growth and Transformation.* New York: Wiley.

Monaghan-Blout, S. (1999). *Choosing to be the exception: A study of parents resisting the intergenerational legacy of maltreatment.* Unpublished dissertation, Antioch New England Graduate School.

Monk, G. (1997). How narrative therapy works. In G. Monk, J. Winslade, K. Crocket, & D. Epston (Eds.), *Narrative Therapy in Practice: The Archaeology of Hope.* San Francisco: Jossey-Bass.

Monk, G., Winslade, J., Crocket, K., & Epston, D. (Eds.). (1997). *Narrative Therapy in Practice: The Archaeology of Hope.* San Francisco: Jossey-Bass.

Neal, J. (1996). Narrative therapy training and supervision. *Journal of Systemic Therapies, 15,* 63–78.

Nichols, M. P. (1984). *Family Therapy: Concepts and Methods.* Boston: Allyn & Bacon.

Nichols, M. P. (1987). *The Self in the System: Expanding the Limits of Family Therapy.* New York: Brunner/Mazel.

Nichols, T., & Jacques, C. (1995). Family reunions: Communities celebrate new possibilities. In S. Friedman (Ed.), *The Reflecting Team in Action: Collaborative Practice in Family Therapy.* New York: Guilford Press.

Nylund, D., & Corsiglia, V. (1994). Becoming solution-focused forced in brief therapy: Remembering something important we already knew. *Journal of Systemic Therapies, 13,* 5–12.

Nylund, D., & Thomas, J. (1994). The economics of narrative. *Family Therapy Networker, 18,* 38–39.

Nylund, D., & Thomas, J. (1997). Situating therapist's questions in the presence of the family: A qualitative inquiry. *Journal of Systemic Therapies, 16*, 211–228.

O'Hanlon B., & Beadle, S. (1994). *A Field Guide to Possibility Land: Possibility Therapy Methods.* Omaha, NB: Center Press.

O'Hanlon, B., & Wilk, J. (1987). *Shifting Contexts: The Generation of Effective Psychotherapy.* New York: Guilford Press.

O'Hanlon, W. H., & Weiner-Davis, M. (1989). *In Search of Solutions: A New Direction in Psychotherapy.* New York: Norton.

O'Neill, M., & Stockell, G. (1991). Worthy of discussion: Collaborative group therapy. *Australian and New Zealand Journal of Family Therapy, 12*, 201–206.

Palazzoli, M. S., Boscolo, L., Cecchin, G., & Prata, G. (1981). *Paradox and Counterparadox: A New Model in the Therapy of the Family in Schizophrenic Transaction.* New York: Jason Aronson.

Pare, D. A. (1995). Of families and other cultures: The shifting paradigm of family therapy. *Family Process, 34*, 1–19.

Pare, D. A. (1996). Culture and meaning: Expanding the metaphorical repertoire of family therapy. *Family Process, 35*, 21–42.

Parry, A., & Doan, R. E. (1994). *Story Re-visions: Narrative Therapy in the Postmodern World.* New York: Guilford Press.

Patterson, C. H. (1984). Empathy, warmth, and genuineness in psychotherapy: A review of reviews. *Psychotherapy, 21*, 431–438.

Penn, P. (1982). Circular questioning. *Family Process, 21*, 267–280.

Penn, P. (1985). Feed-forward: Future questions, future maps. *Family Process, 24*, 299–310.

Penn, P., & Sheinberg, M. (1991). Stories and conversations. *Journal of Strategic and Systemic Therapies, 10*, 30–37.

Petr, C. (1999). The Family-Centered Behavior Scale (BCBS): A tool for assessing the quality of partnership with families. *Empowering Families: The Newsletter of the National Association for Family-Based Services (NAFBS), 6*, 1–3.

Random House Dictionary of the English Language (1987). S. B. Flexner & L. C. Hauk (Eds.). (2nd ed.). New York: Random House.

Ransom, D. C. (1982). Resistance: Family- or therapist-generated? In A. S. Gurman (Ed.), *Questions and Answers in the Practice of Family Therapy.* New York: Brunner/Mazel.

Rappaport, J. (1993). Narrative studies, personal stories, and identity transformation in the mutual help context. *Journal of Behavioral Science, 29*, 239–256.

Rappaport, J., Seidman, E., Toro, P., McFadden, L., Reischl, T., Roberts, L., Salem, D., Stein, C., & Zimmerman, M. (1985). Collaborative research with a mutual help organization. *Social Policy, 12*, 12–24.

Ravella, N. F. (1994). Guest editor's introduction. *Journal of Systemic Therapies, 13*, 1–9.

Roberts, J. (1988). Setting the frame: Definitions, functions and typology of rituals. In E. Imber-Black, J. Roberts, & R. Whiting (Eds.), *Rituals in Families and Family Therapy.* New York: Norton.

Rogers, C. (1957). The necessary and sufficient conditions of therapeutic personality change. *Journal of Consulting Psychology, 21*, 95–103.

Rogers, C. (1961). *On Becoming a Person*. Boston: Houghton Mifflin.

Roth, S., & Epston, D. (1996). Consulting the problem about the problematic relationship: An exercise for experiencing a relationship with an externalized problem. In M. F. Hoyt (Ed.), *Constructive Therapies* (Vol. 2). New York: Guilford Press.

Salzer, M. S., McFadden, L., & Rappaport, J. (1994). Professional views of self-help groups: A comparative and contextual analysis. *Administration and Policy in Mental Health, 22,* 85–95.

Sandau-Beckler, P. A., Salcido, R., & Ronneau, J. (1993). Culturally competent family preservation services: An approach for first-generation Hispanic families in an international border community. *The Family Journal: Counseling and Therapy for Couples and Families, 1,* 312–323.

Sanders, C. (1997). Re-authoring problem identities: Small victories with young persons captured by substance misuse. In C. Smith & D. Nylund (Eds.), *Narrative Therapies with Children and Adolescents*. New York: Guilford Press.

Sanders, C. (1998). Substance misuse dilemmas. In S. Madigan & I. Law (Eds.), *Praxis: Situating Discourse, Feminism and Politics in Narrative Therapies*. Vancouver, BC, Canada: Yaletown Family Therapy.

Schwartz, B. K., & Cellini, H. R. (1997). *The Sex Offender: New Insights, Treatment Innovations and Legal Developments* (Vol. II). Kingston, NJ: Civic Research Institute.

Sennett, R., & Cobb, J. (1972). *The Hidden Injuries of Class*. New York: Random House.

Sheinberg, M. (1992). Navigating treatment impasses at the disclosure of incest: Combining ideas from feminism and social constructionism. *Family Process, 31,* 201–217.

Simblett, G. J. (1997). Leila and the tiger: Narrative approaches to psychiatry. In G. Monk, J. Winslade, K. Crocket, & D. Epston (Eds.), *Narrative Therapy in Practice: The Archaeology of Hope*. San Francisco: Jossey-Bass.

Stacey, K. (1997). Alternative metaphors for externalizing conversations. *Gecko, 1,* 29–51.

Stiles, W. B., Shapiro, D. A., & Ellliot, R. (1986). Are all psychotherapies equivalent? *American Psychologist, 41,* 165–180.

Sullivan, H. S. (1953). *The Interpersonal Theory of Psychiatry*. New York: Norton.

Tamasese, K., & Waldegrave, C. (1993). Cultural and gender accountability in the "Just Therapy" approach. *Journal of Feminist Family Therapy, 5,* 29–45.

Tamasese, K., Waldegrave, C., Tuhaka, F., & Campbell, W. (1998). Further conversation about partnerships of accountability. *Dulwich Centre Journal, 4,* 50–62.

Tomm, K. (1984a). One perspective on the Milan systemic approach: Part I. Overview of development, theory and practice. *Journal for Marital and Family Therapy, 10,* 113–125.

Tomm, K. (1984b). One perspective on the Milan systemic approach: Part II. Description of session format, interviewing style and interventions. *Journal for Marital and Family Therapy, 10,* 253–271.

Tomm, K. (1987a). Interventive interviewing: Part I. Strategizing as a fourth guideline for the therapist. *Family Process, 26,* 3–13.

Tomm, K. (1987b). Interventive interviewing: Part II. Reflexive questioning as a means to enable self-healing. *Family Process, 26,* 167–183.

Tomm, K. (1988). Interventive interviewing: Part III. Intending to ask lineal, circular, strategic or reflexive questions. *Family Process, 27,* 1–15.

Tomm, K. (1989). Externalizing the problem and internalizing personal agency. *Journal of Strategic and Systemic Therapies, 8,* 54–59.

Tomm, K. (1990). A critique of the DSM. *Dulwich Centre Newsletter, 3,* 5–8.

Tomm, K. (1991). Beginnings of a "HIPs and PIPs" approach to psychiatric assessment. *Calgary Participator, 1,* 21–24.

Tomm, K. (with Karl, Cynthia, Andrew, & Vanessa). (1992). Therapeutic distinctions in an on-going therapy. In S. McNamee & K. J. Gergen (Eds.), *Therapy as Social Construction.* London: Sage.

Tomm, K. (1993). The courage to protest: A commentary on Michael White's work. In S. Gilligan & R. Price (Eds.), *Therapeutic Conversations.* New York: Norton.

Tomm, K. (1995). *Co-constructing therapeutic practices.* Presentation at National Association for Family-Based Services Conference, Chicago, IL.

Tomm, K., Suzuki, K., & Suzuki, K. (1990). The Ka-no-Mushi: An inner externalization that enables compromise? *Australian and New Zealand Journal of Family Therapy, 11,* 104–107.

Truax, C. B., & Carkhuff, R. R. (1964). Significant developments in psychotherapy research. In *Progress in Clinical Psychology* (Vol. II). New York: Grune & Stratton.

Twain, M. (1980). *The Adventures of Tom Sawyer.* New York: Penguin Books. (Original work published 1876)

van Gennep, A. (1908). *The Rites of Passage.* London: Routledge & Kegan Paul.

Walsh, F. (1996). The concept of family resilience: Crisis and challenge. *Family Process, 35,* 261–282.

Walsh, F. (1998). *Strengthening Family Resilience.* New York: Guilford Press.

Warshaw, C. (1995). Violence and women's health: Old models, new challenges. In M. Pritchard (Ed.), *Dare to Vision: Shaping the National Agenda for Women, Abuse, and Mental Health Services: Proceedings of a Conference held July 14–16, 1994 in Arlington, VA. Co-sponsored by the Center for Mental Health Services and Human Resource Association of the Northeast.* Holyoke, MA: Human Resource Association.

Waters, D. B., & Lawrence, E. C. (1993). *Competence, Courage and Change: An Approach to Family Therapy.* New York: Norton.

Watson, B. (1995, March 15). Parents move from despair to self-confidence. *Daily Hampshire Gazette,* pp. 15–16.

Watzlawick, P., Bavelas, J., & Jackson, D. D. (1967). *Pragmatics of Human Communication.* New York: Norton.

Watzlawick, P., Weakland, J., & Fisch, R. (1974). *Change: Principles of Problem Formation and Problem Resolution.* New York: Norton.

Weingarten, K. (1995). Radical listening: Challenging cultural beliefs for and about mothers. In K. Weingarten (Ed.), *Cultural Resistance: Challenging Beliefs about Men, Women, and Therapy*. Binghamton, NY: Haworth Press.

Weingarten, K. (1997). *The Mother's Voice: Strengthening Intimacy in Families*. New York: Guilford Press.

Weingarten, K. (1998). The small and the ordinary: The daily practice of a post-modern narrative therapy. *Family Process, 37*, 3–16.

White, J. (1996). *A Phenomenological Study of the Experiences of Child Protective Social Workers: Don't Shoot the Messenger*. Unpublished dissertation, Massachusetts School of Professional Psychology, Dedham, MA.

White, M. (1988, Winter). The process of questioning: A therapy of literary merit? *Dulwich Centre Newsletter*, 3–20.

White, M. (1989, Summer). The externalizing of the problem and the re-authoring of lives and relationships. *Dulwich Centre Newsletter*, 3–20.

White, M. (1993). Deconstruction and therapy. In S. Gilligan & R. Price (Eds.), *Therapeutic Conversations*. New York: Norton.

White, M. (1995). *Re-Authoring Lives: Interviews and Essays*. Adelaide, Australia: Dulwich Centre Publications.

White, M. (1997). *Narratives of Therapists' Lives*. Adelaide, Australia: Dulwich Centre Publications.

White, M., & Epston, D. (1990). *Narrative Means to Therapeutic Ends*. New York: Norton.

Winslade, J., Crocket, K., & Monk, G. (1997). The therapeutic relationship. In G. Monk, J. Winslade, K. Crocket, & D. Epston (Eds.), *Narrative Therapy in Practice: The Archaeology of Hope*. San Francisco: Jossey-Bass.

Wright, L. M. (1990). Research as a family therapy intervention technique. *Contemporary Family Therapy, 12*, 477–484.

Wright, L. M., & Levac, A. M. (1992). The non-existence of non-compliant families: The influence of Humberto Maturana. *Journal of Advanced Nursing, 17*, 913–917.

Zehr, H. (1990). *Changing Lenses: A New Focus on Crime and Justice*. Scottsdale, PA: Herald Press.

Zimmerman, J. L., & Dickerson, V. C. (1993). Bringing forth the restraining influence of pattern in couples therapy. In S. Gilligan & R. Price (Eds.), *Therapeutic Conversations*. New York: Norton.

Zimmerman, J. L., & Dickerson, V. C. (1994). Using a narrative metaphor: Implications for theory and clinical practice. *Family Process, 33*, 233–246.

Zimmerman, J. L., & Dickerson, V. C. (1996a). *If Problems Talked: Narrative Therapy in Action*. New York: Guilford Press.

Zimmerman, J. L., & Dickerson, V. C. (Eds.). (1996b). Special issue on narrative. *Journal of Systemic Therapies, 15*.

Index

DATE DUE